The Era of Good Feelings and The Age of Jackson, 1816-1841

compiled by

Robert V. Remini

University of Illinois, Chicago Circle

and

Edwin A. Miles

University of Houston

AHM Publishing Corporation
Arlington Heights, Illinois 60004

ISBN: 0-88295-579-9 paper
ISBN: 0-88295-578-0 cloth

Library of Congress Card Number:
79-84211

PRINTED IN THE UNITED STATES OF AMERICA
729

Contents

CONTENTS

CONTENTS

CONTENTS

CONTENTS

Preface

The literature of the first half of the nineteenth century is enormous, for that half-century was one of the most exciting, creative and dynamic segments of the American past and has proved an enduring fascination for all those who read and write and enjoy history. Because there were so many extraordinary, larger-than-life size figures crowding the American scene between the War of 1812 and the Civil War, from politicians and military heroes to social reformers and literary giants, it would be virtually impossible to construct a bibliography that did total justice to this period, particularly if we attempted to include the contemporary as well as the secondary literature. Moreover, since there are a number of other Goldentree Bibliographies that single out specific areas and treat them in depth, such as those concerned with the frontier and the American west, the Indian, education, constitutional development, and social, economic and diplomatic history, we have directed our attention to those areas not covered by these other volumes. And although we have not consciously minimized the importance of any one phase of American life during the Era of Good Feelings and the Jacksonian Era, we have concentrated our efforts on political history, particularly biographical studies. We have tried to cover the administrations of each president during this period in depth, both in domestic and foreign affairs. We have also concentrated on the problem of slavery and the condition of Blacks, both free and slave. Regional and state history enjoyed a priority because of their particular importance in the antebellum era. We were also anxious to provide a complete listing of travel accounts and personal narratives. And because considerable controversy among historians has raged for years over virtually all aspects of the Age of Jackson, we have sought to provide a full guide to the bibliographical, historiographical and methodological literature.

Although this is one of the longest Goldentree Bibliographies to date, we have followed several guidelines to keep the number of entries within reason. If an author subsequently published his dissertation, we cited only the published work; or if a series of articles appeared later in book form we have listed the book only. Due to in-process revision, there are no entries 191 through 199.

PREFACE

As an aid to the reader we have attempted to cross list as extensively as possible before most of the major categories. Therefore, the index at the end of this book is simply an index by author, not by subject, except in a very few instances such as "antimasonry."

We are under a great obligation to many staffs of many libraries and to several of our students who aided in the search for titles and the preparation of the final list. It is not possible to cite every name because of the number involved, but it must be recorded that they have our deepest thanks.

Robert V. Remini
Edwin A. Miles
June, 1978

Abbreviations

Ag Hist	Agricultural History
Ala Hist Q	Alabama Historical Quarterly
Ala Hist Soc Trans	Alabama Historical Society Transactions
Ala Rev	Alabama Review
Am Econ Rev	American Economic Review
Am Hist Assn Pamphlets	American Historical Association Pamphlets
Am Hist Assn Papers	American Historical Association Papers
Am Hist Rev	American Historical Review
Am Jew Archiv	American Jewish Archives
Am J Econ Soc	American Journal of Economics and Sociology
Am J Leg Hist	American Journal of Legal History
Am J Pol Sci	American Journal of Political Science
Am J Soc	American Journal of Sociology
Am Lit	American Literature
Am Neptune	American Neptune
Am Phil Soc Proc	American Philosophical Society Proceedings
Am Phil Soc Trans	American Philosophical Society Transactions
Am Pol Sci Rev	American Political Science Review
Am Q	American Quarterly
Am Soc Rev	American Sociological Review
Am Stud	American Studies
Am W	The American West
Ann Med Hist	Annals of Medical History
Ann Rep Am Hist Assn	American Historical Association Annual Report
Antioch Rev	Antioch Review
Ariz W	Arizona and the West
Ark Hist Assn Pub	Arkansas Historical Association Publications
Ark Hist Q	Arkansas Historical Quarterly
Bibliog Soc Am Papers	Bibliographical Society of America Papers
Branch Hist Papers	John P. Branch Historical Society Papers
Buff Hist Soc Pub	Buffalo Historical Society Publications
Bull Friends Hist Assn	Bulletin of the Friends Historical Association
Bull Hist Med	Bulletin of the History of Medicine (title varies)
Bull Hist Phil Soc Ohio	Bulletin of the Historical and Philosophical Society of Ohio
Bus Hist Rev	Business History Review
Bus Hist Soc Bull	Bulletin of the Business Historical Society
Calif Hist Q	California Historical Quarterly

Calif Hist Soc Q	California Historical Society Quarterly
Calif Law Rev	California Law Review
Can Hist Rev	Canadian Historical Review
Can Rev Am Stud	Canadian Review of American Studies
Cap Stud	Capitol Studies
Cath Hist Rev	Catholic Historical Review
Chron Okla	Chronicles of Oklahoma
Church Hist	Church History
Cincinnati Hist Soc Bull	Cincinnati Historical Society Bulletin
C W Hist	Civil War History
Col Law Rev	Columbia Law Review
Comp Stud Soc Hist	Comparative Studies in Society and History
Conn Hist Soc Bull	Connecticut Historical Society Bulletin
Daed	Daedalus
Del Hist	Delaware History
Econ Hist Rev	Economic History Review
Econ Stud Q	Economic Studies Quarterly
Essex Inst Hist Coll	Essex Institute Historical Collections
E Tenn Hist Soc Pub	East Tennessee Historical Society Publications
E Tex Hist J	East Texas Historical Journal
Explo Econ Hist	Explorations in Economic History
Explo Entrep Hist	Explorations in Entrepreneurial History
Fem Stud	Feminist Studies
Filson Club Hist Q	Filson Club Historical Quarterly
Fla Hist Q	Florida Historical Quarterly
Fr Hist Stud	French Historical Studies
Ga Hist Q	Georgia Historical Quarterly
Ga Rev	Georgia Review
Geo Law Rev	Georgetown Law Journal
Great Plains J	Great Plains Journal
Har Ed Rev	Harvard Educational Review
Har Law Rev	Harvard Law Review
His-Am Hist Rev	Hispanic-American Historical Review
Hist	The Historian
Hist Educ Q	History of Education Quarterly
Hist J	Historical Journal
Hist Mag P E Ch	Historical Magazine of the Protestant Episcopal Church
Hist Methods Newsl	Historical Methods Newsletter
Hist N H	Historical New Hampshire
Hist Teacher	History Teacher
Hist Today	History Today
Hunt Lib Bull	Huntington Library Bulletin
Hunt Lib Q	Huntington Library Quarterly
Ill Hist Soc Trans	Illinois Historical Society Transactions
Ill St Hist J	Illinois State Historical Journal
Ind Hist	Indian Historian
Ind Hist Coll	Indiana Historical Collections
Ind Hist Soc Pub	Indiana Historical Society Publications

ABBREVIATIONS

Ind Mag Hist	Indiana Magazine of History
J Am Hist	Journal of American History
J Am Stud	Journal of American Studies
J Black Stud	Journal of Black Studies
J Econ Bus Hist	Journal of Economic and Business History
J Econ Hist	Journal of Economic History
J Hist Ideas	Journal of the History of Ideas
J Interdis Hist	Journal of Interdisciplinary History
J Miss Hist	Journal of Mississippi History
J Neg Educ	Journal of Negro Education
J Neg Hist	Journal of Negro History
J Pol	Journal of Politics
J Pol Econ	Journal of Political Economy
J Pop Cult	Journal of Popular Culture
J Presby Hist	Journal of Presbyterian History
J Presby Hist Soc	Journal of the Presbyterian Historical Society
J Pub Law	Journal of Public Law
J S Hist	Journal of Southern History
J Soc Hist	Journal of Social History
J Urban Hist	Journal of Urban History
J W	Journal of the West
Jour Q	Journalism Quarterly
Kan Hist Q	Kansas Historical Quarterly
Labor Hist	Labor History
La Hist	Louisiana History
La Hist Q	Louisiana Historical Quarterly
La Stud	Louisiana Studies
Mass Hist Soc Proc	Massachusetts Historical Society Proceedings
Md Hist Mag	Maryland Historical Magazine
Mich Hist	Michigan History
Mich Law Rev	Michigan Law Review
Mid-Am	Mid-America
Mil Aff	Military Affairs
Minn Hist	Minnesota History
Miss Hist Soc Pub	Mississippi Historical Society Publications
Miss Q	Mississippi Quarterly
Miss Val Hist Assn Proc	Mississippi Valley Historical Association Proceedings
Miss Val Hist Rev	Mississippi Valley Historical Review
Mo Hist Rev	Missouri Historical Review
Mo Hist Soc Bull	Missouri Historical Society Bulletin
N C Hist Rev	North Carolina Historical Review
Neb Hist	Nebraska History
Neg Hist Bull	Negro History Bulletin
N Eng Q	New England Quarterly
N J Hist	New Jersey History
Notes Qu	Notes and Queries
N Y Hist	New York History
N Y Hist Soc Q	New York Historical Society Quarterly

ABBREVIATIONS

Ohio Arch Hist Q	Ohio Archaeological and Historical Quarterly
Ohio Hist	Ohio History
Ore Hist Q	Oregon Historical Quarterly
Pac Hist Rev	Pacific Historical Review
Pac N W Q	Pacific Northwest Quarterly
Pa Hist	Pennsylvania History
Pa Mag Hist Biog	Pennsylvania Magazine of History and Biography
Perspectives Am Hist	Perspectives in American History
Pol Aff	Political Affairs
Polish Am Stud	Polish American Studies
Pol Sci Q	Political Science Quarterly
Popl Stud	Population Studies
Pres Stud Q	Presidential Studies Quarterly
Proc Am Ant Soc	Proceedings, American Antiquarian Society
Proc N J Hist Soc	Proceedings, New Jersey Historical Society
Proc Vt Hist Soc	Proceedings, Vermont Historical Society
Pub Opin Q	Public Opinion Quarterly
Q J Econ	Quarterly Journal of Economics
Q J Lib Cong	Quarterly Journal of the Library of Congress
Q J Sp	Quarterly Journal of Speech
Quaker Hist	Quaker History
Rec Col Hist Soc	Records of the Columbia Historical Society
Red River Val Hist Rev	Red River Valley Historical Review
Reg Ky Hist Soc	Register of the Kentucky Historical Society
Rev Econ Stat	Review of Economics and Statistics
Rev Pol	Review of Politics
R I Hist	Rhode Island History
Roc Mt Soc Sci J	Rocky Mountain Social Science Journal
S Atl Q	South Atlantic Quarterly
S C Hist Assn Proc	South Carolina Historical Association Proceedings
S C Hist Gen Mag	South Carolina Historical and Genealogical Magazine
S C Hist Mag	South Carolina Historical Magazine
S D Hist	South Dakota History
S Econ J	Southern Economic Journal
S Hist Assn Pub	Southern History Association Publications
S Sp Com J	Southern Speech Communications Journal
S Sp J	Southern Speech Journal
S W Hist Q	Southwestern Historical Quarterly
S W Rev	Southwest Review
S W Soc Sci Q	Southwestern Social Science Quarterly
Soc	Societas
Soc Res	Social Research
Soc Sci	Social Science
Soc Sci Q	Social Science Quarterly
Soc Stud	Social Studies
S Q	Southern Quarterly

ABBREVIATIONS

Stan Law Rev	Stanford Law Review
Swed Pioneer Hist Q	Swedish Pioneer Historical Quarterly
Tchr Col Rec	Teachers College Record
Tenn Hist Mag	Tennessee Historical Magazine
Tenn Hist Q	Tennessee Historical Quarterly
Tenn Law Rev	Tennessee Law Review
Tex	Texana
Trinity Coll Hist Papers	Trinity College Historical Papers
Tyler's	Tyler's Historical and Genealogical Register
U Chi Law Rev	University of Chicago Law Review
Va Mag Hist Biog	Virginia Magazine of History and Biography
Va Q Rev	Virginia Quarterly Review
Vand Law Rev	Vanderbilt Law Review
Vt Hist	Vermont History
W Econ J	Western Economics Journal
W Hist Q	Western Historical Quarterly
W Hum Rev	Western Humanities Review
W Pa Hist Mag	Western Pennsylvania Historical Magazine
W Pol Q	Western Political Quarterly
W Tenn Hist Soc Papers	West Tennessee Historical Society Papers
W Va Hist	West Virginia History
Winterthur Port	Winterthur Portfolio
Wis Acad Sci Trans	Wisconsin Academy of Society, Arts and Letters, Transactions
Wis Mag Hist	Wisconsin Magazine of History
Wm Mar Q	William and Mary Quarterly
Yale Law Rev	Yale Law Review
Yale Rev	Yale Review
Yivo Ann Jew Soc Sci	Yivo Annual of Jewish Social Science

NOTE: The publisher and compilers invite suggestions for new entries in future editions of this bibliography.

I. Guides and General Studies

1. Bibliographies and Selected Reference Works

1 ADAMS, James Truslow, et al., eds. *Album of American History.* 6 vols. New York, 1944.

2 ADAMS, James Truslow, et al., eds. *Dictionary of American History.* 6 vols. New York, 1940–1963.

3 ADAMS, James Truslow, and R. V. COLEMAN, eds. *Atlas of American History.* New York, 1943.

4 American Bibliographic Center. *America: History and Life.* Santa Barbara, Calif., 1964–.

5 ANDREWS, Wayne, ed. *Concise Dictionary of American History.* New York, 1962.

6 *Appleton's Cyclopaedia of American Biography.* Ed. James Grant WILSON and John FISKE. 7 vols. New York, 1888–1901.

7 BEERS, Henry P. *Bibliographies in American History.* Rev ed. New York, 1942.

8 *Bibliographic Index.* New York, 1945–.

9 *Biography Index.* New York, 1949–.

10 *Book Review Digest.* New York, 1905–.

11 *Book Review Index.* Detroit, 1965–.

12 BOYD, Annie M. *United States Government Publications.* 2d ed. New York, 1941.

13 CARMAN, Harry J., and Arthur W. THOMPSON, eds. *A Guide to the Principal Sources for American Civilization, 1800–1900, in the City of New York: Printed Materials.* New York, 1962.

14 CARRUTH, Gordon, et al. *The Encyclopedia of American Facts and Dates.* 4th ed. New York, 1966.

15 *A Catalog of Books Represented by Library of Congress Printed Cards.* 167 vols. Ann Arbor, 1942–1946. [It should be used in conjunction with the *Supplement,* 42 vols. (Ann Arbor, 1948); *The Library of Congress Author Catalog, 1948–1952,* 24 vols. (Ann Arbor, 1953); and *The National Union Catalog, a Cumulative Author List, 1953–1957,* 28 vols. (Ann Arbor, 1958), and several subsequent series bearing the same title. *The National Union Catalog, Pre-1956 Imprints* (London, 1968–.), a comprehensive retrospective series currently being published, will comprise more than 610 volumes when completed. A companion series, *Library of Congress Catalog—Books: Subjects,* providing a subject index for books published since 1950, has also been published in several series.]

16 *Checklist of United States Public Documents, 1789–1909.* Washington, D.C., 1911.

17 COHEN, Hennig, ed. *Articles in American Studies: 1954–1968; A Cumulation of the Annual Bibliographies from American Quarterly.* 2 vols. Ann Arbor, 1972.

1

18 *Combined Retrospective Index to Journals in History, 1838–1974.* 11 vols. Washington, D.C., 1977–.

19 COULTER, Edith M. and Melanie GERSTENFELD, eds. *Historical Bibliographies: A Systematic and Annotated Guide.* Berkeley, 1935.

20 CRICK, Bernard R., and Miriam ALMAN. *A Guide to Manuscripts Relating to America in Great Britain and Ireland.* London, 1961.

21 DARGAN, Marion. *Guide to American Biography.* 2 vols. Albuquerque, 1949–1952.

22 *Dissertation Abstracts International.* Ann Arbor, 1938–. [Title varies: vols. 1–11 (1938–1951) *Microfilm Abstracts;* vols. 12–29 (1952–1969) *Dissertation Abstracts.* An indispensable guide to this series is the *Comprehensive Dissertation Index, 1861–1972,* 37 vols. (Ann Arbor, 1973), which lists virtually all dissertations accepted for academic doctoral degrees by United States and Canadian universities during those years. Vols. 1–32 are computer-generated indexes (by disciplines) based on keywords from dissertation titles. Vols. 33–37 constitute an author index for all disciplines.]

23 *Essay and General Literature Index.* New York, 1934–.

24 *Doctoral Dissertations Accepted by American Universities 1933/34–1954/55,* 22 vols. New York, 1934–1955. [This series is followed by *Index to American Doctoral Dissertations, 1955/56–1966/67,* 12 vols. (Ann Arbor, 1957–1967) and *American Doctoral Dissertations 1967/68–1971/72,* 6 vols. (Ann Arbor, 1968–1973).]

25 FREIDEL, Frank, ed. *Harvard Guide to American History.* Rev. ed. 2 vols. Cambridge, Mass., 1974.

26 GARRATY, John A., ed. *Encyclopedia of American Biography.* New York, 1974.

27 GOHDES, Clarence. *Bibliographical Guide to the Study of the Literature of the U.S.A.* 3d ed. Durham, N.C., 1970.

28 HALE, Richard W., Jr., ed. *Guide to Photocopied Historical Materials in the United States and Canada.* Ithaca, N.Y., 1961.

29 HAMER, Philip M., ed., *A Guide to Archives and Manuscripts in the United States.* New Haven, 1961.

30 HOWE, George F., et al., eds. *The American Historical Association's Guide to Historical Literature.* New York, 1961.

31 *Index to Book Reviews in the Humanities.* Detroit, 1960–.

32 *International Index to Periodicals.* New York, 1916–. [Title varies: Vols. 1–18 (1907–March 1965) *International Index;* vols. 19–27 (April 1965–March 1974) *Social Sciences & Humanities Index.* Superseded by two separate publications, *Social Sciences Index* and *Humanities Index* (April 1974–).]

33 JAMES, Edward T.; Janet Wilson JAMES; and Paul S. BOYER, eds. *Notable American Women, 1607–1950: A Biographical Dictionary.* 3 vols. Cambridge, Mass., 1971.

34 JOHNSON, Allen, and Dumas MALONE, eds. *Dictionary of American Biography.* 23 vols. plus index. New York, 1928–1973.

35 JOHNSON, Thomas H. *The Oxford Companion to American History.* New York, 1966.

36 KAPLAN, Louis, et al., eds. *A Bibliography of American Autobiographies.* Madison, Wis., 1961.

37 KUEHL, Warren F., ed. *Dissertations in History: An Index to Dissertations Completed in History Departments of United States and Canadian Universities.* 2 vols. Lexington, Ky., 1965–1972. [Vol. 1 covers the period from 1873 through 1960; vol. 2 the period from 1961 through June 1970.]

38 LARNED, J. N., ed. *The Literature of American History: A Bibliographic Guide.* Boston, 1902.

39 LELAND, Waldo G. *Guide to Materials for American History in the Libraries and Archives of Paris.* Washington, D.C., 1943.

40 LILLARD, Richard G. *American Life in Autobiography: A Descriptive Guide.* Stanford, Calif., 1956.

41 MATTHEWS, William. *American Diaries in Manuscript, 1580–1954: A Descriptive Bibliography.* Athens, Ga., 1974.

42 MATTHEWS, William. *American Diaries: An Annotated Bibliography of American Diaries Written Prior to the Year 1861.* Berkeley, 1945.

43 MORRIS, Richard B., ed. *Encyclopedia of American History.* Rev ed. New York, 1970.

44 *National Cyclopedia of American Biography.* New York, 1893–.

45 *National Union Catalog of Manuscript Collections.* 12 vols. to date. Washington, D.C., 1962–.

46 *Nineteenth Century Readers' Guide to Periodical Literature, 1890–1899.* 2 vols. New York, 1944.

47 O'NEILL, Edward H. *Biography by Americans, 1658–1936: A Subject Bibliography.*

48 PAULLIN, Charles O. *Atlas of the Historical Geography of the United States.* Ed. John K. WRIGHT. Washington, D.C., 1932.

49 POOLE, William F., et al., eds. *Poole's Index to Periodical Literature,* [1802–1906]. 6 vols. Boston, 1882–1908. [Use with *Cumulative Author Index* (Ann Arbor, 1971).]

50 POORE, Benjamin P. *A Descriptive Catalogue of the Government Publications of the United States, September 5, 1775–March 4, 1881.* Washington, D.C., 1885.

51 *Readers' Guide to Periodical Literature.* New York, 1901–.

52 SABIN, Joseph, et al. *Bibliotheca Americana: A Dictionary of Books Relating to America from Its Discovery to the Present Time.* 29 vols. New York, 1868–1936.

53 SCHMECKEBIER, Laurence, and Roy B. EASTIN. *Government Publications and Their Use.* 2d rev. ed. Washington, D.C., 1969.

54 SOBEL, Robert, comp. *The Biographical Directory of the United States Executive Branch, 1774–1971.* Westport, Conn., 1971.

55 SPILLER, Robert E., et al., eds. *Literary History of the United States.* Rev ed. 3 vols. New York, 1963–1972.

56 United States Congress. *Biographical Directory of the American Congress, 1774–1971.* Washington, D.C., 1971.

57 United States Library of Congress. *A Guide to the Study of the United States of America.* Ed. Donald H. MUGRIDGE and Blanche MCCRUM. Washington, D.C., 1960. *Supplement, 1956–1965.* Ed. Oliver H. ORR, Jr. Washington, D.C., 1976.

58 WINCHELL, Constance M. *Guide to Reference Books*. 8th ed. Chicago, 1967.

59 *Writings on American History, 1902–1903, 1906–1940, 1948–1960*. Washington D.C., 1904, 1941, 1961. [This series, a comprehensive guide to books and articles sponsored by the American Historical Association, will be concluded with the publication of the volume for 1961. A valuable supplement is the *Index to the Writings on American History, 1902–1904* (Washington, D.C., 1956). This series is being succeeded by *Writings on American History: A Subject Bibliography of Articles* (Washington, D.C., 1974–). Yearly volumes, beginning with 1973–1974, have been issued, as well as *Writings on American History, 1962–1973: A Subject Bibliography of Articles*, 4 vols. (Washington, D.C., 1976.)]

2. *Statistical and Documentary Compilations*

60 *Abridgment of the Debates of Congress from 1789 to 1856*. 16 vols. New York, 1857–1861.

61 ALEXANDER, Thomas B. *Sectional and Party Strength: A Computer Analysis of Roll-Call Voting Patterns in the United States House of Representatives, 1836–1860*. Nashville, 1967.

62 BAIN, Richard C., and Judith H. PARRIS. *Convention Decisions and Voting Records*. 2d ed. Washington, D.C., 1973.

63 BURNHAM, Walter D. *Presidential Ballots, 1836–1892*. Baltimore, 1955.

64 *Congressional Globe*. 46 vols. Washington, D.C., 1834–1873.

65 *Debates and Proceedings in the Congress of the United States, 1789–1824* Annals of Congress. 42 vols. Washington, D.C., 1834–1856.

66 GOLDMAN, Perry M., and James S. YOUNG, eds. *The United States Congressional Directories, 1789–1840*. New York, 1973.

67 JOHNSTON, Alexander, and James A. WOODBURN, eds. *American Orations: Studies in American Political History*. 4 vols. New York, 1896–1897.

68 *Journal of the Executive Proceedings of the Senate of the United States, 1789–1905*. 90 vols. Washington, D.C., 1828–1948.

69 *Journal of the House of Representatives of the United States*. Philadelphia and Washington, D.C., 1789–.

70 *Journal of the Senate of the United States*. Philadelphia and Washington, D.C., 1789–.

71 LOWRIE, Walter, et al., eds. *American State Papers: Documents, Legislative and Executive of the Congress of the United States*. 38 vols. Washington, D.C., 1832–1861.

72 *New American States Papers*. Ed Thomas C. COCHRAN. 176 vols. Wilmington, Del., 1972–1973.

73 *Register of Debates in Congress*. 14 Vols in 29. Washington, D.C., 1825–1837.

74 *Reports of Cases Argued and Decided in the Supreme Court of the United States*. 178 vols. in 44. Newark, 1882–1900. [IX Cranch, I–XII Wheaton, and I–XIV Peters are applicable to the period 1816–1841.]

75 RICHARDSON, James D., comp. *A Compilation of the Messages and Papers of the Presidents, 1789–1897.* 10 vols. Washington, D.C., 1896–1899.

76 *Statutes at Large of the United States of America.* 17 vols. Boston, 1845–1873.

77 THORPE, Francis Newton, comp. *The Federal and State Constitutions, Colonial Charters, and Other Organic Laws of the States, Territories and Colonies Now or Heretofore Forming the United States of America.* 7 vols. Washington, D.C., 1909.

78 United States Bureau of the Census. *The Statistical History of the United States from Colonial Times to the Present.* Stamford, Conn., 1965.

3. The Jacksonian Era: Bibliographical, Historiographical, and Methodological Studies

See also **1309–1350, 1909, 1941, 2182, 2230, 2238, 2246, 2293, 2613, 2710, 2877, 2956, 3002, 3076, 3232, 3243, 3246, 3247, 3509, 3736, 3739, 3914, 3948, 4025, 4274, 4284, 4293, 4296.**

79 BENSON, Lee. "Middle Period Historiography: What Is to Be Done?" *American History: Retrospect and Prospect.* Ed. George A. BILLIAS and Gerald N. GROB. New York, 1971.

80 CAVE, Alfred A. *Jacksonian Democracy and the Historians.* Gainesville, 1964.†

81 ERIKSSON, Erik McKinley. "New Viewpoints on the Jacksonian Period." *Soc Stud,* XXV (1934), 167–171.

82 FLATT, Donald Franklin. "Historians View Jacksonian Democracy: A Historiographical Study." Doctoral dissertation, University of Kentucky, 1974.

83 FORMISANO, Ronald P. "Toward a Reorientation of Jacksonian Politics: A Review of the Literature, 1959–1975," *J Am Hist,* LXIII (1976), 42–65.

84 GATELL, Frank O. "Beyond Jacksonian Consensus." *The State of American History.* Ed. Herbert J. BASS. Chicago, 1970.

85 GATELL, Frank O. "The Jacksonian Era, 1824–1848. *The Reinterpretation of American History and Culture.* Ed. William H. CARTWRIGHT and Richard L. WATSON, Jr. Washington, D.C., 1973.

86 MILES, Edwin A. "The Jacksonian Era." *Writing Southern History: Essays in Historiography in Honor of Fletcher M. Green.* Ed. Arthur S. LINK and Rembert W. PATRICK. Baton Rouge, 1965.†

87 MOSS, Richard J. "Jacksonian Democracy: A Note on the Origins and Growth of the Term." *Tenn Hist Q,* XXXIV (1975), 145–153.

88 PESSEN, Edward. "Bibliographical Essay." *Jacksonian America: Society, Personality, and Politics.* Rev. ed. Homewood, Ill., 1978.†

89 PESSEN, Edward. "Jacksonian Quantification: On Asking the Right Questions." *The State of American History.* Ed. Herbert J. BASS. Chicago, 1970.

90 PESSEN, Edward. "The 'Pessen Thesis': Brief Reflections by Its Author." *N Y Hist,* LVI (1975), 456–460.

91 RADER, Benjamin G. "Jacksonian Democracy: Myth or Reality?" *Soc Stud,* LXV (1974), 17–22.

92 ROPER, Donald M. "Beyond the Jacksonian Era: A Comment on the Pessen Thesis." *N Y Hist,* LVI (1975), 226–233.

93 SELLERS, Charles G., Jr. "Andrew Jackson Versus the Historians." *Miss Val Hist Rev,* XLIV (1958), 615–634.

94 SELLERS, Charles G., Jr. *Jacksonian Democracy.* Am Hist Assn Pamphlets. Washington, D.C., 1958.†

95 STERNSHER, Bernard. "Democrats and Whigs." *Consensus, Conflict, and American Historians.* Bloomington, 1975.

96 STEVENS, Harry R. "Jacksonian Democracy, 1825–1849. *Interpreting and Teaching American History.* Ed. William H. CARTWRIGHT and Richard L. WATSON, Jr. Washington, D.C., 1961.

97 VAN DEUSEN, Glyndon G. "Bibliographical Essay." *The Jacksonian Era, 1828–1848.* New York, 1959.†

98 WARD, John W. "The Age of the Common Man," *The Reconstruction of American History.* Ed. John HIGHAM. New York, 1962.†

99 WISE, W. Harvey, Jr., and JOHN W. CRONIN. *A Bibliography of Andrew Jackson and Martin Van Buren.* Washington, D.C., 1935.

4. General United States History, 1816–1841

100 AARON, Daniel, ed. *America in Crisis.* New York, 1952.·

101 ALLMENDINGER, David F., comp. *The American People in the Antebellum North.* West Haven, Conn., 1973.

102 BAKER, Paul R. *The Fortunate Pilgrims: Americans in Italy, 1800–1860.* Cambridge, Mass., 1964.

103 BHAGAT, G. *Americans in India, 1784–1860.* New York, 1970.

104 BILLIAS, George A., and Gerald N. GROB, eds. *American History: Retrospect and Prospect.* New York, 1971.†

105 BINKLEY, Wilfred E. *American Political Parties: Their Natural History.* New York, 1943.

106 BOGUE, Allan G., and Mark Paul MARLAIRE. "Of Mess and Men: The Boardinghouse and Congressional Voting, 1821–1842." *Am J Pol Sci,* XIX (1975), 207–230.

107 BOLES, John B., ed. *America, The Middle Period: Essays in Honor of Bernard Mayo.* Charlottesville, Va., 1973.

108 BOORSTIN, Daniel J. *The Americans: The National Experience.* New York, 1965.

109 BROWN, Richard D. *Modernization: The Transformation of American Life, 1600–1865.* New York, 1976.†

110 BURGESS, John W. *The Middle Period, 1817–1858.* New York, 1897.

111 CHANNING, Edward. *A History of the United States.* 6 vols. New York, 1904–1925.

112 CHAPLIN, Alta B., comp. *Political Parties in the United States, 1800–1914.* New York, 1915.

113 CHASE, James S. *Emergence of the Presidential Nominating Convention, 1789–1832.* Urbana, 1973.

114 CHUTE, Marchette. *The First Liberty: A History of the Right to Vote in America, 1619–1850.* New York, 1969.

115 COBEN, Stanley, and Lorman RATNER, eds. *The Development of an American Culture.* Englewood Cliffs, N.J., 1970.

116 CRAVEN, Avery O. *The Coming of the Civil War.* New York, 1942.†

117 CRAVEN, Avery O. *Democracy in American Life.* Chicago, 1941.

118 CUNLIFFE, Marcus. *The Nation Takes Shape, 1789–1837.* Chicago, 1959.†

119 CUNNINGHAM, Noble E., Jr., ed. *The Early Republic, 1789–1828.* Columbia, S.C., 1968.

120 DALLINGER, Frederick W. *Nominations for Elective Office in the United States.* New York, 1897.

121 DAVIS, David Brion. "Some Ideological Functions of Prejudice in Ante-Bellum America." *The American Experience: Approaches to the Study of the United States.* Ed. Hennig COHEN. Boston, 1968.

122 EKIRCH, Arthur A., Jr. *The Challenge of American Democracy: A Concise History of Social Thought and Political Action.* Belmont, Calif., 1973.

123 FEHRENBACHER, Don E. *The Era of Expansion, 1800–1848.* New York 1969.†

124 FORMISANO, Ronald P. "Deferential-Participant Politics: The Early Republic's Political Culture, 1789–1840." *Am Pol Sci Rev,* LXVIII (1974), 473–487.

125 GATELL, Frank Otto, and John M. MCFAUL. *Jacksonian America, 1815–1840: New Society, Changing Politics.* Englewood Cliffs, N.J., 1970.†

126 GOLDMAN, Perry M. "The Republic of Virtue and Other Essays on the Politics of the Early National Period." Doctoral dissertation, Columbia University, 1970.

127 GRIFFITH, Elmer C. *The Rise and Development of the Gerrymander.* Chicago, 1907.

128 GRIMSTED, David, ed. *Notions of the Americans, 1820–1860.* New York, 1970.

129 GROB, Gerald N. "The Political System and Social Policy in the Nineteenth Century: Legacy of the Revolution." *Mid-Am,* LXVIII (1976), 5–19.

130 HARLOW, Ralph V. *The History of Legislative Methods in the United States before 1825.* New Haven, 1915.

131 HART, Albert B., ed. *American History Told by Contemporaries.* 5 vols. New York, 1897–1929.

132 HARTZ, Louis. *The Liberal Tradition in America: An Interpretation of American Political Thought since the Revolution.* New York, 1955.†

133 HOFSTADTER, Richard. *The Idea of a Party System: The Rise of Legitimate Opposition in the United States, 1780–1840.* Berkeley, 1969.†

134 HOWE, John R. *From the Revolution through the Age of Jackson: Innocence and Empire in the Young Republic.* Englewood Cliffs, N.J., 1973.†

135 LUETSCHER, George D. *Early Political Machinery in the United States.* Philadelphia, 1903.

136 LYNCH, William O. *Fifty Years of Party Warfare.* Indianapolis, 1931.

137 LYNN, Alvin Willard. "Party Formation and Operation in the House of Representatives, 1824–1837." Doctoral dissertation, Rutgers University, 1972.

138 MCCORMICK, Richard L. "Ethno-Cultural Interpretations of Nineteenth-Century American Voting Behavior." *Pol Sci Q,* LXXXIX (1974), 351–378.

139 MCMASTER, John B. *A History of the People of the United States from the Revolution to the Civil War.* 8 vols. New York, 1883–1913.

140 MILLER, Douglas T. *The Birth of Modern America, 1820–1850.* New York, 1970.†

141 MILLER, Douglas T., ed. *The Nature of Jacksonian America.* New York, 1972.†

142 MORANTZ, Regina Ann Markell. " 'Democracy' and 'Republic' in American Ideology, 1787–1840." Doctoral dissertation, Columbia University, 1971.

143 NICHOLS, Roy F. *The Invention of the American Political Parties.* New York, 1967.†

144 OSTRANDER, Gilman. *The Rights of Man in America, 1606–1861.* Columbia, S.C., 1967.†

145 OSTROGORSKI, M. *Democracy and the Organization of Political Parties.* 2 vols. New York, 1902.

146 PARSONS, Lynn Hudson. "The Hamiltonian Tradition in the United States, 1804–1912." Doctoral dissertation, Johns Hopkins University, 1967.

147 PETERSON, Merrill D. *The Jeffersonian Image in the American Mind.* New York, 1960.†

148 POLE, J. R., ed. *The Advance of Democracy.* New York, 1967.

149 PORTER, Kirk H. *A History of Suffrage in the United States.* Chicago, 1918.

149A RICHARDS, Leonard L. *The Advent of American Democracy, 1815–1848.* Glenview, Ill., 1977.

150 ROBINSON, Raymond H. *The Growing of America: 1789–1848.* Boston, 1973.

151 ROSSITER, Clinton. *The American Quest, 1790–1860: An Emerging Nation in Search of Identity, Unity, and Modernity.* New York, 1971.

152 SANFORD, Charles L., ed. *Quest for America, 1810–1824.* New York, 1964.

153 SCHLESINGER, Arthur M., Jr., ed. *History of U.S. Political Parties.* 4 vols. New York, 1973.

154 SCHLESINGER, Arthur M., Jr.; Fred L. ISRAEL; and William P. HANSEN, eds. *History of American Presidential Elections.* 4 vols. New York, 1971.

155 SCHOULER, James. *History of the United States of America under the Constitution.* 7 vols. New York, 1880–1913.

156 SELLERS, Charles G., Jr. "The Equilibrium Cycle in Two-Party Politics." *Pub Opin Q,* XXIX (1965), 16–38.

157 SHADE, William G. "American Political Development: 1789–1840." *Cur Hist,* LXVII (1974), 5–8, 40.

158 SHORT, Lloyd M. *The Development of National Administrative Organization in the United States.* Baltimore, 1923.

159 SILBEY, Joel H., ed. *National Development and Sectional Crisis, 1815–1860.* New York, 1970.†

160 SMITH, Joseph R., and M. Ogden PHILLIPS. *North America, Its People and the Resources, Development, and Prospects of the Continent.* New York, 1940.

161 STILL, Bayrd. "An Interpretation of the Statehood Process, 1800 to 1850." *Miss Val Hist Rev,* XXIII (1936), 189–204.

162 TURNER, Frederick J. *The Significance of Sections in American History.* New York, 1932.

163 WALLACE, Michael L. "Ideologies of Party in the Ante-Bellum Republic." Doctoral dissertation, Columbia University, 1973.

164 WILLIAMS, William Appleton. *The Contours of American History.* Cleveland, 1961.†

165 WILLIAMSON, Chilton. *American Suffrage: From Property to Democracy, 1760–1860.* Princeton, 1960.

166 WILSON, Woodrow. *A History of the American People.* 5 vols. New York, 1902.

167 WILTSE, Charles M., ed. *Expansion and Reform, 1815–1850.* New York, 1967.

168 WILTSE, Charles M. *The New Nation, 1800–1845.* New York, 1961.†

169 WINSOR, Justin, ed. *Narrative and Critical History of America.* 8 vols. Boston, 1885–1889.

170 WISE, Gene. *American Historical Explanations; A Strategy for Grounded Inquiry.* Homewood, Ill., 1973.

171 WYATT-BROWN, Bertram, comp. *The American People in the Antebellum South.* West Haven, Conn., 1973.†

II. Travel Accounts

1. Bibliographies

172 CLARK, Thomas D., ed. *Travels in the Old South: A Bibliography.* 3 vols. Norman, Okla., 1956–1959.

173 HUBACH, Robert R. *Early Midwestern Travel Narratives: An Annotated Bibliography, 1634–1850.* Detroit, 1961.

174 MONAGHAN, Frank. *French Travellers in the United States, 1765–1932: A Bibliography.* New York, 1933. Reprinted with supplement by Samuel J. Marino. New York, 1961.

175 SMET, Antoine de. *Voyageurs Belges aux États-Unis du XVIIᵉ Siècle à 1900: Notices Bio-bibliographiques.* Brussels, 1959.

176 SMITH, Harold F. *American Travellers Abroad: A Bibliography of Accounts Published before 1900.* Carbondale, Ill., 1969.

9

177 WAGNER, Henry R., ed. *The Plains and the Rockies: A Bibliography of Original Narratives of Travel and Adventure, 1800–1865.* 3d ed., rev. Charles L CAMP. San Francisco, 1937.

2. Anthologies

178 ANGLE, Paul M., ed. *Prairie State: Impressions of Illinois, 1673–1967, by Travelers.* Chicago, 1968.

179 BRANDON, Edgar E., ed. *Lafayette, Guest of the Nation: A Contemporary Account of the Triumphal Tour of General Lafayette through the United States in 1824–1825.* 3 vols. Oxford, Ohio, 1950–1957.

180 CLARK, Thomas D., ed. *South Carolina: The Grand Tour, 1780–1865.* Columbia, S.C., 1973.

181 COMMAGER, Henry S., ed. *America in Perspective: The United States through Foreign Eyes.* New York, 1947.

182 HAFEN, LeRoy R., and Ann W. HAFEN, eds. *To the Rockies and Oregon, 1839–1842; with Diaries and Accounts.* Glendale, Calif., 1955.

183 HANDLIN, Oscar, ed. *This Was America: True Accounts of People and Places, Manners and Customs, as Recorded by European Travelers to the Western Shore in the Eighteenth, Nineteenth and Twentieth Centuries.* Cambridge, Mass., 1949.

184 LINDLEY, Harlow, ed. *Indiana as Seen by Early Travelers: A Collection of Reprints from Books of Travel, Letters and Diaries prior to 1830.* Indianapolis, 1916.

185 MORIZE, André, and Elliott M. GRANT, eds. *Selections from French Travelers in America.* New York, 1929.

186 NEVINS, Allan, ed. *America through British Eyes.* New ed. New York, 1948.

187 PIERCE, Besse L., ed. *As Others see Chicago: Impressions of Visitors, 1673–1933.* Chicago, 1933.

188 PROBST, George E., ed. *The Happy Republic: A Reader in Tocqueville's America.* New York, 1962.

189 SCHWAAB, Eugene L., and Jacqueline BULL, eds. *Travels in the Old South; Selected from Periodicals of the Times.* 2 vols. Lexington, Ky., 1973.

190 STUDLEY, Miriam V., ed. *Historic New Jersey through Visitors' Eyes.* New Brunswick, 1964.

200 THWAITES, Reuben G., ed. *Early Western Travels, 1748–1846.* 32 vols. Cleveland, 1904–1907.

201 TRYON, Warren S., ed. *A Mirror for Americans: Life and Manners in the United States, 1790–1870, as Recorded by American Travelers.* 3 vols. Chicago, 1952.

3. Personal Narratives

202 ABDY, Edward Strutt. *Journal of a Residence and Tour in the United States of America, from April, 1833, to October, 1834.* 3 vols. London, 1835.

203 ADDINGTON, Henry U. *Youthful America; Selections from Henry Unwin Addington's Residence in the United States of America, 1822–1825.* Ed. Bradford PERKINS. Berkeley, 1960.

204 ALEXANDER, James E. *Transatlantic Sketches, Comprising Visits to the Most Interesting Scenes in North and South America.* 2 vols. London, 1833.

205 ANDERSON, William M. *The Rocky Mountain Journals of William Marshall Anderson: The West in 1834.* Ed. Dale L. MORGAN and Eleanor T. HARRIS. San Marino, Calif., 1967.

206 ARESE, Francesco. *A Trip to the Prairies and in the Interior of North America [1837–1838].* New York, 1934.

207 ARFWEDSON, Carl D. *The United States and Canada, in 1832, 1833, and 1834.* 2 vols. London, 1834.

208 ATWATER, Caleb. *Remarks Made on A Tour to Prairie du Chien, there to Washington City.* Columbus, 1831.

209 AUDUBON, John James. *Audubon and His Journals with Zoological and Other Notes.* Ed. Maria R. AUDUBON. Notes by Elliott COUES. 2 vols. New York, 1897.

210 AUDUBON, John James. *Eighteen Twenty Six Journal of John James Audubon.* Ed. Alice FORD. Norman, Okla., 1967.

211 AUDUBON, John James. *Journal of John James Audubon Made during His Trip to New Orleans in 1820–1821.* Ed Howard CORNING. Boston, 1929.

212 BARNARD, Henry. "The South Atlantic States in 1833, as Seen by a New Englander." *Md Hist Mag,* XIII (1918), 267–294, 295–386.

213 BEAUMONT, Gustave de. *Lettres d'Amerique, 1831–1832.* Ed. André JARDIN and George W. PIERSON. Paris, 1973.

214 BELL, John R. *The Journal of Captain John R. Bell, 1820, Official Journalist for the Stephen H. Long Expedition to the Rocky Mountains, 1820.* Ed. Harlin M. FULLER and LeRoy R. HAFEN. Glendale, Calif., 1957.

215 BENTON, Colbee C. *A Visitor to Chicago in Indian Days: "Journal to the 'Far Off West.'"* Ed Paul M. ANGLE and James R. GETZ. Chicago, 1957.

216 BERNHARD KARL, Duke of Saxe-Weimar-Eisenach. *Travels through North America, During the Years 1825 and 1826.* 2 vols. Philadelphia, 1828.

217 BIERCE, Lucius Verus. *Travels in the Southland, 1822–1823; The Journal of Lucius Verus Bierce.* Ed. George W. KNEPPER. Columbus, Ohio, 1966.

218 BILLIGMEIER, Robert H., and Fred A PICARD, eds. and trans. *The Old Land and the New: Journals of Two Swiss Families in America in the 1820's.* Minneapolis, 1965.

219 BIRKBECK, Morris. *Letters from Illinois.* Philadelphia, 1818.

220 BIRKBECK, Morris. *Notes on a Journey in America, from the Coast of Virginia to The Territory of Illinois.* Philadelphia, 1817.

221 BLANE, W. N. *An Excursion through the United States and Canada during the Years 1822–1823.* London, 1824.

222 BOARDMAN, James. *America, and the Americans.* London, 1833.

223 BROMME, Traugott. *Reisen durch die Vereinigten Staaten und Ober-Canada.* 3 vols. Baltimore, 1834–1835.

224 BROTHERS, Thomas. *The United States of North America as They Are: Not as They Are Generally Described, Being a Cure for Radicalism.* London, 1840.

225 BUCKINGHAM, James S. *America, Historical, Statistic and Descriptive.* 2 vols. New York, 1841.

226 BUCKINGHAM, James S. *The Eastern and Western States of America.* 3 vols. London, 1842.

227 BUCKINGHAM, James S. *The Slave States of America.* 2 vols. London, 1842.

228 BULLOCK, W. *Sketch of a Journey through the Western States of North America, from New Orleans . . . to New York, in 1827.* London, 1827.

229 CATHCART, James Leander. "Southern Louisiana and South Alabama in 1819: The Journal of James Leander Cathcart." Ed. Walter PRICHARD; Fred B. KNIFFER; and Clair A. BROWN. *La Hist Q,* XXVIII (1945), 735–921.

230 CATLIN, George. *Episodes from Life among the Indians, and Last Rambles.* Ed. Marvin C. ROSS. Norman, Okla., 1959.

231 CATLIN, George. *Letters and Notes on the Manners, Customs, and Condition of the North American Indians [1832–1839].* Minneapolis, 1965.

232 CHEVALIER, Michel. *Society, Manners and Politics in the United States: Being a Series of Letters on North America.* Boston, 1839.

233 COBBETT, William. *A Year's Residence in the United States of America.* 3 vols. New York, 1818.

234 COKE, Edward T. *A Subaltern's Furlough.* 2 vols. London, 1833.

235 COMBE, George. *Notes on the United States of North America during a Phrenological Visit in 1838–1840.* 2 vols. Philadelphia, 1841.

236 CORRÊA DA SERRA, José Francesco. *The Abbé Corrêa in America, 1812–1820.* Ed. Richard B. DAVIS. Philadelphia, 1955.

237 COX, Ross. *The Columbia River; or Scenes and Adventures during a Residence of Six Years on the Western Side of the Rocky Mountains.* London, 1831. New ed. by Edgar I. STEWART and Jane R. STEWART. Norman, Okla., 1957.†

238 DALE, Harrison C., ed. *The Ashley-Smith Explorations and the Discovery of a Central Route to the Pacific, 1822–1829, with the Original Journals.* Glendale, Calif., 1941.

239 DARBY, William. *A Tour from the City of New York to Detroit, in the Michigan Territory.* New York, 1819.

240 D'ARUSMONT, Frances Wright. *Views of Society and Manners in America.* New York, 1821. New ed. by Paul R. BAKER. Cambridge, Mass., 1963.

241 DAUBENY, Charles G. B. *Journal of a Tour through the United States, and in Canada, Made during the Years 1837–38.* Oxford, 1843.

242 DEAN, Thomas. "Journal of Thomas Dean. A Voyage to Indiana in 1817." *Ind Hist Soc Publ,* VI (1918), 273–345.

243 DERBY, Edward George Geoffrey Smith Stanley, 14th Earl of. *Journal of a Tour in America, 1824–1825.* London, 1930.

244 DEROOS, Frederick F. *Personal Narrative of Travels in the United States and Canada in 1826.* London, 1827.

245 DOUGLAS, David. *Journal Kept by David Douglas during His Travels in North America, 1823–27.* London, 1914.

246 DRESEL, Gustav. *Gustav Dresel's Houston Journal: Adventures in North America and Texas, 1837–1841.* Ed. and trans. Max FREUND. Austin, 1954.

247 DUDEN, Gottfried. *Bericht uber eine Reise nach den westlichen Staaten Nordamerikas.* Elberfelt, 1829.

248 DUNCAN, John M. *Travels through Part of the United States and Canada in 1818 and 1819.* 2 vols. New York, 1823.

249 EVANS, Estwick. *A Pedestrious Tour, of Four Thousand Miles, through the Western States and Territories, during the Winter and Spring of 1818.* Concord, N.H., 1818.

250 EVARTS, Jeremiah. *Through the South and West with Jeremiah Evarts in 1826.* Ed. J. Orin OLIPHANT. Lewisburg, Pa., 1956.

251 FARNHAM, Thomas Jefferson. *Travels in the Great Western Prairies, the Anahuac and Rocky Mountains, and in the Oregon Territory.* New York, 1843.

252 FAUX, William. *Memorable Days in America; Being a Journal of a Tour to the United States.* London, 1823.

253 FEARON, Henry B. *Sketches of America. A Narrative of a Journey of Five Thousand Miles through the Eastern and Western States of America.* London, 1818.

254 FIDLER, Isaac. *Observations on Professions, Literature, Manners, and Emigration in the United States and Canada, Made during a Residence There in 1832.* New York, 1833.

255 FIELD, Matthew C. *Matt Field on the Santa Fe Trail.* Ed. John E. SUNDER. Norman, Okla., 1960.

256 FLAGG, Edmund. *The Far West: or, a Tour beyond the Mountains.* 2 vols. New York, 1838.

257 FLINT, James *Letters from America.* Edinburgh, 1822.

258 FORDHAM, Elias P. *Personal Narrative of Travels in Virginia, Maryland, Pennsylvania, Ohio, Indiana, Kentucky; and of a Residence in the Illinois Territory, 1817–1818.* Cleveland, 1906.

259 FOWLER, Jacob. *The Journal of Jacob Fowler, Narrating an Adventure from Arkansas through the Indian Territory.* Ed. Elliott COUES. New York, 1898.

260 FRÉMONT, John C. *Expeditions of John Charles Frémont.* Vol I: *Travels from 1838 to 1844.* Ed. Donald JACKSON and Mary Lee SPENCE. Urbana, Ill., 1970.

261 GAILLARDET, Frederic. *Sketches of Early Texas and Louisiana.* Ed. and trans. James L. SHEPHERD, III. Austin, 1966.

262 GILPIN, Henry D. "A Glimpse of Baltimore Society in 1827: Letters of Henry D. Gilpin." Ed. Ralph D. GRAY and Gerald E. HARTDAGEN. *Md Hist Mag,* LXIX (1974), 256–270.

263 GILPIN, Henry D. "A Tour of Virginia in 1827: Letters of Henry D. Gilpin to His Father." Ed. Ralph D. GRAY. *Va Mag Hist Bio,* LXXVI (1968), 444–471.

264 GILPIN, Henry D. "Washington in 1825: Observations by Henry D. Gilpin." Ed. Ralph D. GRAY. *Del Hist,* XI (1965), 240–250.

265 GRASSI, Giovanni. *Notizie varie sullo stato presente della republica degli Stati Uniti.* Rome, 1818.

266 GREENE, Elizabeth V. T. "Going West: A Journey to Illinois in 1835." *Vt Hist,* XXXI (1973), 95–100.

267 GREENE, Welcome Arnold. *The Journals of Welcome Arnold Greene: Journeys to the South, 1822–1824.* Ed Alice E. SMITH. Madison, 1957.

268 GRUND, Francis J. *The Americans in Their Moral, Social, and Political Relations.* 2 vols. London, 1837.

269 GRUND, Francis J. *Aristocracy in America: From the Sketch-Book of a German Nobleman.* 2 vols. London, 1839.

270 HALL, Basil. *Travels in North America, in the Years 1827 and 1828.* 3 vols. Edinburgh, 1829.

271 HALL, Francis, *Travels in Canada and the United States, in 1816 and 1817.* London, 1818.

272 HALL, James. *Notes on the Western States.* Philadelphia, 1838.

273 HALL, Margaret. *The Aristocratic Journey; Being the Outspoken Letters of Mrs. Basil Hall Written during a Fourteen Month Sojourn in America, 1827–1828.* Ed. Una POPE-HENNESSY. New York, 1931.

274 HALL, William. "From England to Illinois in 1821: The Journal of William Hall." Ed. Jay MONAGHAN. *Ill State Hist J,* XXXIX (1946), 21–67, 208–53.

275 HAMILTON, Thomas. *Men and Manners in America.* 2 vols. Philadelphia, 1833.

276 HODGSON, Adam. *Remarks during a Journey through North America, in the Years 1819, 1820, and 1821.* New York, 1823.

277 HOFFMAN, Charles Fenno. *A Winter in the Far West.* 2 vols. London, 1835.

278 HOLMES, Isaac. *An Account of the United States of America, Derived from Actual Observation, during a Residence of Four Years in the Republic.* London, 1823.

279 INGRAHAM, Joseph Holt. *The South-West, by a Yankee.* 2 vols. New York, 1835.

280 IRVING, Washington. *A Tour on the Prairies.* Philadelphia, 1835. New ed. by John F. McDERMOTT. Norman, Okla., 1956.

281 JAMES, Edwin, comp. *Account of an Expedition from Pittsburgh to the Rocky Mountains, Performed in the Years 1819 and '20.* 2 vols. Philadelphia, 1822–1823.

282 JANSSENS, Agustín. *The Life and Adventures of Don Agustín Janssens, 1834–1856.* Ed. William H. ELLISON and Francis PRICE. San Marino, Calif., 1953.

283 KEATING, William H., comp. *Narrative of an Expedition to the Source of St. Peter's River, Lake Winnepeek, Lake of the Woods, &c. Performed in the Year 1823.* 2 vols. Philadelphia, 1824.

284 KEMBLE, Frances A. *Journal.* 2 vols. London, 1835.

285 KEMBLE, Frances A. *Journal of a Residence on a Georgian Plantation in 1838–39.* New York, 1863. New ed. by John A. SCOTT. New York, 1961.†

286 KIRKLAND, Caroline M. S. *A New Home—Who'll Follow? or, Glimpses of Western Life.* New York, 1839.

287 KLINKOWSTRÖM, Baron Axel Leonhard, *Baron Klinkowström's America, 1818–1820.* Ed. Franklin D. SCOTT. Evanston, Ill., 1952.

288 LARPENTEUR, Charles. *Forty Years a Fur Trader on the Upper Missouri.* 2 vols. New York, 1898.

289 LATROBE, Benjamin H. *Impressions Respecting New Orleans: Diary and Sketches, 1818–1820.* Ed. Samuel WILSON, Jr. New York, 1951.

290 LATROBE, Benjamin H. *The Journal of Latrobe . . . from 1796 to 1820.* New York, 1905.

291 LATROBE, Charles J. *The Rambler in North America, 1832–33.* 2 vols. New York, 1835.

292 LIEBER, Francis. *The Stranger in America.* Philadelphia, 1835.

293 MARRYAT, Frederick. *A Diary in America, with Remarks on Its Institutions.* 2 parts, 3 vols. each. London, 1839. New ed. by Jules ZANGER. Bloomington, Ind., 1960. New ed. by Sydney JACKMAN. New York, 1962.

294 MARTINEAU, Harriet. *Retrospect of Western Travel.* 3 vols. London, 1838.

295 MARTINEAU, Harriet. *Society in America.* 3 vols. London, 1838.

296 MASON, Richard L. *Narrative of Richard Lee Mason in the Pioneer West, 1819.* New York, 1915.

297 MAXIMILIAN ALEXANDER PHILIPP, Prinz von Wiedneuwied. *Travels in the Interior of North America [1832–1834].* London, 1843.

298 MONTLEZUN, Baron de. *Voyage fait dans les années 1816 et 1817, de New York à la Nouvelle Orléans.* 2 vols. Paris, 1818.

299 MONTULÉ, Edouard de. *Travels in America, 1816–1817.* Bloomington, Ind., 1950.

300 MUIR, Andrew Forest, ed. *Texas in 1837: An Anonymous, Contemporary Narrative.* Austin, 1958.

301 MURAT, Achille. *A Moral and Political Sketch of the United States of North America.* London, 1833.

302 MURRAY, Charles A. *Travels in North America during the Years 1834, 1835, and 1836.* 2 vols. London, 1839.

303 NEILSON, Peter. *Recollections of Six Years' Residence in the United States.* Glasgow, 1830.

304 NUTTALL, Thomas. *A Journal of Travels into the Arkansas Territory during the Year 1819.* Philadelphia, 1821.

305 OGDEN, Peter S. *Snake Country Journal, 1826–27.* Ed Kenneth G. DAVIES. London, 1961.

306 OWEN, Robert D. *To Holland and New Harmony: Robert Dale Owen's Travel Journal, 1825–1826.* Ed Josephine M. ELLIOTT. Indianapolis, 1969.

307 PARKER, Amos A. *A Trip to the West and Texas.* Concord, 1835.

308 PARKER, Samuel. *Journal of an Exploring Tour beyond the Rocky Mountains . . ., Performed in the Years 1835, '36, and '37.* Ithaca, N.Y., 1838.

309 PATTIE, James O. *The Personal Narrative of James O. Pattie, of Kentucky.* Cincinnati, 1833.

310 PAULDING, James K. *Letters from the South, Written during an Excursion in the Summer of 1816.* 2 vols. New York, 1817.

311 PAVIE, Théodore. *Souvenirs Atlantiques; Voyage aux États-Unis et au Canada.* 2 vols. Paris, 1833.

312 PIKE, Albert. "Narrative of a Journey in the Prairie." *Ark Hist Assoc Publ,* IV (1917), 66–139.

313 POURTALES, Albert-Alexandre De. *On the Western Tour with Washington Irving: The Journal and Letters of Count de Pourtales.* Ed. George F. SPAULDING and trans. Seymour FEILER. Norman, Okla., 1968.

314 POWER, Tyrone. *Impressions of America; during the Years 1833, 1834, and 1835.* 2 vols. Philadelphia, 1836.

315 ROYALL, Anne N. *The Black Book; or a Continuation of Travels.* 3 vols. Washington, D. C., 1828–1829.

316 ROYALL, Anne N. *Letters from Alabama on Various Subjects.* Washington, D.C., 1830. New ed. by Lucille GRIFFITH. University, Ala., 1969.

317 ROYALL, Anne N. *Mrs. Royall's Pennsylvania, or, Travels Continued in the United States.* 2 vols. Washington, D.C., 1829.

318 ROYALL, Anne N. *Mrs. Royall's Southern Tour, or Second Series of the Black Book.* 3 vols. Washington, D.C., 1830–1831.

319 ROYALL, Anne N. *Sketches of History, Life, and Manners in the United States.* New Haven, 1826.

320 RUSSELL, Osborne. *Journal of a Trapper; or, Nine Years in the Rocky Mountains, 1834–1843.* Boise, Idaho, 1914. New ed. by Aubrey L. HAINES. Lincoln, Neb., 1965†

321 SCHOOLCRAFT, Henry R. *Journal of a Tour into the Interior of Missouri and Arkansas in the Years 1818 and 1819.* London, 1821.

322 SCHOOLCRAFT, Henry R. *The Literary Voyager, or Muzzeniegun.* Ed. Philip P. MASON. East Lansing, Mich., 1962.

323 SCHOOLCRAFT, Henry R. *Narrative Journal of Travels through the Northwestern Regions of the United States Extending from Detroit through the Great Chain of American Lakes to the Sources of the Mississippi River in the Year 1820.* Albany, N. Y., 1821.

324 SCHOOLCRAFT, Henry R. *Narrative of an Expedition through the Upper Mississippi to Itasca Lake.* New York, 1834. New ed. by Philip P. MASON. East Lansing, Michigan, 1958.

325 SCHOOLCRAFT, Henry R. *Scenes and Adventures in the Semi-Alpine Region of the Missouri and Arkansas [in 1818].* Philadelphia, 1853.

326 SEALSFIELD, Charles. *The Americans As They Are; Described in a Tour through the Valley of the Mississippi.* London, 1828.

327 SHERIDAN, Francis C. *Galveston Island; or, a Few Months off the Coast of Texas: the Journal of Francis C. Sheridan, 1839–1840.* Ed Willis W. PRATT. Austin, 1954.

328 SHIRREFF, Patrick. *A Tour through North America.* Edinburgh, 1835.

329 SIBLEY, George C., et al. *The Road to Santa Fe: the Journal and Diaries of George Champlin Sibley and others . . . , 1825–1827.* Ed. Kate L. GREGG. Albuquerque, 1952.

330 SMET, Pierre Jean de. *Letters and Sketches, with a Narrative of a Year's Residence among the Indian Tribes of the Rocky mountains.* Philadelphia, 1843.

331 SMITH, Jedediah S. *The Travels of Jedediah Smith.* Ed. Maurice S. SULLIVAN Santa Anna, Calif., 1934.

332 STUART, James. *Three Years in North America.* 2 vols. Edinburgh, 1833.

333 TANNER, Henry S. *The American Traveler; or Guide through the United States.* Philadelphia, 1834. [Ten editions published through 1846.]

334 TANNER, John. *A Narrative of Captivity and Adventures of John Tanner.* Ed. Edwin JAMES. New York, 1830.

335 TOCQUEVILLE, Alexis de. *Democracy in America.* 4 vols. London, 1835–1840. New ed. by J. P. MAYER and Max LERNER. 2 vols. New York, 1966. [Numerous other editions.]

336 TOCQUEVILLE, Alexis de. *Journey to America.* Ed. J. P. MAYER. New Haven, 1960.

337 TOLMIE, William F. *The Journals of William Fraser Tolmie, Physician and Fur Trader.* Vancouver, 1963.

338 TROLLOPE, Frances M. *Domestic Manners of the Americans.* 2 vols. London, 1832. New ed. by Donald SMALLEY. New York, 1949.

339 TUDOR, William. *Letters on the Eastern States.* New York, 1820.

340 WILHELM, Paul. *Travels in North America, 1822–1824.* Ed. Savoie LOTTIN-VILLE and trans. W. Robert NISKE. Norman, Okla., 1974.

341 WISLIZENUS, F. A. *A Journey to the Rocky Mountains in the Year 1839.* St. Louis, 1912.

342 WYETH, Nathaniel J. *The Correspondence and Journals of Captain Nathaniel Wyeth, 1831–1836.* Eugene, Ore., 1899.

343 YOUNT, George C. *George C. Yount and His Chronicles of the West.* Ed. Charles L. CAMP. Denver, 1966.

344 ZAVALA, Lorenzo de. *Viaje a los Estados-Unidas.* Paris, 1834.

4. Secondary Works

345 ADAMS, Ephraim D. "The Point of View of the British Traveler in America." *Pol Sci Q,* XXIX (1914), 244–264.

346 ADAMS, Herbert Baxter. *Jared Sparks and Alexis de Tocqueville.* Baltimore, 1898.

347 ALFORD, Terry L. "The West as a Desert in American Thought Prior to Long's 1819–1820 Expedition." *J W,* VIII (1969), 515–525.

348 ASHBY, Clifford. "Fanny Kemble's 'Vulgar' Journal." *Pa Mag Hist Biog,* XCVIII (1974), 58–66.

349 BERGER, Max. *The British Traveller in America, 1836–1860.*

350 BRINK, Florence Roos. "Literary Travelers in Louisiana between 1803 and 1860." *La Hist Q,* XXXI (1948), 394–424.

351 BROOKS, John G. *As Others See Us: A Study of Progress in the United States.* New York, 1908.

352 BURNS, Francis P. "Lafayette Visits New Orleans." *La Hist Q,* XXIX (1946), 296–340.

353 CAMP, Charles L. "Jedediah Smith's First Far-Western Expedition." *W Hist Q,* IV (1973), 151–170.

354 CATE, Margaret Davis. "Mistakes in Fanny Kemble's Journal." *Ga Hist Q,* XLIX (1960), 1–17.

355 CLARK, Thomas D. "The Great Visitation to American Democracy." *Miss Val Hist Rev,* XLIV (1957), 3–28.

356 DILLON, Richard H. "Stephen Long's Great American Desert." *Am Phil Soc Proc,* CXI (1967), 93–108.

357 DRESCHER, Seymour. "Tocqueville's Two Démocraties." *J Hist Ideas,* XXV (1964), 201–216.

358 EARNEST, Grace Elvira. "City Life in the Old South: The British Travelers' Image." Doctoral dissertation, Florida State University, 1966.

359 FRANKLIN, John Hope. *A Southern Odyssey: Travelers in the Antebellum North.* Baton Rouge, 1976.

360 GERSHAM, Sally. "Alexis de Tocqueville and Slavery." *Fr Hist Stud,* IX (1976), 467–483.

361 GRIBBIN, William. "A Greater than Lafayette is Here: Dissenting Views of the Last American Visit." *S Atl Q,* LXXIII (1974), 348–362.

362 HAMILTON, Holman, and James L. CROUTHAMEL. "A Man for Both Parties: Francis J. Grund as Political Cameleon." *Pa Mag Hist Biog,* XCVII (1973), 465–484.

363 HAY, Robert P. "The American Revolution Twice Recalled: Lafayette's Visit and the Election of 1824." *Ind Mag Hist,* LXIX (1973), 43–62.

364 HEINEMAN, Helen L. "Frances Trollope in the New World: *Domestic Manners of the Americans.*" *Am Q,* XXI (1969), 544–559.

365 HEINEMAN, Helen L. " 'Starving in That Land of Plenty': New Backgrounds to Frances Trollope's *Domestic Manners of the Americans.*" *Am Q,* XXIV (1972), 643–660.

366 HEWITT, David Gerald. "Slavery in the Old South: The British Travelers' Image, 1825–1860." Doctoral dissertation, Florida State University, 1968.

367 HILLBRUNER, Anthony. "Frances Wright: Egalitarian Reformer." *S Sp J,* XXIII (1958), 193–203.

368 HORWITZ, Morton J. "Tocqueville and the Tyranny of the Majority." *Rev Pol,* XXVIII (1966), 293–307.

369 HOSKINS, Janina W. "The Image of America in Accounts of Polish Travelers of the 18th and 19th Centuries." *Q J Lib Cong,* XXII (1965), 226–245.

369A JAKLE, John A. *Images of the Ohio Valley: A Historical Geography of Travel, 1740–1860.* New York, 1977.

370 LERNER, Max. "Tocqueville's *Democracy in America:* Politics, Law and the Elites." *Antioch Rev,* XXV (1965–1966), 543–563.

371 MARSHALL, Lynn L., and Seymour DRESCHER. "American Historians and Tocqueville's *Democracy.*" *J Am Hist* LV (1968), 512–532.

372 MARTIN, John M. "The People of New Orleans as Seen by Her Visitors, 1803–1860." *La Stud,* VI (1967), 361–375.

373 MCWILLIAMS, Tennant S. "The Marquis and the Myth: Lafayette's Visit to Alabama, 1825." *Ala Rev,* XXII (1969), 135–146.

374 MESICK, Jane L. *The English Traveller in America, 1785–1835.* New York, 1922.

375 MEYERS, Marvin. "The Basic Democrat: A Version of Tocqueville." *Pol Sci Q,* LXXII (1957), 50–70.

376 MILES, Wyndham D. "A Versatile Explorer: A Sketch of William H. Keating." *Minn Hist,* XXXVI (1959), 294–299.

377 MURPHY, William J., Jr. "Alexis de Tocqueville in New York: The Formulation of the Egalitarian Thesis." *N Y Hist Soc Q,* LXI (1977), 69–79.

378 PATTON, James W. "Glimpses of North Carolina in the Writings of Northern and Foreign Travelers, 1783–1860." *N C Hist Rev,* XLV (1968), 298–323.

379 PIERSON, George Wilson. *Tocqueville and Beaumont in America.* New York, 1938.

380 RESH, Richard W. "Alexis de Tocqueville and the Negro: *Democracy in America* Reconsidered." *J Neg Hist,* XLVIII (1963), 251–259.

381 SCHLEIFER, James Thomas. "The Making of Tocqueville's *Democracy:* Studies in the Development of Alexis de Tocqueville's Work on America with Particular Attention to His Sources, His Ideas, and His Methods." Doctoral dissertation, Yale University, 1972.

382 SCOTT, John A. "On the Authenticity of Franny Kemble's Journal of a Residence on a Georgian Plantation in 1838–39." *J Neg Hist,* XLVI (1961), 233–242.

383 SEMMES, Raphael. *Baltimore as Seen by Visitors, 1783–1860.* Baltimore, 1953.

384 SHINGLETON, Royce Gordon. "Rural Life in the Old South: The British Traveller's Image, 1820–1860." Doctoral dissertation, Florida State University, 1971.

385 SIBLEY, Marilyn M. *Travelers in Texas, 1761–1860.* Austin, 1967.

386 SONGY, Benedict G. "Alexis de Tocqueville and Slavery: Judgments and Predictions." Doctoral dissertation, St. Louis University, 1969.

387 STROUT, Cushing. "Tocqueville's Duality: Describing America and Thinking of Europe." *Am Q,* XXI (1969), 87–99.

388 TUCKERMAN, Henry T. *America and Her Commentators. With a Critical Sketch of Travel in the United States.* New York, 1964.

III. Biographies, Autobiographies, Journals, Correspondence, and Collected Works of Political Leaders and Selected Public Figures

Adair, John [1757–1840]

389 LEGER, William Garrard. "The Public Life of John Adair." Doctoral dissertation, University of Kentucky, 1953.

Adams, Charles Francis [1807–1886]

See also **1538**

390 ADAMS, Charles Francis. *Diary.* Ed. Aida DiPace DONALD; David DONALD; Marc FRIEDLANDER; and L. H. BUTTERFIELD. 6 vols. to date. Cambridge, Mass., 1964–.

391 ADAMS, Charles Francis. *Charles Francis Adams.* Boston, 1900.

392 DUBERMAN, Martin. *Charles Francis Adams, 1807–1886.* Boston, 1961.†

Adams, John [1735–1826]

393 ADAMS, Charles Francis, ed. *The Works of John Adams.* 10 vols. Boston, 1850–1856.

394 ALLISON, John Murray. *Adams and Jefferson: The Story of a Friendship.* Norman, 1966.

395 CAPPON, Lester J., ed. *The Adams-Jefferson Letters: The Complete Correspondence between Thomas Jefferson and Abigail and John Adams.* 2 vols. Chapel Hill, 1959.

396 CHINARD, Gilbert. *Honest John Adams.* Boston, 1933.

397 HEDGES, James B., ed. "John Adams Speaks His Mind [1817]." *Am Hist Rev,* XLVII (1942), 806–809.

398 KOCH, Adrienne, ed. *Adams and Jefferson: "Posterity Must Judge."* Chicago, 1963.

399 KOCH, Adrienne, and William PEDEN, eds. *The Selected Writings of John and John Quincy Adams.* New York, 1946.

400 PETERSON, Merrill D. *Adams and Jefferson: A Revolutionary Dialogue.* Athens, Ohio, 1976.†

401 RODESCH, Jerold Clarence. "America and the Middle Ages: A Study in the Thought of John and John Quincy Adams." Doctoral dissertation, Rutgers University, 1971.

402 SMITH, Page. *John Adams.* 2 vols. Garden City, N.Y., 1961.

403 STEWART, Donald H., and George P. CLARK. "Misanthrope or Humanitarian? John Adams in Retirement." *N Eng Q,* XXVIII (1955), 216–236.

Adams, John Quincy [1767–1848]

See also **399, 1159, 1168, 1169, 1199, 1208, 1220, 1239, 1277–1308, 1467, 3484, 3487, 3545, 3732**

404 ADAMS, Charles Francis, ed. *Memoirs of John Quincy Adams, Comprising Portions of His Diary from 1795 to 1848.* 12 vols. Philadelphia, 1874–1877.

405 BEMIS, Samuel Flagg. *John Quincy Adams and the Foundations of American Foreign Policy.* New York, 1949.†

406 BEMIS, Samuel Flagg. *John Quincy Adams and the Union.* New York, 1956.

407 CALLANAN, Harold John. "The Political Economy of John Quincy Adams." Doctoral dissertation, Boston University, 1975.

408 CLARK, Bennett Champ. *John Quincy Adams, "Old Man Eloquent."* Boston, 1932.

409 FORD, Worthington C., ed. *The Writings of John Quincy Adams.* 7 vols. New York, 1913–1917.

410 HECHT, Marie B. *John Quincy Adams: A Personal History of an Independent Man.* New York, 1972

411 LIPSKY, George A. *John Quincy Adams: His Theory and Ideas.* New York, 1950†

412 MCLAUGHLIN, Andrew C., ed. "Letters of John Quincy Adams to Alexander Hamilton Everett, 1811–1837." *Am Hist Rev,* XI (1905), 88–116.

413 MACLEAN, William Jerry. "John Quincy Adams and Reform." Doctoral dissertation, University of North Carolina at Chapel Hill, 1971.

414 MACOLL, John Douglas. "Congressman John Quincy Adams, 1831–1833." Doctoral dissertation, Indiana University, 1973.

415 MORSE, John T., Jr. *John Quincy Adams.* New York, 1882.

416 NEVINS, Allan, ed. *The Diary of John Quincy Adams, 1794–1845.* New York, 1928.

417 OWENS, Patrick James. "John Quincy Adams and American Utilitarianism." Doctoral dissertation, University of Notre Dame, 1976.

418 RODESCH, Jerold Clarence. "America and the Middle Ages: A Study in the Thought of John and John Quincy Adams." Doctoral dissertation, Rutgers University, 1971.

419 STENBERG, Richard R. "J. Q. Adams: Imperialist and Apostate." *S W Soc Sci Q*, XVI (1936), 37–49.

420 WILTSE, Charles M. "John Quincy Adams and the Party System: A Review Article." *J Pol*, IV (1942), 407–414.

Allen, William [1803–1879]

421 MCGRANE, Reginald Charles. *William Allen, a Study in Western Democracy.* Columbus, 1925.

Anderson, Richard Clough [1788–1826]

422 TISCHENDORF, Alfred, and E. Taylor PARKS, eds. *The Diary and Journal of Richard Clough Anderson, Jr., 1814–1826.* Durham, 1964.

Appleton, Nathan [1779–1861]

423 GREGORY, Frances W. *Nathan Appleton, Merchant and Entrepreneur, 1779–1861.* Charlottesville, 1976.

Ashley, William H. [1778–1838]

424 CLOKEY, Richard M. "The Life of William H. Ashley." Doctoral dissertation, University of Wisconsin, Madison, 1969.

425 MORGAN, Dale L., ed. *The West of William H. Ashley: The International Struggle for the Fur Trade of the Missouri, the Rocky Mountains, and the Columbia, with Explorations beyond the Continental Divide, Recorded in the Diaries and Letters of William H. Ashley and His Contemporaries, 1822–1838.* Denver, 1964.

Atkinson, Henry [1782–1842]

426 NICHOLS, Roger L. *General Henry Atkinson: A Western Military Career.* Norman, 1965.

Austin, Moses [1761–1821]

See also **2402**

427 GARDNER, James Alexander. "The Life of Moses Austin, 1761–1821." Doctoral dissertation, Washington University, 1963.

428 GARDNER, James Alexander. "The Business Career of Moses Austin, 1798–1821." *Mo Hist Rev,* L (1956), 235–247.

Austin, Stephen F. [1793–1836]

See also **2405, 2439**

429 BARKER, Eugene C. *The Life of Stephen F. Austin, Founder of Texas.* Nashville, 1925.†

430 BARKER, Eugene C., ed. *The Austin Papers.* 3 vols. Washington, Austin, 1924–1927.

431 BEERS, Henry P., ed. "Stephen F. Austin and Anthony Butler Documents." *S W Hist Q,* LXII (1958), 233–240.

432 RASBURY, Ruth Grandstaff. *The Broad Land; The Life and Times of Stephen Fuller Austin.* Philadelphia, 1972.

Baldwin, Simeon [1761–1851]

433 BALDWIN, Simeon E. *Life and Letters of Simeon Baldwin.* New Haven, 1919.

Bancroft, George [1800–1891]

434 HOWE, M. A. De Wolfe, *The Life and Letters of George Bancroft.* 2 vols. New York, 1908.

435 NYE, Russel B. *George Bancroft, Brahmin Rebel.* New York, 1944.

Barbour, James [1775–1842]

436 LOWERY, Charles Douglas. "James Barbour, A Politician and Planter of Ante-Bellum Virginia." Doctoral dissertation, University of Virginia, 1966.

Barnard, Daniel D. [1796–1821]

437 PENNEY, Sherry. *Patrician in Politics: Daniel Dewey Barnard of New York.* Port Washington, N. Y., 1974.

Bates, Frederick [1777–1825]

438 MARSHALL, Thomas Maitland. *The Life and Papers of Frederick Bates.* 2 vols. St. Louis, 1926.

Bell, John [1797–1869]

439 PARKS, Joseph Howard. *John Bell of Tennessee.* Baton Rouge, 1950.

440 PARKS, Norman L. "The Career of John Bell as Congressman from Tennessee, 1827–1841." *Tenn Hist Q,* I (1942), 229–249.

Bennett, James Gordon [1795–1872]

See also **4553**

441 CARLSON, Oliver. *The Man Who Made News, James Gordon Bennett.* New York, 1942.

442 SEITZ, Don C. *The James Gordon Bennetts, Father and Son.* Indianapolis, 1928.

Benton, Thomas Hart [1782–1858]

See also **2396, 2557, 2591**

443 BENTON, Thomas Hart. *Thirty Years' View.* New York, 1854–1856.

444 CHAMBERS, William Nisbet. *Old Bullion Benton: Senator from the New West.* Boston, 1956.

445 MCCANDLESS, Perry G. "Thomas Hart Benton: His Source of Political Strength in Missouri from 1815–1838." Doctoral dissertation, University of Missouri, Columbia, 1953.

446 MCCANDLESS, Perry G. "The Rise of Thomas Hart Benton in Missouri Politics." *Mo Hist Rev,* L (1955), 16–29.

447 MCCANDLESS, Perry G. "The Political Philosophy and Political Personality of Thomas Hart Benton." *Mo Hist Rev,* L (1956), 145–158.

448 MEIGS, William M. *The Life of Thomas Hart Benton.* Philadelphia, 1904.

449 ROGERS, Joseph M. *Thomas Hart Benton.* Philadelphia, 1905.

450 ROOSEVELT, Theodore. *Life of Thomas Hart Benton.* New York, 1887.

451 SHALHOPE, Robert E. "Thomas Hart Benton and Missouri State Politics: A Re-Examination." *Mo Hist Soc Bull,* XXV (1969), 171–191.

452 SMITH, Elbert B. *Magnificent Missourian: The Life of Thomas Hart Benton.* Philadelphia, 1958.

Berrien, John MacPherson [1781–1856]

See also **1390, 2225**

453 MCCRARY, Royce Coggins. "John MacPherson Berrien of Georgia: A Political Biography." Doctoral dissertation, University of Georgia, 1971.

Bibb, George M. [1776–1859]

454 GOFF, John S. "The Last Leaf: George Mortimer Bibb." *Reg Ky Hist Soc,* LIX (1961), 331–342.

Biddle, Nicholas [1786–1844]

See also **1496, 1501, 1519**

455 GOVAN, Thomas Payne. *Nicholas Biddle: Nationalist and Public Banker, 1786–1844.* Chicago, 1959.†

456 MCGRANE, Reginald, C., ed. *The Correspondence of Nicholas Biddle Dealing with National Affairs, 1807–1844.* Boston, 1919.

Binney, Horace [1780–1875]

457 BINNEY, Charles C. *Life of Horace Binney, with Selections from His Letters.* Philadelphia, 1903.

Birney, James G. [1792–1857]

458 BIRNEY, William. *James G. Birney and His Times.* New York. 1890.

459 DUMOND, Dwight, L., ed. *Letters of James Gillespie Birney, 1831–1857.* 2 vols., New York, 1938.

460 FLADELAND, Betty L. *James Gillespie Birney: Slaveholder to Abolitionist.* Ithaca, 1955.

Black Hawk [1767–1838]

461 BLACK HAWK. *Life of Ma-Ka-Tai-Me-She-Kia-Kiak, or Black Hawk.* Cincinnati, 1833. New ed. by Donald Jackson. Urbana, Ill., 1964.

462 COLE, Cyrenus. *I am a Man: The Indian Black Hawk.* Iowa City, 1938.

Blair, Francis P. [1791–1876]

See also **1377–1379**

463 SMITH, William Ernest. *The Francis Preston Blair Family in Politics.* New York, 1933.

Borden, Gail [1801–1874]

464 FRANTZ, Joe B. *Gail Borden: Dairyman to a Nation.* Norman, 1951.

Bradish, Luther [1783–1863]

465 GIMELLI, Louis B. "Luther Bradish, 1783–1863." Doctoral dissertation, New York University, 1964.

Brackenridge, Henry Marie [1786–1871]

466 KELLER, William F. *The Nation's Advocate: Henry Marie Brackenridge and Young America.* Pittsburgh, 1956.

Brown, Bedford [1792–1870]

467 JONES, Houston, G. "Bedford Brown: State Rights Unionist." *N C Hist Rev* XXXI (1955), 321–345, 483–511.

Bown, James [1766–1835]

468 PADGETT, James A., ed. "Letters of James Brown to Henry Clay, 1804–1835." *La Hist Q,* XXIV (1941), 921–1177.

Brownson, Orestes A. [1803–1876]

469 BROWNSON, Henry F. *Orestes A. Brownson's Early Life.* Detroit, 1898.

470 BROWNSON, Henry F., ed. *Works of Orestes A. Brownson.* 20 vols. 1882–1907.

471 GILMORE, William James. "Orestes Brownson and New England Religious Culture, 1803–1827." Doctoral dissertation, University of Virginia, 1971.

472 LAPATI, Americo D. *Orestes Brownson.* New York, 1965.†

473 SCHLESINGER, Arthur, M., Jr. *Orestes A. Brownson: A Pilgrim's Progress.* Boston, 1939.

Buchanan, James [1791–1868]

See also **1174, 1555**

474 CURTIS, George T. *Life of James Buchanan.* 2 vols. New York, 1883.

475 HILLMAN, Franklin P. "The Diplomatic Career of James Buchanan." Doctoral dissertation, George Washington University, 1953.

476 KLEIN, Philip Shriver. *President James Buchanan.* University Park, Penna., 1962

477 MOORE, John Bassett. *The Works of James Buchanan.* 12 vols. Philadelphia, 1908–1911.

Bullard, Henry A [1788–1851]

478 BONQUOIS, Dora J. "The Career of Henry Adams Bullard, Louisiana Jurist, Legislator, and Educator." *La Hist Q,* XXIII (1940), 999–1106.

Burnet, David G. [1788–1870]

479 CHAMBLESS, Beauford. The First President of Texas: The Life of David Gouverneur Burnet." Doctoral dissertation, Rice University, 1954.

480 CLARKE, Mary Whatley. *David G. Burnet.* Austin, 1969.

Butler, Benjamin Franklin [1795–1858]

481 DRISCOLL, William Dennis. "Benjamin F. Butler: Lawyer and Regency Politician." Doctoral dissertation, Fordham University, 1965.

482 EKIRCH, Arthur A., Jr. "Benjamin F. Butler of New York: A Personal Portrait." *N Y Hist,* LVIII (1977), 47–68.

Calhoun, John C. [1782–1850]

See also **1112, 1115, 1116, 1121, 1172, 1395–1396, 1684, 2191, 2197, 2201, 2270, 3652, 3677, 4337**

483 ANDERSON, John M., ed. *Calhoun: Basic Documents.* State College, Penna., 1952.

484 ATWELL, Priscilla Ann. "Freedom and Diversity: Continuity in the Political Tradition of Thomas Jefferson and John C. Calhoun." Doctoral dissertation, University of California, Los Angeles, 1967.

485 BOLLER, Paul F., Jr. "Calhoun on Liberty." *S Atl Q,* LXVI (1967), 395–408.

486 BOUCHER, Chauncey, S., and Robert P. Brooks, eds. *Correspondence Addressed to John C. Calhoun, 1837–1849.* Ann Rep Am Hist Assn, 1929. Washington, D.C., 1931.

487 CAPERS, Gerald M. "A Reconsideration of John C. Calhoun's Transition from Nationalism to Nullification." *J S Hist,* XIV (1948), 34–48.

488 CAPERS, Gerald M. *John C. Calhoun—Opportunist: A Reappraisal.* Gainesville, 1960.†

489 COIT, Margaret L. *John C. Calhoun: American Portrait.* Boston, 1950.†

490 CRALLÉ, Richard K., ed. *The Works of John C. Calhoun.* 6 vols. New York, 1851–1856.

491 CURRENT, Richard N. "John C. Calhoun, Philosopher of Reaction." *Antioch Rev,* III (1943), 223–234.

492 CURRENT, Richard N. *John C. Calhoun.* New York, 1963.

493 DONOGHUE, Francis John. "The Economic and Social Philosophies of John C. Calhoun." Doctoral dissertation, Columbia University, 1969.

494 DRUCKER, Peter F. "A Key to American Politics: Calhoun's Pluralism." *Rev Pol,* X (1948), 412–426.

495 FREEHLING, William W. "Spoilsmen and Interests in the Thought and Career of John C. Calhoun." *J Am Hist,* LII (1965), 25–42.

496 HAY, Thomas R., ed. "John C. Calhoun and the Presidential Campaign of 1824: Some Unpublished Calhoun Letters." *Am Hist Rev,* XL (1934–1935), 82–96, 287–300.

497 HAY, Thomas R. "John C. Calhoun and the Presidential Campaign of 1824." *N C Hist Rev,* XII (1935), 20–44.

498 HOFSTADTER, Richard. "John C. Calhoun: the Marx of the Master Class." *The American Political Tradition and the Men Who Made it.* New York, 1948.†

499 HUNT, Gaillard. *John C. Calhoun.* Philadelphia, 1908.

500 HUNTER, Robert M. T. *Life of John C. Calhoun.* New York, 1843.

501 JAMESON, J. Franklin, ed. *Correspondence of John C. Calhoun.* Ann Rep Am Hist Assn, 1899. Vol. II. Washington, D.C., 1900.

502 KATEB, George. "The Majority Principle: Calhoun and His Antecedents." *Pol Sci Q,* LXXXIV (1969), 583–605.

503 LERNER, Ralph. "Calhoun's New Science of Politics." *Am Pol Sci Rev,* LVII (1963), 918–932.

504 MARMOR, Theodore Richard. "The Career of John C. Calhoun: Politician, Social Critic, Political Philosopher." Doctoral dissertation, Harvard University, 1966.

505 MARMOR, Theodore, R. "Anti-Industrialism and the Old South: The Agrarian Perspective of John C. Calhoun." *Comp Stud Soc Hist,* IX (1967), 377–406.

506 MEIGS, William M. *The Life of John Caldwell Calhoun.* 2 vols. New York, 1917.

507 MERIWETHER, Robert L.; W. Edwin HEMPHILL; and Clyde N. WILSON, eds. *The Papers of John C. Calhoun.* 10 vols to date. Columbia, S.C., 1959–.

508 MERRIAM, Charles E. "The Political Philosophy of John C. Calhoun." *Studies in Southern History and Politics, Inscribed to William Archibald Dunning.* New York, 1914.

509 MOORE, F. W. "Calhoun as Seen by His Political Friends." *S Hist Assn Pub*, VII (1903), 159–169, 269–291, 353–361, 419–426.

510 OGBURN, Charlton. "The Constitutional Principles of John C. Calhoun." *J Pub Law*, II (1953), 303–313.

511 SPAIN, August O. *The Political Theory of John C. Calhoun.* New York, 1951.

512 STEPHENSON, Nathaniel W. "Calhoun, 1812, and After." *Am Hist Rev*, XXXI (1926), 701–707

513 STYRON, Arthur. *The Cast-Iron Man: John C. Calhoun and American Democracy.* New York, 1935.

514 THOMAS, John L., ed. *John C. Calhoun.* New York, 1968.†

515 WARING, Alice Noble, ed. "Letters of John C. Calhoun to Patrick Noble, 1812–1837." *J S Hist*, XVI (1950), 64–73.

516 WILTSE, Charles M. "Calhoun's Democracy." *J Pol*, III (1941), 210–223.

517 WILTSE, Charles M. "Calhoun and the Modern State." *Va Q Rev*, XIII (1937), 396–408.

518 WILTSE, Charles M. *John C. Calhoun.* 3 vols. Indianapolis, 1944–1951.

Call, Richard Keith [1791–1862]

519 DOHERTY, Herbert J. *Richard Keith Call: Southern Unionist.* Gainesville, 1961.

Campbell, David [1779–1859]

520 MITCHELL, David. "The Political Career of Governor David Campbell of Virginia." Doctoral dissertation, Duke University, 1968.

Campbell, George Washington [1769–1848]

521 JORDAN, Weymouth T. *George Washington Campbell of Tennessee: Western Statesman.* Tallahassee, 1955.

Cardozo, Jacob N. [1786–1873]

522 LEIMAN, Melvin M. *Jacob N. Cardozo: Economic Thought in the Antebellum South.* New York, 1966.

Carey, Henry C. [1793–1879]

523 BAILY, Nathan A. "Henry Charles Carey—Forgotten Prophet." Doctoral dissertation, Columbia University, 1946.

524 ELDER, William. *A Memoir of Henry C. Carey.* Philadelphia, 1880.

525 GREEN, Arnold W. *Henry Charles Carey, Nineteenth Century Sociologist.* Philadelphia, 1951.

526 SMITH, George W. *Henry C. Carey and the American Sectional Conflict.* Albuquerque, 1951.

Carey, Mathew [1760–1839]

527 BRADSHER, Earl L. *Mathew Carey, Editor, Author and Publisher.* New York, 1912.

528 ROWE, Kenneth W. *Mathew Carey, a Study in American Economic Development.* Baltimore, 1933.

Cass, Lewis [1782–1866]

See also **1437, 1440, 3760**

529 DUNBAR, Willis F. *Lewis Cass.* Grand Rapids, 1970.

530 MCLAUGHLIN, Andrew C. *Lewis Cass.* Boston, 1891.

531 WOODFORD, Frank B. *Lewis Cass: The Last Jeffersonian.* New Brunswick, 1950.

Cheves, Langdon [1776–1857]

532 HUFF, Archie Vernon, Jr. *Langdon Cheves of South Carolina.* Columbia, S.C., 1977.

Chilton, Thomas [1796–1853]

533 HANNUM, Sharon Elaine. "Thomas Chilton: Lawyer, Politician, Preacher." *Filson Club Hist Q,* XXXVIII (1964), 97–114.

Choate, Rufus [1799–1859]

534 BROWN, Samuel G., ed. *The Works of Rufus Choate, with a Memoir of His Life.* 2 vols. Boston, 1862.

535 FUESS, Claude M. *Rufus Choate, the Wizard of the Law.* New York, 1928.

536 WALKER, David Bradstreet. "Rufus Choate: A Case Study in Old Whiggery." *Essex Inst Hist Coll,* XCIV (1958), 334–355.

Claiborne, John F. H. [1807–1884]

537 WILLIAMS, Frederick D. "The Career of J. F. H. Claiborne, States' Rights Unionist." Doctoral dissertation, Indiana University, 1953.

Clark, William [1770–1838]

See also 2395

538 STEFFEN, Jerome O. *William Clark: Jeffersonian Man on the Frontier*. Norman, 1977.

Clay, Clement Comer [1789–1866]

539 NUERMBERGER, Ruth Ketring. *The Clays of Alabama: A Plantation-Lawyer-Politician Family*. Lexington, 1958

Clay, Henry [1777–1852]

See also 1106, 1107, 1145, 1169, 1170, 1173, 1175, 1226, 1281, 1295, 2244, 3625, 4336

540 CAMPBELL, Randolph Bluford. "Henry Clay and the Emerging Nations of Spanish America, 1815–1829." Doctoral dissertation, University of Virginia, 1966.

541 CLAY, Thomas Hart. *Henry Clay*. Philadelphia, 1910.

542 COLTON, Calvin, ed. *The Works of Henry Clay*. 6 vols. New York, 1857.

543 EATON, Clement. *Henry Clay and the Art of American Politics*. Boston, 1957.†

544 HOPKINS, James F., and Mary W. M. HARGREAVES, eds. *The Papers of Henry Clay*. 5 vols to date. Lexington, 1959–.

545 JONES, Thomas B. "Henry Clay and Continental Expansion, 1820–1844." *Reg Ky Hist Soc*, LXXIII (1975), 241–262.

546 MORLEY, Margaret Ruth. "The Edge of Empire: Henry Clay's American System and the Formulation of American Foreign Policy, 1810–1833." Doctoral dissertation, University of Wisconsin, Madison, 1972.

547 POAGE, George R. *Henry Clay and the Whig Party*. Chapel Hill, 1936.

548 ROGERS, Joseph M. *The True Henry Clay*. Philadelphia, 1904.

549 SCHURZ, Carl. *Life of Henry Clay*. 2 vols. Boston, 1887.

550 VAN DEUSEN, Glyndon G. *The Life of Henry Clay*. Boston, 1937.

551 WINKLER, James E. "Henry Clay: A Current Assessment." *Reg Ky Hist Soc*, LXX (1972), 179–186.

Clay, John Randolph [1808–1885]

552 OESTE, George I. *John Randolph Clay: America's First Career Diplomat.* Philadelphia, 1966.

Clayton, John M. [1796–1856]

See also **2075, 2076**

553 WIRE, Richard Arden. "John M. Clayton and the Search for Order: A Study in Whig Politics and Diplomacy." Doctoral dissertation, University of Maryland, 1971.

Clinch, Duncan L. [1787–1849]

554 PATRICK, Rembert W. *Aristocrat in Uniform: General Duncan L. Clinch.* Gainesville, 1963.

Clinton, De Witt [1769–1828]

See also **1992, 1998, 2004, 2012, 3811, 4701**

555 CAMPBELL, William W. *The Life and Writings of De Witt Clinton.* New York, 1933.

555A BOBBÉ, Dorothie. *De Witt Clinton.* New York, 1933.

Coffee, John [1772–1833]

556 CHAPPELL, Gordon T. "The Life and Activities of General John Coffee." *Tenn Hist Q,* I (1942), 125–146.

557 CHAPPELL, Gordon T. "John Coffee: Surveyor and Land Agent." *Ala Rev,* XIV (1961), 180–195, 243–250.

558 CHAPPELL, Gordon T. "John Coffee: Land Speculator and Planter." *Ala Rev,* XXII (1969), 24–43.

Coles, Edward [1786–1868]

See also **2511**

559 ALVORD, Clarence W., ed. *Governor Edward Coles.* Springfield, 1920.

Colton, Calvin [1789–1857]

See also **3493**

560 CAVE, Alfred A. *An American Conservative in the Age of Jackson: The Political and Social Thought of Calvin Colton.* Fort Worth, 1969.

Cooper, Thomas [1759–1839]

561 "Letters of Dr. Thomas Cooper, 1825–1832." *Am Hist Rev,* VI (1901), 725–736.
562 MALONE, Dumas. *The Public Life of Thomas Cooper, 1783–1839.* New Haven, 1926.

Corcoran, William W. [1798–1888]

563 COHEN, Henry. *Business and Politics in America from the Age of Jefferson to the Civil War: The Career Biography of W. W. Corcoran.* Westport, 1971.

Corning, Erastus [1794–1872]

564 NEU, Irene D. *Erastus Corning: Merchant and Financier, 1794–1872.* Ithaca, 1960.

Crawford, George W. [1798–1872]

565 CLEVELAND, Len Gibson. "George W. Crawford of Georgia." Doctoral dissertation, University of Georgia, 1974.

Crawford, William H. [1772–1834]

See also **1115, 1288**

566 CUTLER, Everette Wayne. "William H. Crawford: A Contextual Biography." Doctoral dissertation, University of Texas at Austin, 1971.
567 GREEN, Philip Jackson. *The Life of William Harris Crawford.* Charlotte, 1965.
568 MOONEY, Chase C. *William H. Crawford, 1772–1834.* Lexington, 1974.
569 SHIPP, J. E. D. *Giant Days; or the Life and Times of William H. Crawford.* Americus, Ga., 1909.
570 WILLIAMS, William Henry, ed. "Ten Letters from William Harris Crawford to Martin Van Buren." *Ga Hist Q,* XLIX (1965), 65–81.

Crittenden, John J. [1787–1863]

571 COLEMAN, Ann Mary Butler. *Life of John J. Crittenden.* 2 vols. Philadelphia. 1871.

572 KIRWAN, Albert D. *John J. Crittenden: The Struggle for the Union.* Lexington, 1962.

Crockett, David [1786–1836]

573 ARPAD, Joseph John. "David Crockett, An Original Eccentricity and Early American Character." Doctoral dissertation, Duke University, 1969.

574 CROCKETT, David. *A Narrative of the Life of David Crockett of the State of Tennessee.* Ed. James A. SHACKFORD and Stanley J. FOLMSBEE. Knoxville, 1973.

575 FOLMSBEE, Stanley J., and Anna Grace CATRON. "The Early Career of David Crockett." *E Tenn Hist Soc Pub,* no. 28 (1956), 58–85.

576 FOLMSBEE, Stanley J., and Anna Grace CATRON. "David Crockett: Congressman." *E Tenn Hist Soc Pub,* no. 29 (1957), 40–78.

577 FOLMSBEE, Stanley J., and Anna Grace CATRON. "David Crockett in Texas." *E Tenn Hist Soc Pub,* no. 30 (1958), 48–74.

578 FOLMSBEE, Stanley J. "David Crockett and His Autobiography." *E Tenn Hist Soc Pub,* no. 43 (1971), 3–17.

579 FOLMSBEE, Stanley J. "David Crockett and West Tennessee." *W Tenn Hist Soc Papers,* no. 28 (1974), 5–24.

580 HEALE, M. J. "The Role of the Frontier in Jacksonian Politics: David Crockett and the Myth of the Self-Made Man." *W Hist Q,* IV (1973), 405–423.

581 SHACKFORD, James Atkins. *David Crockett: The Man and the Legend.* Chapel Hill, 1956.

Cushing, Caleb [1800–1879]

582 FUESS, Claude M. *The Life of Caleb Cushing.* 2 vols. New York, 1923.

Dallas, Alexander James [1759–1817]

See also **1475, 1476**

583 DALLAS, George M. *Life and Writings of Alexander James Dallas.* Philadelphia, 1871.

584 WALTERS, Raymond, Jr. *Alexander James Dallas: Lawyer-Politician-Financier.* Philadelphia, 1943.

Dallas, George Mifflin [1792–1864]

585 AMBACHER, Bruce Irwin. "George M. Dallas: Leader of the Family Party." Doctoral dissertation, Temple University, 1971.

586 BELOHLAVEK, John M. *George Mifflin Dallas: Jacksonian Patrician.* University Park, Penna, 1977.

Daniel, Peter V. [1784–1860]

See also **1693**

587 FRANK, John P. *Justice Daniel Dissenting: A Biography of Peter V. Daniel, 1784–1860.* Cambridge, Mass., 1964.

D'Arusmont, Frances Wright [1795–1852]

See also **2774, 3178**

588 PERKINS, Alice J. G., and Theresa WOLFSON. *Frances Wright, Free Enquirer.* New York, 1939.

589 WATERMAN, William R. *Frances Wright.* New York, 1924.

Desha, Joseph [1768–1842]

See also **2261**

590 PADGETT James A., ed. "Joseph Desha, Letters and Papers." *Reg Ky Hist Soc,* LI (1953), 286–304.

Dew, Thomas Roderick [1802–1846]

591 HARRISON, Lowell H., "Thomas Roderick Dew: Philosopher of the Old South." *Va Mag Hist Biog,* LVII (1949), 390–404.

592 MANSFIELD, Stephen. "Thomas Roderick Dew at William and Mary: 'A Main Prop of that Venerable Institution.' " *Va Mag Hist Biog,* LXXV (1967), 429–442.

593 MANSFIELD, Stephen. "Thomas Roderick Dew: Defender of the Southern Faith." Doctoral dissertation, University of Virginia, 1968.

Dickerson, Mahlon [1770–1853]

594 BECKWITH, Robert Russell. "Mahlon Dickerson of New Jersey, 1770–1853." Doctoral dissertation, Columbia University, 1964.

Dickins, Asbury [1780–1861]

595 NUERMBERGER, Ruth Ketring. "Asbury Dickins: A Career in Government Service." *N C Hist Rev*, XXIV (1947), 281–314.

Dix, John A. [1798–1879]

596 DIX, Morgan. *Memoirs of John A. Dix.* 2 vols. New York, 1883.
597 LICHTERMAN, Martin. "John Adams Dix, 1798–1879." Doctoral dissertation, Columbia University, 1952.

Donelson, Andrew Jackson [1799–1871]

598 SATTERFIELD, Robert Beeler. "Andrew Jackson Donelson: A Moderate Nationalist Jacksonian." Doctoral dissertation, Johns Hopkins University, 1962.

Du Pont, Eleuthère Irénée [1771–1834]

599 Du Pont, Bessie G. *Life of Eleuthère Irénée du Pont.* 12 vols. Newark, Del., 1923–1926.

Eaton, John H. [1790–1856]

See also **1387–1396, 2294**

600 LOWE, Gabriel L., Jr. "John H. Eaton, Jackson's Campaign Manager." *Tenn Hist Q*, XI (1952), 99–147.

Eaton, Margaret O'Neale [1796–1879]

See also **1387–1389, 1391, 1393**

601 CLARK, Allen C. "Margaret Eaton (Peggy O'Neal)." *Rec Col Hist Soc*, XLIV–XLV (1942–1943), 1–33.
602 EATON, Peggy. *Autobiography.* New York, 1932.

603 POLLACK, Queena. *Peggy Eaton, Democracy's Mistress.* New York, 1931.

Edwards, Ninian [1775–1833]

604 BAKALIS, Michael John. "Ninian Edwards and Territorial Politics in Illinois: 1775–1818." Doctoral dissertation, Northwestern University, 1966.

605 EDWARDS, N. W. *History of Illinois from 1778 to 1833; and Life and Times of Ninian Edwards.* Springfield, 1870.

Elliott, William [1788–1863]

606 JONES, Lewis Pinckney. "William Elliott, South Carolina Nonconformist." *J S Hist,* XVII (1951), 361–381.

Everett, Edward [1794–1865]

607 FROTHINGHAM, Paul R. *Edward Everett, Orator and Statesman.* Boston, 1925.

608 HORN, Stuart Joel. "Edward Everett and American Nationalism." Doctoral dissertation, City University of New York, 1973.

Fairfield, John [1797–1847]

609 STAPLES, Arthur G., ed. *The Letters of John Fairfield.* Lewiston, Me., 1922.

Fillmore, Millard [1800–1874]

610 GRIFFIS, William E. *Millard Fillmore,* Ithaca, 1915.

611 RAYBACK, Robert J. *Millard Fillmore: Biography of a President.* Buffalo, 1959.

612 SCHELIN, Robert C. "Millard Fillmore, Anti-Mason to Know-Nothing: A Moderate in New York Politics, 1828–1856." Doctoral dissertation, State University of New York, Binghamton, 1975.

613 SEVERANCE, Frank H., ed. *Millard Fillmore Papers.* 2 vols. Buffalo, 1907.

Flagg, Azariah C. [1790–1873]

614 FOURNIER, Sister Theresa Lorraine. "The Political Career of Azariah Cutting Flagg: 1823–1847." Doctoral dissertation, Middle Tennessee State University, 1975.

Fletcher, Calvin [1798–1866]

615 THORNBROUGH, Gayle, and Dorothy L. RIKER, eds. *The Diary of Calvin Fletcher*. 5 vols to date. Indianapolis, 1972–.

Floyd, John [1783–1837]

616 AMBLER, Charles H. *The Life and Diary of John Floyd, Governor of Virginia, an Apostle of Secession, and the Father of the Oregon Country*. Richmond, 1918.

Foote, Henry Stuart [1804–1880]

617 FOOTE, Henry S. *Casket of Reminiscences*. St. Louis, 1876.

618 GONZALES, John E. "The Public Career of Henry Stuart Foote." Doctoral dissertation, University of North Carolina at Chapel Hill, 1957.

Forsyth, John [1780–1841]

619 DUCKETT, Alvin Laroy. *John Forsyth, Political Tactician*. Athens, 1962.

Gaines, Edmund Pendleton [1777–1849]

See also **1790**

620 SILVER, James W. *Edmund Pendleton Gaines: Frontier General*. Baton Rouge, 1949.

Gales, Joseph [1761–1841]

621 EATON, Clement. "Winifred and Joseph Gales, Liberals in the Old South." *J S Hist*, X (1944), 461–474.

Gallatin, Albert [1761–1849]

See also **1866**

622 ADAMS, Henry. *Life of Albert Gallatin*. Philadelphia, 1879.

623 ADAMS, Henry., ed. *The Writings of Albert Gallatin*. 3 vols. Philadelphia, 1879.

624 BOXALL, James Alexander, Jr. "Albert Gallatin and American Foreign Policy: A Study in Thought and Action." Doctoral dissertation, Michigan State University, 1967.

625 THRONBROUGH, Gayle, ed. *The Correspondence of John Badolett and Albert Gallatin, 1804–1836.* Indianapolis, 1963.

626 WALTERS, Raymond, Jr. *Albert Gallatin: Jeffersonian Financier and Diplomat.* New York, 1957.

Garrison, William Lloyd [1805–1879]

See also **3608, 3616, 3633**

627 FREDRICKSON, George M., ed. *William Lloyd Garrison.* Englewood Cliffs, N.J., 1969.†

628 GARRISON, Wendell, P., and Francis J. GARRISON. *William Lloyd Garrison, 1805–1879.* 4 vols. New York, 1885–1889.

629 MERRILL, Walter M. *Against Wind and Tide: A Biography of Wm. Lloyd Garrison.* Cambridge, Mass., 1963.

630 MERRILL, Walter M., and Louis Ruchames, eds. *The Letters of William Lloyd Garrison.* 4 vols to date. Cambridge, Mass., 1971–.

631 NYE, Russel B. *William Lloyd Garrison and the Humanitarian Reformers.* Boston, 1955.†

632 SWIFT, Lindsay. *William Lloyd Garrison.* Philadelphia, 1911.

633 THOMAS, John L. *The Liberator: William Lloyd Garrison, a Biography.* Boston, 1964.

Gaston, William [1778–1844]

634 SCHAUINGER, J. Herman. *William Gaston: Carolinian.* Milwaukee, 1949.

Giddings, Joshua R. [1795–1864]

635 JULIAN, George W. *Life of Joshua Giddings.* Chicago, 1892.

636 SOLBERG, Richard W. "Joshua Giddings, Politician and Idealist." Doctoral dissertation, University of Chicago, 1952.

637 STEWART, James Brewer. *Joshua R. Giddings and the Tactics of Radical Politics.* Cleveland, 1970.

Giles, William B. [1762–1830]

638 ANDERSON, Dice Robins. *William Branch Giles: A Study in the Politics of Virginia and the Nation from 1790 to 1830.* Menasha, 1914.

Gilpin, Henry D. [1801–1860]

See also **1517, 1527**

639 GRAY, Ralph D. "Henry D. Gilpin, a Pennsylvania Jacksonian." *Pa Hist,* XXVII (1970), 340–351.

Gilmer, George R. [1790–1859]

640 GILMER, George R. *Sketches of Some of the First Settlers of Upper Georgia, of the Cherokees, and the Author.* New York, 1855.

Gilmer, Thomas Walker [1802–1844]

See also **2219**

641 "Letters of Thomas Walker Gilmer." *Tyler's,* VI (1924–1925), 15–22, 187–199, 240–249.

Goodell, William [1792–1878]

642 PERKAL, Meyer Leon. "William Goodell: A Life of Reform." Doctoral dissertation, City University of New York, 1972.

Gordon, William F. [1787–1858]

643 GORDON, Armistead. *William Fitzhugh Gordon, a Virginian of the Old School.* New York, 1909.

Graham, William Alexander [1804–1875]

644 HAMILTON, J. G. de Roulhac, and Max R. WILLIAMS, eds. *The Papers of William Alexander Graham.* 5 vols to date. Raleigh, 1957–.

645 WILLIAMS, Max R. "William A. Graham, North Carolina Whig Party Leader, 1804–1849." Doctoral dissertation, University of North Carolina at Chapel Hill, 1965.

646 WILLIAMS, Max R. "The Education of William A. Graham." *N C Hist Rev,* XL (1963), 1–14.

Green, Duff [1791–1875]

647 GREEN, Fletcher M. "Duff Green, Militant Journalist of the Old School." *Am Hist Rev,* LII (1946), 247–264.

Grimké, Angelina [1805–1879] and Grimké, Sarah [1792–1873]

648 BARNES, Gilbert H., and Dwight L. DUMOND, eds. *Letters of Theodore Dwight Weld, Angelina Grimké Weld, and Sarah Grimké, 1822–1844.* 2 vols. New York, 1934

649 BIRNEY, Catherine H. *The Grimké Sisters.* Boston, 1885.

650 LERNER, Gerda. *The Grimké Sisters from South Carolina: Rebels against Slavery.* Boston, 1967.†

651 LUMPKIN, Katharine Du Pre. *The Emancipation of Angelina Grimké.* Chapel Hill, 1974.

652 MELDER, Keith E. "Forerunners of Freedom: The Grimké Sisters in Massachusetts, 1837–38." *Essex Inst Hist Coll,* CIII (1967), 223–249.

Grimké, Frederick [1792–1863] and Grimké, Thomas Smith [1786–1834]

653 KOCH, Adrienne. "Two Charlestonians in Pursuit of Truth: the Grimké Brothers." *S C Hist Mag,* LXIX (1968), 159–170.

Grundy, Felix [1777–1840]

See also **2289**

654 PARKS, Joseph Howard. *Felix Grundy, Champion of Democracy.* Baton Rouge, 1940.

Hamilton, James, Jr. [1786–1857]

655 GLENN, Virginia L. "James Hamilton, Jr., of South Carolina: A Biography." Doctoral dissertation, University of North Carolina at Chapel Hill, 1964.

656 KELL, Carl Lewis. "A Rhetorical History of James Hamilton, Jr.: The Nullification Era in South Carolina." Doctoral dissertation, University of Kansas, 1971.

Hamilton, James A. [1788–1878]

657 HAMILTON, James A. *Reminiscences.* New York, 1869.

Hammond, Charles [1779–1840]

658 MURDOCH, James Murray. "Charles Hammond: Egalitarian Whig: An Analysis of the Political Philosophy of a Federalist-Whig Editor and Its Implications Concerning the Traditional Concept of Jacksonian Democracy." Doctoral dissertation, Northwestern University, 1971.

659 WEISENBERGER, Francis P. "A Life of Charles Hammond, the First Great Journalist of the Old Northwest." *Ohio Arch Hist Q,* XLIII (1934), 337–427.

Hammond, James H. [1807–1864]

660 MERRITT, Elizabeth. *James Henry Hammond, 1807–1864.* Baltimore, 1923.

661 TUCKER, Robert C. "James Henry Hammond, South Carolinian." Doctoral dissertation, University of North Carolina at Chapel Hill, 1958.

Harper, Robert G. [1765–1825]

662 COX, Joseph W. *Champion of Southern Federalism; Robert Goodloe Harper of South Carolina.* Port Washington, N.Y., 1972.

Harrison, William Henry [1773–1841]

See also **1113**

663 CLEAVES, Freeman. *Old Tippecanoe: William Henry Harrison and His Time.* New York, 1939.

664 GOEBEL, Dorothy Burne. *William Henry Harrison, a Political Biography.* Indianapolis, 1926.

665 GREEN, James A. *William Henry Harrison: His Life and Times.* Richmond, 1941.

Hayne, Robert Y. [1791–1839]

666 JERVEY, Theodore D. *Robert Y. Hayne and His Times.* New York, 1909.

Hone, Philip [1780-1851]

667 KRIEDMAN, Herbert. "New York's Philip Hone: Businessman—Politician—Patron of Arts and Letters." Doctoral dissertation, New York University, 1965.

668 NEVINS, Allan., ed. *The Diary of Philip Hone, 1828-1851.* New York, 1927.

Hopkinson, Joseph [1770-1842]

669 KONKLE, Burton A. *Joseph Hopkinson, 1770-1842.* Philadelphia, 1931.

Houston, Samuel [1793-1863]

See also **1424, 1428, 1543-1553, 2272**

670 BRAIDER, Donald. *Solitary Star: A Biography of Sam Houston.* New York, 1974.

671 DAY, Donald, and Harry Herbert ULLOM, eds. *The Autobiography of Sam Houston.* Norman, 1954.

672 FRIEND, Llerena. *Sam Houston: The Great Designer.* Austin, 1954.†

673 JAMES, Marquis. *The Raven, a Biography of Sam Houston.* Indianapolis, 1929.†

674 WILLIAMS, Amelia W., and Eugene C. BARKER, eds. *The Writings of Sam Houston.* 8 vols. Austin, 1938-1943.

675 WISEHART, M. K. *Sam Houston, American Giant.* Washington, D.C., 1962.

Howe, Samuel Gridley [1801-1876]

676 RICHARDS, Laura E. *Samuel Gridley Howe.* New York, 1935.

677 RICHARDS, Laura E., ed. *Letters and Journals of Samuel Gridley Howe.* 2 vols. Boston, 1906-1909.

678 SANBORN, Franklin B. *Dr. S. G. Howe, the Philanthropist.* New York, 1891.

679 SCHWARTZ, Harold. *Samuel Gridley Howe: Social Reformer.* Cambridge, Mass., 1956.

Hughes, Christopher [1786-1849]

680 DUNHAM, Chester Gray. "The Diplomatic Career of Christopher Hughes." Doctoral dissertation, Ohio State University, 1968.

Hunter, Robert M. T. [1809–1887]

See also **2138**

681 AMBLER, Charles H., ed. *Correspondence of R. M. T. Hunter, 1826–1876.* Ann Rep Am Hist Assn, 1916. Vol. II. Washington, D.C., 1918.

682 SIMMS, Henry H. *Life of Robert M. T. Hunter; A Study in Sectionalism and Secession.* Richmond, 1935.

Huntsman, Adam [1786–1849]

683 MOONEY, Chase C. "The Public Career of Adam Huntsman." *Tenn Hist Q,* X (1951), 99–126.

Ingersoll, Charles Jared [1782–1862]

684 MEIGS, William M. *The Life of Charles Jared Ingersoll.* Philadelphia, 1897.

Jackson, Andrew [1767–1845]

See also **1165, 1168, 1174, 1192, 1286–1293, 1356–1569, 2169, 2222, 2235, 2287, 2339, 2521, 3985, 4281**

685 ABERNETHY, Thomas P. "Andrew Jackson and the Rise of Southwestern Democracy." *Am Hist Rev,* XXXIII (1927), 64–77.

686 BASSETT, John Spencer. *The Life of Andrew Jackson.* 2 vols. New York, 1911.

687 BASSETT, John Spencer, ed. *Correspondence of Andrew Jackson.* 7 vols. Washington, D.C., 1926–1935.

687A BUELL, Augustus C. *History of Andrew Jackson.* 2 vols. New York, 1904.

688 BURKE, John Emmett. "Andrew Jackson as Seen by Foreigners." *Tenn Hist Q,* X (1951), 25–45.

689 CRAVEN, Avery O., ed. "Letters of Andrew Jackson." *Hunt Lib Bull,* no. 3 (1933), 109–134.

690 CURTIS, James C. *Andrew Jackson and the Search for Vindication.* Boston, 1976.†

691 DAVIS, Burke. *Old Hickory: A Life of Andrew Jackson.* New York, 1977.

692 DOHERTY, Herbert J., Jr., ed. "Andrew Jackson on Manhood Suffrage." *Tenn Hist Q,* XV (1956), 57–60.

693 FELLMAN, Michael. "The Earthbound Eagle: Andrew Jackson and the American Pantheon." *Am Stud,* XII (1971), 67–76.

694 GOFF, Reda C. "A Physical Profile of Andrew Jackson." *Tenn Hist Q,* XXVIII (1969), 297–309.

695 HOFSTADTER, Richard. "Andrew Jackson and the Rise of Liberal Capitalism." *The American Political Tradition and the Men Who Made It.* New York, 1948.†

696 HORN, Stanley F., ed. "Some Jackson-Overton Correspondence." *Tenn Hist Q,* VI (1947), 161–175.

697 JAMES, Marquis. *Andrew Jackson: The Border Captain.* Indianapolis, 1933.

698 JAMES, Marquis. *Andrew Jackson: Portrait of a President.* Indianapolis, 1937.

699 LINDSAY, David. *Andrew Jackson and John C. Calhoun.* New York, 1973.†

700 PARTON, James. *Life of Andrew Jackson.* 3 vols. New York, 1860.

701 PARTON, James. *The Presidency of Andrew Jackson.* Ed. Robert V. REMINI. New York, 1967.

702 READ, Allen Walker. "Could Andrew Jackson Spell?" *Am Sp,* XXXVIII (1963), 188–195.

703 REID, John, and John Henry EATON. *The Life of Andrew Jackson.* Ed. Frank L. OWSLEY, Jr. University, Ala., 1974.

704 REMINI, Robert V. *Andrew Jackson.* New York, 1966.†

705 REMINI, Robert V. *Andrew Jackson and the Course of American Empire, 1767–1821.* New York, 1977.

706 ROGIN, Michael Paul. *Fathers and Children: Andrew Jackson and the Subjugation of the American Indian.* New York, 1975.†

707 SELLERS, Charles G., Jr., ed. *Andrew Jackson: A Profile.* New York, 1971.†

708 SOMIT, Albert. "Andrew Jackson: Legend and Reality." *Tenn Hist Q,* VII (1948), 291–313.

709 SOMIT, Albert. "Andrew Jackson as Political Theorist." *Tenn Hist Q,* VIII (1949), 99–126.

710 STARK, Cruce. "The Historical Irrelevance of Heroes: Henry Adams's Andrew Jackson." *Am Lit,* XLVI (1974), 170–181.

711 SUMNER, William Graham. *Andrew Jackson.* Boston, 1882.

712 SYRETT, Harold C., ed. *Andrew Jackson: His Contribution to the American Tradition.* Indianapolis, 1953.

713 WALKER, Arda S. "Andrew Jackson: Planter." *E Tenn Hist Soc Pub,* no. 15 (1943), 19–34.

714 WALKER, Arda S. "The Educational Training and Views of Andrew Jackson." *E Tenn Hist Soc Pub,* no. 16 (1944), 22–29.

715 WALKER, Arda S. "The Religious Views of Andrew Jackson." *E Tenn Hist Soc Pub,* no. 17 (1945), 61–70.

716 WALKER, Arda S. "Andrew Jackson: Frontier Democrat." *E Tenn Hist Soc Pub,* no. 18 (1946), 59–86.

717 WARD, John William. *Andrew Jackson: Symbol for an Age.* New York, 1955.†

718 WHEATEN, John J., ed. "The Jackson-[Moses] Dawson Correspondence." *Bull Hist Phil Soc Ohio,* XVI (1958), 3–30.

Jackson, Andrew, Jr. [1809–1865]

719 GALLOWAY, Linda Bennett. "Andrew Jackson, Junior." *Tenn Hist Q*, IX (1950), 195–216, 306–343.

Jackson, Rachel Donelson [1767–1828]

720 OWSLEY, Harriet C. "The Marriages of Rachel Donelson." *Tenn Hist Q*, XXXVI (1978), 479–492.

Jay, William [1789–1858]

721 TRENDEL, Robert A., Jr. "William Jay: Churchman, Public Servant and Reformer." Doctoral dissertation, Southern Illinois University, 1972.

Jefferson, Thomas [1743–1826]

See also **1078, 1083, 2103, 2625, 3135**

722 LIPSCOMB, Andrew A., and Albert E. BERGH, eds. *The Writings of Thomas Jefferson.* 20 vols. Washington, D.C., 1903.

723 PETERSON, Merrill D. *Thomas Jefferson and the New Nation: A Biography.* New York, 1970.†

Johnson, Cave [1793–1866]

724 GRANT, C. L. "The Public Career of Cave Johnson." *Tenn Hist Q*, X (1951), 195–223.

Johnson, Richard M. [1780–1850]

725 MEYER, Leland Winfield. *The Life and Times of Colonel Richard M. Johnson of Kentucky.* New York, 1932.

726 BOLT, Robert. "Vice President Richard M. Johnson of Kentucky: Hero of the Thames—Or the Great Amalgamator?" *Reg Ky Hist Soc*, LXXV (1977), 191–203.

727 PADGETT, James A., ed. "The Letters of Colonel Richard M. Johnson of Kentucky." *Reg Ky Hist Soc*, XXXVIII (1940), 186–201, 323–339, XXXIX (1941), 22–46, 172–188, 260–274, 358–367, XL (1942), 69–91.

Johnson, William [1771–1834]

See also **1716, 2193**

728 BEDFORD, Henry F. "William Johnson and the Marshall Court." *S C Hist Mag*, LXII (1961), 165–171.

729 MORGAN, Donald G. *Justice William Johnson, the First Dissenter: The Career and Constitutional Philosophy of a Jeffersonian Judge.* Columbia, 1964.

Jones, Anson [1798–1858]

730 GAMBRELL, Herbert P. *Anson Jones: The Last President of Texas.* Garden City, 1948.

Jones, William [1760–1831]

731 CORRIGAN, Sister M. Saint Pierre. "William Jones of the Second Bank of the United States: A Reappraisal." Doctoral dissertation, University of St. Louis, 1966.

Kavanagh, Edward [1795–1844]

732 LUCEY, William L. *Edward Kavanagh, Catholic, Statesman, Diplomat, from Maine, 1795–1844.* Francestown, N.H., 1947.

Kendall, Amos [1789–1869]

See also **1500, 2255, 2261**

733 DANIELS, James Douglas. "Amos Kendall: Cabinet-Politician, 1829–1841." Doctoral dissertation, University of North Carolina at Chapel Hill, 1968.

733A DANIELS, James D. "Amos Kendall: Kentucky Journalist, 1819–1829." *Filson Club Hist Q*, LII (1978), 46–65

734 MARSHALL, Lynn La Due. "The Early Career of Amos Kendall: The Making of a Jacksonian." Doctoral dissertation, University of California, Berkeley, 1962.

735 STICKNEY, William, ed. *The Autobiography of Amos Kendall.* Boston, 1872.

Kennedy, John Pendleton [1795–1870]

736 BOHNER, Charles H. *John Pendleton Kennedy: Gentleman from Baltimore.* Baltimore, 1961.

737 RIDGELY, J. V. *John Pendleton Kennedy.* New York, 1966.†

738 SPELMAN, Georgia Peterman. "The Whig Rhetoric of John Pendleton Kennedy." Doctoral dissertation, Indiana University, 1974.

Kent, James [1763–1847]

739 HORTON, John Theodore. *James Kent: A Study in Conservatism.* New York, 1939.

740 KENT, William. *Memoirs and Letters of James Kent, LL.D., Late Chancellor of the State of New York.* Boston, 1898.

Key, Francis Scott [1779–1843]

See also **2313, 2319**

741 DELAPLAINE, Edward S. *Francis Scott Key: Life and Times.* New York, 1937.

King, Rufus [1755–1827]

See also **1135, 1140–1142**

742 ERNST, Robert. *Rufus King: American Federalist.* Chapel Hill, 1968.

743 KING, Charles R., ed. *Life and Correspondence of Rufus King.* 6 vols. New York, 1894–1900.

King, Thomas Butler [1800–1864]

744 STEEL, Edward M., Jr. *T. Butler King of Georgia.* Athens, 1964.

King, William R. [1786–1853]

745 MARTIN, John M. "William Rufus King: Southern Moderate." Doctoral dissertation, University of North Carolina at Chapel Hill, 1955.

746 MARTIN, John M. "William R. King: Jacksonian Senator." *Ala Rev,* XVIII (1965), 243–267.

Lamar, Mirabeau Buonaparte [1798–1859]

747 GAMBRELL, Herbert P. *Mirabeau Buonaparte Lamar, Troubadour and Crusader.* Dallas, 1934.

748 GULLICK, Charles A., ed. *The Papers of Mirabeau Buonaparte Lamar.* 6 vols. Austin, 1921–1927.

749 SIEGEL, Stanley. *The Poet President of Texas: The Life of Mirabeau B. Lamar, President of the Republic of Texas.* Austin, Tex., 1977.

Lee, Jason [1803–1845]

750 BORSNAN, Cornelius J. *Jason Lee, Prophet of the New Oregon.* New York, 1932.

Lee, William [1772–1840]

751 MANN, Mary Lee, ed. *A Yankee Jeffersonian: Selections from the Diary and Letters of William Lee of Massachusetts, Written from 1796 to 1840.* Cambridge, Mass., 1958.

Legaré, Hugh S. [1797–1843]

752 BULLEN, Mary S. Legaré., ed. *Writings of Hugh Swinton Legaré.* 2 vols. Charleston, 1845–1846.

753 RHEA, Linda. *Hugh Swinton Legaré, a Charleston Intellectual.* Chapel Hill, 1934.

Leggett, William [1801–1839]

754 HOFSTADTER, Richard. "William Leggett, Spokesman of Jacksonian Democracy." *Pol Sci Q,* LVIII (1943), 581–594.

755 RIFKIN, Lester Harvey. "William Leggett: Journalist-Philosopher of Agrarian Democracy in New York." *N Y Hist,* XXXII (1951), 45–60.

756 SEDGWICK, Theodore, Jr., ed. *A Collection of the Political Writings of William Leggett.* New York, 1840.

Letcher, Robert Perkins [1788–1861]

757 GILLIAM, William D., Jr. "The Public Career of Robert Perkins Letcher." Doctoral dissertation, University of Indiana, 1941.

Lewis, William B. [1784–1866]

758 HARLAN, Louis R. "Public Career of William Berkeley Lewis." *Tenn Hist Q,* VII (1948), 3–37, 118–151.

Lieber, Francis [1800–1872]

759 FREIDEL, Frank. *Francis Lieber: Nineteenth Century Liberal.* Baton Rouge, 1947.

760 GILMAN, Daniel C. *The Miscellaneous Writings of Francis Lieber.* 2 vols. Philadelphia, 1881.

Livingston, Edward [1764–1836]

See also **1463, 1558, 2808**

761 HATCHER, William B. *Edward Livingston: Jeffersonian Republican and Jacksonian Democrat.* Baton Rouge, 1940.

Lovejoy, Elijah P. [1802–1837]

762 DILLON, Merton L. *Elijah P. Lovejoy, Abolitionist Editor.* Urbana, 1961.

763 GILL, John. *Tide without Turning: Elijah P. Lovejoy and Freedom of the Press.* Boston, 1958.

Lowndes, William [1782–1822]

See also **4371**

764 RAVENEL, Harriott H. *Life and Times of William Lowndes of South Carolina.* Boston, 1901.

765 VIPPERMAN, Carl Jackson. "William Lowndes: South Carolina Nationalist." Doctoral dissertation, University of Virginia, 1966.

Lundy, Benjamin [1789–1839]

766 DILLON, Merton L. *Benjamin Lundy and the Struggle for Negro Freedom.* Urbana, 1966.

767 EARLE, Thomas, ed. *The Life, Travels and Opinions of Benjamin Lundy, Including His Journeys to Texas and Mexico.* Philadelphia, 1847.

Lyon, Lucius [1800–1851]

768 SHIRIGAN, John. "Lucius Lyon: His Place in Michigan History." Doctoral dissertation, University of Michigan, 1961.

McCoy, Isaac [1784–1846]

769 SCHULTZ, George A. *An Indian Canaan: Isaac McCoy and the Vision of an Indian State.* Norman, 1972.

McDonogh, John [1779–1850]

770 NUHRAH, Arthur G. "John McDonogh: Man of Many Facets." *La Hist Q,* XXXIII (1950), 5–144.

McDowell, James [1795–1851]

771 COLLIER, James Glen. "The Political Career of James McDowell, 1830–1851." Doctoral dissertation, University of North Carolina at Chapel Hill, 1963.

McDuffie, George [1790–1851]

772 GREEN, Edwin L. *George McDuffie.* Columbia, 1936.

McKenney, Thomas L. [1785–1859]

See also **1439**

773 MCKENNEY, Thomas L. *Memoirs, Official and Personal.* Lincoln, 1973. Introduction by Herman J. Viola.

774 VIOLA, Herman J. *Thomas L. McKenney: Architect of America's Early Indian Policy: 1816–1830.* Chicago, 1974.

McKinley, John [1780–1852]

775 HICKS, Jimmie. "Associate Justice John McKinley: A Sketch." *Ala Rev,* XVIII (1965), 227–233.

776 MARTIN, John M. "John McKinley: Jacksonian Phase." *Ala Hist Q,* XXVIII (1966), 7–32.

McLane, Louis [1786–1857]

777 MUNROE, John A. *Louis McLane: Federalist and Jacksonian.* New Brunswick, 1973.

McLean, John [1785–1861]

See also **1285**

778 WEISENBURGER, Francis P. *The Life of John McLean: A Politician on the United States Supreme Court.* Columbus, 1937.

McLoughlin, John [1784–1857]

779 HOLMAN, Frederick V. *Dr. John McLoughlin, the Father of Oregon.* Cleveland, 1907.

780 JOHNSON, Robert C. *John McLoughlin, Patriarch of the Northwest.* Portland, 1935.

781 MONTGOMERY, Richard G. *The White-Headed Eagle, John McLoughlin, Builder of an Empire.* New York, 1934.

Macon, Nathaniel [1758–1837]

See also **1079, 4345**

782 BASSETT, John S., ed. "Some Unpublished Letters of Nathaniel Macon." *Trinity Coll Hist Papers,* VI (1906), 57–65.

783 BATTLE, Kemp P., ed. *Letters of Nathaniel Macon, John Steele and William Barry Grove.* Chapel Hill, 1902.

784 DODD, William E. *The Life of Nathaniel Macon.* Chicago, 1903.

785 DODD, William E. "Nathaniel Macon Correspondence." *Branch Hist Papers,* III (1909), 27–93.

786 MCPHERSON, Elizabeth Gregory, ed. "Letters from Nathaniel Macon to John Randolph of Roanoke." *N C Hist Rev,* XXXIX (1962), 195–211.

Madison, James [1751–1836]

See also **1460**

787 ADAIR, Douglass, ed. "James Madison's Autobiography." *Wm Mar Q,* 3d ser., II (1945), 191–209.

788 BRANT, Irving. *James Madison.* 6 vols. Indianapolis, 1948–1961.

789 BRANT, Irving. *The Fourth President: The Life of James Madison.* Indianapolis, 1970.

790 BRANT, Irving. *James Madison and American Nationalism.* Princeton, 1968.

791 BRANT, Irving. "James Madison and His Times." *Am Hist Rev,* LVII (1952), 853–870.

792 BURNS, Edward McNall. *James Madison, Philosopher of the Constitution.* New Brunswick, 1938.

793 DEWEY, Donald O. "The Sage of Montpelier: James Madison's Constitutional and Political Thought, 1817–1836." Doctoral dissertation, University of Chicago, 1961.

794 DEWEY, Donald O. "Madison's Views on Electoral Reform [1823]." *W Pol Q,* XV (1962), 140–145.

795 DEWEY, Donald O. "James Madison Helps Clio Interpret the Constitution." *Am J Leg Hist,* XV (1971), 38–55.

796 HUNT, Gaillard. *The Life of James Madison.* 1902.

797 HUNT, Gaillard, ed. *The Writings of James Madison.* 9 vols. New York, 1900–1910.

798 KETCHAM, Ralph. *James Madison: A Biography.* New York, 1971.

799 KOCH, Adrienne. *Madison's "Advice to My Country."* Princeton, 1966.†

800 PADOVER, Saul K., ed. *The Complete Madison: His Basic Writings.* New York, 1953.

801 RIEMER, Neal. "The Republicanism of James Madison." *Pol Sci Q,* LXIX (1954), 45–64.

802 RIVES, William C. *History of the Life and Times of James Madison.* 3 vols. Boston, 1859–1868.

803 SCHULTZ, Harold S. *James Madison.* New York, 1970.

804 SMITH, Abbot E. *James Madison: Builder.* New York, 1937.

Mangum, Willie P. [1792–1861]

See also **1529**

805 SHANKS, Henry T., ed. *The Papers of Willie Persons Mangum.* 5 vols. Raleigh, 1950–1956.

Mann, Horace [1796–1859]

See also **3054, 3077**

806 MESSERLI, Jonathan. *Horace Mann: A Biography.* New York, 1972.

Marcy, William L. [1786–1857]

See also **2020**

807 MATTINA, Benjamin J. "The Early Life of William Learned Marcy, 1789–1832." Doctoral dissertation, Georgetown University, 1949.

808 SPENCER, Ivor Debenham. *The Victor and the Spoils: A Life of William L. Marcy.* Providence, 1959.

Marshall, John [1755–1835]

See also **1082, 1125, 1126, 1436, 1692, 1694, 1696, 1697, 1701, 1703, 1704, 1721, 1728, 1729, 1733, 1736, 1742, 2137**

809 ADAMS, John Stokes, ed. *An Autobiographical Sketch of John Marshall.* Ann Arbor, 1937.

810 BAKER, Leonard. *John Marshall: A Life in Law.* New York, 1974.

811 BEVERIDGE, Albert J. *The Life of John Marshall.* 4 vols. Boston, 1916–1919.

812 CROSSKEY, William W. "Mr. Chief Justice Marshall." *Mr. Justice.* Ed. Allison DUNHAM and Philip B. KURLAND. Rev. ed. Chicago, 1964.

813 FAULKNER, Robert Kenneth. *The Jurisprudence of John Marshall.* Princeton, 1968.

814 FRANKFURTER, Felix. "John Marshall and the Judicial Function." *Har Law Rev,* LXIX (1955), 217–238.

815 JONES, W. Melville, ed. *Chief Justice John Marshall: A Reappraisal.* Ithaca, 1956.

816 KONEFSKY, Samuel. *John Marshall and Alexander Hamilton: Architects of the American Constitution.* New York, 1964.

817 KUTLER, Stanley I., ed. *John Marshall.* Englewood Cliffs, 1972.†

818 LERNER, Max. "John Marshall and the Campaign of History." *Col Law Rev,* XXXIX (1939), 396–431.

819 LOTH, David. *Chief Justice: John Marshall and the Growth of the Republic.* New York, 1949.

820 MARSHALL, John. *The Writings of John Marshall.* Boston, 1839.

821 PADOVER, Saul K. "The Political Ideas of John Marshall." *Soc Res,* XXVI (1959), 47–70.

822 SERVIES, James A. *A Bibliography of John Marshall.* Washington, D.C., 1956.

823 THAYER, James B. *John Marshall.* Boston, 1901.

Mason, James M. [1798–1871]

824 BUGG, James L., Jr. "The Political Career of James Murray Mason: The Legislative Phase." Doctoral dissertation, University of Virginia, 1950.

Mason, Jeremiah [1768–1848]

825 HILLIARD, George S., ed. *Memoir, Autobiography and Correspondence of Jeremiah Mason.* Cambridge, Mass., 1873.

Mason, Stevens Thomson [1811–1843]

826 HEMANS, Lawton T. *Life and Times of Stevens Thomson Mason, the Boy Governor of Michigan.* Lansing, 1920.

827 SAGENDORPH, Kent. *Stevens Thomson Mason, Misunderstood Patriot.* New York, 1947.

Monroe, James [1758–1831]

See also 1109–1110, 1119–1120, 1158–1160, 1215, 1366, 2012

828 AMMON, Harry. *James Monroe: The Quest for National Identity.* New York, 1971.

829 BROWN, Stuart G., ed. *The Autobiography of James Monroe.* Syracuse, 1959.

830 CRESSON, William P. *James Monroe.* Chapel Hill, 1946.

831 GILMAN, Daniel C. *James Monroe.* Boston, 1883.

832 HAMILTON, Stanislaus Murray, ed. *The Writings of James Monroe.* 7 vols., New York, 1898–1903.

833 STYRON, Arthur. *The Last of the Cocked Hats: James Monroe and the Virginia Dynasty.* Norman, 1945.

834 WILMERDING, Louis, Jr. *James Monroe: Public Claimant* New Brunswick, 1960.

Moore, Ely [1798–1860]

835 HUGINS, Walter E. "Ely Moore: The Case History of a Jacksonian Labor Leader." *Pol Sci Q,* LXV (1950), 105–125.

Moore, Gabriel [1785–1845]

836 MARTIN, John M. "The Early Career of Gabriel Moore." *Ala Hist Q,* XXIX (1967), 89–105.

837 MARTIN, John M. "The Senatorial Career of Gabriel Moore." *Ala Hist Q,* XXVI (1964), 249–281.

Morehead, John Motley [1796–1866]

838 KONKLE, Burton Alva. *John Motley Morehead and the Development of North Carolina, 1796–1866.* Philadelphia, 1922.

Murphey, Archibald D. [1777?–1832]

839 HOYT, William H. *The Papers of Archibald D. Murphey.* 2 vols. Raleigh, 1914.

840 LERCHE, Margaret E. "The Life and Public Career of Archibald D. Murphey." Doctoral dissertation, University of North Carolina at Chapel Hill, 1948.

Niles, Hezekiah [1777–1839]

See also 4574, 4575

841 SCHMIDT, Philip Redding. "Hezekiah Niles and American Economic Nationalism: A Political Biography." Doctoral dissertation, University of Kansas, 1974.

Noah, Mordecai M. [1785–1851]

842 GAPPELBERG, Leonard I. "M. M. Noah and the *Evening Star:* Whig Journalism, 1833–1840." Doctoral dissertation, Yeshwa University, 1970.

843 GOLDBERG, Isaac. *Major Noah: American-Jewish Pioneer.* Philadelphia, 1936.

Otis, Harrison Gray [1765–1848]

844 MORISON, Samuel Elliot. *Harrison Gray Otis, 1765–1848: The Urbane Federalist.* Boston, 1969.

Overton, John [1766–1833]

845 CLIFTON, Frances. "John Overton as Andrew Jackson's Friend." *Tenn Hist Q,* XI (1952), 23–40.

Owen, Robert Dale [1801–1887]

846 LEOPOLD, Richard W. *Robert Dale Owen: A Biography.* Cambridge, Mass., 1940.

847 PANCOAST, Elinor, and Anne E. LINCOLN. *The Incorrigible Idealist: Robert Dale Owen in America.* Bloomington, 1940.

Paulding, James K. [1778–1860]

848 ADERMAN, Ralph M., ed. *The Letters of James Kirke Paulding.* Madison, 1962.

849 HEROLD, Amos L. *James Kirke Paulding, Versatile American.* New York, 1926.

850 PAULDING, William I. *Literary Life of James K. Paulding.* New York, 1867.

Perkins, Thomas H. [1764–1854]

851 SEABURG, Carl, and Stanley PATERSON. *Merchant Prince of Boston: Colonel T. H. Perkins.* Cambridge, Mass., 1971.

Perry, Benjamin F. [1805–1886]

852 KIBLER, Lillian A. *Benjamin F. Perry, South Carolina Unionist.* Durham, S.C., 1946.

853 PERRY, Benjamin F. *Reminiscences of Public Men.* Philadelphia, 1883. Second series, Greenville, S.C., 1889.

Petigru, James L. [1789–1863]

854 CARSON, James P., ed. *Life, Letters and Speeches of James Louis Petigru, the Union Man of South Carolina.* Washington, D.C., 1920.

Pickens, Francis W. [1805–1869]

855 EDMUNDS, John Boyd, Jr. "Francis W. Pickens: A Political Biography." Doctoral dissertation, University of South Carolina, 1967.

Pickens, Israel [1780–1827]

856 BAILEY, Hugh C. "Israel Pickens, People's Politician." *Ala Rev,* XVII (1964), 83–101.

Pierce, Franklin [1804–1869]

857 NICHOLS, Roy F. *Franklin Pierce.* Philadelphia, 1931.

Pinkney, William [1764–1822]

See also **1070**

858 IRELAND, Robert M. "The Legal Career of William Pinkney." Doctoral dissertation, University of Nebraska, 1967.

859 IRELAND, Robert M. "William Pinkney: A Revision and Re-emphasis." *Am J Leg Hist,* XIV (1970), 235–246.

Pitchlynn, Peter [1806–1881]

860 BAIRD, W. David. *Peter Pitchlynn: Chief of the Choctaws.* Norman, 1972.

Plumer, William [1795–1850]

861 PLUMER, William, Jr. *Life of William Plumer.* Boston, 1856.

862 TURNER, Lynn W. *William Plumer of New Hampshire.* Chapel Hill, 1962.

Plumer, William, Jr. [1789–1854]

863 BROWN, Everett Somerville, ed. *The Missouri Compromise and Presidential Politics, 1820–1825, from the Letters of William Plumer, Jr.* St. Louis, 1926.

Plummer, Franklin E. [1805?–1852]

864 MILES, Edwin A. "Franklin E. Plummer: Piney Woods Spokesman of the Jackson Era." *J. Miss Hist,* XIV (1952), 11–34.

Poindexter, George [1779–1833]

See also **2327, 2339**

865 SWEARINGEN, Mack. *The Early Life of George Poindexter.* New Orleans, 1934.

Poinsett, Joel R. [1779–1851]

See also **1306, 1307**

866 HRUNENI, George Anthony, Jr. "Palmetto Yankee: The Public Life and Times of Joel Roberts Poinsett." Doctoral dissertation, University of California, Santa Barbara, 1972.

867 PUTNAM, Herbert Everett. *Joel Roberts Poinsett: A Political Biography.* Washington, D.C., 1935.

868 RIPPY, J. Fred. *Joel R. Poinsett, Versatile American.* Durham, 1935.

869 STONEY, Samuel Gaillard, ed. "The Poinsett–[James B.] Campbell Correspondence." *S C Hist Gen Mag,* XLVII (1941), 31–52, 122–136, 149–168, XLVIII (1942), 27–34.

Polk, James K [1795–1849]

See also **2268, 2286, 2298**

870 BASSETT, John Spencer, ed. "James K. Polk and His Constituents, 1831–1832." *Am Hist Rev,* XXVIII (1922), 69–77.

871 MCCORMAC, Eugene Irving. *James K. Polk: A Political Biography.* Berkeley 1922.

872 MOORE, Powell. James K. Polk: Tennessee Politician." *J S Hist,* XVII (1951), 493–516.

873 SELLERS, Charles G., Jr. *James K. Polk, Jacksonian, 1795–1843.* Princeton, 1957.

874 WEAVER, Herbert; Paul H. BERGERON; Kermit L. HALL; and Wayne CUTLER, eds. *Correspondence of James K. Polk.* 4 vols. to date. Nashville, 1969–.

Poore, Benjamin Perley [1820–1887]

875 POORE, Benjamin Perley. *Reminiscences of Sixty Years in the National Metropolis.* 2 vols. Philadelphia, 1886.

Pope, John [1770–1845]

See also **2244**

876 BAYLOR, Orval W. *John Pope: Kentuckian.* Cynthiana, 1943.

Porter, Alexander [1785–1844]

See also **2356**

877 STEPHENSON, Wendell Holmes. *Alexander Porter, Whig Planter of Old Louisiana.* Baton Rouge, 1953.

Porter, David [1780–1843]

See also **1882**

878 LONG, David F. *Nothing Too Daring: A Biography of Commodore David Porter, 1780–1843.* Annapolis, 1970.

879 PORTER, David D. *Memoir of Commodore David Porter of the United States Navy.* Albany, 1875.

880 TURNBULL, Archibald Douglas. *Commodore David Porter, 1780–1843.* New York, 1929.

Porter, Peter B. [1773–1844]

881 GRANDE, Joseph Anthony. "The Political Career of Peter Buell Porter, 1797–1829." Doctoral dissertation, University of Notre Dame, 1971.

Prentiss, Seargent S. [1808–1850]

882 DICKEY, Dallas C. *Seargent S. Prentiss: Whig Orator of the Old South.* Baton Rouge, 1945.

883 PRENTISS, George L. *A Memoir of S. S. Prentiss.* 2 vols. New York, 1855.

Quincy, Josiah [1772–1864]

884 MCCAUGHEY, Robert A. *Josiah Quincy, 1772–1864: The Last Federalist.* Cambridge, Mass., 1974.

885 QUINCY, Edmund. *Life of Josiah Quincy of Massachusetts.* Boston, 1867.

Quincy, Josiah [1802–1882]

886 QUINCY, Josiah. *Figures of the Past from the Leaves of Old Journals.* Boston, 1883.

Quitman, John A. [1798–1858]

887 CLAIBORNE, J. F. H. *Life and Correspondence of John A. Quitman.* 2 vols. New York, 1860.

888 MCLENDON, James H. "John A. Quitman." Doctoral dissertation, University of Texas at Austin, 1949.

Randolph, John [1773–1833]

See also **1281**

889 ADAMS, Henry. *John Randolph.* Boston, 1882.

890 BRUCE, William Cabell. *John Randolph of Roanoke, 1773–1833.* 2 vols. New York, 1922.

891 DAWIDOFF, Robert. "The Education of John Randolph." Doctoral dissertation, Cornell University, 1975.

892 GARLAND, Hugh A. *The Life of John Randolph of Roanoke.* 2 vols. New York, 1850.

893 HINES, Jack W. "John Randolph and the Growth of Federal Power: The Opinion of a States' Righter on the Political Issues of His Time." Doctoral dissertation, University of Kansas, 1957.

894 KIRK, Russell. *Randolph of Roanoke: A Study in Conservative Thought.* Chicago, 1951.

Randolph, Thomas J. [1792–1875]

895 VANCE, Joseph C. "Thomas Jefferson Randolph." Doctoral dissertation, University of Virgina, 1957.

Randolph, Thomas M. [1768–1828]

896 GAINES, William H., Jr. *Thomas Mann Randolph: Jefferson's Son-in-Law.* Baton Rouge, 1966.

Rantoul, Robert [1805–1852]

897 BULKLEY, Robert D. "Robert Rantoul, Jr., 1805–1852: Politics and Reform in Antebellum Massachusetts." Doctoral dissertation, Princeton University, 1971.

898 BULKLEY, Robert D. "A Democrat and Slavery: Robert Rantoul, Jr." *Essex Inst Hist Coll,* CX (1974), 216–238.

899 HAMILTON, Luther, ed. *Memoirs, Speeches, and Writings of Robert Rantoul, Jr.* Boston, 1854.

Rhett, Robert Barnwell [1802–1876]

See also **2191**

900 WHITE, Laura A. *Robert Barnwell Rhett, Father of Secession.* New York, 1931

Ritchie, Thomas [1778–1834]

901 AMBLER, Charles Henry. *Thomas Ritchie: A Study in Virginia Politics.* Richmond, 1913.

902 MUTERSBAUGH, Bert M. "Jeffersonian Journalist: Thomas Ritchie and the *Richmond Enquirer,* 1804–1820." Doctoral dissertation, University of Missouri, Columbia, 1973.

Rives, William Cabell [1793–1868]

903 DINGLEDINE, Raymond C. "The Political Career of William Cabell Rives." Doctoral dissertation, University of Virginia, 1947.

904 "Letters of William C. Rives, 1823–1829." *Tyler's,* V (1924), 223–237, VI (1924), 6–15, 97–106, VII (1926), 203–207.

905 LISTON, Ann Elizabeth. "W. C. Rives: Diplomat and Politician, 1829–53." Doctoral dissertation, Ohio State University, 1972.

Roane, Spencer [1762–1834]

906 BEACH, Rex. "Spencer Roane and the Richmond Junto." *Wm Mar Q,* 2d ser., XXII (1942), 1–17.

907 GELBACK, Clyde C. "Spencer Roane of Virginia, 1768–1822, A Judicial Advocate of State Rights." Doctoral dissertation, University of Pittsburgh, 1955.

908 HORSNELL, Margaret Eileen. "Spencer Roane: Judicial Advocate of Jeffersonian Principles." Doctoral dissertation, University of Minnesota, 1967.

909 "Judge Spencer Roane of Virginia—Champion of States' Rights—Foe of John Marshall." *Har Law Rev,* LXVI (1953), 1242–1259.

Rodgers, John [1773–1838]

910 PAULLIN, Charles O. *Commodore John Rodgers, Captain, Commodore, and Senior Officer of the American Navy, 1773–1838.* Cleveland, 1910.

Ross, John [1790–1866]

See also **1430**

911 EATON, Rachael Caroline. *John Ross and the Cherokee Indians.* Menasha, 1914.

912 MOULTON, Gary E. *John Ross: Cherokee Chief.* Athens, 1978.

Royall, Anne N. [1769–1854]

913 JACKSON, George Stuyvesant. *Uncommon Scold: The Story of Anne Royall.* Boston, 1937.

914 JAMES, Bessie Rowland. *Anne Royall's U.S.A.* New Brunswick, 1972.

915 PORTER, Sarah Harvey. *The Life and Times of Anne Royall.* Cedar Rapids, 1909.

Ruffin, Edmund [1794–1865]

916 CRAVEN, Avery O. *Edmund Ruffin, Southerner.* New York, 1932.

Ruffin, Thomas [1787–1870]

917 HAMILTON, J. G. de Roulhac, ed. *The Papers of Thomas Ruffin.* 4 vols. Raleigh, 1918–1920 .

Rush, Richard [1780–1859]

See also **1178, 1800**

918 POWELL, J. H. *Richard Rush: Republican Diplomat, 1780–1859.* Philadelphia, 1942.

919 RUSH, Richard. *Narrative of a Residence at the Court of London.* London, 1833.

920 RUSH, Richard. *Memoranda of a Residence at the Court of London.* Philadelphia, 1845.

Sargent, Nathan [1794–1875]

921 SARGENT, Nathan. *Public Men and Events.* 2 vols. Philadelphia, 1875.

Scott, Winfield [1786–1866]

See also **1603**

922 ELLIOTT, Charles Winslow. *Winfield Scott: The Soldier and the Man.* New York, 1937.

923 SCOTT, Winfield. *Memoirs of Lieutenant-General Scott, LL.D.* 2 vols. New York, 1864.

924 SMITH, Arthur D. Howden. *Old Fuss and Feathers: The Life and Exploits of Lt.-General Winfield Scott.* New York, 1937.

Seward, William H. [1801–1872]

See also **2008, 3093, 3094, 3117, 3141**

925 BAKER, George E., ed. *The Workers of William H. Seward.* 5 Vols. New York, 1853–1884.

926 BANCROFT, Frederic. *The Life of William H. Seward.* 2 vols. New York, 1900.

927 SCHEIDENHELM, Richard J. "The Legal and Political Rhetoric of William Henry Seward." Doctoral dissertation, University of Wisconsin, Madison, 1970.

928 SEWARD, Frederick W., ed. *William H. Seward; an Autobiography from 1801 to 1834. With a Memoir of His Life, and Selections from His Letters.* 3 vols. New York, 1877–1891.

929 VAN DEUSEN, Glyndon G. *William Henry Seward.* New York, 1967.

Shaw, Lemuel [1781–1861]

930 CHASE, Frederic H. *Lemuel Shaw, Chief Justice of the Supreme Judicial Court of Massachusetts.* Boston, 1918.

931 LEVY, Leonard W. *The Law of the Commonwealth and Chief Justice Shaw.* Cambridge, Mass., 1957.

Simms, William Gilmore [1806–1870]

932 OLIPHANT, Mary C. Simms; Alfred Taylor ODELL; and T. C. Duncan EAVES, eds. *The Letters of William Gilmore Simms.* 5 vols. Columbia, 1952–1956.

933 TRENT, William P. *William Gilmore Simms.* Boston, 1892.

934 WAKELYN, Jon L. *The Politics of a Literary Man: William Gilmore Simms.* Westport, 1973.

Skinner, John Stuart [1788–1851]

935 BERRYMAN, Jack William. "John Stuart Skinner and Early American Sport Journalism." Doctoral dissertation, University of Maryland, 1976.

Smith, Gerrit [1797–1874]

936 HARLOW, Ralph V. *Gerrit Smith, Philanthropist and Reformer.* New York, 1939.

Smith, Margaret Bayard [1778–1844]

937 HUNT, Gaillard, ed. *The First Forty Years of Washington Society.* New York, 1906.

Smith, Samuel [1752–1839]

938 CASSELL, Frank A. *Merchant Congressman in the Young Republic: Samuel Smith of Maryland, 1752–1839.* Madison, 1971.

939 PANCAKE, John S. *Samuel Smith and the Politics of Business: 1752–1839.* University, Ala., 1972.

Snyder, Simon [1759–1819]

940 DERR, Emerson L. "Simon Snyder, Governor of Pennsylvania, 1808–1817." Doctoral dissertation, Pennsylvania State University, 1960.

Southard, Samuel L. [1787–1842]

941 ERSHKOWITZ, Herbert. "Samuel L. Southard: A Case Study of Whig Leadership in the Age of Jackson." *N J Hist,* LXXXVIII (1970), 5–24.

Stanly, Edward [1810–1872]

942 BROWN, Norman D. *Edward Stanly: Whiggery's Tarheel "Conqueror."* University, Ala., 1975.

Stanton, Henry B. [1805–1887]

943 STANTON, Henry B. *Random Recollections.* New York, 1886.

Stevenson, Andrew [1785–1857]

944 Wayland, Francis Fry. *Andrew Stevenson: Democrat and Diplomat, 1785–1857.* Philadelphia, 1949.

Story, Joseph [1779–1845]

See also **1698, 1699, 1714, 1719, 1722, 1723, 1725, 1726, 1734**

945 DUNNE, Gerald T. *Justice Joseph Story and the Rise of the Supreme Court.* New York, 1970.

946 DUNNE, Gerald T., ed. "The Story–[Brockholst] Livingston Correspondence, 1812–1822." *Am J Leg Hist,* X (1966), 224–236.

947 MCCLELLAN, James. *Joseph Story and the American Constitution: A Study in Political and Legal Thought.* Norman, 1971.

948 NEWMYER, R. Kent. "Justice Joseph Story: A Political and Constitutional Study." Doctoral dissertation, University of Nebraska, 1959.

949 NEWMYER, R. Kent. "A Note on the Whig Politics of Justice Joseph Story." *Miss Val Hist Rev,* XLVIII (1961), 480–491.

950 SCHWARTZ, Mortimer D., and John C. HOGAN, eds. *Joseph Story: Eminent Jurist.* New York, 1959.

951 STORY, William W. *Life and Letters of Joseph Story.* 2 vols. Boston, 1851.

952 STORY, William W., ed. *The Miscellaneous Writings of Joseph Story.* Boston, 1852.

953 WARREN, Charles, ed. "The Story–[John] Marshall Correspondence." *Wm Mar Q,* 2d ser., XXI (1941), 1–25.

Swain, David L. [1801–1868]

See also **2185**

954 WALLACE, Carolyn A. "David Lowry Swain." Doctoral dissertation, University of North Carolina at Chapel Hill, 1954.

Tait, Charles [1768–1835]

955 MOFFAT, Charles H. "Charles Tait, Planter, Politician, and Scientist of the Old South." *J S Hist,* XIV (1948), 206–233.

Taney, Roger B. [1777–1864]

See also **1477, 1486, 1488, 1510, 1692, 1701, 1712, 1713, 1715, 1721, 1724, 1735, 2118**

956 ARMSTRONG, Walter P. "The Rehabilitation of Roger B. Taney." *Tenn Law Rev,* XIV (1936), 205–218.

957 BORCHARD, Edwin. "Taney's Influence on Constitutional Law." *Geo Law J,* XXIV (1936), 848–863.

958 HARRIS, Robert J. "Chief Justice Taney: Prophet of Reform and Reaction." *Vand Law Rev,* X (1957), 227–257.

959 LEWIS, Walker. *Without Fear or Favor: A Biography of Chief Justice Roger Brooke Taney.* Boston, 1965.

960 RANSOM, William L. "Roger Brooke Taney: Chief Justice of the Supreme Court of the United States." *Geo Law J,* XXIV (1936), 809–847.

961 SMITH, Charles W. *Roger B. Taney: Jacksonian Jurist.* Chapel Hill, 1937.

962 STEINER, Bernard C. *Life of Roger Brooke Taney, Chief Justice of the United States.* Baltimore, 1922.

963 SWISHER, Carl Brent. *Roger B. Taney.* New York, 1935.

964 SWISHER, Carl B. "Mr. Chief Justice Taney." *Mr. Justice.* Ed. Allison DUNHAM and Philip P. KURLAND. Rev. ed. Chicago, 1964.

965 WINITSKY, Marvin Laurence. "The Jurisprudence of Roger B. Taney." Doctoral dissertation, University of California, Los Angeles, 1973.

966 WINITSKY, Marvin Laurence. "Roger B. Taney: A Historiographical Inquiry." *Md. Hist Mag,* LXIX (1974), 1–26.

Tappan, Arthur [1786–1865]

See also **3607**

967 TAPPAN, Lewis. *The Life of Arthur Tappan.* New York, 1870.

Tappan, Lewis [1788–1873]

968 WYATT-BROWN, Bertram. *Lewis Tappan and the Evangelical War against Slavery.* Cleveland, 1969.

Taylor, John. [1753–1824]

See also **2135, 2149**

969 BAILOR, Keith M. "John Taylor of Caroline: Continuity, Change, and Disconti-
nuity in Virginia's Sentiments toward Slavery, 1790–1820." *Va Mag Hist Biog,*
LXXV (1967), 290–304.

970 MUDGE, Eugene TenBroeck. *The Social Philosophy of John Taylor of Caroline:
A Study in Jeffersonian Democracy.* New York, 1937.

971 SIMMS, Henry H. *Life of John Taylor: The Story of a Brilliant Leader in the Early
Virginia State Rights School.* Richmond, 1932.

972 WRIGHT, Benjamin F., Jr. "The Philosopher of Jeffersonian Democracy." *Am
Pol Sci Rev,* XXII (1928), 870–892.

Taylor, John W. [1784–1854]

See also **1118**

973 SPANN, Edward K. "John W. Taylor, the Reluctant Partisan, 1784–1854."
Doctoral dissertation, New York University, 1957.

Taylor, Zachary [1784–1850]

974 DYER, Brainerd. *Zachary Taylor.* Baton Rouge, 1946.

975 HAMILTON, Holman. *Zachary Taylor.* 2 vols. Indianapolis, 1941–1951.

Tazewell, Littleton W. [1774–1860]

976 SAWERS, Timothy R. "The Public Career of Littleton Waller Tazewell, 1824–
1836." Doctoral dissertation, Miami University, 1972.

Thompson, Smith [1768–1843]

See also **2017**

977 ROPER, Donald M. "Mr. Justice Thompson and the Constitution." Doctoral
dissertation, Indian University, 1963.

Tompkins, Daniel D. [1774–1825]

978 IRWIN, Ray W. *Daniel D. Tompkins: Governor of New York and Vice President
of the United States.* New York, 1968.

Tipton, John [1786–1839]

979 ROBERTSON, Nellie Armstrong, and Dorothy RIKER, eds. *The John Tipton Papers.* 3 vols. Indianapolis, 1942.

Travis, William B. [1809–1836]

980 MCDONALD, Archie P. *Travis.* Austin, 1976.

981 TURNER, Martha Anne. *William Barret Travis: His Sword and His Pen.* Waco, 1972.

Troup, George M. [1780–1856]

982 FORTUNE, Porter L., Jr. "George M. Troup: Leading State Rights Advocate." Doctoral dissertation, University of North Carolina at Chapel Hill, 1949.

983 HARDEN, Edward J. *The Life of George McIntosh Troup.* Savannah, 1859.

Tucker, George [1775–1861]

984 MCLEAN, Robert Colin. *George Tucker: Moral Philosopher and Man of Letters.* Chapel Hill, 1961.

985 SNAVELY, Tipton R. *George Tucker as Political Economist.* Charlottesville, 1964.

Tucker, Nathaniel Beverley [1784–1851]

986 BRUGGER, Robert J. *Beverley Tucker: Heart over Head in the Old South.* Baltimore, 1978.

987 WILSON, Gerald Lee. "Nathaniel Beverley Tucker, 'Aristocratic Paternalist': The Search for Order and Stability in the Antebellum South." Doctoral dissertation, University of North Carolina at Chapel Hill, 1973.

Tyler, John [1790–1862]

988 CHITWOOD, Oliver Perry. *John Tyler, Champion of the Old South.* New York, 1939.

989 SEAGER, Robert, II. *And Tyler Too: A Biography of John & Julia Gardiner Tyler.* New York, 1963.

990 TYLER, Lyon G. *The Letters and Times of the Tylers.* 3 vols. Richmond, 1884–1896.

Upshur, Abel P. [1791–1844]

991 HALL, Claude H. *Abel Parker Upshur, Conservative Virginian.* Madison, 1963.

992 MILLER, Russell E. "Abel Parker Upshur: A Study in Ante-Bellum Social and Political Philosophy." Doctoral dissertation, Princeton University, 1951.

Van Buren, Martin [1782–1862]

See also **1284, 1376, 1487, 1570–1606**

993 ALEXANDER, Holmes. *The American Talleyrand.* New York, 1935.

994 BROWN, Richard H. " 'Southern Planters and Plain Republicans of the North': Martin Van Buren's Formula for National Politics." Doctoral dissertation, Yale University, 1955.

995 BUTLER, William A. *Martin Van Buren: Lawyer, Statesman and Man.* New York, 1862.

996 CONE, Leon W., Jr. "Martin Van Buren: The Architect of the Democratic Party, 1837–1840." Doctoral dissertation, Chicago, 1951.

997 CROCKETT, David. *The Life of Martin Van Buren.* Philadelphia, 1835.

998 CURTIS, James C. *The Fox at Bay: Martin Van Buren and the Presidency.* Lexington, Ky., 1970.

999 EMMONS, William. *Biography of Martin Van Buren.* Washington, D.C., 1835.

1000 FITZPATRICK, John C., ed. *Autobiography of Martin Van Buren.* Washington, D.C., 1920.

1001 IRELAN, John R. *History of the Life, Administration and Times of Martin Van Buren, Eighth President of the United States.* Chicago, 1887.

1002 LYNCH, Denis T. *An Epoch and a Man, Martin Van Buren and His Times.* New York, 1929.

1003 MACKENZIE, William L. *Life and Times of Martin Van Buren.* Boston, 1846.

1004 MINTZ, Max M. "The Political Ideas of Martin Van Buren." *N Y Hist,* XXX (1949), 422–448.

1005 REMINI, Robert V. *Martin Van Buren and the Making of the Democratic Party.* New York, 1959.†

1006 SHEPARD, Edward M. *Martin Van Buren.* Boston, 1889.

1007 SMITH, Richard Williams. "The Career of Martin Van Buren in Connection with the Slavery Controversy through the Election of 1840." Doctoral dissertation, Ohio State University, 1959.

1008 VAN BUREN, Martin. *Inquiry into the Origins and Course of Political Parties in the United States.* New York, 1867.

Verplanck, Gulian C. [1786–1870]

1009 JULY, Robert W. *The Essential New Yorker: Gulian Crommelin Verplanck.* Durham, 1951.

Walker, John W. [1783–1823]

See also **1111, 2304**

1010 BAILEY, Hugh C. *John Williams Walker: A Study in the Political, Social, and Cultural Life of the Old Southwest.* University, Ala., 1964.

1011 OWSLEY, Frank L. "John Williams Walker." *Ala Rev,* IX (1956), 100–119.

Walker, Robert J. [1801–1869]

1012 DODD, William E. *Robert J. Walker, Imperialist.* Chicago, 1914.

1013 SHENTON, James P. *Robert John Walker: A Politician from Jackson to Lincoln.* New York, 1961.

1014 TICK, Frank H. "The Political and Economic Policies of Robert J. Walker." Doctoral dissertation, University of California, Los Angeles, 1947.

Wayne, James M. [1790–1867]

1015 LAWRENCE, Alexander A. *James Moore Wayne: Southern Unionist.* Chapel Hill, 1943.

Webb, James Watson [1802–1884]

See also **4551**

1016 CROUTHAMEL, James L. *James Watson Webb: A Biography.* Middletown, 1969.

Webster, Daniel [1782–1852]

See also **1128, 1459, 4335, 4344**

1017 BARTLETT, Irving H. "Daniel Webster as a Symbolic Hero." *N. Eng Q,* XLV (1972), 484–507.

1018 BARTLETT, Irving H. *Daniel Webster.* New York, 1978.

1019 BAXTER, Maurice G. *Daniel Webster & the Supreme Court.* Amherst, 1966.

1020 BROWN, Norman D. *Daniel Webster and the Politics of Availability.* Athens, 1969.

1021 CAREY, Robert Lincoln. *Daniel Webster as an Economist.* New York, 1929.

1022 CURRENT, Richard N. *Daniel Webster and the Rise of National Conservatism.* Boston, 1955.†

1023 CURTIS, George T. *Life of Daniel Webster.* 2 vols. New York, 1870.

1024 FUESS, Claude M. *Daniel Webster.* 2 vols. Boston, 1930.

1025 LEWIS, Walker, ed. *Speak for Yourself, Daniel: A Life of Webster in His Own Words.* Boston, 1969.

1026 LODGE, Henry Cabot. *Daniel Webster.* Boston, 1883.

1027 MCINTYRE, J. W., ed. *The Writings and Speeches of Daniel Webster.* 18 vols. Boston, 1903.

1028 MCMASTER, John Bach. *Daniel Webster.* New York, 1902.

1029 MONDALE, Clarence. "Daniel Webster and Technology." *Am Q,* XIV (1962), 37–47.

1030 NATHANS, Sydney H. *Daniel Webster and Jacksonian Democracy.* Baltimore, 1973.

1031 NATHANS, Sydney H. "Daniel Webster, Massachusetts Man." *N Eng Q,* XXXIX (1966), 161–181.

1032 OGG, Frederic Austin. *Daniel Webster.* Philadelphia, 1914.

1033 PARISH, Peter J. "Daniel Webster, New England, and the West." *J Am Hist,* LIV (1967), 524–549.

1034 VAN TYNE, C. H., ed. *The Letters of Daniel Webster.* New York, 1902.

1035 WILTSE, Charles M.; Harold D. MOSER; and David G. ALLEN, eds. *The Papers of Daniel Webster.* 3 vols. to date. Hanover, N.H., 1974–.

1036 WILTSE, Charles M. "Daniel Webster and the British Experience." *Mass Hist Soc Proc,* LXXXV (1973), 58–77.

Weed, Thurlow [1797–1882]

See also **2023**

1037 BARNES, Thurlow W. *Memoir of Thurlow Weed.* Boston, 1884.

1038 VAN DEUSEN, Glyndon G. *Thurlow Weed: Wizard of the Lobby.* Boston, 1947.

1039 WEED, Harriet H., ed. *Autobiography of Thurlow Weed.* Boston, 1883.

Weld, Theodore D. [1803–1895]

1040 THOMAS, Benjamin P. *Theodore Weld: Crusader for Freedom.* New Brunswick, 1950.

Wheaton, Henry [1785–1848]

1041 BAKER, Elizabeth F. *Henry Wheaton, 1785–1848.* Philadelphia, 1937.

White, Hugh L. [1773–1840]

See also **2280**

1042 GRESHAM, L. Paul. "The Public Career of Hugh Lawson White." *Tenn Hist Q*, III (1944), 291–318.

1043 SCOTT, Nancy N. *Memoir of Hugh Lawson White.* Philadelphia, 1856.

Whitman, Marcus [1802–1847] & Whitman, Narcissa P. [1808–1847]

1044 DRURY, Clifford M. *Marcus and Narcissa Whitman and the Opening of Old Oregon.* 2 vols. Glendale, 1973.

1045 JONES, Nard. *The Great Command: The Story of Marcus and Narcissa Whitman and the Oregon Country Pioneers.* Boston, 1960.

Whittlesey, Elisha [1783–1863]

1046 DAVISON, Kenneth E. "Forgotten Ohioan: Elisha Whittlesey." Doctoral dissertation, Western Reserve University, 1953.

Wilkes, Charles [1798–1877]

1047 HENDERSON, Daniel. *The Hidden Coasts: a Biography of Admiral Charles Wilkes.* New York, 1953.

Williams, David R. [1776–1830]

1048 COOK, Harvey Toliver. *The Life and Legacy of David Rogerson Williams.* New York, 1916.

Williams, Samuel May [1795–1858]

1049 HENSON, Margaret Swett. *Samuel May Williams: Early Texas Entrepreneur.* College Station, Texas, 1976.

Wirt, William [1772–1834]

See also **1450, 1520**

1050 BURKE, Joseph Charles. "William Wirt: Attorney General and Constitutional Lawyer." Doctoral dissertation, Indiana University, 1965.

1051 KENNEDY, John P. *Memoirs of the Life of William Wirt, Attorney General of the United States.* 2 vols. Philadelphia, 1849.

1052 ROBERT, Joseph C. "William Wirt, Virginian." *Va Mag Hist Biog,* LXXX (1972), 387–441.

Wise, Henry A. [1806–1876]

1053 ADKINS, Edwin P. "Henry A. Wise in Sectional Politics, 1833–1860." Doctoral dissertation, Ohio State University, 1948.

1054 WISE, Barton H. *The Life of Henry A. Wise of Virginia, 1806–1876.* New York, 1899.

1055 WISE, Henry A. *Seven Decades of the Union.* Philadelphia, 1872.

Woodbury, Levi [1789–1851]

See also **1367, 1928**

1056 CAPOWSKI, Vincent Julian. "The Making of a Jacksonian Democrat: Levi Woodbury, 1789–1831." Doctoral dissertation, Fordham University, 1966.

1057 WHEATON, Philip D. "Levi Woodbury, Jacksonian Financier." Doctoral dissertation, University of Maryland, 1955.

1058 WOODBURY, Levi. *Writings of Levi Woodbury.* 3 vols. Boston, 1852.

Worcester, Samuel A. [1798–1859]

1059 BASS, Althea. *Cherokee Messenger.* Norman, 1936.

1060 KILPATRICK, Jack F., and Anna G. KILPATRICK, eds. *New Echota Letters: Contributions of Samuel A. Worcester to the Cherokee Phoenix.* Dallas, 1968.

Worthington, Thomas [1773–1827]

1061 SEARS, Alfred Byron. *Thomas Worthington: Father of Ohio Statehood.* Columbus, 1958.

Wright, Silas [1795–1847]

1062 GARRATY, John A. *Silas Wright.* New York, 1949.

1063 HAMMOND, Jabez D. *Life and Times of Silas Wright.* Syracuse, 1848.

1064 KENNEDY, Mary C. "Silas Wright and New York Politics, 1795–1847." Doctoral dissertation, University of Chicago, 1950.

IV. The Era of Good Feelings and After, 1816-1828

1. The Twilight of the Madison Administration

See also **2016**

1065 ADAMS, Henry. *History of the United States during the Administrations of Jefferson and Madison.* 9 vols. New York, 1889–1891. [Abridged 1 vol. ed.†]

1066 BAKER, Maury. "The Spanish War Scare of 1816." *Mid-Am,* XLV (1963), 67–78.

1067 BROWN, Kenneth L. "Stephen Girard, Promoter of the Second Bank of the United States." *J Econ Hist,* II (1942), 125–148.

1068 FRITZ, Harry William. "The Collapse of Party; President, Congress, and the Decline of Party Action, 1807–1817." Doctoral dissertation, Washington University, 1971.

1069 IRWIN, Ray W. *The Diplomatic Relations of the United States with the Barbary Powers, 1776–1816.* Chapel Hill, 1931.

1070 MARRARO, Howard R. "William Pinkney's Mission to the Kingdom of the Two Sicilies, 1816." *Md Hist Mag,* XLII (1948), 235–365.

1071 MORGAN, William G. "The Congressional Nominating Caucus of 1816: The Struggle against the Virginia Dynasty." *Va Mag Hist Biog,* LXXX (1972), 461–475.

1072 NICHOLS, Roy F. "Diplomacy in Barbary." *Pa Mag Hist Biog,* LXXIV (1950), 113–141.

1073 PREYER, Norris, W. "Southern Support of the Tariff of 1816—A Reappraisal." *J S Hist,* XXV (1959), 306–322.

1074 TURNER, Lynn W. "Elections of 1816 and 1820." *History of American Presidential Elections.* 4 vols. Ed. Arthur M. SCHLESINGER, Jr.; Fred L. ISRAEL; and William P. HANSEN. New York, 1971. I, 299–345.

1075 WALTERS, Raymond, Jr., "The Origins of the Second Bank of the United States." *J Pol Econ,* LIII (1945), 115–131.

2. Political History

See also **787–804, 1918, 2022, 2056, 2063**

1076 BABCOCK, Kendric C. *The Rise of American Nationality, 1811–1819.* New York, 1906.

1077 BOGART, E. L. "Taxation of the Second Bank of the United States by Ohio." *Am Hist Rev,* XVII (1912), 312–331.

1078 COOPER, Joseph. "Jeffersonian Attitudes toward Executive Leadership and Committee Development in the House of Representatives, 1789–1829." *W Pol Q,* XVIII (1965), 45–63.

1079 CUNNINGHAM, Noble E., Jr. "Nathaniel Macon and the Southern Protest against National Consolidation." *N C Hist Rev,* XXXII (1955), 376–384.

1080 DANGERFIELD, George. *The Era of Good Feelings.* New York, 1952.†

1081 DANGERFIELD, George. *The Awakening of American Nationalism, 1815–1828.* New York, 1965.†

1082 DODD, William E. "Chief Justice Marshall and Virginia, 1813–1821." *Am Hist Rev,* XII (1907), 776–787.

1083 JOHNSON, Allen. *Jefferson and His Colleagues: A Chronicle of the Virginia Dynasty.* New Haven, 1921.

1084 LIVERMORE, Shaw. *The Twilight of Federalism: The Disintegration of the Federalist Party, 1815–1830.* Princeton, 1962.

1085 MORGAN, William G. "Presidential Nominations in the Federal Era." Doctoral dissertation, University of Southern California, 1969.

1086 MORGAN, William G. "The Origin and Development of the Congressional Nominating Caucus." *Am Phil Soc Proc,* CXIII (1969), 184–196.

1087 NAGEL, Paul C. "The Era of Good Feeling: Foundation for Disunion." Doctoral dissertation, University of Minnesota, 1952.

1088 NIELSEN, George Raymond. "The Indispensable Institution: the Congressional Party during the Era of Good Feelings." Doctoral dissertation, University of Iowa, 1968.

1089 OSTROGORSKI, M. "The Rise and Fall of the Nominating Caucus, Legislative and Congressional." *Am Hist Rev,* V (1900), 252–283.

1090 PETERSON, Merrill D., ed. *Democracy, Liberty, and Property: The State Constitutional Conventions of the 1820's.* Indianapolis, 1966.†

1091 RISJORD, Norman K. *The Old Republicans: Southern Conservatism in the Age of Jefferson.* New York, 1965.

1092 RUSSO, David John. "The Southern Republicans and American Political Nationalism, 1815–1825." Doctoral dissertation, Yale University, 1966.

1093 STAUDENRAUS, P. J. " 'Era of Good Feelings' Reconsidered." *Mid-Am,* XXXVIII (1956), 180–194.

1094 SYDNOR, Charles S. "The One-Party Period of American History." *Am Hist Rev,* LI (1946), 439–451.

1095 TAYLOR, George R., ed. *The Great Tariff Debate, 1820–1830.* Boston, 1953.†

1096 THOMPSON, C. S. *An Essay on the Rise and Fall of the Congressional Caucus.* New Haven, 1902.

1097 TURNER, Frederick J. *Rise of the New West, 1819–1829.* New York, 1906.

1098 TURNER, Frederick J. "The Colonization of the West, 1820–1830." *Am Hist Rev,* XI (1906), 303–327.

1099 TURNER, Frederick J. "The South, 1820–1830." *Am Hist Rev,* XI (1906), 559–573.

1100 WALTERS, Raymond, J., Jr., ed. *The Virginia Dynasty.* Princeton, 1965.

1101 WESLEY, Edgar Bruce. *Guarding the Frontier: A Study of Frontier Defense from 1815 to 1825.* Minneapolis, 1935.

1102 WHITE, Leonard D. *The Jeffersonians: A Study in Administrative History, 1801–1829.* New York, 1951.

1103 YOUNG, James Sterling. *The Washington Community, 1800–1828.* New York, 1966.†

3. Diplomatic History

1104 BENNS, F. Lee. *The American Struggle for the British West India Carrying-Trade, 1815–1830.* Bloomington, 1923.

1105 BERQUIST, Harold Edward, Jr. "Russian-American Relations, 1820–1830: The Diplomacy of Henry Middleton, American Minister at St. Petersburg." Doctoral dissertation, Boston University, 1970.

1106 CAMPBELL, Randolph Bluford. "The Spanish American Aspect of Henry Clay's American System." *Americas,* XXIV (1967), 3–17.

1107 MORLEY, Margaret Ruth. "The Edge of Empire: Henry Clay's American System and the Formulation of American Foreign Policy, 1810–1833." Doctoral dissertation, University of Wisconsin, Madison, 1972.

1108 WEBSTER, Charles K. *The Foreign Policy of Castlereagh, 1815–1822.* London, 1925.

4. The Administrations of James Monroe, 1817–1825

Domestic Politics

A. The President, Cabinet, and Congress

See also **828–834**

1109 AMMON, Harry. "James Monroe and the Era of Good Feelings." *Va Mag Hist Biog,* LXVI (1958), 387–398.

1110 AMMON, Harry. "Executive Leadership in the Monroe Administration." *America, the Middle Period: Essays in Honor of Bernard Mayo.* Ed. John B. BOLES. Charlottesville, 1973.

1111 BAILEY, Hugh C. "John W. Walker and the Land Laws of the 1820's." *Ag Hist,* XXXII (1958), 120–126.

1112 BARSNESS, Richard W. "John C. Calhoun and the Military Establishment, 1817–1825. *Wis Mag Hist,* L (1966), 43–53.

1113 CARTER, Clarence E., ed. "William Henry Harrison and the Mexican Appointment, 1823–1824." *Miss Val Hist Rev,* XXV (1938), 251–262.

1114 CUTLER, Wayne E. "The A. B. Controversy." *Mid-Am,* LI (1969), 24–37.

1115 SKEEN, C. Edward. "Calhoun, Crawford, and the Politics of Retrenchment." *S C Hist Mag,* LXXIII (1972), 141–155.

1116 SMITH, Carlton B. "John C. Calhoun, Secretary of War, 1817–25: The Cast Iron Man as Administrator." *America, the Middle Period: Essays in Honor of Bernard Mayo.* Ed. John B. BOLES. Charlottesville, 1973.

1117 SMITH, Carlton B. "Congressional Attitudes toward Military Preparedness during the Monroe Administration." *Mil Aff,* XL (1976), 22–25.

1118 SPANN, Edward K. "The Souring of Good Feelings: John W. Taylor and the Speakership Election of 1821." *N Y Hist,* XLI (1960), 379–399.

1119 STATHIS, Stephen W. "Dr. Barton's Case and the Monroe Precedent of 1818." *Wm Mar Q,* 3rd ser., XXXII (1975), 465–474.

1120 WILMERDING, Louis, Jr. "James Monroe and the Furniture Fund." *N Y Hist Soc Q,* XLIV (1960), 133–149.

1121 WILTSE, Charles M. "John C. Calhoun and the 'A. B.' Plot." *J S Hist,* XIII (1947), 46–61.

B. The Supreme Court and Judicial Nationalism

1122 BAXTER, Maurice G. "Should the *Dartmouth Case* Have Been Reargued?" *N Eng Q,* XXXIII (1960), 19–36.

1123 BAXTER, Maurice G. *The Steamboat Monopoly:* Gibbons v. Odgen, 1824. New York, 1972.†

1124 CAMPBELL, Bruce A. "Law and Experience in the Early Republic: The Evolution of the *Dartmouth College* Doctrine, 1780–1819." Doctoral dissertation, Michigan State University, 1973.

1125 CAMPBELL, Bruce A. "John Marshall, the Virginia Political Economy, and the *Dartmouth College* Decision." *Am J Leg Hist,* XIX (1975), 40–65.

1126 MARSHALL, John. " 'A Friend of the Constitution': In Defense and Elaboration of *McCulloch v. Maryland.* " Ed. Gerald GUNTHER. *Stan Law Rev,* XXI (1969), 449–499.

1127 MENDELSON, Wallace. "New Light on *Fletcher v. Peck* and *Gibbons v. Ogden.* " *Yale L Rev,* LVIII (1949), 567–573.

1128 NEWMYER, R. Kent. "Daniel Webster as Tocqueville's Lawyer: The *Dartmouth College* Case Again." *Am J Leg Hist,* XI (1967), 127–147.

1129 NORTH, William G. "The Political Background of the *Dartmouth College* Case." *N Eng Q,* XVIII (1945), 181–203.

1130 NOVAK, Steven J. "The College in the *Dartmouth College* Case: A Reinterpretation." *N Eng Q,* XLVII (1974), 550–563.

1131 PLOUS, Harold J., and Gordon BAKER. "*McCulloch vs. Maryland,* Right Principle, Wrong Case." *Stan Law Rev,* IX (1957), 710–730.

1132 SHIRLEY, John M. *The* Dartmouth College *Causes and the Supreme Court of the United States.* St Louis, 1877.

1133 STITES, Francis N. *Private Interest & Public Gain: The Dartmouth College Case, 1819.* Amherst, 1972.†

1134 TREON, John Alfred. "*Martin v. Hunter's Lessee:* A Case History." Doctoral dissertation, University of Virginia, 1970.

C. The Missouri Controversy, 1819–1821

See also **1915, 1917, 2303, 2386, 2394**

1135 ARBENA, Joseph L. "Politics or Principle? Rufus King and the Opposition to Slavery, 1785–1825." *Essex Inst Hist Coll,* CI (1965), 56–77.

1136 BROWN, Richard H. "The Missouri Crisis, Slavery, and the Politics of Jacksonianism." *S Atl Q,* LXV (1966), 55–72.

1137 BURNS, Zed H. "Sectional Controversy and the Missouri Compromise." *S Q,* V (1967), 335–345.

1138 DETWEILER, Philip. "Congressional Debate on Slavery and the Declaration of Independence, 1819–1821." *Am Hist Rev,* LXIII (1958), 598–616.

1139 DIXON, Mrs. Archibald. *The True History of the Missouri Compromise and Its Repeal.* Cincinnati, 1899.

1140 EGERTON, Cecil Baker. "Rufus King and the Missouri Question: A Study in Political Mythology." Doctoral dissertation, Claremont University, 1968.

1141 ERNST, Robert. "Rufus King, Slavery, and the Missouri Crisis." *N Y Hist Soc Q,* XLVI (1962), 357–382.

1142 HOCKETT, Homer C. "Rufus King and the Missouri Compromise." *Mo Hist Rev,* II (1908), 211–220.

1143 HODDER, Frank H. "Side Lights on the Missouri Compromises." *Ann Rep Am Hist Assn, 1909.* Washington, D.C., 1911, pp. 151–161.

1144 JOHNSON, William R. "Prelude to the Missouri Compromise: A New York Congressman's Effort to Exclude Slavery from Arkansas Territory." *N Y Hist Soc Q,* XLVIII (1964), 31–50.

1145 LIGHTFOOT, Alfred. "Henry Clay and the Missouri Question, 1819–1821." *Mo Hist Rev,* LXI (1967), 143–165.

1146 MOORE, Glover. *The Missouri Controversy, 1819–1821.* Lexington, 1953.†

1147 ROBINSON, Donald L. *Slavery in the Structure of American Politics, 1765–1820.* New York, 1971.

1148 SIMPSON, Albert F. "The Political Significance of Slave Representation, 1787–1821." *J S Hist,* VII (1941), 315–342.

1149 WILSON, Major L. "The Two Free Soils in the Missouri Controversy, 1819–1820. Memphis State University, *MVC Bulletin,* no. 5 (1972), 50–60.

1150 WOODBURN, James A. "The Historical Significance of the Missouri Compromise." *Ann Rep Am Hist Assn, 1893.* Washington, D.C., 1894, pp. 249–297.

D. The Panic of 1819 and Its Aftermath

See also **2255, 2257, 2263, 2289, 2291, 2375**

1151 DORSEY, Dorothy B. "The Panic of 1819 in Missouri." *Mo Hist Rev,* XXIX (1935), 79–91.

1152 GREER, Thomas H. "Economic and Social Effects of the Depression in the Old Northwest." *Ind Mag Hist,* XLIX (1948), 227–243.

1153 HAMILTON, W. J. "The Relief Movement in Missouri, 1820–1822." *Mo Hist Rev.,* XXII (1927), 51–92.

1154 JONES, Thomas Bard. "Legacy of Change: The Panic of 1819 and Debtor Relief Legislation in the Western States." Doctoral dissertation, Cornell University, 1968.

1155 REZNECK, Samuel. "The Depression of 1819–1822, A Social History." *Am Hist Rev,* XXXIX (1933), 28–47.

1156 ROTHBARD, Murray N. *The Panic of 1819: Reactions and Policies.* New York, 1962.

1157 SCHUR, Leon M. "The Second Bank of the United States and the Inflation after the War of 1812. *J Pol Econ,* LXVIII (1960), 118–134.

E. The Presidential Election of 1820

See also **1074**

1158 MOORE, Glover. Monroe's Re-Election in 1820." *Miss Q,* XI (1958), 131–140.

1159 PAULLIN, Charles O. "The Electoral Vote for John Quincy Adams in 1820." *Am Hist Rev,* XXI (1916), 318–319.

1160 TURNER, Lynn W. "The Electoral Vote against Monroe in 1820—An American Legend." *Miss Val Hist Rev,* XLII (1955), 250–273.

F. The Presidential Election of 1824–1825

See also **496, 497, 2026, 2178, 2396, 2467, 2468**

1161 AMES, William E., and S. Dean OLSON. "Washington's Political Press and the Election of 1824." *Jour Q,* XL (1963), 343–350.

1162 BROWN, Everett S. "The Presidential Election of 1824–1825." *Pol Sci Q,* XL (1925), 384–403.

1163 FINK, William B. "Stephen Van Rensselaer and the House Election of 1825." *N Y Hist,* XXXII (1951), 323–330.

1164 HAY, Robert P. " 'The Presidential Question': Letters to Southern Editors, 1823–24." *Tenn Hist Q,* XXXI (1972), 170–186.

1165 HAY, Robert P. "The Case for Andrew Jackson in 1824: Eaton's 'Wyoming Letters.' " *Tenn Hist Q,* XXIX (1970), 139–151.

1165A HAY, Robert P. "The American Revolution Twice Recalled: Lafayette's Visit and the Election of 1824." *Ind Mag Hist,* LXIX (1973), 43–62.

1166   HOPKINS, James F. "Election of 1824." *History of American Presidential Elections.* 4 vols. Ed. Arthur M. SCHLESINGER, Jr.; Fred L. ISRAEL; and William P. HANSEN. New York, 1971. I, 349–408.

1166A   LATHROP, Barnes F., comp. "Monroe on the Adams-Clay 'Bargain'." *Am Hist Rev,* XLII (1937), 273–276.

1167   MORGAN, William G. "The Decline of the Congressional Nominating Caucus." *Tenn Hist Q,* XXIV (1965), 245–255.

1168   MORGAN, William G. "John Quincy Adams versus Andrew Jackson: Their Biographers and the 'Corrupt Bargain' Charge." *Tenn Hist Q,* XXVI (1967), 43–58.

1169   MORGAN, William G. The 'Corrupt Bargain' Charge against Clay and Adams: An Historiographical Analysis." *Filson Club Hist Q,* XLII (1968), 132–149.

1170   MORGAN, William G. "Henry Clay's Biographers and the 'Corrupt Bargain' Charge." *Reg Ky Hist Soc,* LXVI (1968), 242–258.

1171   NAGEL, Paul C. "The Election of 1824: A Reconsideration Based on Newspaper Opinion." *J S Hist,* XXVI (1960), 315–329.

1172   NEWSOME, Albert R., ed. "Correspondence of John C. Calhoun, George McDuffie and Charles Fisher, Relating to the Presidential Campaign of 1824." *N C Hist Rev,* VII (1930), 477–504.

1173   SELLERS, Charles Grier, Jr. "Jackson Men with Feet of Clay." *Am Hist Rev,* LXII (1957), 537–551.

1174   STENBERG, Richard R. "Jackson, Buchanan, and the 'Corrupt Bargain' Calumny." *Pa Mag Hist Biog,* LVIII (1934), 61–85.

1175   STEVENS, Harry R. "Henry Clay, the Bank, and the West in 1824." *Am Hist Rev,* LX (1955), 843–848.

1176   TANKARD, James W., Jr. "Public Opinion Polling by Newspapers in the Presidential Election Campaign of 1824." *Jour Q,* XLIX (1972), 361–365.

Foreign Relations

A. United States–British Relations: The American–Canadian Border

See also **1822, 1844, 1861, 1863**

1177   CALLAHAN, James Morton. *The Neutrality of the American Lakes and Anglo-American Relations.* Baltimore, 1898.

1178   FAY, Terence James. "Rush-Bagot Agreement; A Reflection of the Anglo-American Detente, 1815–1818." Doctoral dissertation, Georgetown University, 1974.

1179   GOLLADAY, V. Dennis. "The United States and British North American Fisheries, 1815–1818." *Am Neptune,* XXXIII (1973), 246–257.

1180   LASS, William E. "How the Forty-Ninth Parallel Became the International Boundary." *Minn Hist,* XLIV (1975), 209–219.

1181   MCELROY, Robert, and Thomas RIGGS, eds. *The Unfortified Boundary: A Diary of the First Survey of the Canadian Boundary Line.* New York, 1943.

1182 MERK, Frederick. "The Genesis of the Oregon Question." *Miss Val Hist Rev,* XXXVI (1950), 583–612.

1183 MERK, Frederick. "The Ghost River Caledonia in the Oregon Negotiation of 1818." *Am Hist Rev,* LV (1950), 530–551.

1184 MERK, Frederick. *The Oregon Question: Essays in Anglo-American Diplomacy and Politics.* Cambridge, Mass., 1967.

B. The Acquisition of Florida and the Adams-Onis Treaty

1185 AMOS, Alcione M. "Captain Hugh Young's Map of Jackson's 1818 Seminole Campaign in Florida." *Fla Hist Q,* LV (1977), 336–346.

1186 BISCEGLIA, Louis R. "The Florida Treaty and the [Albert] Gallatin–[Gen. Francisco] Vives Misunderstanding." *Fla Hist Q,* XLVII (1970), 247–263.

1187 BOWMAN, Charles H. "Vicente Pazos and the Amelia Island Affair, 1817." *Fla Hist Q,* LIII (1975), 273–295.

1188 BOWMAN, Charles H. "Vicente Pazos, Agent for the Amelia Island Filibusters, 1818." *Fla Hist Q,* LIII (1975), 528–442.

1189 BROOKS, Philip Coolidge. *Diplomacy and the Borderlands: The Adams-Onis Treaty of 1819.* Berkeley, 1939.

1190 FULLER, Hubert Bruce. *The Purchase of Florida; Its History and Development.* Cleveland, 1906.

1191 LOWE, Richard G. "American Seizure of Amelia Island." *Fla Hist Q,* XLV (1966), 18–30.

1192 MCQUEEN, Ray A. "The Role of Andrew Jackson in the Acquisition of the Floridas." Doctoral dissertation, University of Pittsburgh, 1942.

1193 ONIS, Luis de. *Memoir upon the Negotiations between Spain and the United States of America, Which Led to the Treaty of 1819.* Washington, D.C., 1921.

1194 PORTER, Kenneth Wiggins. "Negroes and the Seminole War, 1817–1818." *J Neg Hist,* XXXVI (1951), 249–280.

C. United States–Russian Relations: The Pacific Northwest

See also **1839, 1851, 2550, 2593**

1195 BOLKHOVITINOV, Nikolai N., and Basil DMYTRYSHYIZ. "Russia and the Declaration of the Non-Colonization Principle: New Archival Evidence." *Ore Hist Q,* LXX (1971) 101–126.

1196 BROOKS, Philip C. "The Pacific Coast's First International Boundary Delineation, 1816–1819." *Pac Hist Rev,* III (1934), 62–79.

1197 FORD, Worthington, C., ed. "Correspondence of the Russian Ministers in Washington, 1818–1825." *Am Hist Rev,* XVIII (1913), 309–345, 537–562.

1198 HILDT, J. C. *Early Diplomatic Relations of the United States and Russia.* Baltimore, 1906.

1199 HINES, Clarence. "Adams, Russia and the Northwest Trade, 1824." *Ore Hist Q,* XXXVI (1935), 348–358.

1200 HUCULAK, Mykhaylo. *When Russia Was America: The Alaskan Treaty Negotiations, 1824–1825, and the Role of Pierre de Poletica.* Vancouver, 1971.

1201 JORDAN, Weymouth T. "Excerpts from the Diary of a Tennesseean [George Washington Campbell] at the Court of the Tsar, 1818–1820." *E Tenn Hist Soc Pub,* no. 15 (1943), 104–109.

1202 KUSHNER, Howard I. "The Russian-American Diplomatic Contest for the Pacific Basin and the Monroe Doctrine." *J W,* XV (1976), 65–80.

1203 MAZOUR, Anatole G. "The Russian-American and Anglo-Russian Conventions, 1824–1825: An Interpretation." *Pac Hist Rev,* XIV (1945), 303–310.

1204 NICHOLS, Irby C., Jr. "The Russian Ukase and the Monroe Doctrine: A Reevaluation." *Pac Hist Rev,* XXXVI (1967), 13–26.

1205 NICHOLS, Irby C., Jr., and Richard A. WARD. "Anglo-American Relations and the Russian Ukase: A Reassessment." *Pac Hist Rev,* XLI (1972), 444–459.

1206 TOMPKINS, S. R. "Drawing the Alaska Boundary [1824]." *Can Hist Rev,* XXVI (1945), 1–24.

D. The Independence of Latin America and The Monroe Doctrine

1207 BEMIS, Samuel F. "Early Diplomatic Missions from Buenos Aires to the United States, 1811–1824." *Proc Am Ant Soc,* XLIX (1939), 11–101.

1208 BERQUIST, Harold E., Jr. "John Quincy Adams and the Promulgation of the Monroe Doctrine." *Essex Inst Hist Coll,* CXI (1975), 37–52.

1209 BILLINGSLEY, Edward Baxter. *In Defense of Neutral Rights: the United States Navy and the Wars of Independence in Chile and Peru.* Chapel Hill, 1967.

1210 BORNHOLDT, Laura. "The Abbe de Pradt and the Monroe Doctrine." *His-Am Hist Rev,* XXIV (1944), 201–221.

1211 BRACKENRIDGE, Henry M. *Voyage to South America, Performed by Order of the American Government, in the Years 1817 and 1818.* 2 vols. Baltimore, 1819.

1212 BRADLEY, Phillips. *A Bibliography of the Monroe Doctrine, 1919–1929.* London, 1929.

1213 CRAVEN, Wesley F. "The Risk of the Monroe Doctrine." *His-Am Hist Rev,* VII (1927), 320–333.

1214 CRESSON, W. P. *The Holy Alliance: The European Background of the Monroe Doctrine.* New York, 1922.

1215 DAVIS, T. B., Jr. "Carlos de Alvear and James Monroe: New Light on the Origin of the Monroe Doctrine." *His-Am Hist Rev,* XXIII (1943), 632–649.

1216 EDGINGTON, T. B. *The Monroe Doctrine.* Boston, 1904.

1217 FALK, Stanley L. "Some Contemporary Views of the Monroe Doctrine: The United States Press in 1823." *Americas,* XII (1955), 183–193.

1218 FISHER, Lillian E. "American Influence upon the Movement for Mexican Independence." *Miss Val Hist Rev,* XVIII (1932), 463–478.

1219 FORD, Worthington C. "Some Original Documents on the Genesis of the Monroe Doctrine." *Mass Hist Soc Proc,* 2d ser., XV (1902), 373–436

1220 FORD, Worthington C. "John Quincy Adams and the Monroe Doctrine." *Am Hist Rev,* VII (1902), 676–696, VIII (1902), 28–52.

1221 GRIFFIN, Charles Carroll. *The United States and the Disruption of the Spanish Empire, 1810–1822: A Study of the Relations of the United States with Spain and with the Rebel Spanish Colonies.* New York, 1937.

1222 GRONET, Richard W. "Early Latin American-United States Contacts: An Analysis of Jeremy Robinson's Communications to the Monroe Administration, 1817–1823." Doctoral dissertation, Catholic University, 1970.

1223 HART, Albert B. *The Monroe Doctrine: An Interpretation.* Boston, 1916.

1224 HEINZ, Georg. *Die Beziehungen zwischen Russland, England, und Nordamerika im Jahre 1823.* Berlin, 1911.

1225 HIMELOCH, Myra. "Heman Allen's Mission to Chile, 1823–1827." *Vt Hist,* XLII (1974), 155–169.

1226 HOSKINS, Halford L. "The Hispanic American Policy of Henry Clay, 1816–1828." *His-Am Hist Rev,* VII (1927), 460–478.

1227 JOHNSON, J. J. "Early Relations of the United States with Chile." *Pac Hist Rev,* XIII (1944), 260–270.

1228 KAUFMANN, William R. *British Policy and the Independence of Latin America, 1801–1828.* New Haven, 1951.

1229 LOGAN, John A., Jr. *No-Transfer: An American Security Principle.* New Haven, 1961.

1230 MACCORKLE, William A. *The Personal Genesis of the Monroe Doctrine.* New York, 1923.

1231 MANNING, William R., ed. *Diplomatic Correspondence of the United States concerning the Independence of the Latin American Nations.* 3 vols. New York, 1925.

1231A MCELHANNON, J. C. "Relations between Inperial Mexico and the United States, 1821–1823." *Essays in Mexican History.* Ed. Thomas E. COTNER and Carlos E. CASTANEDA. Austin, 1958.

1232 MCGEE, Gale W. "The Monroe Doctrine—A Stopgap Measure." *Miss Val Hist Rev,* XXXVIII (1951), 233–250.

1233 MAY, Ernest R. *The Making of the Monroe Doctrine.* Cambridge, Mass., 1975.

1234 MEYER, H. H. B. *List of References on the Monroe Doctrine.* Washington, D.C., 1919.

1235 NEUMANN, William L. "United States Aid to the Chilean War of Independence." *His-Am Hist Rev,* XXVII (1947), 205–219.

1236 OLIPHANT, J. Orin. "The Parvin-Brigham Mission to Spanish America, 1823–1826." *Church Hist,* XIV (1945), 85–103.

1237 PAXSON, Frederic L. *The Independence of the South American Republics. A Study in Recognition and Foreign Policy.* Philadelphia, 1903.

1238 PERKINS, Bradford. "The Suppressed Dispatch of H. U. Addington, Washington, November 3, 1823." *His-Am Hist Rev,* XXXVII (1957), 480–485.

1239 PERKINS, Bradford. *Castlereagh and Adams: England and the United States, 1812–1823.* Berkeley, 1964.

1240 PERKINS, Dexter. "Europe, Spanish America, and the Monroe Doctrine." *Am Hist Rev,* XXVII (1922), 207–218.

1241 PERKINS, Dexter. *The Monroe Doctrine, 1823–1826.* Cambridge, Mass., 1927.

1242 PERKINS, Dexter. *The Monroe Doctrine, 1826–1867.* Baltimore, 1933.

1243 PERKINS, Dexter. *A History of the Monroe Doctrine.* Rev. ed. Boston, 1963.†

1244 PHILLIPS, W. A. *The Confederation of Europe: A Study of the European Alliance, 1813–1823.* London, 1920.

1245 POTTER, Kenneth. "The Hispanic American Policy of John Quincy Adams, 1817–1825." Doctoral dissertation, University of California, Berkeley, 1935.

1246 PRATT, E. J. "Anglo-American Commercial and Political Rivalry on the Plata, 1820–1830." *His-Am Hist Rev,* XI (1931), 302–335.

1247 RAPPAPORT, Armin, ed. *The Monroe Doctrine.* New York, 1964.†

1248 REDDAWAY, W. F. *The Monroe Doctrine.* Cambridge, Mass., 1898.

1249 RIPPY, J. Fred. *Rivalry of the United States and Great Britain over Latin America.* Baltimore, 1929.

1250 ROBERTSON, William S. "The Monroe Doctrine Abroad, 1823–1824. *Am Pol Sci Rev,* VI (1912), 546–563.

1251 ROBERTSON, William S. "The United States and Spain in 1822." *Am Hist Rev,* XX (1915), 781–800.

1252 ROBERTSON, William S. "South America and the Monroe Doctrine, 1824–1828." *Pol Sci Q,* XXX (1915), 82–105.

1253 ROBERTSON, William S. "The First Legations of the United States in Latin America." *Miss Val Hist Rev,* II (1915), 183–212.

1254 ROBERTSON, William S. "The Recognition of the Hispanic American Nations by the United States." *His-Am Hist Rev,* I (1918), 239–269.

1255 ROBERTSON, William S. *France and Latin-American Independence.* Baltimore, 1939.

1256 ROBERTSON, William S. "Russia and the Emancipation of Spanish America." *His-Am Hist Rev,* XXI (1941), 196–221.

1257 SCHELLENBERG, T. R. "Jeffersonian Origins of the Monroe Doctrine." *His-Am Hist Rev,* XIV (1934), 1–31.

1258 STEWART, Watt. "The South American Commission, 1817–1818." *His-Am Hist Rev,* IX (1929), 31–59.

1259 STEWART, Watt. "Argentina and the Monroe Doctrine, 1824–1828." *His-Am Hist Rev,* X (1930), 26–32.

1260 TATUM, Edward Howland, Jr. *The United States and Europe, 1815–1823; a Study in the Background of the Monroe Doctrine.* Berkeley, 1936.

1261 TEMPERLEY, H. W. V., ed. "Documents Illustrative of the Reception and Interpretation of the Monroe Doctrine in Europe, 1823–4." *Eng Hist Rev,* XXXIX (1924), 390–393.

1262 TEMPERLEY, H. W. V. *The Foreign Policy of Canning, 1822–1827.* London, 1925.

1263 THOMAS, David Y. *One Hundred Years of the Monroe Doctrine, 1823–1923.* New York, 1923.

1264 TUCKER, G. F. *The Monroe Doctrine: A Concise History of Its Origin and Growth.* Boston, 1885.

1265 WEBSTER, Charles K., ed. *Britain and the Independence of Latin America, 1812–1830; Select Documents.* 2 vols. London, 1938.

1266 WHITAKER, Arthur Preston. *The United States and the Independence of Latin America, 1800–1830.* Baltimore, 1941.

1267 WINN, Wilkins B. "The Issue of Religious Liberty in the United States Commercial Treaty with Colombia, 1824." *Americas,* XXVI (1970), 291–301.

E. Relations with Other Nations

See also **1815–1855**

1268 CLINE, Myrtle A. *American Attitude toward the Greek War of Independence, 1821–1828.* Atlanta, 1930.

1269 DOTSON, Lloyd Clay. "The Diplomatic Mission of Baron Hyde de Neuville to the United States, 1816–1822." Doctoral dissertation, University of Georgia, 1970.

1270 DUNHAM, Chester Gray. "A Nineteenth Century Baltimore Diplomat: Christopher Hughes Goes to Sweden." *Md Hist Mag,* LXX (1977), 387–400.

1271 EARLE, Edward M. "American Interest in the Greek Cause, 1821–1827." *Am Hist Rev,* XXXIII (1927), 44–63.

1272 EARLE, Edward M. "Early American Policy concerning Ottoman Minorities." *Pol Sci Q,* XLII (1927), 337–367.

1273 HYDE DE NEUVILLE, Guillaume. *Memoires et Souvenirs du Baron Hyde de Neuville.* 3 vols. Paris, 1912.

1274 PAPPAS, Paul C. "The *Wheeling Gazette* and the Question of Greek Independence in Western Virginia, 1821–1828." *W Va Hist,* XXXV (1973), 40–55.

1275 PAPPAS, Paul C. "The Question of Greek Independence in Kentucky, 1821–1828." *Reg Ky Hist Soc,* LXXII (1974), 143–170.

1276 WINN, Thomas Howard. "To Embrace a Corpse: American Diplomacy and the Greek War of Independence, 1821–1833." Doctoral dissertation, Ball State University, 1974.

5. The Administration of John Quincy Adams, 1825–1829

Domestic Politics

A. The President, Cabinet, and Congress

1277 BEMIS, Samuel F. "The Scuffle in the Rotunda: A Footnote to the Presidency of John Quincy Adams and to the History of Dueling." *Mass Hist Soc Proc* LXXI (1959), 156–166.

1278 BUTTERFIELD, L. H. "The Jubilee of Independence, July 4, 1826." *Va Mag Hist Biog,* LXI (1953), 119–140.

1279 BUTTERFIELD, L. H. "Tending a Dragon-Killer: Notes for the Biographer of Mrs. John Quincy Adams." *Am Phil Soc Proc,* CXVIII (1974), 165–178.

1280 CARROLL, Eber M. "Politics during the Administration of John Quincy Adams." *S Atl Q,* XXIII (1924), 141–154.

1281 CORTS, Paul R. "Randolph vs. Clay: A Duel of Words and Bullets." *Filson Club Hist Q,* XLIII (1969), 151–157.

1282 HAY, Robert P. "The Glorious Departure of the American Patriarchs: Contemporary Reactions to the Deaths of Jefferson and Adams." *J S Hist,* XXXV (1969), 543–555.

1283 MILES, Edwin A. "President Adams's Billiard Table." *N Eng Q,* XLV (1972), 31–43.

1284 REMINI, Robert V. "Martin Van Buren and the Tariff of Abominations." *Am Hist Rev,* LXIII (1958), 903–917.

1285 WEISENBURGER, Francis P. "John McLean, Postmaster-General." *Miss Val Hist Rev,* XVIII (1931), 23–33.

B. The Presidential Election of 1828

See also **600, 2014, 2248, 2376**

1286 JOHNSON, Patricia Givens. "William P. Anderson and 'The May Letters.' " *Filson Club Hist Q,* XLVII (1973), 171–178.

1287 KELSAY, Isabel Thompson. "The Presidential Campaign of 1828." *E. Tenn Hist Soc Pub,* no 5 (1933), 69–80.

1288 RABUN, James Z., and James Harvey YOUNG, eds. "William H. Crawford on the Election of 1828; Two Letters." *Ga Hist Q,* XXXVII (1953), 340–345.

1289 REMINI, Robert V. *The Election of Andrew Jackson.* Philadelphia, 1963.†

1290 REMINI, Robert V. "Election of 1828." *History of American Presidential Elections.* 4 vols. Ed. Arthur M. SCHLESINGER, Jr.; Fred L. ISRAEL; and William P. HANSEN. New York, 1971. I, 413–492.

1291 SMITH, Culver H. "Propaganda Technique in the Jackson Campaign of 1828." *E Tenn Hist Soc Pub,* no. 6 (1934), 44–66.

1292 SULLIVAN, John. "Jackson Caricatured: Two Historical Errors." *Tenn Hist Q,* XXXI (1972), 39–44.

1293 WESTON, Florence. *The Presidential Election of 1828.* Washington, 1938.

Foreign Relations

See also **540, 546, 1815**

1294 BOLKHOVITINOV, N. N. "The Decembrists and America." *Pol Aff,* CIV (1975), 31–50.

1295 CAMPBELL, Randolph. "Henry Clay and the Poinsett Pledge Controversy of 1826." *Americas,* XXVIII (1972), 429–440.

1296 CLEVEN, Andrew N. "The First Panama Mission and the Congress of the United States." *J Neg Hist,* XIII (1928), 225–254.

1297 HACKETT, Charles W. "The Development of John Quincy Adams's Policy with Respect to an American Confederation and the Panama Congress, 1822–1825." *His-Am Hist Rev,* VIII (1928), 496–525.

1298 MANNING, William R. "An Early Diplomatic Controversy between the United States and Brazil." *His-Am Hist Rev,* I (1918), 123–145.

1299 MANNING, William R. "Diplomacy concerning the Santa Fe Road." *Miss Val Hist Rev,* I (1915), 516–531.

1300 NIELSEN, George R. "Ben Milam and United States and Mexican Relations [1825]." *S W Hist Q,* LXXIII (1970), 393–396.

1301 REINHOLD, Frances L. "New Research on the First Pan-American Congress Held at Panama in 1826." *His-Am Hist Rev,* XVIII (1938), 342–363.

1302 RIPPY, J. Fred. "Britain's Role in the Early Relations of the United States and Mexico." *His-Am Hist Rev,* VII (1927), 2–24.

1303 SANDERS, Ralph. "Congressional Reaction in the United States to the Panama Congress of 1826." *Americas,* XI (1954), 141–154.

1304 SHEPHERD, William R. "Bolivar and the United States." *His-Am Hist Rev,* I (1918), 270–298.

1305 VERLARDE, Fabian, and Felipe J. ESCOBAR. *El Congreso de Panama en 1826.* Panama, 1922.

1306 WEBER, Ralph E. "Your Obedient Servant, Joel R. Poinsett." *Prologue,* II (1970), 185–188.

1307 WEBER, Ralph E. "Joel R. Poinsett's Secret Mexican Dispatch Twenty." *S C Hist Mg,* LXXV (1974), 67–76.

1308 WINN, Wilkins B. "The Efforts of the United States to Secure Religious Liberty in a Commercial Treaty with Mexico, 1825–1831." *Americas,* XXVIII (1972), 311–332.

V. The Age of Jackson, 1829–1841

1. General Works

See also 2027, 2028, 2033, 2036, 2064, 2066, 2092, 2110, 2117, 2165, 2169, 2215, 2242, 2267–2272, 2297, 2354, 2459, 2470, 2478

1309 ASHFORD, Gerald. "Jacksonian Liberalism and Spanish Law." *S W Hist Q,* LVII (1953), 1–37.

1310 BLAU, Joseph L., ed. *Social Theories of Jacksonian Democracy.* New York, 1947.†

1311 BOWERS, Claude G. *The Party Battles of the Jackson Period.* Boston, 1922.

1312 BRASINGTON, George Figures, Jr. "Representative Government in Jacksonian Political Thought." Doctoral dissertation, University of Illinois, Urbana-Champaign, 1958.

1313 BRENT, Robert A. "The Triumph of Jacksonian Democracy in the United States." *S Q*, VII (1968), 43–57.

1314 BROWN, Richard H. *The Hero and the People: the Meaning of Jacksonian Democracy.* New York, 1963.

1315 BUGG, James L., Jr., ed. *Jacksonian Democracy: Myth or Reality?* 2d ed. New York, 1976.†

1316 CRENSON, Matthew A. *The Federal Machine: Beginnings of Bureaucracy in Jacksonian America.* Baltimore, 1975.

1317 EATON, Clement, ed. *The Leaven of Democracy: The Growth of the Democratic Spirit in the Time of Jackson.* New York, 1963.†

1318 ERSHKOWITZ, Herbert, and William G. SHADE. "Consensus or Conflict? Political Behavior in the State Legislatures during the Jacksonian Era." *J Am Hist*, LVIII (1971), 591–621.

1319 FISH, Carl Russell. *The Rise of the Common Man, 1830–1850.* New York, 1929.†

1320 FORMISANO, Ronald P. "Analyzing American Voting, 1830–1860: Methods." *Hist Methods Newsl*, II (1969), 1–12.

1321 FORMISANO, Ronald P. "Political Character, Antipartyism, and the Second Party System." *Am Q*, XXI (1969), 683–709.

1322 FRASER, Hugh Russell. *Democracy in the Making: the Jackson-Tyler Era.* Indianapolis, 1938.

1323 GATELL, Frank O., comp. *Essays on Jacksonian America.* New York, 1970.

1324 GOETZMANN, William H. "The Mountain Man as Jacksonian Man." *Am Q*, XV (1963), 402–415.

1325 GOLDMAN, Perry M. "Political Rhetoric in the Age of Jackson." *Tenn Hist Q*, XXIX (1970–1971), 360–371.

1326 GOLDMAN, Perry M. "Political Virtue in the Age of Jackson." *Pol Sci Q*, LXXXVII (1972), 46–62.

1327 HARKNESS, Donald Ray. "Crosscurrents: American Anti-Democracy from Jackson to the Civil War (1829–1860)." Doctoral dissertation, University of Minnesota, 1955.

1328 HOLT, Michael F. "The Democratic Party, 1828–1860." *History of U.S. Political Parties.* 4 vols. Ed. Arthur M. SCHLESINGER, Jr. New York, 1973. I, 497–571.

1329 LEBOWITZ, Michael A. "The Jacksonians: Paradox Lost." *Towards a New Past: Dissenting Essays in American History.* Ed. Barton J. BERNSTEIN. New York, 1968.

1330 LILLIBRIDGE, G. D. *Beacon of Freedom: The Impact of American Democracy upon Great Britain, 1830–1870.* Philadelphia, 1954.†

1331 MCCORMICK, Richard P. "Suffrage Classes and Party Alignments: A Study in Voter Behavior." *Miss Val Hist Rev*, XLVI (1959), 397–410.

1332 MCCORMICK, Richard P. "New Perspectives on Jacksonian Politics." *Am Hist Rev*, LXV (1960), 288–301.

1333 MCCORMICK, Richard P. *The Second American Party System: Party Formation in the Jacksonian Era.* Chapel Hill, 1966.†

1334 MCCORMICK, Richard P. "Political Development and the Second Party System." *The American Party Systems: Stages of Political Development.* Ed. William Nisbet CHAMBERS and Walter Dean BURNHAM. New York, 1967.

1335 MEYERS, Marvin. *The Jacksonian Persuasion: Politics and Belief.* Stanford, 1957.†

1336 OGG, Frederic Austin. *The Reign of Andrew Jackson: a Chronicle of the Frontier in Politics.* New Haven, 1919.

1337 PECK, Charles H. *The Jacksonian Epoch.* New York, 1899.

1338 PESSEN, Edward. *Jacksonian America: Society, Personality, and Politics.* Rev. ed., Homewood, Ill, 1978.†

1339 PESSEN, Edward, ed. *New Perspectives on Jacksonian Parties and Politics.* Boston, 1969.

1340 PESSEN, Edward, ed. *The Many-Faceted Jacksonian Era: New Interpretations.* Westport, Conn., 1977.

1341 PESSEN, Edward. "The Egalitarian Myth and the American Social Reality: Wealth, Mobility, and Equality in the 'Era of the Common Man." *Am Hist Rev,* LXXVI (1971) 989–1034.

1342 REMINI, Robert V., comp. *The Age of Jackson.* New York, 1972.†

1343 REMINI, Robert V. *The Revolutionary Age of Andrew Jackson.* New York, 1976.†

1344 RIEGEL, Robert E. *Young America, 1830–1840.* Norman, 1949.

1345 ROZWENC, Edwin C., ed. *The Meaning of Jacksonian Democracy.* Boston, 1963.

1346 ROZWENC, Edwin C., ed. *Ideology and Power in the Age of Jackson.* New York, 1964.†

1347 RUSSO, David J. "The Major Political Issues of the Jacksonian Period and the Development of Party Loyalty in Congress, 1830–1840." *Am Phil Soc Trans,* LXII (1972), 1–51.

1348 SCHLESINGER, Arthur M., Jr. *The Age of Jackson.* Boston, 1945.†

1349 SHIELDS, Johanna Nicol. "The Making of American Congressional Mavericks: A Contrasting of the Cultural Attitudes of Mavericks and Conformists in the United States House of Representatives, 1836–1860." Doctoral dissertation, University of Alabama, 1973.

1350 SILBEY, Joel H., ed. *Political Ideology and Voting Behavior in the Age of Jackson.* Englewood Cliffs, N. J., 1973.†

1351 TURNER, Frederick Jackson. *"The United States, 1830–1850: the Nation and Its Sections."* New York, 1935.†

1352 VAN DEUSEN, Glyndon G. *The Jacksonian Era, 1828–1845.* New York, 1959.†

1353 WARD, John William. "Jacksonian Democratic Thought: 'A Natural Charter of Privilege.' " *The Development of an American Culture.* Ed. Stanley COBEN and Lorman RATNER. Englewood Cliffs, N. J., 1970.

1354 WHITE, Leonard D. *The Jacksonians: A Study in Administrative History, 1829–1861.* New York, 1954.

1355 WYATT-BROWN, Bertram. "Prelude to Abolitionism: Sabbatarian Politics and the Rise of the Second Party System." *J Am Hist,* LVIII (1971), 316–341.

2. The Administrations of Andrew Jackson, 1829–1837

Domestic Politics

A. The President, Cabinet, and Congress

1356 AHL, Frances Norene. *Andrew Jackson and the Constitution.* Boston, 1939.

1357 BASSETT, John S. "Notes on Jackson's Visit to New England, June, 1833." *Mass Hist Soc Proc,* LVI (1923), 244–260.

1358 BUSFIELD, Roger M. "The Hermitage Walking Stick: First Challenge to Congressional Immunity." *Tenn Hist Q,* XXI (1962), 122–130.

1359 CANFIELD, Frederick A. "The Figurehead of Jackson." *Tenn Hist Mag,* VIII (1924), 144–145.

1360 CHAMBERS, William N. "Andrew Jackson." *America's Eleven Greatest Presidents.* Ed. Morton BORDEN. Chicago, 1971.

1361 COX, I. J., contr. "Letters of William T. Barry, 1806–1810, 1829–1831." *Am Hist Rev,* XVI (1911), 327–336.

1362 CURTIS, James C. "Andrew Jackson and His Cabinet—Some New Evidence." *Tenn Hist Q,* XXVII (1968), 157–164.

1363 DAVIS, Andrew McFarland. "A Tempest in a Teapot: Jackson's 'LL.D.' " *Tenn Hist Mag,* VIII (1924), 191–210.

1364 ERIKSSON, Erik M. "President Jackson's Propaganda Agencies." *Pac Hist Rev,* VI (1937), 47–57.

1365 GREEN, Fletcher M. "On Tour with President Andrew Jackson." *N Eng Q,* XXXVI (1963), 209–228.

1366 HAY, Robert P. "The Meaning of Monroe's Death: The Contemporary Response." *W Va Hist,* XXX (1969), 427–435.

1367 HOOGENBOOM, Ari, and Herbert ERSHKOWITZ, ed. "Levi Woodbury's 'Intimate Memoranda' of the Jackson Administration." *Pa Mag Hist Biog,* XCII (1968), 507–515.

1368 JACKSON, Carlton L. "The Internal Improvement Vetoes of Andrew Jackson." *Tenn Hist Q,* XXV (1966), 261–280.

1369 JACKSON, Carlton L. "Another Time, Another Place: The Attempted Assassination of Andrew Jackson." *Tenn Hist Q,* XXVI (1967), 184–190.

1370 LATNER, Richard B. "Andrew Jackson and His Advisers: White House Politics, 1829–1837." Doctoral dissertation, University of Wisconsin, 1972.

1371 LATNER, Richard B. "A New Look at Jacksonian Politics." *J Am Hist,* LXI (1975), 943–969.

1372 LONGAKER, Richard P. "Andrew Jackson and the Presidency." Doctoral dissertation, Cornell University, 1954.

1373 LONGAKER, Richard P. "Andrew Jackson and the Judiciary." *Pol Sci Q,* LXXI (1956), 341–364.

1374 LONGAKER, Richard P. "Was Jackson's Kitchen Cabinet a Cabinet?" *Miss Val Hist Rev,* XLIV (1957), 94–108.

1375 MACDONALD, William *Jacksonian Democracy, 1829–1837.* New York, 1906.

1376 NIGRO, Felix A. "The Van Buren Confirmation before the Senate." *W Pol Q,* XIV (1961), 148–159.

1377 SINGLETARY, Michael W. "The New Editorial Voice for Andrew Jackson: Happenstance or Plan?" *Jour Q,* LIII (1976), 672–678.

1378 SMITH, Elbert B. "Francis P. Blair and the Globe: Nerve Center of the Jacksonian Democracy." *Reg Ky Hist Soc,* LVIII (1959), 340–353.

1379 SMITH, William E. "Francis P. Blair, Pen-Executive of Andrew Jackson." *Miss Val Hist Rev,* XVII (1931), 543–556.

1380 SOMIT, Albert. "The Political and Administrative Ideas of Andrew Jackson." Doctoral dissertation, University of Chicago, 1947.

1381 SOMIT, Albert. "Andrew Jackson as an Administrative Reformer." *Tenn Hist Q,* XIII (1954), 204–233.

1382 SOMIT, Albert. "New Papers: Some Sidelights upon Jacksonian Administration." *Miss Val Hist Rev,* XXXV (1948), 91–99.

1383 TUCKER, Edward L., ed. "The Attempted Assassination of President Jackson: A Letter by Richard Henry Wilde." *Ga Hist Q,* LVIII (1974), 193–199.

1384 WALLACE, Sarah Agnes, ed. "Opening Days of Jackson's Presidency as Seen in Private Letters." *Tenn Hist Q,* IX (1950), 367–371.

1385 WARREN, Charles. "How Politics Intruded into the Washington Centenary of 1832." *Mass Hist Soc Proc,* LXV (1940), 37–62.

1386 WATSON, Richard L., Jr. "Congressional Attitudes toward Military Preparedness, 1829–1835." *Miss Val Hist Rev,* XXXIV (1948), 611–636.

B. The Peggy Eaton Affair and the Dissolution of Jackson's First Cabinet

1387 BARBEE, David Rankin. "Andrew Jackson and Peggy O'Neale." *Tenn Hist Q,* XV (1956), 37–52.

1388 CRAWFORD, Charles W., ed. " 'The Subject is a Painful One to Me.' " *Tenn Hist Q,* XXVI (1967), 23–42.

1389 DAHL, Curtis. "The Clergyman, the Hussy, and Old Hickory: Ezra Stiles Ely and the Peggy Eaton Affair." *J Presby Hist Soc,* LII (1974), 137–155.

1390 GOVAN, Thomas P. "John M. Berrien and the Administration of Andrew Jackson." *J S Hist,* V (1939), 447–467.

1391 LATNER, Richard B. "The Eaton Affair Reconsidered." *Tenn Hist Q,* XXXVI (1977), 330–351.

1392 MCCRARY, Royce C., Jr. " 'The Long Agony is Nearly Over': Samuel D. Ingham Reports on the Dissolution of Andrew Jackson's First Cabinet." *Pa Mag Hist Biog,* C (1976), 231–242.

1393 MUNROE, John A. "Mrs. [Louis] McLane's Colored Boy and Peggy O'Neal." *Del Hist,* X (1963), 361–366.

1394 STENBERG, Richard R. "Jackson's 'Rhea Letter' Hoax." *J S Hist,* II (1936), 480–496.

1395 STENBERG, Richard R. "A Note on the Jackson-Calhoun Breach of 1830–31." *Tyler's,* XXI (1939), 65–69.

1396 STENBERG, Richard R. "Jackson's Quarrel with the Alleged 'Calhounite' Cabinet Members in 1830–31." *Tyler's,* XXII (1941), 208–228.

C. Patronage and the Spoils System

See also **2004, 2011, 2123, 2240, 2241, 4151**

1397 ARONSON, Sidney H. *Status and Kinship in the Higher Civil Service: Standards of Selection in the Administrations of John Adams, Thomas Jefferson, and Andrew Jackson.* Cambridge, Mass., 1964.

1398 ERIKSSON, Erik McKinley. "The Federal Civil Service under President Jackson." *Miss Val Hist Rev,* XIII (1927), 517–540.

1399 FISH, Carl Russell. *The Civil Service and the Patronage.* New York, 1905.

1400 FOWLER, Dorothy G. *The Cabinet Politician: The Postmasters General, 1829–1909.* New York, 1943.

1401 FREIDEL, Frank. "Jackson's Political Removals as Seen by Historians." *Hist,* II (1939), 41–52.

1402 FULLER, Wayne E. *The American Mail: Enlarger of the Common Life.* Chicago, 1972.

1403 MUGLESTON, William F. "Andrew Jackson and the Spoils System: An Historiographical Essay." *Mid-Am,* LIX (1977), 113–125.

1404 RICH, Wesley Everett. *The History of the United States Post Office to the Year 1829.* Cambridge, Mass., 1924.

1405 VAN RIPER, Paul. *History of the United States Civil Service.* Evanston, 1958.

D. Indian Affairs and Indian Removal

See also **1194, 2213, 2319, 3654–3771**

1406 AGNEW, Ramon Bradford. "Fort Gibson: Terminal on the Trail of Tears." Doctoral dissertation, Oklahoma University, 1976.

1407 ANSON, Bert. "Variations of the Indian Conflict: The Effects of the Emigrant Indian Removal Policy, 1830–1854." *Mo Hist Rev,* LIX (1964), 64.

1408 BRANNON, Peter A. "Removal of the Indians from Alabama." *A'n ist Q,* XII (1950), 91–117.

1409 BITTLE, George C. "First Campaign of the Second Seminole War." *Fla Hist Q,* XLVI (1967), 39–45.

1410 BURKE, Joseph C. "The Cherokee Cases: A Study in Law, Politics, and Morality." *Stan Law Rev,* XXI (1969), 500–531.

1411 CHROUST, Anton-Hermann. "Did President Jackson Actually Threaten the Supreme Court of the United States with the Nonenforcement of Its Injunction against the State of Georgia?" *Am J Leg Hist,* IV (1960), 76–78.

1412 DAVIS, Kenneth Penn. "The Cherokee Removal, 1835–1838." *Tenn Hist Q,* XXXII (1973), 311–331.

1413 DEBO, Angie. *And Still the Waters Run.* Princeton, 1940.

1414 DEROSIER, Arthur H., Jr. "Negotiations for the Removal of the Choctaw." *Chron Okla,* XXXVIII (1960), 85–100.

1415 DEROSIER, Arthur H., Jr. "The Choctaw Removal of 1831, A Civilian Effort." *J W,* VI (1967), 237–247.

1416 DEROSIER, Arthur H., Jr. "Andrew Jackson and Negotiations for the Removal of the Choctaw Indians." *Hist,* XXIX (1967), 343–362.

1417 DEROSIER, Arthur H., Jr. *The Removal of the Choctaw Indians.* Knoxville, 1970.

1418 EBY, Cecil. *"That Disgraceful Affair": The Black Hawk War.* New York, 1973.

1419 EDMUNDS, R. David. "The Prairie Potawatomi Removal of 1833." *Ind Mag Hist,* LXVIII (1972), 240–253.

1420 FILLER, Louis, and Allen GUTTMAN, eds. *The Removal of the Cherokee Nation: Manifest Destiny or National Dishonor?* Boston, 1962.†

1421 FOREMAN, Grant. *Indian Removal: The Emigration of the Five Civilized Tribes.* Norman, 1953.

1422 GERWING, Anselm J. "The Chicago Indian Treaty of 1833." *Ill St Hist J,* LVIII (1964), 117–142.

1423 HAGAN, William T. "The Black Hawk War." Doctoral dissertation, University of Wisconsin, 1950.

1424 HALL, Kermit L. "New Light on an Old Enigma: Sam Houston and the Grand Saline." *Chron Okla,* LI (1973), 335–342.

1425 HOFFMANN, William S. "Andrew Jackson, State Rightist: The Case of the Georgia Indians." *Tenn Hist Q,* XI (1952), 329–345.

1426 HORN, Stanley F., ed. "Tennessee Volunteers in the Seminole Campaign of 1836: The Diary of Henry Hollingsworth." *Tenn His Q,* I (1942), 269–274, 344–366, II (1943), 61–73, 163–178, 236–256.

1427 JACK, Theodore H. "Alabama and the Federal Government: The Creek Indian Controversy." *Miss Val Hist Rev,* III (1916), 301–317.

1428 JONES, Robert L., and Pauline H. JONES. "Houston's Politics and the Cherokees, 1829–1833." *Chron Okla,* XLVI (1969), 418–432.

1429 LUMPKIN, Wilson. *The Removal of the Cherokee Indians from Georgia.* 2 vols. New York, 1907.

1430 MAHON, John K. *History of the Second Seminole War, 1835–1842.* Gainesville, 1967.

1431 MAHON, John K. "Two Seminole Treaties: Payne's Landing, 1832, and Ft. Gibson, 1833." *Fla Hist Q,* XLI (1962), 1–21.

1432 MAHON, John K. "The Second Seminole War, 1835–1842." *U.S. Army Military History Research Collections, Special Bibliography Series,* IV (1976), 106–122.

1433 MELTZER, Milton. *Hunted Like a Wolf: The Story of the Seminole War.* New York, 1972.

1434 MILES, Edwin A. "After John Marshall's Decision: *Worcester v. Georgia* and the Nullification Crisis." *J S Hist,* XXXIX (1973), 519–544.

1435 MIRIANA, Ronald Gregory. "Lewis Cass and Indian Administration in the Old Northwest, 1815–1836." Doctoral dissertation, University of Michigan, 1974.

1436 MOULTON, Gary E. "Chief John Ross and Cherokee Removal Finances." *Chron Okla,* LII (1974), 342–359.

1437 MOULTON, Gary E. "Cherokees and the Second Seminole War." *Fla Hist Q,* LIII (1975), 296–305.

1438 PORTER, Kenneth W. "Florida Slaves and Free Negroes in the Seminole War, 1835–1842." *J Neg Hist,* XXVIII (1943), 390–421.

1439 PRUCHA, Francis Paul. "Thomas L. McKenney and the New York Indian Board." *Miss Val Hist Rev,* LXVIII (1962), 635–655.

1440 PRUCHA, Francis Paul. *Lewis Cass and American Indian Policy.* Detroit, 1967.

1441 PRUCHA, Francis Paul. "Andrew Jackson's Indian Policy: A Reassessment." *J Am Hist,* LVI (1969), 527–539.

1442 QUAIFE, M. M., ed. "Journals and Reports of the Black Hawk War." *Miss Val Hist Rev,* XII (1925), 392–409.

1443 ROONEY, Elizabeth B. "The Story of the Black Hawk War." *Wis Mag Hist,* XL (1957), 274–283.

1444 SATZ, Ronald N. *American Indian Policy in the Jacksonian Era.* Lincoln, 1975.†

1445 SATZ, Ronald N. "Indian Policy in the Jacksonian Era: The Old Northwest as a Test Case." *Mich Hist,* LX (1976), 71–93.

1446 SILVER, James W. "A Counter-Proposal to the Indian Removal Policy of Andrew Jackson." *J Miss Hist,* IV (1942), 207–215.

1447 STEINER, Bernard C. "Jackson and the Missionaries." *Am Hist Rev,* XXIX (1924), 722–723.

1448 STEVENS, Frank E. *The Black Hawk War, including a Review of Black Hawk's Life.* Chicago, 1903.

1449 SYNDERGAARD, Rex. "The Final Move of the Choctaws, 1825–1830." *Chron Okla,* LII (1974), 207–219.

1450 TREACY, Kenneth W. "Another View on Wirt in *Cherokee Nation."* *Am J Leg Hist,* IV (1961), 358–388.

1451 WALLACE, Anthony F. *Prelude to Disaster: The Course of Indian-White Relations Which Led to the Black Hawk War of 1832.* Springfield, 1970.

1452 WHITNEY, Ellen M., comp. and ed. *The Black Hawk War: 1831–1832.* Vol I: *Illinois Volunteers.* Vol II: *Letters and Papers.* Springfield, 1970–1975.

1453 WRIGHT, Muriel H. "The Removal of the Choctaws to the Indian Territory, 1830–1833." *Chron Okla,* VI (1928), 103–128.

1454 YOUNG, Mary E. "The Creek Frauds: A Study in Conscience and Corruption." *Miss Val Hist Rev,* XLII (1955), 411–437.

1455 YOUNG, Mary E. "Indian Removal and Land Allotment: The Civilized Tribes and Jacksonian Justice." *Am Hist Rev,* LXIV (1958), 31–45.

1456 YOUNG, Mary E. *Redskins, Ruffleshirts and Rednecks: Indian Allotments in Alabama and Mississippi, 1830–1860.* Norman, 1961.

E. The Tariff and Nullification

See also **487, 655–656, 2082, 2189, 2190, 2192, 2199, 2200, 2205, 2206, 2220, 2226, 2253, 2270, 2271, 2336**

1457 BANCROFT, Frederic. *Calhoun and the South Carolina Nullification Movement.* Baltimore, 1928.

1458 BOUCHER, Chauncey Samuel. *The Nullification Controversy in South Carolina.* Chicago, 1916.

1459 BROWN, Norman D. "Webster-Jackson Movement for a Constitution and Union Party in 1833." *Mid-Am,* XLVI (1964), 147–171.

1460 DEWEY, Donald O. "Madison's Response to Jackson's Foes." *Tenn Hist Q,* XX (1961), 167–176.

1461 FREEHLING, William W. *Prelude to Civil War: The Nullification Movement in South Carolina, 1816–1836.* New York, 1966.†

1462 FREEHLING, William W., ed. *The Nullification Era: A Documentary Record.* New York, 1967.†

1463 HATCHER, William B. "Edward Livingston's View of the Nature of the Union." *La Hist Q,* XXIV (1941), 698–728.

1464 HOFFER, Peter C. "Sectionalism and National History: American History in the Debate over Foote's Resolution." *Mo Hist Rev,* LXVI (1972), 520–538.

1465 HOUSTON, David Franklin. *A Critical Study of Nullification in South Carolina.* New York, 1896.

1466 LATNER, Richard B. "The Nullification Crisis and Republican Subversion." *J S Hist,* XLIII (1977), 19–38.

1467 MACOLL, John D. "Representative John Quincy Adams's Compromise Tariff of 1832." *Cap Stud,* I (1972), 41–58.

1468 MILLER, Richard G. "The Tariff of 1832: The Issue that Failed." *Filson Club Hist Q,* XLIX (1975), 221–230.

1469 NUSSBAUM, Frederick L. "The Compromise Tariff of 1833: a Study in Practical Politics." *S Atl Q,* XI (1912), 337–349.

1470 SELLERS, Charles G., Jr., ed. *Andrew Jackson, Nullification, and the State-Rights Tradition.* Chicago, 1963.

1471 STENBERG, Richard R. "The Jefferson Birthday Dinner, 1830." *J S Hist,* IV (1938), 334–345.

1472 WILSON, Major L. " 'Liberty and Union': An Analysis of Three Concepts Involved in the Nullification Controversy." *J S Hist,* XXXIII (1967), 331–355.

1473 WILSON, Major L. "A Preview of Irrepressible Conflict." *Miss Q,* XIX (1966) 184–193.

1474 WILSON, Major L. "Andrew Jackson: The Great Compromiser." *Tenn Hist Q,* XXVI (1967), 64–78.

F. Banking and Currency

See also 455, 456, 1921, 1963, 2043, 2060, 2173, 2460, 4103, 4111

1475 AMBACHER, Bruce. "George M. Dallas and the Bank War." *Pa Hist,* XLII (1975), 117–136.

1476 BELOHLAVEK, John M. "Dallas, the Democracy, and the Bank War of 1832." *Pa Mag Hist Biog,* XCVI (1972), 377–390.

1477 BRUCHEY, Stuart, ed. "Roger Brooke Taney's Account of His Relations with Thomas Ellicott in the Bank War." *Md Hist Mag,* LIII (1958), 58–74, 131–152.

1478 CATTERALL, Ralph C. H. *The Second Bank of the United States.* Chicago, 1903.

1479 CLARKE, Matthew St. Clair, and David A. HALL. *Legislative and Documentary History of the Bank of the United States.* Washington, 1832.

1480 CROUTHAMEL, James L. "Three Philadelphians in the Bank War: A Neglected Chapter in American Lobbying." *Pa Hist,* XXVII (1960), 361–378.

1481 CROUTHAMEL, James L. "Did the Second Bank of the United States Bribe the Press?" *Jour Q,* XXXVI (1959), 35–44.

1482 DUANE, William John. *Narrative and Correspondence concerning the Removal of the Deposites, and Occurrences Connected Therewith.* Philadelphia, 1838.

1483 ENGERMAN, Stanley L. "A Note on the Economic Consequences of the Second Bank of the United States." *J Pol Econ,* LXXVIII (1970), 725–728.

1484 FRAAS, Arthur. "The Second Bank of the United States: An Instrument for an Interregional Monetary Union." *J Econ Hist,* XXXIV (1974), 447–467.

1485 GATELL, Frank O. "Spoils of the Bank War: Political Bias in the Selection of Pet Banks." *Am Hist Rev,* LXX (1964), 35–58.

1486 GATELL, Frank O. "Secretary Taney and the Baltimore Pets: A Study in Banking and Politics." *Bus Hist Rev,* XXXIX (1965), 205–227.

1487 GATELL, Frank O. "Sober Second Thoughts on Van Buren, the Albany Regency, and the Wall Street Conspiracy." *Miss Val Hist Rev,* LIII (1966), 19–40.

1488 GATELL, Frank O., ed. "Roger B. Taney, the Bank of Maryland Rioters, and a Whiff of Grapeshot." *Md Hist Mag,* LIX (1964), 262–267.

1489 GATELL, Frank O., ed. *The Jacksonians and the Money Power, 1829–1840.* Chicago, 1967.†

1490 GILBERT, Abby L. "Thomas Ewing, Sr.: Ohio's Advocate for a National Bank." *Ohio Hist,* LXXXII (1973), 4–24.

1491 GORDON, Thomas F. *The War on the Bank of the United States.* Philadelphia, 1834.

1492 GOUGE, William M. *A Short History of Paper Money and Banking in the United States.* Philadelphia, 1833.

1493 GOVAN, Thomas P. "Fundamental Issues of the Bank War." *Pa Mag Hist Biog,* LXXXII (1958), 305–315.

1494 GRACE MADELEINE, Sister. *Monetary and Banking Theories of Jacksonian Democracy.* Philadelphia, 1943.

1495 HAMMOND, Bray. "Public Policy and National Banks." *J Econ Hist,* VI (1946), 79–84.

1496 HAMMOND, Bray. "Jackson, Biddle, and the Bank of the United States." *J Econ Hist,* VII (1947), 1–23.

1497 HAMMOND, Bray. *Banks and Politics in America from the Revolution to the Civil War.* Princeton, 1957.

1498 MCFAUL, John M. *The Politics of Jacksonian Finance.* Ithaca, 1972.

1499 MCFAUL, John M., and Frank Otto GATELL. "The Outcast Insider: Reuben M. Whitney and the Bank War." *Pa Mag Hist Biog,* XCI (1967), 115–144.

1500 MARSHALL, Lynn L. "The Authorship of Jackson's Bank Veto Message." *Miss Val Hist Rev,* L (1963), 466–477.

1501 MEERMAN, Jacob P. "The Climax of the Bank War: Biddle's Contraction, 1833–1834." *J Pol Econ,* LXXI (1963), 378–388.

1502 PLOUS, Harold J. "Jackson, the Bank War and Liberalism." *S W Soc Sci Q,* XXXVIII (1957), 99–110.

1503 RADER, Benjamin G. "William M. Gouge: Jacksonian Economic Theorist." *Pa Hist,* XXX (1963), 443–453.

1504 REMINI, Robert V. *Andrew Jackson and the Bank War: A Study in the Growth of Presidential Power.* New York, 1967.†

1505 ROCKOFF, Hugh. "Money, Prices, and Banks in the Jacksonian Era." *The Reinterpretation of American Economic History.* Ed. Robert W. FOGEL and Stanley L. ENGERMAN. New York, 1971.

1506 SCHEIBER, Harry N. "Some Documents on Jackson's Bank War." *Pa Hist,* XXX (1963), 46–55.

1507 SCHEIBER, Harry N. "The Pet Banks in Jacksonian Politics and Finance, 1833–1841." *J Econ Hist,* XXIII (1963), 196–214.

1508 SCHEIBER, Harry N. "A Jacksonian as Banker and Lobbyist: New Light on George Bancroft." *N Eng Q,* XXXVII (1964), 363–372.

1509 SMITH, Walter Buckingham. *Economic Aspects of the Second Bank of the United States.* Cambridge, Mass., 1953.

1510 SWISHER, Carl Brent, ed. "Roger B. Taney's 'Bank War Manuscript.' *Md Hist Mag,* LIII (1958), 103–130, 215–237.

1511 TAYLOR, George R., ed. *Jackson Versus Biddle's Bank: The Struggle over the Second Bank of the U.S.* 2d ed. Boston, 1967.†

1512 TEMIN, Peter. "The Economic Consequences of the Bank War." *J Pol Econ,* LXXVI (1968), 257–274.

1513 TEMIN, Peter. *The Jacksonian Economy.* New York, 1969.†

1514 TIMBERLAKE, Richard H., Jr. "The Specie Circular and Distribution of the Surplus." *J Pol Econ,* LXVIII (1960), 109–117.

1515 TIMBERLAKE, Richard H., Jr. "The Specie Circular and Sales of Public Lands: A Comment." *J Econ Hist,* XXV (1965), 414–416.

1516 TIMBERLAKE, Richard H., Jr. "The Specie Standard and Central Banking in the United States before 1860." *J Econ Hist,* XXI (1961), 318–341.

1517 TOBIAS, Clifford Ian. " 'A Rale Sharp Fellow': Henry D. Gilpin and the Bank War, a Study in Reform Politics." Doctoral dissertation, Case Western Reserve University, 1975.

1518 VENIT, Abraham H. "Isaac Bronson: His Banking Theory and the Financial Controversies of the Jacksonian Period." *J Econ Hist,* V (1945), 201-214.

1519 WILBURN, Jean Alexander. *Biddle's Bank: The Crucial Years.* New York, 1967.

G. *The Presidential Campaign of 1832*

See also **1919**. For *Antimasonry,* see **1929, 1974, 2031, 2044, 2049, 2729, 2912, 4564**

1520 CAIN, Marvin R. "William Wirt against Andrew Jackson: Reflection of an Era." *Mid-Am,* XLVII (1965), 113-138.

1521 CHASE, James Staton. "Jacksonian Democracy and the Rise of the Nominating Convention." *Mid-Am,* XLV (1963), 229-249.

1522 CHASE, James Staton. "Genesis of the First National Political Convention: A Case Study in the Development of an American Institution." *Soc Sci Q,* L (1969), 92-105.

1523 ERICKSSON, Erik McKinley. "Official Newspaper Organs and Jackson's Re-Election, 1832." *Tenn Hist Mag,* IX (1925), 37-58.

1524 GAMMON, Samuel Rhea, Jr. *The Presidential Campaign of 1832.* Baltimore, 1922.

1525 HOLT, Michael F. "The Antimasonic and Know Nothing Parties." *History of U.S. Political Parties.* 4 vols. Ed. Arthur M. SCHLESINGER, Jr. New York, 1973. I, 575-737.

1526 MCCARTHY, Charles. *The Anti-Masonic Party.* Ann Rep Am Hist Assn, 1902. Washington, 1903.

1527 REMINI, Robert V. "Election of 1832." *History of American Presidential Elections.* 4 vols. Ed. Arthur M. SCHLESINGER, Jr.; Fred L. ISRAEL; and William P. HANSEN. New York, 1971. I, 495-574.

H. *Rise of the Whig Opposition*

See also **1847, 1942, 1949, 1971, 1972, 2007, 2008, 2028, 2029, 2036, 2061, 2084, 2100, 2115, 2128, 2155, 2180, 2187, 2228, 2245, 2265, 2300, 2310, 2315, 2343-2346, 2351, 2358, 2359, 2387, 2389, 2458, 2513**

1528 CARROLL, E. Malcolm. *Origins of the Whig Party.* Durham, 1925.

1529 HOFFMANN, William S. "Willie P. Mangum and the Whig Revival of the Doctrine of Instructions.' *J S Hist,* XXII (1956), 338-354.

1530 HOWE, Daniel Walker, ed. *The American Whigs: An Anthology.* New York, 1973.

1531 MARSHALL, Lynn L. "The Strange Stillbirth of the Whig Party." *Am Hist Rev,* LXXII (1967) 425-444.

1532 MILES, Edwin A. "The Whig Party and the Menace of Caesar." *Tenn Hist Q,* XXVII (1968), 361-379.

1533 STOKES, William S. "Whig Conceptions of Executive Power." *Pres Stud Q,* VI (1976), 16-35.

1534 VAN DEUSEN, Glyndon G. "The Whig Party." *History of U.S. Political Parties.* 4 vols. Ed. Arthur M. SCHLESINGER, Jr. New York, 1973. I, 333-493.

1535 VAN DEUSEN, Glyndon G. "Some Aspects of Whig Thought and Theory in the Jacksonian Period." *Am Hist Rev.* LXIII (1958), 305–322.

1536 WALKER, Franklin A. "The Whig Party and Domestic Politics, 1830–1841." Doctoral dissertation, Cornell University, 1954.

I. The Presidential Campaign of 1836

See also **2171**

1537 BARTUS, Sister Mary Raimonde. "The Presidential Election of 1836." Doctoral dissertation, Fordham University, 1967.

1538 DUBERMAN, Martin B. "Charles Francis Adams, Anti-Masonry and the Presidential Election of 1836." *Mid-Am,* XLIII (1961), 114–126.

1539 ERIKSSON, Erik McKinley. "Official Newspaper Organs and the Presidential Election of 1836." *Tenn Hist Mag,* IX (1925), 115–130.

1540 PRITCHETT, John Perry, ed. "Friends of the Constitution, 1836." *N Eng Q,* IX (1936), 679–683.

1541 SILBEY, Joel H. "Election of 1836." *History of American Presidential Elections.* 4 vols. Ed. Arthur M. SCHLESINGER, Jr.; Fred L. ISRAEL; and William P. HANSEN. New York, 1971. I, 577–640.

1542 SILBEY, Joel H. "The Election of 1836." *Crucial American Elections: Symposium Presented at the Autumn General Meeting of the American Philosophical Society, November 10, 1972.* Philadelphia, 1973.

Foreign Relations

A. Relations with Mexico and Texas

See also **1873–1878, 1882, 1886, 1889, 1891, 1897–1901, 1905, 1907, 1911, 2398–2444, 2605**

1543 BARKER, Eugene C. "President Jackson and the Texas Revolution." *Am Hist Rev,* XII (1907), 788–809.

1544 BARKER, Eugene C. "The United States and Mexico, 1835–1837." *Miss Val Hist Rev,* I (1914), 3–30.

1545 BAUER, K. Jack. "The United States and Texas Independence: A Study in Jacksonian Integrity." *Mil Aff,* XXXIV (1970), 44–48.

1546 GARRISON, George P. "The First Stage of the Movement for the Annexation of Texas." *Am Hist Rev,* X (1904), 72–96.

1547 GIBSON, Joe. "A Butler: What a Scamp!" *J W,* XI (1972), 235–247.

1548 MCNIELL, Sarah Brown. "Andrew Jackson and Texas Affairs, 1819–1836." *E Tenn Hist Soc Pub,* no. 28 (1956), 86–101.

1549 SMITH, Justin H. *The Annexation of Texas.* New York, 1911

1550 STENBERG, Richard R. "Jackson, Anthony Butler and Texas." *S W Soc Sci Q,* XIII (1932), 264–287.

1551 STENBERG, Richard R. "The Texas Schemes of Jackson and Houston." *S W Soc Sci Q,* XV (1934), 229–250.

1552 STENBERG, Richard R., ed. "President Jackson and Anthony Butler." *S W Rev,* XXII (1937), 391–404.

1553 WINSTON, James E. "The Attitude of the Newspapers of the United States towards Texan Independence." *Miss Val Hist Assn Proc,* VIII (1914–1915), 160–175.

B. Relations with Other Nations

See also **1104, 1815–1872, 2059**

1554 ASTOLFI, Douglas M. "Foundations of Destiny: A Foreign Policy of the Jacksonians, 1824–1837." Doctoral dissertation, Northern Illinois University, 1972.

1555 BAYLEN, Joseph O. "James Buchanan's 'Calm of Despotism' [in Russia]." *Pa Mag Hist Biog,* LXXVII (1953), 294–310.

1556 BELOHLAVEK, John M. "Andrew Jackson and the Malaysian Pirates: A Question of Diplomacy and Politics." *Tenn Hist Q,* XXXVI (1977), 19–30.

1557 BLUMENTHAN, Henry. *A Reappraisal of Franco-American Relations, 1830–1871.* Chapel Hill, 1959.

1558 CAROSSO, Vincent P., and Lawrence H. LEDER, eds. "Edward Livingston and Jacksonian Diplomacy." *La Hist,* VII (1966), 241–248.

1559 COX, Henry Bartholomew. " 'To the Victor': A History of the French Spoliation Claims Controversy, 1793–1955." Doctoral dissertation, George Washington University, 1967.

1560 DOYLE, John A., ed. "The Papers of Sir Charles Vaughan." *Am Hist Rev,* VII (1902), 304–329, 500–533.

1561 LERSKI, Jerzy Jan. *A Polish Chapter in Jacksonian America: The United States and the Polish Exiles of 1831.* Madison, 1958

1562 MCGRANE, Reginald C. "Jacksonian America as Seen by the British Minister [Charles Vaughan]." *Bull Hist Phil Soc Ohio,* XII (1954), 194–208.

1563 MCLEMORE, Richard A. "The French Spoliation Claims, 1816–1836: A Study in Jacksonian Diplomacy." *Tenn Hist Mag,* 2d ser., II (1932), 234–254.

1564 MCLEMORE, Richard A. *Franco-American Diplomatic Relations, 1816–1836.* Baton Rouge, 1941.

1565 MARRARO, Howard R. "John Nelson's Mission to the Kingdom of the Two Sicilies [1831–1832]." *Md Hist Mag,* XLIV (1949), 149–176.

1566 MARRARO, Howard R. "Auguste Davezac's Mission to the Kingdom of the Two Sicilies, 1833–1834." *La Hist Q,* XXXII (1949), 791–808.

1567 REZNECK, Samuel, ed. "An American Diplomat [Francis Baylies] Writes about Latin America in 1832." *Americas,* XXVIII (1971), 206–211.

1568 THOMAS, Robert Charles. "Andrew Jackson versus France: American Policy toward France, 1834–1836." *Tenn Hist Q,* XXXV (1976), 51–64.

1569 WEBSTER, C. K. "British Mediation between France and the United States, 1834–36." *Eng Hist Rev,* XLII (1927), 58–78.

3. The Administration of Martin Van Buren, 1837–1841

Domestic Politics

A. The Panic of 1837 and Its Aftermath

See also **996, 998, 1975, 1995, 2020, 2021, 2133, 2171, 3871, 4263, 4334**

1570 BEESLEY, David. "The Politics of Bankruptcy in the United States, 1837–1845." Doctoral dissertation, University of Utah, 1968.

1571 BOURNE, Edward G. *The History of the Surplus Revenue of 1837.* New York, 1885.

1572 CARLETON, William G. "Political Aspects of the Van Buren Era." *S Atl Q,* L (1951), 167–185.

1573 DEGLER, Carl N. "The Locofocos: Urban 'Agrarians.'" *J Econ Hist,* XVI (1956), 322–333.

1574 FRIEDMAN, Jean Elizabeth. "The Revolt of the Conservative Democrats: An Essay on American Political Culture and Political Development, 1837–1844." Doctoral dissertation, Lehigh University, 1976.

1575 HURST, Lawrence. "National Party Politics, 1837–1840." *Studies in American History Inscribed to James Albert Woodburn.* Bloomington, 1926.

1576 KINLEY, David. *The Independent Treasury of the United States and Its Relations to the Banks of the Country.* Washington, D.C., 1910.

1577 MCGRANE, Reginald C. *The Panic of 1837: Some Financial Problems of the Jacksonian Era.* Chicago, 1924.

1578 MCGRANE, Reginald C. *Foreign Bondholders and American State Debts.* New York, 1935.

1579 REZNECK, Samuel. "The Social History of an American Depression, 1837–1843." *Am Hist Rev,* XL (1935), 662–687.

1580 SCOTT, William Amasa. *The Repudiation of State Debts.* New York, 1893.

1581 SHARP, James Roger. *The Jacksonians Versus the Banks: Politics in the States after the Panic of 1837.* New York, 1970.

1582 TIMBERLAKE, Richard H., Jr. "Independent Treasury and Monetary Policy before the Civil War." *S Econ J,* XXVII (1960), 92–103.

1583 TRIMBLE, William. "The Social Philosophy of the Loco-Foco Democracy." *Am J Soc,* XXVI (1921), 705–715.

B. The Presidential Campaign of 1840

See also **1933, 2025, 2247, 2267, 2307, 2481, 2501**

1584 CHAMBERS, William N. "Election of 1840." *History of American Presidential Elections.* 4 vols. Ed. Arthur M. SCHLESINGER, Jr.; Fred L. ISRAEL; and William P. HANSEN. New York, 1971. I, 643–744.

1585 GILBERT, Abby L. "Of Banks and Politics: The Bank Issue and the Election of 1840." *W Va Hist*, XXXIV (1972), 18–45.

1586 GUNDERSON, Robert Gray. *The Log-Cabin Campaign*. Lexington, 1957.

1587 KRADITOR, Aileen S. "The Liberty and Free Soil Parties." *History of U. S. Political Parties*. 4 vols. Ed. Arthur M. SCHLESINGER, Jr. New York, 1973. I, 741–882.

1588 PRICHARD, Walter. "The Presidential Campaign and Election of 1840." *Studies in American History Inscribed to James Albert Woodburn*. Bloomington, 1926.

Foreign Relations

See also **1815–1911, 1916**

1589 COREY, Albert B. *The Crisis of 1830–1842 in Canadian-American Relations*. New Haven, 1941.

1590 CRAIG, G. M. "The American Impact on the Upper Canadian Reform Movement before 1837." *Can Hist Rev*, XXIX (1948), 333–352.

1591 EILTS, Hermann Frederick. "Ahmad Bin Na'aman's Mission to the United States in 1840, the Voyage of Al-Sultanah to New York City." *Essex Inst Hist Coll*, XCVIII (1962), 219–277.

1592 FRANK, Douglas. "The Canadian Rebellion and the American Public." *Niagara Frontier*, XVI (1969), 96–104.

1593 JONES, Howard. "Anglophobia and the Aroostook War." *N Eng Q*, XLVIII (1975), 519–539.

1594 JONES, Howard. "The *Caroline* Affair." *Hist*, XXXVIII (1976), 485–502.

1595 JONES, Howard. *To the Webster-Ashburton Treaty: A Study in Anglo-American Relations, 1783–1843*. Chapel Hill, 1977.

1596 LAURENT, Pierre-Henri. "Anglo-American Diplomacy and the Belgian Indemnities Controversy, 1836–1842." *Hist J*, X (1967), 197–217.

1597 LAURENT, Pierre-Henri. "Belgium's Relations with Texas and the United States, 1839–1844." *S W Hist Q*, LXVIII (1964), 220–236.

1598 LE DUC, Thomas. "The Maine Frontier and the Northeastern Boundary Controversy." *Am Hist Rev*, LIII (1947), 30–41.

1599 LINK, Eugene P. "Vermont Physicians and the Canadian Rebellion of 1837." *Vt Hist*, XXXVII (1969), 177–183.

1600 LOWENTHAL, David. "The Maine Press and the Aroostook War." *Can Hist Rev*, XXXII (1951), 315–336.

1601 MARTIN, Thomas P. "The Upper Mississippi Valley in Anglo-American Anti-Slavery and Free Trade Relations, 1837–1842." *Miss Val Hist Rev*, XV (1928), 204–220.

1602 SHORTRIDGE, Wilson P. "The Canadian-American Frontier during the Rebellion of 1837–1838." *Can Hist Rev*, VII (1926), 13–26.

1603 STACEY, C. P., ed. "A Private Report of General Winfield Scott on the Border Situation in 1839." *Can Hist Rev*, XXI (1940), 407–414.

1604 TEMPERLEY, Harold W. V. "The O'Connell–Stevenson Contretemps: A Reflection of the Anglo-American Slavery Issue." *J Neg Hist,* XLVII (1962), 217–233.

1605 TIFFANY, Orrin E. "Relations of the United States to the Canadian Rebellion of 1837–1838." *Buff Hist Soc Pub,* VIII (1905), 1–147.

1606 WATT, Alastair. "The Case of Alexander McLeod." *Can Hist Rev,* XII (1931), 145–167.

VI. Government and Politics

1. Constitutional History

See also **906–909, 1122–1134, 1356, 1690–1717, 1955, 1962, 1977, 2003, 2095, 2119, 2141–2143, 2151, 2156, 2164, 2192, 2231, 2233, 2250, 2253, 2273, 2285, 2314, 2331–2333, 2514**

1607 AMES, Herman V. *State Documents on Federal Relations: The States and the United States.* Philadelphia, 1906.

1608 AMES, Herman V. *The Proposed Amendments to the Constitution of the United States during the First Century of its History.* Ann Rep Am Hist Assn, 1896. II. Washington, D.C., 1897.

1609 ASSOCIATION OF AMERICAN LAW SCHOOLS. *Selected Essays in Constitutional Law.* 4 vols. Chicago, 1938.

1610 BAUER, Elizabeth Kelley. *Commentaries on the Constitution, 1790–1860.* New York, 1952.

1611 BORGEAUD, Charles. *Adoption and Amendment of Constitutions in Europe and America.* New York, 1895.

1612 BURDICK, Charles K. *The Law of the American Constitution.* New York, 1926.

1613 CORWIN, Edward S. "The Doctrine of Due Process before the Civil War." *Har Law Rev,* XXIV (1911), 366–385, 460–479.

1614 CORWIN, Edward S. "The Basic Doctrine of American Constitutional Law." *Mich Law Rev,* XII (1914), 247–276.

1615 CORWIN, Edward S. "National Power and State Interposition, 1787–1861." *Mich Law Rev,* X (1912), 535–551.

1616 CORWIN, Edward S. *The Commerce Power Versus State Rights.* Princeton, 1936.

1617 CROSSKEY, William W. *Politics and the Constitution in the History of the United States.* 2 vols. Chicago, 1953.

1618 DEALEY, James Q. *Growth of American State Constitutions From 1776 to the End of the Year 1914.* Boston, 1915.

1619 DODD, Walter F. *The Revision and Amendment of State Constitutions.* Baltimore, 1910.

1620 ELAZAR, Daniel J. "Federal-State Collaboration in the Nineteenth Century United States." *Pol Sci Q,* LXXIX (1964), 248–281.

1621 FAIRLIE, John A. *Local Government in Counties, Towns and Villages.* New York, 1906.

1622 HAINES, Charles G. *The Conflict over Judicial Powers in the United States to 1870.* New York, 1909.

1623 HAINES, Charles G. *The Revival of Natural Law Concepts.* Cambridge, Mass., 1930.

1624 HENDERSON, Gerald C. *The Position of Foreign Corporations in American Constitutional Law.* Cambridge, Mass., 1918.

1625 HOCKETT, Homer Carey. *The Constitutional History of the United States, 1776–1876.* 2 vols. New York, 1939.

1626 HUNTING, Warren B. *The Obligation of Contracts Clauses of the United States Constitution.* Baltimore, 1919.

1627 JOHNSON, Allen, Ed. *Readings in American Constitutional History.* Boston, 1912.

1628 KELLY, Alfred H. and Winfred A. HARBISON. *The American Constitution.* 5th ed. New York, 1976.

1629 KEMPIN, Frederick G., Jr. "Precedent and Stare Decisis: The Critical Years, 1800 to 1850." *Am J Leg Hist,* III (1959), 28–54.

1630 KUTLER, Stanley I. "John Bannister Gibson: Judicial Restraint and the Positive State." *J Pub Law,* XIV (1965), 181–197.

1631 MCLAUGHLIN, Andrew C. *A Constitutional History of the United States.* New York, 1935.

1632 MCLAUGHLIN, Andrew C. *The Courts, the Constitution and Parties; Studies in Constitutional History and Politics.* Chicago, 1912.

1633 MCLAUGHLIN, Andrew C. *The Foundations of American Constitutionalism.* New York, 1932.

1634 MILLETT, Stephen M., comp. *A Selected Bibliography of American Constitutional History.* Santa Barbara, Calif., 1975.

1635 NETTLES, Curtis. "The Mississippi Valley and the Constitution." *Miss Val Hist Rev,* XI 1924, 332–357.

1636 PARKINSON, George Phillip, Jr. "Antebellum State Constitution-Making: Retention, Circumvention, Revision." Doctoral dissertation, University of Wisconsin, 1972.

1637 SCHOULER, James. *Constitutional Studies, State and Federal.* New York, 1897.

1638 SCHWARTZ, Bernard. *From Confederation to Nation: The American Constitution, 1835–1877.* Baltimore, 1973.

1639 SHOLLEY, John B. "The Negative Implications of the Commerce Clause." *U Chi L Rev,* III (1936), 556–596.

1640 STILL, Bayrd. "State Constitutional Development in the United States, 1829–1851." Doctoral dissertation, University of Wisconsin, 1933.

1641 SWISHER, Carl B. *American Constitutional Development.* Boston, 1954.

1642 TAYLOR, John. *Constitution Construed, and Constitutions Vindicated.* Richmond, 1820.

1643 THORPE, Francis Newton. *A Constitutional History of the American People, 1776–1850.* 2 vols. New York, 1898.

1644 THORPE, Francis Newton. *The Constitutional History of the United States.* 3 vols. Chicago, 1901.

1645 WENDELL, Mitchell. *Relations between the Federal and State Courts.* New York, 1949.

1646 WRIGHT, Benjamin F. *The Contract Clause of the Constitution.* Cambridge, Mass., 1938.

1647 WRIGHT, Benjamin F. *The Growth of American Constitutional Law.* Boston, 1942†

2. Legal History

See also **739–740, 858–859, 930–931, 1050–1052, 1410, 1922, 1990, 2148, 2150, 2251, 2515, 2521, 2525, 3206, 3273 3494**

1648 BLOOMFIELD, Maxwell. *American Lawyers in a Changing Society, 1776–1876.* Cambridge, Mass., 1976.

1649 BLOOMFIELD, Maxwell. "Law vs. Politics: The Self-Image of the American Bar (1830–1860)." *Am J Leg Hist,* XII (1968), 306–323.

1650 BLOOMFIELD, Maxwell. "Lawyers and Public Criticism: Challenge and Response in Nineteenth Century America." *Am J Leg Hist,* XV (1971), 269–277.

1651 BLOOMFIELD, Maxwell. "William Sampson and the Codifiers: The Roots of American Legal Reform, 1820–1830." *Am J Leg Hist,* X (1967), 234–252.

1652 BROWN, Elizabeth Gaspar. "The Bar on a Frontier: Wayne County, [Michigan], 1796–1836." *Am J Leg Hist,* XIV (1970), 136–156.

1653 BROWN, Elizabeth Gaspar. "Frontier Justice: Wayne County, [Michigan], 1792–1836." *Am J Leg Hist,* XVI (1972), 126–153.

1654 CHROUST, Anton-Herman. *The Rise of the Legal Profession in America.* 2 vols. Norman, Okla., 1965.

1655 COOK, Charles Malcolm. "The American Codification Movement: A Study of Antebellum Legal Reform." Doctoral dissertation, University of Maryland, 1974.

1656 FRIEDMAN, Lawrence M. *A History of American Law.* New York, 1973.†

1657 GAWALT, Gerald W. "Massachusetts Legal Education in Transition, 1766–1840." *Am J Leg Hist,* XVII (1973), 27–50.

1658 HORWITZ, Morton J. *The Transformation of American Law, 1780–1860.* Cambridge, Mass., 1977.

1659 HURST, James Willard. *The Growth of American Law: The Law Makers.* Boston, 1950.

1660 HURST, James Willard. *Law and Conditions of Freedom in the Nineteenth Century United States.* Madison, 1956.

1661 LEWIS, William D., ed. *Great American Lawyers.* 8 vols. Philadelphia, 1907–1909.

1662 LYONS, Grant. "Louisiana and the Livingston Criminal Codes." *La Hist,* XV (1974), 243–272.

1663 MILLER, Perry. "The Common Law and Codification in Jacksonian America." *Am Phil Soc Proc,* CIII (1959), 463–468.

1664 NASH, Gary B. "The Philadelphia Bench and Bar, 1800–1861." *Comp Stud Soc Hist,* VII (1965), 203–220.

1665 NELSON, William E. *Americanization of the Common Law: The Impact of Legal Change on Massachusetts Society, 1760–1830.* Cambridge, Mass., 1975.

1666 POUND, Roscoe. *The Formative Era of American Law.* Boston, 1938.

1667 SCHLOSSMAN, Steven L. "Juvenile Justice in the Age of Jackson." *Tchr Col Rec,* LXXVI (1974), 119–133.

1668 SENESE, Donald Joseph. "Legal Thought in South Carolina, 1800–1860." Doctoral dissertation, University of South Carolina, 1970.

1669 WARREN, Charles. *A History of the American Bar.* Boston, 1911.

1670 WYLLIE, Irvin G. "The Search for an American Law of Charity, 1776–1844." *Miss Val Hist Rev,* XLVI (1959), 203–221.

1671 YOUNGER, Richard D. *The People's Panel: The Grand Jury in the United States, 1634–1941.* Providence, 1963.

3. Political Thought

1672 CARPENTER, William S. *The Development of American Political Thought.* Princeton, 1930.

1673 EKIRCH, Arthur A., Jr. *The American Democratic Tradition: A History.* New York, 1963.

1674 EKIRCH, Arthur A., Jr. *The Decline of American Liberalism.* New York, 1955.

1675 GETTELL, Raymond G. *History of American Political Thought.* New York, 1928.

1676 GRIMES, Alan P. *American Political Thought.* Rev. ed. New York, 1960.

1677 KORITANSKY, John C. "Two Forms of the Love of Equality in Tocqueville's Practical Teaching for Democracy." *Polity,* VI (1973), 488–499.

1678 MERRIAM, Charles E. *A History of American Political Theories.* New York, 1903.

1679 MEYERS, Marvin. "Louis Hartz, *The Liberal Tradition in America:* An Appraisal." *Comp Stud Soc Hist,* V (1963), 261–268.

1680 NAGEL, Paul C. *This Sacred Trust: American Nationality, 1798–1898.* New York, 1971.

1681 NAGEL, Paul C. *One Nation Indivisible; the Union in American Thought, 1776–1861.* New York, 1964.

1682 ROSSITER, Clinton L. *Conservatism in America; the Thankless Persuasion.* 2d ed. New York, 1962.†

1683 *State Papers on Nullification: Including the Public Acts of the Convention of the People of South Carolina (1832–1833), The Proclamation of the President of the United States, The Proceedings of the Several State Legislatures Which Have Acted on the Subject.* Boston, 1834.

1684 VOLPE, Michael. "The Logic of Calhoun's Constitutional Theory." *S Sp Com J,* XXXIX (1973), 161–172.

1685 WILSON, Major L. "An Analysis of the Ideas of Liberty and Union as Used by Members of Congress and the Presidents from 1828 to 1861." Doctoral dissertation, University of Kansas, 1964.

1686 WILSON, Major L. "The Concept of Time and the Political Dialogue in the United States, 1828–48." *Am Q,* XIX (1967), 619–644.

1687 WILSON, Major L. *Space, Time and Freedom: The Quest for Nationality and the Irrepressible Conflict, 1815–1861.* Westport, Conn., 1974.

1688 WILTSE, Charles M. *The Jeffersonian Tradition in American Democracy.* Chapel Hill, N.C., 1935.†

1689 WRIGHT, Benjamin F. *American Interpretations of Natural Law: A Study in the History of Political Thought.* Cambridge, Mass., 1931.

4. Supreme Court

See also **587, 728, 729, 775, 776, 778, 809–823, 945–953, 956–966, 1015, 1019, 1090, 1122–1134, 1373, 1410, 1411, 1425, 1436, 1450, 1607–1647, 2193, 2521**

1690 BALDWIN, Simeon E. *The American Judiciary.* New York, 1905.

1691 BOUDIN, Louis B. *Government by Judiciary.* 2 vols. New York, 1932.

1692 BOUDIN, Louis B. "John Marshall and Roger B. Taney." *Geo Law J,* XXIV (1930), 864–909.

1693 BURNETTE, O. Lawrence, Jr. "Peter V. Daniel: Agrarian Justice." *Va Mag Hist Biog,* LXII (1954), 289–305.

1694 CORWIN, Edward S. *John Marshall and the Constitution: A Chronicle of the Supreme Court.* New Haven, 1919.

1695 CORWIN, Edward S. *The Twilight of the Supreme Court.* New Haven, 1934.

1696 COTTON, Joseph P., Jr., ed. *The Constitutional Decisions of John Marshall.* 2 vols. New York, 1905.

1697 CUSTER, Lawrence B. "Bushrod Washington and John Marshall: A Preliminary Inquiry." *Am J Leg Hist,* IV (1960), 34–78.

1698 DUNNE, Gerald T. "Joseph Story: The Lowering Storm." *Am J Leg Hist,* XIII (1969), 1–41.

1699 DUNNE, Gerald T. "Mr. Joseph Story and the American Law of Banking." *Am. J. Leg Hist,* V (1961), 205–229.

1700 EWING, Cortez A. M. *The Judges of the Supreme Court, 1789–1937.* Minneapolis, 1938.

1701 FRANKFURTER, Felix. *The Commerce Clause under Marshall, Taney, and Waite.* Chapel Hill, 1937.

1702 FRANKFURTER, Felix, and James M. LANDIS. *The Business of the Supreme Court.* New York, 1927.

1703 FRISCH, Morton J. "John Marshall's Philosophy of Constitutional Republicanism." *Rev Pol,* XX (1958), 34–45.

1704 GARVEY, Gerald. "The Constitutional Revolution of 1837 and the Myth of Marshall's Monolith." *W Pol Q,* XVIII (1965), 27–34.

1705 GASS, Edmund C. "The Constitutional Opinions of Justice John Catron." *E Tenn Hist Soc Pub,* no. 8 (1936), 54–81.

1706 GOFF, John S. "Mr. Justice Trimble of the United States Supreme Court." *Reg Ky Hist Soc,* LVIII (1960), 6–28.

1707 GRAHAM, Howard Jay. "Procedure to Substance—Extra-Judicial Rise of Due Process, 1830–1860." *Calif Law Rev,* XL (1952–1953), 483–500.

1708 HAINES, Charles G. *The American Doctrine of Judicial Supremacy.* Berkeley, 1932.

1709 HAINES, Charles Grove. *The Role of the Supreme Court in American Government and Politics, 1789–1835.* Berkeley, 1944.

1710 HAINES, Charles Grove, and Foster H. SHERWOOD. *The Role of the Supreme Court in American Government and Politics, 1835–1864.* Berkeley and Los Angeles, 1957.

1711 HALE, Robert L. "The Supreme Court and the Contract Clause." *Har Law Rev,* LVII (1944), 512–557, 621–674, 852–892.

1712 HALL, Kermit Lance. "The Taney Court in the Second Party System: The Congressional Response to Federal Judicial Reform." Doctoral dissertation, University of Minnesota, 1972.

1713 KUTLER, Stanley I. *Privilege and Creative Destruction: The Charles River Bridge Case.* New York, 1971.†

1714 LESLIE, William R. "The Influence of Joseph Story's Theory of the Conflict of Laws on Constitutional Nationalism." *Miss Val Hist Rev,* XXXV (1948), 203–220.

1715 MONKKONEN, Eric. "*Bank of Augusta* v. *Earle:* Corporate Growth v. States' Rights." *Ala Hist Q,* XXXIV (1972), 113–130.

1716 MORGAN, Donald G. "Mr. Justice William Johnson and the Constitution." *Harv Law Rev,* LVII (1944), 328–361.

1717 MORGAN, Donald G. "The Origin of Supreme Court Dissent." *Wm Mar Q,* X (1953), 353–377.

1718 MYERS, Gustavus. *History of the Supreme Court of the United States.* Chicago, 1912.

1719 NADELMAN, Kurt H. "Joseph Story's Contribution to American Conflict Law: A Comment." *Am J Leg Hist,* V (1961), 230–253.

1720 NETTLES, Curtis. "The Mississippi Valley and the Federal Judiciary, 1807–1837." *Miss Val Hist Rev,* XII (1925), 202–226.

1721 NEWMYER, R. Kent. *The Supreme Court Under Marshall and Taney.* Arlington Heights, Ill., 1968.†

1722 NEWMYER, R. Kent. "Justice Joseph Story on Circuit and a Neglected Phase of American Legal History." *Am J Leg Hist,* XIV (1970), 112–135.

1723 NEWMYER, R. Kent. "Justice Story, The Charles River Bridge Case and the Crisis of Republicanism." *Am J Leg Hist,* XVII (1973), 232–245.

1724 PALMER, Benjamin W. *Marshall and Taney: Statesmen of the Law.* New York, 1966.

1725 PRAGER, Frank D. "The Influence of Mr. Justice Story on American Patent Law." *Am J Leg Hist,* V (1961), 254–264.

1726 PRAGER, Frank D. "The Changing Views of Justice Story on the Construction of Patents." *Am J Leg Hist,* IV (1960), 1–21.

1727 PRAGER, Frank D. "Trends and Developments in American Patent Law from Jefferson to Clifford (1790–1870)." *Am J Leg Hist,* VI (1963), 45–62.

1728 ROPER, Donald M. "In Quest of Judicial Objectivity: The Marshall Court and the Legitimation of Slavery." *Stan Law Rev,* XXI (1969), 532–549.

1729 ROPER, Donald M. "Judicial Unanimity and the Marshall Court: A Road to Reappraisal." *Am J Leg Hist,* IX (1965), 118–134.

1730 SCHMIDHAUSER, John R. "Judicial Behavior and the Sectional Crisis of 1837–1860." *J Pol,* XXIII (1961), 615–640.

1731 SCHMIDHAUSER, John R. *The Supreme Court as Final Arbiter in Federal-State Relations, 1789–1957.* Chapel Hill, 1958.

1732 SENIOR, Mildred R., comp. *The Supreme Court: Its Power of Judicial Review with Respect to Congressional Legislation.* Washington, D.C., 1937.

1733 STEAMER, Robert. "Congress and the Supreme Court during the Marshall Era." *Rev Pol,* XXVII (1965), 364–385.

1734 STORY, Joseph. *Commentaries on the Constitution of the United States.* 5th ed. Boston, 1891.

1735 SWISHER, Carl S. "The Taney Period, 1835–1864." *History of the Supreme Court of the United States.* Ed. Fred ISRAEL and Arthur M. SCHLESINGER, Jr. New York, 1974.

1736 UMBANHOWAR, Charles E. "Marshall on Judging." *Am J Leg Hist,* VII (1963), 210–227.

1737 WARREN, Charles. *Congress, the Constitution, and the Supreme Court.* Boston, 1925.

1738 WARREN, Charles. *The Supreme Court in United States History.* 2 vols. Boston, 1922.

1739 WHATLEY, George C. "Jackson's Justices and the Federal System, 1830–1856." Doctoral dissertation, University of Alabama, 1969.

1740 WHITE, G. Edward. *The American Judicial Tradition: Profiles of Leading American Judges.* New York, 1976.†

1741 WILLOUGHBY, Westel W. *The Supreme Court of the United States: Its Influence on Our Constitutional System.* Baltimore, 1890.

1742 ZIEGLER, Benjamin Munn. *The International Law of John Marshall: A Study of First Principles.* Chapel Hill, 1939.

5. President and Congress

See also **1078, 1088, 1118, 1368, 1372, 1374, 1381, 1382, 1533, 2217, 4360, 4580**

1743 ALEXANDER, DeAlva Stanwood. *History and Procedure of the House of Representatives.* Boston, 1916.

1744 BATES, Ernest Sutherland. *The Story of Congress, 1789–1935.* New York, 1936.

1745 BINKLEY, Wilfred E. *The Powers of the President.* Garden City, N.Y., 1937.

1746 BINKLEY, Wilfred E. *President and Congress.* 3d ed. New York, 1962.

1747 BINKLEY, Wilfred E. *The Man in the White House: His Powers and Duties.* Baltimore, 1959.†

1748 CORWIN, Edward S. *The President, Office and Powers.* 4th rev. ed. New York, 1974.

1749 CORWIN, Edward S. *The President's Control of Foreign Relations.* Princeton, 1917.

1750 CORWIN, Edward S. "The Spending Power of Congress—Apropos the Maternity Act." *Har Law Rev,* XXXVI (1923), 548–582.

1751 CUNLIFFE, Marcus. *American Presidents and the Presidency.* 2d rev. ed. New York, 1976.

1752 GALLOWAY, George B. *History of the United States House of Representatives.* Rev. ed. Washington, D.C., 1965.

1753 HAYNES, George H. *The Senate of the United States; Its History and Practice.* Boston, 1938.

1754 HINSDALE, Mary L. *A History of the President's Cabinet.* Ann Arbor, 1911.

1755 KOENIG, Louis W. *The Invisible Presidency.* New York, 1960.

1756 LEARNED, Henry Barrett. *The President's Cabinet: Studies in the Origin, Formation, and Structure of an American Institution.* New Haven, 1912.

1757 MILTON, George Fort. *The Use of Presidential Power, 1789–1943.* Boston, 1944.

1758 ROSEBOOM, Eugene H. *A History of Presidential Elections.* New York, 1957.

1759 ROSSITER, Clinton L. *The American Presidency.* New York, 1963.†

1760 SALMON, Lucy M. "History of the Appointing Power of the President." *Am Hist Assn Papers,* I (1886), 299–419.

1761 STANWOOD, Edward. *A History of the Presidency.* 2 vols. Boston, 1928.

6. The Armed Forces

A. General Studies and Civilian-Military Relationships

1762 BERNARDO, C. Joseph, and Eugene H. BACON. *American Military Policy, Its Development since 1775.* 2d ed. Harrisburg, 1961.

1763 CUNLIFFE, Marcus. *Soldiers and Civilians: The Martial Spirit in America, 1775–1865.* New York, 1973.†

1764 DAVIES, Wallace Evan. *Patriotism on Parade; the Story of Veterans' and Hereditary Organizations in America, 1783–1900.* Cambridge, Mass., 1955.

1765 DUPUY, Richard Ernest, and Trevor N. DUPUY. *Military Heritage of America.* New York, 1956.

1766 EKIRCH, Arthur A. *The Civilian and the Military.* New York, 1956.†

1767 HOLMES, Joseph J. "The Decline of the Pennsylvania Militia, 1815–1870." *W Pa Hist Mag,* LVII (1974), 199–217.

1768 HUNTINGTON, Samuel P. *The Soldier and the State: The Theory and Politics of Civil-Military Relations.* Cambridge, Mass., 1957.†

1769 MARRO, Anthony. "Vermont's Local Militia Units, 1815–1860." *Vt Hist,* XL (1972), 28–42.

1770 PALMER, John McAuley. *America in Arms; the Experience of the United States with Military Organization.* New Haven, 1941.

1771 UPTON, Emory. *The Military Policy of the United States.* Washington, D.C., 1917.

1772 WEIGLEY, Russell Frank. *The American Way of War: A History of United States Military Strategy and Policy.* New York, 1973.†

B. The Army

1773 AGNEW, Brad. "The Dodge-Leavenworth Expedition of 1834." *Chron Okla,* LIII (1975), 376–396.

1774 BEERS, Henry P. *The Western Military Frontier, 1815–1846.* Philadelphia, 1935.

1775 BITTLE, George C. "The Florida Militia's Role in the Battle of Withlacoochee." *Fla Hist Q,* XLIV (1966), 303–311.

1776 CHILDRESS, David Ted. "The Army in Transition: The United States Army, 1815–1846." Doctoral dissertation, Mississippi State University, 1974.

1777 DENTON, Edgar, III. "The Formative Years of the United States Military Academy, 1775–1833." Doctoral dissertation, Syracuse University, 1964.

1778 DUPUY, Richard Ernest. *The Compact History of the United States Army.* Rev. ed. New York, 1961.

1779 FORMAN, Sidney. *West Point: A History of the United States Military Academy.* New York, 1950.

1780 GRAHAM, Stanley Silton. "Life of the Enlisted Soldier on the Western Frontier, 1815–1845." Doctoral dissertation, North Texas State University, 1972.

1781 HAGAN, William T. "General Henry Atkinson and the Militia." *Mil Aff,* XXIII (1959), 194–197.

1782 HARRISON, Joseph H., Jr. "Simon Bernard, the American System, and the Ghost of the French Alliance." *America, the Middle Period: Essays in Honor of Bernard Mayo.* Ed. John B. Boles. Charlottesville, 1973.

1783 HUGHES, J. Patrick. "The Adjutant General's Office, 1821–1861: A Study in Administrative History." Doctoral dissertation, Ohio State University, 1977.

1784 JOHNSON, Leland R. "Army Engineers on the Cumberland and Tennessee, 1824–1854." *Tenn Hist Q,* XXXI (1972), 149–169.

1785 MORRISON, James Lunsford, Jr. "The United States Military Academy, 1833–1866." Doctoral dissertation, Columbia University, 1970.

1786 MORRISON, James Lunsford, Jr. "The Struggle between Sectionalism and Nationalism at Ante-Bellum West Point, 1830–1861." *C W Hist,* XIX (1973), 138–148.

1787 MOTTE, Jacob Rhette. *Journey into Wilderness: An Army Surgeon's Account of Life in Camp and Field during the Creek and Seminole Wars, 1836–1838.* Ed. James F. SUNDERSON. Gainesville, 1953.

1788 PRUCHA, Francis Paul. *Broadax and Bayonet: The Role of the United States Army in the Development of the Northwest, 1815–1860.* Madison, 1953.†

1789 PRUCHA, Francis Paul. *The Sword of the Republic: The United States Army on the Frontier, 1783–1846.* New York, 1969.†

1790 SILVER, James W. "Edmund Pendleton Gaines and Frontier Problems, 1801–1840." *J S Hist,* I (1935), 320–344.

1791 SKELTON, William B. "The United States Army, 1821–1837: An Institutional History." Doctoral dissertation, University of Virginia, 1968.

1792 SKELTON, William B. "The Commanding General and the Problem of Command in the United States Army, 1821–1841." *Mil Aff,* XXXIV (1970), 117–122.

1793 SKELTON, William B. "Army Officers' Attitudes toward Indians, 1830–1860." *Pac N W Q,* LXVII (1976), 113–124.

1794 SMITH, Carlton Bruce. "The United States War Department, 1815–1842." Doctoral dissertation, University of Virginia, 1967.

1795 WEIGLEY, Russell F. *Towards an American Army: Military Thought from Washington to Marshall.* New York, 1962.

1796 WINTON, George Peterson. "Ante-Bellum Military Instruction of West Point Officers, and Its Influence upon Confederate Military Organization and Operations." Doctoral dissertation, University of South Carolina, 1972.

1797 YOUNG, Otis E. "The United States Mounted Ranger Battalion, 1832–1833." *Miss Val Hist Rev,* XLI (1954), 453–470.

1798 YOUNG, Tommy Richard, II. "The United States Army in the South, 1789–1835." Doctoral dissertation, Louisiana State University, 1973.

C. The Navy

See also **426, 554, 556, 620, 878–880, 910, 922–924, 974–975, 1047, 1112, 1117, 1185, 1194, 1386, 1409, 1418, 1423, 1426, 1431–1435, 1438, 1442–1443, 1451–1452, 1593, 1600, 1602, 1605, 1815, 1906, 2409, 2434, 2552, 2587, 3729, 3743, 3937, 4381, 4416, 4440, 4765**

1799 ALLEN, Gardner W. *Our Navy and the West Indian Pirates.* Salem, Mass., 1929.

1799A BAUER, K. Jack. "Naval Shipbuilders Programs, 1794–1860." *Mil Aff,* XXIX (1965), 29–40.

1800 BORTHWICK, Doris Esch. "Outfitting the United States Exploring Expedition: Lieutenant Charles Wilkes' European Assignment, August–November, 1836." *Am Phil Soc Proc,* CIX (1965), 159–172.

1801 BRESICA, Anthony M. "The American Navy, 1817–1822: Comments of Richard Rush." *Am Neptune,* XXXI (1971), 217–225.

1802 BUKER, George E. "Riverine Warfare: Naval Combat in the Second Seminole War, 1835–1842." Doctoral dissertation, University of Florida, 1969.

1803 CHAPELLE, Howard I. *The History of the American Sailing Navy; the Ships and Their Development.* New York, 1949.

1804 HARMON, Judd Scott. "Marriage of Convenience: The United States Navy in Africa, 1820–1843." *Am Neptune,* XXXII (1972), 264–276.

1805 KNOX, Dudley W. *A History of the United States Navy.* Rev ed. New York, 1948.

1806 LANGLEY, Harold David. *Social Reform in the United States Navy, 1798–1862.* Urbana, 1967.

1807 LONG, David F. " 'Martial Thunder': The First Official American Armed Intervention in Asia." *Pac Hist Rev,* XLII (1973), 143–162.

1808 PONKO, Vincent, Jr. *Ships, Seas, and Scientists: U.S. Naval Exploration and Discovery in the Nineteenth Century.* Annapolis, 1974.

1809 PRATT, Fletcher. *The Compact History of the United States Navy.* Rev. ed. New York, 1962.

1810 SMITH, Geoffrey Sutton. "The Navy before Darwinism: Science, Exploration, and Diplomacy in Antebellum America." *Am Q,* XXVIII (1976), 41–55.

1811 SMITH, Myron J., Jr., ed. *The American Navy, 1789–1860: A Bibliography.* Metuchen, N.J., 1974.

1812 SPROUT, Harold H., and Margaret SPROUT. *The Rise of American Naval Power, 1776–1918.* Rev. ed. Princeton, 1942.

1813 STANTON, William. *The Great United States Exploring Expedition of 1838–1842.* Berkeley, 1975.

1814 WOOD, James Benjamin. "The American Response to China, 1784–1844: Consensus Policy and the Origin of the East India Squadron." Doctoral dissertation, Duke University, 1969.

7. Foreign Affairs

A. General Studies

See also **475, 552, 624, 680, 732, 1069, 1070, 1072, 1104–1108, 1113, 1177–1276, 1294–1309, 1543–1569, 1578, 1589–1606, 1782, 1799, 1800, 1804, 1807, 1814, 2858, 2987, 4117–4154, 4316**

1815 ALLEN, Gardner W. *Our Navy and the Barbary Corsairs.* Boston, 1905.

1816 BAILEY, Thomas A. *America Faces Russia: Russian-American Relations from Early Times to Our Day.* Ithaca, N.Y., 1950.

1817 BARRAGY, Terrence Joseph. "American Maritime Otter Diplomacy [1808–1824]." Doctoral dissertation, University of Wisconsin, Madison, 1974.

1818 BEMIS, Samuel Flagg, ed. *The American Secretaries of State and Their Diplomacy.* 10 vols. New York, 1927–1929.

1819 BEMIS, Samuel Flagg, and Grace Gardner GRIFFIN. *Guide to the Diplomatic History of the United States, 1775–1921.* Washington, D.C., 1935.

1820 BRADLEE, Francis B. *Piracy in the West Indies and Its Suppression.* Salem, 1923.

1821 BRADLEY, Harold W. "Hawaii and the American Penetration of the Northeastern Pacific, 1800–1845." *Pac Hist Rev,* XII (1943), 277–286.

1822 CALLAHAN, James M. *American Foreign Policy in Canadian Relations.* New York, 1937.

1823 COLE, Allan B., ed. "Captain David Porter's Proposed Expedition to the Pacific and Japan, 1815." *Pac Hist Rev,* IX (1940), 61–65.

1824 COUGHLIN, Sister Magdalen. "California Ports: A Key to Diplomacy for the West Coast, 1820–1845." *J W,* V (1966), 153–172.

1825 DANIEL, Robert L. "American Influence in the Near East before 1861." *Am Q,* XVI (1964), 72–84.

1826 DENNETT, Tyler. *Americans in Eastern Asia.* New York, 1922.

1827 DUIGNAN, Peter, and Clarence CLENDENEN. *The United States and the African Slave Trade.* Stanford, 1963.

1828 DUNCAN, Bingham. "Franco-American Tobacco Diplomacy, 1784–1860." *Md Hist Mag,* LI (1956), 273–301.

1829 FARNHAM, Thomas Javery. "The State and the Nation: The History of the Federal-State Issue in American Diplomacy, 1789–1860." Doctoral dissertation, University of North Carolina, 1965.

1830 GILBERT, Felix. *To the Farewell Address: Ideas of Early American Foreign Policy.* Princeton, 1961.†

1831 GOEBEL, Julius. *The Recognition Policy of the United States.* New York, 1915.

1832 GOETZMANN, William H. *When the Eagle Screamed: The Romantic Horizon in American Diplomacy, 1800–1860.* New York, 1966.†

1833 GORDON, Leland James. *American Relations with Turkey, 1830–1930.* Philadelphia, 1932.

1834 HESS, Sister Mary Anthonita. *American Tobacco and Central European Policy: Early Nineteenth Century.* Washington, D.C., 1948.

1835 HILL, C. E., ed. *Leading American Treaties.* New York, 1931.

1836 HYDEN, Ralston. *The Senate and Treaties, 1789–1817: The Development of the Treaty-Making Functions of the United States Senate during Their Formative Period.* New York, 1920.

1837 ISRAEL, Fred, ed. *Major Peace Treaties of Modern History, 1648–1967.* 4 vols. New York, 1967.

1838 KUEBEL, Mary Veronica. "Merchants and Mandarins: The Genesis of American Relations with China." Doctoral dissertation, University of Virginia, 1974.

1839 KUSHNER, Howard I. *Conflict on the Northwest Coast: American-Russian Rivalry in the Pacific Northwest, 1790–1867.* Westport, Conn., 1975.

1840 LASERSON, Max M. *The American Impact on Russia, Diplomatic and Ideological, 1784–1917.* New York, 1950.

1841 LATOURETTE, Kenneth Scott. *The History of Early Relations between the United States and China, 1784–1844.* New Haven, 1917.

1842 LINGELBACH, W. E. "Saxon-American Relations, 1778–1828." *Am Hist Rev,* XVII (1912), 517–539.

1843 LIVERMORE, Seward W. "Early Commercial and Consular Relations with the East Indies." *Pac Hist Rev,* XV (1946), 31–58.

1844 MANNING, William R., ed. *Diplomatic Correspondence of the United States: Canadian Relations, 1784–1860.* 4 vols. Washington, D.C., 1940–1945.

1845 MILLER, Hunter, ed. *Treaties and Other International Acts of the United States of America, 1776–1863.* 8 vols. Washington, D.C., 1931–1948.

1846 MOORE, John Bassett. *History and Digest of the International Arbitrations to Which the United States Has Been a Party.* 6 vols. Washington, D.C., 1898.

1847 PUDELKA, Leonard William. "American Whig Party's Far Eastern Foreign Policy: A Prelude to Imperialism." Doctoral dissertation, Syracuse University, 1972.

1848 ROONEY, John W., Jr. *Belgian-American Diplomatic and Consular Relations, 1830–1850: A Study in American Foreign Policy in Mid-Nineteenth Century.* Louvain, Belgium, 1969.

1849 STELLE, Charles C. "American Trade in Opium to China, 1821–1839." *Pac Hist Rev,* X (1941), 57–74.

1850 TATE, E. Mowbray. "American Merchant and Naval Contacts with China, 1784–1850." *Am Neptune,* XXXI (1971), 177–191.

1851 THOMAS, Benjamin P. *Russo-American Relations, 1815–1867.* Baltimore, 1930.

1852 VAN ALSTYNE, R. W. *The Rising American Empire.* New York, 1960.†

1853 WHARTON, Francis, ed. *A Digest of the International Law of the United States.* 3 vols. Washington, D.C., 1886.

1854 WRISTON, Henry M. *Executive Agents in American Foreign Relations.* Baltimore, 1929.

1855 ZAHNISER, Marvin R. *Uncertain Friendship: American-French Diplomatic Relations through the Cold War.* New York, 1975.†

B. United States–British Relations

1856 ALLEN, Harry C. *Conflict and Concord: the Anglo-American Relationship since 1783.* New York, 1959.

1857 BREBNER, John B. *North Atlantic Triangle: the Interplay of Canada, the United States and Great Britain.* New Haven, 1945.

1858 CROOK, David Paul. *American Democracy in English Politics, 1815–1850.* Oxford, 1965.

1859 DUNNING, William A. *The British Empire and the United States: A Review of Their Relations during the Century of Peace following the Treaty of Ghent.* New York, 1914.

1860 DURAM, James C. "A Study of Frustration: Britain, the USA, and the African Slave Trade, 1815–1870." *Soc Sci,* XL (1965), 220–225.

1861 GALBRAITH, John S. "British-American Competition in the Border Trade of the 1820s." *Minn Hist,* XXXVI (1959), 241–249.

1862 HAMER, Philip M. "Great Britain, the United States, and the Negro Seamen Acts, 1822–1848." *J S Hist,* I (1935), 3–28.

1863 KEENLEYSIDE, Hugh Llewellyn, and Gerald S. BROWN. *Canada and the United States.* Rev. ed. New York, 1952.

1864 LINDSAY, Arnett G. "Diplomatic Relations between the United States and Great Britain bearing on the Return of Negro Slaves, 1788–1828." *J Neg Hist,* V (1920), 391–419.

1865 MACMASTER, Richard Kerwin. "The United States, Great Britain and the Suppression of the Cuban Slave Trade, 1835–1860." Doctoral dissertation, Georgetown University, 1968.

1866 MERK, Frederick. *Albert Gallatin and the Oregon Problem: A Study in Anglo-American Diplomacy.* Cambridge, Mass., 1950.

1867 MYERS, Gustavus. *America Strikes Back: A Record of Contrasts.* New York, 1935.

1868 SCHAFER, Joseph. "The British Attitude toward the Oregon Question, 1815–1846." *Am Hist Rev,* XVI (1911), 273–299.

1869 SOULSBY, Hugh G. *The Right of Search and the Slave Trade in Anglo-American Relations, 1814–1862.* Baltimore, 1933.

1870 STACEY, C. P. "The Myth of the Unguarded Frontier, 1815–1871." *Am Hist Rev,* LVI (1950), 1–18.

1871 THISTLETHWAITE, Frank. *The Anglo-American Connection in the Early Nineteenth Century.* Philadelphia, 1959.

1872 WILLIAMS, Mary Wilhelmine. *Anglo-American Isthmian Diplomacy, 1815–1915.* Washington, D.C., 1916.

C. United States–Latin American Relations

See also **1104–1108, 1177–1276, 1294–1308, 1543–1569, 1589–1606**

1873 BEMIS, Samuel Flagg. *The Latin American Policy of the United States, an Historical Interpretation.* New York, 1943.†

1874 BIERCK, Harold A., Jr. "Spoils, Soils and Skinner." *Md Hist Mag,* XLIX (1954), 21–40, 143–155.

1875 BRACK, Gene M. "Mexican Opinion and the Texas Revolution." *S W Hist Q,* LXXII (1968), 170–182.

1876 BRACK, Gene M. "Imperious Neighbor: The Mexican View of the United States, 1821–1846." Doctoral dissertation, University of Texas, 1967.

1877 BROWN, Lee Francis. "The Explorer, the United States Government, and the Approaches to Santa Fe: A Study of American Policy Relative to the Spanish Southwest, 1800–1819." Doctoral dissertation, Loyola University, Chicago, 1972.

1878 CALLAHAN, James M. *American Foreign Policy in Mexican Relations.* New York, 1932.

1879 CRISP, James Ernest. "Anglo-Texas Attitudes toward the Mexican, 1821–1845." Doctoral dissertation, Yale University, 1976

1880 DE LEON, Arnoldo. "White Racial Attitudes toward Mexicans in Texas, 1821–1900." Doctoral dissertation, Texas Christian University, 1974.

1881 EVANS, Henry C. *Chile and Its Relations with the United States.* Durham, N.C., 1927.

1882 FLACCUS, Elmer W. "Commodore David Porter and the Mexican Navy." *His-Am Hist Rev,* XXXIV (1954), 365–373.

1883 GANTENBEIN, James W. *Evolution of Our Latin-American Policy, a Documentary Record.* New York, 1950.

1884 HILL, Lawrence F. *Diplomatic Relations between the United States and Brazil.* Durham, N.C., 1932.

1885 LANGLEY, Lester D. *Struggle for the American Mediterranean: United States-European Rivalry in the Gulf-Caribbean, 1776–1904.* Athens, 1976.

1886 LEARY, David T. "The Attitudes of Certain United States Citizens toward Mexico, 1821–1846." Doctoral dissertation, University of Southern California, 1969.

1887 LOCKEY, J. B. *Pan-Americanism: Its Beginnings.* New York, 1920.

1888 MANNING, William R. *Diplomatic Correspondence of the United States: Inter-American Affairs, 1831–1860.* 12 vols. Washington, D.C., 1932–1939.

1889 MANNING, William R. *The Early Diplomatic Relations between the United States and Mexico.* Baltimore, 1916.

1890 MARSHALL, Thomas M. *A History of the Western Boundary of the Louisiana Purchase, 1819–1841.* Berkeley, Calif., 1914.

1891 MCELROY, M. D. "Colonial Propaganda for Northern Mexico." *J W,* IX (1970), 505–518.

1892 MONTAGUE, Ludwell Lee. *Haiti and the United States, 1714–1938.* Durham, N.C., 1940.

1893 OLIPHANT, J. Orin. "A Philadelphia Editor Looks at Latin America, 1823–1834." *Pa Hist,* XII (1945), 115–146.

1894 ONIS, José de. *The United States as Seen by Spanish American Writers, 1776–1890.* New York, 1952.

1895 PARKS, E. Taylor. *Colombia and the United States, 1765–1934.* Durham, N.C., 1935.

1896 PETERSON, Harold F. *Argentina and the United States, 1810–1960.* New York, 1964.

1897 PICHARDO, José A. *Pichardo's Treatise on the Limits of Louisiana and Texas.* Ed. C. W. Hackett. 4 vols. Austin, 1931–1946.

1898 PITCHFORD, Louis Cleveland, Jr. "The Diplomatic Representatives from the United States to Mexico from 1836 to 1848." Doctoral dissertation, University of Colorado, 1965.

1899 REYNOLDS, Curtis R. "The Deterioration of Mexican-American Diplomatic Relations, 1833–1845." *J W,* XI (1972), 213–224.

1900 RIPPY, J. Fred. *The United States and Mexico.* New York, 1931.

1901 RIVES, George L. *The United States and Mexico, 1821–1848.* 2 vols. New York, 1913.

1902 ROBERTSON, William S., ed. "Documents Concerning the Consular Service of the United States in Latin America, with Introductory Note." *Miss Val Hist Rev,* II (1916), 560–568.

1903 ROBERTSON, William S. *Hispanic-American Relations with the United States.* New York, 1923.

1904 RYDJORD, John. *Foreign Interest in the Independence of New Spain.* Durham, N.C., 1935.

1905 SCHMITT, Karl M. *Mexico and the United States, 1821–1973: Conflict and Coexistence.* New York, 1974.†

1906 SHOEMAKER, Raymond Leroy. "Diplomacy from the Quarterdeck: The United States Navy in the Caribbean, 1815–1830. Doctoral dissertation, Indiana University, 1976.

1907 SMITH, Ralph A. "Indians in American-Mexican Relations Before the War of 1846." *His-Am Hist Rev,* XLIII (1963), 34–64.

1908 TANSILL, Charles C. *The United States and Santo Domingo, 1798–1873: A Chapter in Caribbean Diplomacy.* Baltimore, 1938.

1909 TRASK, David F.; Michael C. MEYER; and Roger R. TRASK, comps. *A Bibliography of United States–Latin American Relations since 1810.* Lincoln, 1968.

1910 ULIBARRI, Richard Onofre. "American Interest in the Spanish-American Southwest, 1803–1848." Doctoral dissertation, University of Utah, 1963.

1911 WEBER, David J. "Mexico's Far Northern Frontier, 1821–1854: Historiography Askew." *W Hist Q,* VII (1976), 279–293.

8. The Regions, States, and Territories

New England

A. Regional Studies.

See also **2851, 2861, 2944, 3061, 3064, 3067, 3170A, 3387–3455, 3896, 4178, 4192, 4241, 4304–4327, 4427, 4599, 4635**

1912 ADAMS, James Truslow. *New England in the Republic, 1776–1850.* Boston, 1926.

1913 ELKINS, Stanley, and Eric MCKITRICK. "A Meaning for Turner's Frontier: The Southwest Frontier and New England." *Pol Sci Q,* LXIX (1954), 565–602.

1914 GRANT, Philip A., Jr. "The Elections of 1834–1835 in New England: A Judgment of Jacksonian Democracy." Doctoral dissertation, Georgetown University, 1960.

B. Maine

See also **609, 732, 1593, 1595, 1598, 1600, 3910, 4098, 4201, 4244**

1915 BANKS, Ronald F. *Maine Becomes a State: The Movement to Separate Maine from Massachusetts, 1785–1820.* Middletown, 1970.†

1916 BURRAGE, Henry S. *Maine in the Northeastern Boundary Controversy.* Augusta, 1919.

1917 LEVINE, Robert. "The Separation of the District of Maine from Massachusetts, 1785 to 1820. Doctoral dissertation, Clark University, 1933.

C. New Hampshire

See also **825, 857, 861–863, 1056–1058, 3886**

1918 CAPOWSKI, Vincent J. "The Era of Good Feelings in New Hampshire." *Hist N H,* XXI (Winter 1966), 3–30.

1919 COLE, Donald B. "The Presidential Election of 1832 in New Hampshire." *Hist N H, XXI (Winter 1966), 32–50.*

1920 COLE, Donald B. *Jacksonian Democracy in New Hampshire, 1800–1851.* Cambridge, Mass., 1970.

1921 GRANT, Philip A., Jr. "The Bank Controversy and New Hampshire Politics, 1834–1835. *Hist N H,* XXIII (Autumn 1968), 19–36.

1922 McLOUGHLIN, William G. "The Bench, the Church, and the Republican Party in New Hampshire, 1790 to 1820." *Hist N H,* XX (Summer 1965), 3–31.

192. MORISON, Elizabeth Forbes, and Elting E. MORISON. *New Hampshire: A Bicentennial History.* New York, 1976.

1924 TASHOFF, Sue. "New Hampshire State Politics and the Concept of a Party System, 1800–1840." *Hist N H,* XXXI (Spring-Summer 1976), 17–43.

D. Vermont

See also **1599, 1769, 2910**

1925 BASSETT, T. D. Seymour. "The Rise of Cornelius Peter Van Ness, 1782–1826." *Proc Vt Hist Soc,* n. s. X (1942), 3–20.

1926 BECKLEY, Hosea. *The History of Vermont.* Brattleboro, Vt., 1846.

1927 DUFFY, John, and Nicholas MULLER. "The Great Wolf Hunt: The Popular Response in Vermont to the *Patriote* Uprising of 1837." *J Am Stud,* VIII (1974), 153–169.

1928 FANT, H. B. ed. "Levi Woodbury's Week in Vermont, May 1819." *Vt Hist,* XXXIV (1966), 36–62.

1929 GRANT, Philip A., Jr. "The Antimasons Retain Control of the Green Mountain State." *Vt Hist,* XXXIV (1966), 169–187.

1930 LUDLUM, David M. *Social Ferment in Vermont, 1791–1850.* New York, 1939.

1931 STILWELL, Lewis D., *Migration from Vermont, 1776–1860.* Montpelier, 1937.

1932 WILLIAMSON, Chilton. *Vermont in Quandry, 1763–1825.* Montpelier, 1949.

1933 WRIGHT, Martha R. "The Log Cabin Convention of 1840 Sixty Years Later: Vermonters Correct the Record." *Vt Hist,* XL (1972), 237–245.

E. Massachusetts

See also **390–420, 423, 434, 435, 534–536, 582, 607, 608, 751, 806, 844, 851, 884–886, 897–899, 930–931, 1017–1036, 1657, 1665, 1915, 1917, 1969, 2754, 2756, 2791, 2803, 3030, 3054, 3065–3086, 3100, 3126, 3130, 3142, 3164, 3778, 3792, 3802, 3806, 3816, 3825, 4091, 4097, 4132, 4157, 4180, 4187, 4191, 4192, 4200, 4229, 4262, 4319, 4545, 4720**

1934 BOWER, Robert T. "Note on 'Did Labor Support Jackson?: The Boston Story.' " *Pol Sci Q,* LXV (1950), 441–444.

1935 CARTER, George E. "Democrat in Heaven–Whig on Earth–The Politics of Ralph Waldo Emerson." *Hist N H,* XXVII (1972), 123–140.

1936 DARLING, Arthur B. "Jacksonian Democracy in Massachusetts, 1824–1848." *Am Hist Rev,* XXIX (1924), 271–287.

1937 DARLING, Arthur B. *Political Changes in Massachusetts, 1824–1848.* New Haven, 1925.

1938 DARLING, Arthur B. "The Workingmen's Party in Massachusetts, 1833–1834." *Am Hist Rev,* XXIX (1923), 81–86.

1939 GRANT, Philip A., Jr. "The Elections of 1834 in Essex County, Massachusetts." *Essex Inst Hist Coll,* CVI (1970), 126–141.

1940 HANDLIN, Oscar, and Mary Flug HANDLIN. *Commonwealth: A Study of the Role of Government in the American Economy: Massachusetts, 1774–1861.* New York, 1947.

1941 HASKELL, John D., Jr., comp. *Massachusetts: A Bibliography of Its History.* Boston, 1976.

1942 HAWS, Robert James. "Massachusetts Whigs, 1833–1854." Doctoral dissertation, University of Nebraska, 1973.

1943 PADOVER, Saul K. "Ralph Waldo Emerson: The Moral Voice in Politics." *Pol Sci Q,* LXXIV (1959), 334–350.

1944 PESSEN, Edward. "Did Labor Support Jackson?: The Boston Story." *Pol Sci Q,* LXIV (1949), 262–274.

1945 POLE, J. R. "Suffrage and Representation in Massachusetts: A Statistical Note." *Wm Mar Q,* XIV (1957), 560–592.

1946 RICH, Robert. " 'A Wilderness of Whigs': The Wealthy Men of Boston." *J Soc Hist,* IV (1971), 263–276.

1947 ROBBINS, James H. "Voting Behavior in Massachusetts, 1800–1820: A Case Study." Doctoral dissertation, Northwestern University, 1970.

1948 ROSS, Gordon D. "The Crowninshield Family in Business and Politics, 1790–1830." Doctoral dissertation, Claremont University, 1965.

1949 SCHOULER, James. "The Whig Party in Massachusetts." *Mass Hist Soc Proc,* L (1917), 39–53.

1950 SIRACUSA, Carl Franklin. "A Mechanical People: The Worker's Image in Massachusetts Politics, 1815–1880." Doctoral dissertation, Brandeis University, 1973.

1951 TRUSTY, Norman Lance. "Massachusetts Public Opinion and the Annexation of Texas, 1835–1845." Doctoral dissertation, Boston University, 1964.

F. Rhode Island

See also **2807, 4173, 4234**

1952 ARNOLD, Samuel Greene. *History of the State of Rhode Island and Providence Plantation.* 2 vols. New York, 1860.

1952A CARROLL, Charles. *Rhode Island: Three Centuries of Democracy.* 4 vols. New York, 1932.

1953 CHUDACOFF, Howard P., and Theodore C. HIRT. "Social Turmoil and Governmental Reform in Providence, 1820–1832." *R I Hist,* XXXI (1972), 21–31.

1954 COLEMAN, Peter J. *The Transformation of Rhode Island, 1790–1860.* Providence, 1963.

1955 CONLEY, Patrick Thomas. "Rhode Island Constitutional Development, 1636–1841: Prologue to the Dorr Rebellion." Doctoral dissertation, University of Notre Dame, 1970.

1956 DENNISON, George M. *The Dorr War: Republicanism on Trial, 1831–1861.* Lexington, 1976.

1957 GETTLEMAN, Marvin E. *The Dorr Rebellion: A Study in American Radicalism, 1833–1849.* New York, 1973.

1958 GETTLEMAN, Marvin E., and Noel P. CONLON, eds. "Responses to the Rhode Island Workingmen's Reform Agitation of 1833." *R I Hist,* XXVIII (1969), 75–94.

1959 GRANT, Philip A. "Party Chaos Embroils Rhode Island." *R I Hist,* XXVI (1967), 113–125, XXVII (1968), 24–33.

1960 SWEET, Edward Francis. "The Origin of the Democratic Party in Rhode Island, 1834–1836." Doctoral dissertation, Fordham University, 1971.

G. Connecticut

See also **433, 2976, 4183, 4213, 4260, 4603**

1961 BROWNSWORD, Alan W. "Connecticut Political Patterns, 1817–1828." Doctoral dissertation, University of Wisconsin, 1962.

1962 BROWNSWORD, Alan W. "The Constitution of 1818 and Political Afterthoughts, 1800–1840." *Conn Hist Soc Bull,* XXX (1965), 1–10.

1963 GRANT, Philip A., Jr. "The Bank Controversy and Connecticut Politics." *Conn Hist Soc Bull,* XXXIII (1968), 90–96.

1964 GRANT, Philip A., Jr. "Jacksonian Democracy Triumphs in Connecticut." *Conn Hist Soc Bull,* XXXIII (1968), 117–124.

1965 MORSE, Jarvis Means. *A Neglected Period of Connecticut's History, 1818–1850.* New Haven, 1933.

1966 PURCELL, Richard J. *Connecticut in Transition, 1775–1818.* Washington, D.C., 1918.

1967 STAMPS, Norman L. "Political Parties in Connecticut, 1789–1818." Doctoral dissertation, Yale University, 1952.

1968 THOMAS, Edmund B., Jr. "Politics in the Land of Steady Habits: Connecticut's First Political Party System, 1789–1820." Doctoral dissertation, Clark University, 1972.

Middle Atlantic States

A. Regional Studies

See also **3387–3455, 3783**

1969 REED, John J. "The Emergence of the Whig Party in the North: Massachusetts, New York, Pennsylvania, and Ohio." Doctoral dissertation, University of Pennsylvania, 1953.

B. New York

See also 437, 441, 442, 465, 481, 482, 555, 564, 596–597, 610–614, 667–668, 721, 739–740, 742–743, 754–756, 807, 808, 835, 842–843, 881, 925–929, 973, 978, 993–1009, 1016, 1037–1039, 1062–1064, 1487, 1969, 2701, 2733, 2736, 2754, 2760, 2785, 2787, 2793, 2798, 2799, 2805, 2811, 2812, 2819, 2825, 2842, 2845, 2884, 2984, 2985, 3030, 3085, 3103, 3105, 3117, 3118, 3182, 3807, 3811, 3813, 3815, 3816, 3826, 3828, 3830, 3933, 3974, 3997–3999, 4052, 4126, 4143, 4189, 4270, 4334, 4438, 4445, 4592, 4593, 4620, 4657, 4743

1970 ALEXANDER, DeAlva Standwood. *A Political History of the State of New York.* 3 vols. New York, 1906–1909.

1971 BARKAN, Elliott R. "The Emergence of a Whig Persuasion: Conservatism, Democratism, and the New York State Whigs." *N Y Hist,* LII (1971), 367–395.

1972 BARKAN, Elliott R. "Portrait of a Party: The Origins and Development of the Whig Persuasion in New York State." Doctoral dissertation, Harvard University, 1969.

1973 BENSON, Lee. *The Concept of Jacksonian Democracy: New York as a Test Case.* Princeton, 1961.†

1974 BRACKNEY, William Henry. "Religious Antimasonry: The Genesis of a Political Party." Doctoral dissertation, Temple University, 1976.

1975 BYRDSALL, F. *History of the Loco-Foco, or Equal Rights Party.* New York, 1842.

1976 CARLTON, Frank T. "The Working Men's Party of New York City, 1829–1831." *Pol Sci Q,* XXII (1907), 401–415.

1977 CASAIS, Jack Antony. "The New York State Constitutional Convention of 1821 and Its Aftermath." Doctoral dissertation, Columbia University, 1967.

1978 CHAZANOF, William. "The Political Influence of Joseph Ellicott in Western New York, 1800–1821." Doctoral dissertation, Syracuse University, 1955.

1979 CHRISTMAN, Henry. *Tin Horns and Calico.* New York, 1945.

1980 COHEN, Ira. "The Auction System in the Port of New York, 1817–1837." *Bus Hist Rev,* XLV (1971), 488–510.

1981 COHEN, Ira. "The Auction System in the Port of New York, 1817–1837." Doctoral dissertation, New York University, 1969.

1982 DANFORTH, Brian Joseph. "The Influence of Socioeconomic Factors upon Political Behavior: A Quantitative Look at New York City Merchants, 1828–1844." Doctoral dissertation, New York University, 1974.

1983 DONOVAN, Herbert D. A. *The Barnburners: A Study of the Internal Movements in the Political History of New York State and the Resulting Changes in Poltical Affiliation, 1830–1852.* New York, 1925.

1984 FORMISANO, Ronald P., and Kathleen Smith KUTOLOWSKI. "Antimasonry and Masonry: The Genesis of Protest, 1826–1827." *Am Q,* XXIX (1977), 139–165.

1985 FOX, Dixon Ryan. *The Decline of Aristocracy in the Politics of New York.* New York, 1919.†

1986 GARRATY, John A. "Silas Wright and the Election of 1840 in New York State." *N Y Hist,* XXVIII (1947), 288–303.

1987 GATELL, Frank Otto. "Money and Party In Jacksonian America: A Quantitative Look at New York City's Men of Quality." *Pol Sci Q,* LXXXII (1967), 235–252.

1988 GOLDSTEIN, Kalman. "The Albany Regency: The Failure of Practical Politics." Doctoral dissertation, Columbia University, 1969.

1989 GOTSCH, Charles Edward. "The Albany Workingmen's Party and the Rise of Popular Politics." Doctoral dissertation, State University of New York at Albany, 1976.

1990 GUNN, L. Ray. "Political Implications of General Incorporation Laws in New York to 1860." *Mid-Am,* LIX (1977), 171–191.

1991 HAMMOND, Jabez D. *History of Political Parties in the State of New York.* 3 vols., New York, 1852.

1992 HANYAN, Craig R. "De Witt Clinton and Partisanship: The Development of Clintonianism from 1811 to 1820." *N Y Hist Soc Q,* LVI (1972), 109–131.

1993 HARMOND, Richard. "Ebenezer Sage of Sag Harbor: An Old Republican in Young America, 1812–1834." *N Y Hist Soc Q,* LVII (1973), 309–325.

1994 HENDRICKS, John R. "The Liberty Party in New York State, 1838–1848." Doctoral dissertation, Fordham University, 1959.

1995 HERSHKOWITZ, Leo. "The Loco-Foco Party of New York: Its Origins and Career, 1835–1837." *N Y Hist Soc Q,* XLVI (1962), 305–329.

1996 HERSHKOWITZ, Leo. "The Native American Democratic Association in New York City, 1835–1836." *N Y Hist Soc Q,* XLVI (1962), 41–59.

1997 HERSHKOWITZ, Leo. "New York City, 1834–1840, A Study in Local Politics." Doctoral dissertation, New York University, 1960.

1998 HOPKINS, Vivian C. "The Empire State: De Witt Clinton's Laboratory." *N Y Hist Soc Q,* LIX (1975), 7–49.

1999 HUGINS, Walter. *Jacksonian Democracy and the Working Class: A Study of the New York Workingmen's Movement, 1829–1837.* Stanford, 1960.

2000 JENKINS, J. S. *History of Political Parties in the State of New York.* Auburn, N.Y., 1846.

2001 KASS, Alvin. *Politics in New York State, 1800–1830.* Syracuse, 1965.

2002 KUTOLOWSKI, Kathleen Smith. "The Social Composition of Political Leadership: Genesee County, New York, 1821–1860." Doctoral dissertation, Rochester University, 1973.

2003 LINCOLN, Charles Z. *The Constitutional History of New York.* 5 vols. Rochester, 1906.

2004 MCBAIN, Howard L. *De Witt Clinton and the Origin of the Spoils System in New York.* New York, 1907.

2005 MCGEE, Patricia E. "Issues and Factions: New York State Politics from the Panic of 1837 to the Election of 1848." Doctoral dissertation, St. John's University, 1970.

2006 MILLER, Douglas T. *Jacksonian Aristocracy: Class and Democracy in New York, 1830–1860.* New York, 1967.

2007 MORRIS, John David. "The New York State Whigs, 1834–1842: A Study of Political Organization." Doctoral dissertation, Rochester University, 1970.

2008 MUNTZ, Ernest G. "The First Whig Governor of New York, William H. Seward, 1838–1842." Doctoral dissertation, Rochester University, 1960.

2009 MUSHKAT, Jerome. *Tammany: The Evolution of a Political Machine, 1789–1865.* Syracuse, 1971.

2010 MYERS, Gustavus. *The History of Tammany Hall.* 2d ed. New York, 1917.

2011 NADLER, Solomon. "Federal Patronage and New York Politics, 1801–1830." Doctoral dissertation, New York University, 1973.

2012 NADLER, Solomon. "The Green Bag: James Monroe and the Fall of De Witt Clinton." *N Y Hist Soc Q,* LIX (1975), 202–225.

2013 NORTON, John R. "The New York State Government and the Economy, 1819–1846." *N Y Hist,* XXXIV (1953), 298–314.

2014 PRICE, Harry S., Jr. "The Regions of New York in the Election of 1828." Doctoral dissertation, Columbia University, 1953.

2015 REMINI, Robert V. "The Albany Regency." *N Y Hist,* XXXIX (1958), 341–355.

2016 REMINI, Robert V. "New York and the Presidential Election of 1816." *N Y Hist,* XXXI (1950), 308–324.

2017 ROPER, Donald M. "Justice Smith Thompson: Politics and the New York Supreme Court in the Early Nineteenth Century." *N Y Hist Soc Q,* LI (1967), 119–139.

2018 RUSSO, Raymond Joseph. "The Political Process in New York State, 1816–1824: A Study in Political Morality and Changing Attitudes toward the Party System." Doctoral dissertation, Fordham University, 1973.

2019 SPANN, Edward K. *Ideals & Politics; New York Intellectuals and Liberal Democracy, 1820–1880.* Albany, 1972.

2020 SPENCER, Ivor D. "William L. Marcy Goes Conservative." *Miss Val Hist Rev,* XXXI (1944), 205–224.

2021 TRIMBLE, William. "Diverging Tendencies in New York Democracy in the Period of the Locofocos." *Am Hist Rev,* XXIV (1919), 396–421.

2022 WALLACE, Michael. "Changing Concepts of Party in the United States: New York, 1815–1828." *Am Hist Rev,* LXXIV (1968), 453–491.

2023 WATSON, Richard L., Jr. "Thurlow Weed, Political Boss." *N Y Hist,* XXII (1941), 411–425.

C. New Jersey

See also **594, 941, 2802, 2863, 3963, 4049, 4386, 4387**

2024 CADMAN, John W., Jr. *The Corporation in New Jersey: Business and Politics, 1791–1875.* Cambridge, Mass., 1949.

2025 CHUTE, William J. "The New Jersey Whig Campaign of 1840." *Proc N J Hist Soc,* LXXVII (1959), 223–239.

2026 ERSHKOWITZ, Herbert. "The Election of 1824 in New Jersey." *Proc N J Hist Soc,* LXXXIV (1966), 113–132.

2027 ERSHKOWITZ, Herbert. "New Jersey Politics during the Era of Andrew Jackson." Doctoral dissertation, New York University, 1965.

2028 ERSHKOWITZ, Herbert. "The Origins of the Whig and Democratic Parties in New Jersey." *Papers Presented at the Second Annual New Jersey History Symposium.* Newark, 1971.

2029 FALLAW, Walter Robert, Jr. "The Rise of the Whig Party in New Jersey." Doctoral dissertation, Princeton University, 1967.

2030 FEE, Walter R. *The Transition from Aristocracy to Democracy in New Jersey, 1789–1829.* Somerville, 1933.

2031 HERMANN, Frederick M. "Anti-Masonry in New Jersey." *N J Hist,* XCI (1973), 149–165.

2032 LEVINE, Peter David. *The Behavior of State Legislative Parties in the Jacksonian Era: New Jersey, 1829–1844.* Cranbury, N. J., 1977.

2033 LEVINE, Peter. "The Rise of Mass Parties and the Problem of Organization: New Jersey, 1829–1844." *N J Hist,* XCI (1973), 91–107.

2034 LEVINE, Peter. "State Legislative Parties in the Jacksonian Era: New Jersey, 1829–1844." *J Am Hist,* LXII (1975), 591–608.

2035 MCCORMICK, Richard P. *The History of Voting in New Jersey.* New Brunswick, 1953.

2036 MCCORMICK, Richard P. "Party Formation in New Jersey in the Jackson Era." *Proc N J Hist Soc,* LXXXIII (1965), 161–173.

2037 NADWORNY, Milton J. "New Jersey Workingmen and the Jacksonians." *Proc N J Hist Soc,* LXVII (1949), 185–198.

2038 PASLER, Rudolph J., and Margaret C. PASLER. "Federalist Tenacity in Burlington County, 1810–1824." *N J Hist,* LXXXVII (1969), 197–210.

2039 PASLER, Rudolph J., and Margaret C. PASLER. *The New Jersey Federalists.* Rutherford, Penna., 1975.

2040 POLE, J. R. "The Reform of Suffrage and Representation in New Jersey, 1774–1844." Doctoral dissertation, Princeton University, 1953.

2041 PRINCE, Carl E. "James J. Wilson: Party Leader, 1801–1829." *Proc N J Hist Soc,* LXXXIII (1965), 24–39.

2042 PRINCE, Carl E. *New Jersey's Jeffersonian Republicans: The Genesis of an Early Party Machine, 1789–1817.* Chapel Hill, 1967.

D. Pennsylvania

See also **457, 474–477, 583–586, 639, 669, 918–920, 940, 1664, 1767, 1969, 2755, 2770–2771, 2792, 2829, 2833, 2908, 3044, 3095, 3123, 3124, 3148, 3776, 3777, 3804, 3824, 3845, 3849, 3866, 3915, 4050, 4067, 4163, 4204, 4205, 4207, 4249, 4271, 4275, 4277, 4298, 4300, 4361, 4377, 4378, 4382, 4447, 4455, 4463, 4476, 4569, 4604, 4693, 4774**

2043 AMBACHER, Bruce I. "Urban Response to Jacksonian Democracy: Philadelphia Democrats and the Bank War, 1832–1834." *Essays on Urban America.* Ed. Margaret Francine MORRIS and Elliott WEST. Austin, 1975.

2044 ANDREWS, J. Cutler. "The Antimasonic Movement in Western Pennsylvania." *W Pa Hist Mag,* XVIII (1935), 255–266.

2045 ARKY, Louis H. "The Mechanics' Union of Trade Associations and the Formation of the Philadelphia Workingmen's Movement." *Pa Mag Hist Biog,* LXXVI (1952), 142–176.

2046 BARTLETT, Marguerite G. *The Chief Phases of Pennsylvania Politics in the Jacksonian Period.* Allentown, 1919.

2047 BOWERS, Douglas Eugene. "The Pennsylvania Legislature, 1815–1860: A Study of Democracy at Work." Doctoral dissertation, University of Chicago, 1974.

2048 FRIEDMAN, Jean E., and William G. SHADE. "James M. Porter: A Conservative Democrat in the Jacksonian Era." *Pa Hist,* LXII (1975), 188–204.

2049 GERRITY, Frank. "The Masons, the Antimasons, and the Pennsylvania Legislature, 1834–1836." *Pa Mag Hist Biog,* XCIX (1975), 180–206.

2050 HAILPERIN, Herman. "Pro-Jackson Sentiment in Pennsylvania." *Pa Mag Hist Biog,* L (1926), 193–240.

2051 HARTZ, Louis. *Economic Policy and Democratic Thought: Pennsylvania, 1776–1860.* Cambridge, Mass., 1948.†

2052 HELLEGERS, John F. "Some Bases of Early Pro-Jackson Sentiment in Western Pennsylvania." *W Pa Hist Mag,* XLV (1962), 31–46.

2053 HIGGINBOTHAM, Sanford W. *The Keystone in the Democratic Arch: Pennsylvania Politics, 1800–1816.* Harrisburg, 1952.

2054 HOFFMAN, John Nathan. *Girard Estate Coal Lands in Pennsylvania, 1801–1884.* Washington, D.C., 1972.

2055 HUBNER, Thurman W. "Walter Lowrie (1784–1863), Educator, United States Senator, and Secretary of the United States Senate," *W Pa Hist Mag,* XXXIX (1956), 145–162.

2056 KEHL, James A. *Ill Feeling in the Era of Good Feeling: Western Pennsylvania Political Battles, 1815–1835.* Pittsburgh, 1956.

2057 KLEIN, Philip Shriver. *Pennsylvania Politics, 1817–1832: A Game Without Rules.* Philadelphia, 1940.

2058 KLEIN, Philip S., and Ari HOOGENBOOM. *A History of Pennsylvania.* New York, 1973.

2059 LANGLEY, Harold D. "The Tragic Case of H. G. Rogers, Pennsylvania Politician and Jacksonian Diplomat." *Pa Hist,* XXXI (1964), 30–61.

2060 MADONNA, George Terry. "The Pennsylvania Jacksonians and the Bank War." Doctoral dissertation, University of Delaware, 1975.

2061 MUELLER, Henry R. *The Whig Party in Pennsylvania.* New York, 1922.

2062 PESSEN, Edward. "The Ideology of Stephen Simpson, Upperclass Champion of the Early Philadelphia Workingmen's Movement." *Pa Hist,* XXII (1955), 328–340.

2063 PHILLIPS, Kim T. "Democrats of the Old School in the Era of Good Feelings." *Pa Mag Hist Biog,* XCV (1971), 363–382.

2064 PHILLIPS, Kim T. "The Pennsylvania Origins of the Jackson Movement." *Pol Sci Q,* XCI (1976), 489–508.

2065 SHADE, William G. "Pennsylvania Politics in the Jacksonian Period: A Case Study, Northampton County, 1824–1844." *Pa Hist,* XXXIX (1972), 313–333.

2066 SNYDER, Charles McCool. *The Jacksonian Heritage: Pennsylvania Politics, 1833–1848.* Harrisburg, 1958.

2067 TAYLOR, M. Flavia. "The Political and Civic Career of Henry Baldwin, 1799–1830." *W Pa Hist Mag,* XXIV (1941), 37–50.

2068 WALTON, Joseph S. "Nominating Conventions in Pennsylvania." *Am Hist Rev,* II (1897), 262–278.

E. Delaware

See also **599, 777, 4194, 4550**

2069 BOHNER, Charles H. "Rum and Reform: Temperance in Delaware Politics." *Del Hist,* V (1953), 237–269.

2070 GARRETT, Jane N. "The Delaware College Lotteries." *Del Hist,* VII (1957), 299–318.

2071 MUMFORD, Richard L. "Constitutional Development in the State of Delaware." Doctoral dissertation, University of Delaware, 1968.

2072 MUNROE, John A. "Party Battles, 1789–1850." *Delaware: A History of the First State.* Ed. H. Clay Reed. 2 vols. New York, 1947.

2073 PELTIER, David P. "Nineteenth-Century Voting Patterns in Delaware." *Del Hist,* XIII (1969), 219–233.

2074 REED, H. Clay. "Presidential Electors in Delaware, 1789–1829." *Del Hist,* XIV (1970), 1–21.

2075 WIRE, Richard Arden. "John M. Clayton and the Rise of the Anti-Jackson Party in Delaware, 1824–1828." *Del Hist,* XV (1973), 256–268.

2076 WIRE, Richard Arden. "Young Senator Clayton and the Early Jackson Years." *Del Hist,* XVII (1976), 104–126.

The South

A. Regional Studies

See also **86, 1092, 1099, 1798, 2626–2628, 2630, 2657, 2660, 2674, 2686, 2689, 2695, 2697, 2700, 2707, 2708, 2739, 2746, 2753, 2783, 2862, 2874, 2949, 2950, 2967–2973, 2994, 2996, 3009, 3048, 3049, 3063, 3088, 3196, 3197, 3204–3653, 3671, 3672, 3784, 3785, 3883, 3895, 3906, 3917, 3918, 3920–3922, 3925, 3928, 3932, 3934, 3939, 3953, 3965, 4017, 4019, 4039, 4063, 4064, 4219, 4220, 4226, 4250, 4373, 4465, 4521, 4594, 4629, 4643, 4669, 4680, 4704, 4740, 4764**

2077 ABERNETHY, Thomas Perkins. "Democracy and the Southern Frontier." *J S Hist,* IV (1938), 3–13.

2078 ABERNETHY, Thomas P. "The Political Geography of Southern Jacksonism." *E Tenn His Soc Pub,* no. 3 (1931), 35–41.

2079 ABERNETHY, Thomas P. *The South in the New Nation, 1789–1819.* Baton Rouge, 1961.†

2080 BEAN, William Gleason. "Anti-Jeffersonianism in the Ante-Bellum South." *N C Hist Rev,* XII (1935), 103–124.

2081 BRADEN, Waldo W., ed. *Oratory in the Old South, 1828–1860.* Baton Rouge, 1970.

2082 BROWN, Karmalene Kelso. "The South's Reaction to the Tariffs and the Force Bill, 1828–1833." Doctoral dissertation, Oklahoma State University, 1971.

2083 CARPENTER, Jesse T. *The South as a Conscious Minority, 1789–1861; a Study in Political Thought.* New York, 1930.

2084 COLE, Arthur Charles. *The Whig Party in the South.* Washington, 1913.

2085 DEGLER, Carl N. *The Other South: Southern Dissenters in the Nineteenth Century.* New York, 1974.†

2086 DODD, William E. *Statesmen of the Old South, or From Radicalism to Conservative Revolt.* New York, 1911.

2087 DYER, Gustavus W. *Democracy in the South before the Civil War.* Nashville, 1906.

2088 EATON, Clement. *Freedom of Thought in the Old South.* Durham, 1940.

2089 EATON, Clement. *The Growth of Southern Civilization, 1790–1860.* New York, 1961.

2090 EATON, Clement. *A History of the Old South: The Emergence of a Reluctant Nation.* 3d edition. New York, 1975.

2091 EATON, Clement. "Southern Senators and the Right of Instruction, 1789–1860." *J S Hist,* XVIII (1952), 303–319.

2092 FOLSOM, Burton W. "Party Formation and Development in Jacksonian America: The Old South." *J Am Stud,* VII (1973), 217–229.

2093 FRANKLIN, John Hope. *The Militant South, 1800–1861.* Cambridge, Mass., 1956.

2094 GOVAN, Thomas P. "Was the Old South Different?" *J S Hist,* XXI (1955), 447–455.

2095 GREEN, Fletcher M. *Constitutional Development in the South Atlantic States 1776–1860: A Study in the Evolution of Democracy.* Chapel Hill, 1930.

2096 GREEN, Fletcher M. "Democracy in the Old South." *J S Hist,* XII (1946), 3–23.

2097 GREEN, Fletcher M. *The Role of the Yankee in the Old South.* Athens, 1972.

2098 HARRISON, Joseph Hobson, Jr. "Martin Van Buren and His Southern Supporters." *J S Hist,* XXII (1956), 438–458.

2099 HESSELTINE, William B., and David L. SMILEY. *The South in American History.* 2d ed. Englewood Cliffs, N.J., 1960.

2100 PHILLIPS, Ulrich B. "The Southern Whigs, 1834–1854." *Essays in American History Dedicated to Frederick Jackson Turner.* Ed. Guy S. FORD. New York, 1910.

2101 PHILLIPS, Ulrich B. *The Course of the South to Secession.* Ed. E. Merton Coulter. New York, 1939.†

2102 SELLERS, Charles Grier, Jr. ed. *The Southerner as American.* Chapel Hill, 1960.

2103 SHALHOPE, Robert E. "Thomas Jefferson's Republicanism and Antebellum Southern Thought." *J S Hist,* XLII (1976), 529–556.

2104 SIMKINS, Francis Butler, and Charles Pierce ROLAND. *A History of the South.* 4th ed. New York, 1972.

2105 SINGLETARY, Otis A., and Kenneth K. BAILEY. *The South in American History.* Am Hist Assn Service Center for Teachers Publication. Washington, D.C., 1965.†

2106 SYDNOR, Charles S. *The Development of Southern Sectionalism, 1819–1848.* Baton Rouge, 1948.†

2107 VINSON, John Chalmers. "Electioneering in the South, 1800–1840." *Ga Rev,* X (1956), 265–273.

B. District of Columbia

See also 563, 595, 601–603, 875, 913–915, 937, 1103, 3781, 3788, 4537, 4558, 4581, 4583

2108 ARNOLD, Linda Marion. "Congressional Government of the District of Columbia." Doctoral dissertation, Georgetown University, 1974.

2109 BRYAN, Wilhelmus Bogard. *A History of the National Capital from Its Foundation through the Period of the Adoption of the Organic Act.* 2 vols. New York, 1914–1916.

2110 GREEN, Constance McLaughlin. "The Jacksonian 'Revolution' in the District of Columbia." *Miss Val Hist Rev,* XLV (1959), 591–605.

2111 GREEN, Constance McLaughlin. *Washington: Village and Capital, 1800–1878.* Princeton, 1962.

2112 LEWIS, David L. *District of Columbia: A Bicentennial History.* New York, 1976.

2113 MYERS, Gibbs. "The Founding of Modern Washington, 1790 to 1874." Doctoral dissertation, Yale University, 1943.

C. Maryland

See also 553, 736–738, 858–859, 938–939, 956–966, 1486, 1488, 2763, 3042, 3277, 3779, 3907, 4081, 4197, 4282, 4392, 4403, 4460, 4756

2114 BOHMER, David Alan. "Voting Behavior during the First American Party System: Maryland, 1796–1816." Doctoral dissertation, University of Michigan, 1974.

2115 CRAIG, Willliam H. "The Rise and Early Success of the Whig Party In Maryland." Doctoral dissertation, Johns Hopkins University, 1931.

2116 HAGENSICK, A. Clarke. "Revolution or Reform in 1836: Maryland's Preface to the Dorr Rebellion." *Md Hist Mag,* LVII (1962), 346–366.

2117 HALLER, Mark H. "The Rise of the Jackson Party in Maryland, 1820–1829." *J S Hist,* XXVIII (1962), 307–326.

2118 LEVIN, Alexandria Lee. "Two Jackson Supporters: Roger Brooke Taney and William Murdoch Beall of Frederick." *Md Hist Mag* LV (1960), 221–229.

2119 POLE, J. R. "Constitutional Reform and Election Statistics in Maryland, 1790–1821." *Md Hist Mag,* LV (1960), 275–292.

2120 REMINGTON, Jesse A., Jr. "State-Rights in Maryland, 1787–1832." Doctoral dissertation, University of Maryland, 1940.

2121 RENZULLI, Libero Marx, Jr. *Maryland Federalism, 1787–1819.* Cranbury, N.J., 1972.

2122 RIDGWAY, Whitman H. "Community Leadership: Baltimore during the First and Second Party Systems." *Md Hist Mag,* LXXI (1976), 334–348.

2123 RIDGWAY, Whitman H. "McCulloch vs. the Jacksonians: Patronage and Politics in Maryland." *Md Hist Mag,* LXX (1975), 350–362.

2124 RIDGWAY, Whitman H. "A Social Analysis of Maryland Community Elites, 1827–1836: A Study of the Distribution of Power in Baltimore City, Frederick County, and Talbot County." Doctoral dissertation, University of Pennsylvania, 1973.

2125 ROSEBOOM, Eugene H. "Baltimore as a National Nominating Convention City." *Md Hist Mag,* LXVII (1972), 215–224.

2126 SMITH, W. Wayne. "Jacksonian Democracy on the Chesapeake: The Political Institutions." *Md Hist Mag,* LXII (1967), 381–393.

2127 SMITH, W. Wayne. "Jacksonian Democracy on the Chesapeake: Class, Kinship and Politics." *Md Hist Mag,* LXIII (1968), 55–67.

2128 SMITH, W. Wayne. "The Whig Party in Maryland, 1826–1856." Doctoral dissertation, University of Maryland, 1967.

2129 WALSH, Richard, and William Lloyd FOX, eds. *Maryland: A History, 1632–1974.* Baltimore, 1974.

D. Virginia

See also **436, 520, 587, 591–593, 616, 638, 643, 681–682, 722, 723, 771, 787–804, 809–824, 828–834, 889–896, 901–909, 916, 944, 969–972, 976, 984–992, 1050–1055, 1100, 1274, 2625, 2732, 2816, 3037, 3134, 3352, 3773, 3782, 3862, 3863, 3907, 3945, 3955, 3956, 4162, 4165, 4231, 4424, 4467, 4472–4474, 4544, 4546, 4607, 4731, 4735**

2130 AMBLER, Charles Henry. *Sectionalism in Virginia from 1776 to 1861.* Chicago, 1910.

2131 AMMON, Harry. "The Republican Party in Virginia, 1789 to 1824." Doctoral dissertation, University of Virginia, 1948.

2132 AMMON, Harry. "The Richmond Junto, 1800–1824." *Va Mag Hist Biog,* LXI (1953), 395–418.

2133 BRAVERMAN, Howard. "The Economic and Political Background of the Conservative Revolt in Virginia." *Va Mag Hist Biog,* LX (1952), 266–287.

2134 DABNEY, Virginius. *Virginia: The New Dominion.* Garden City, 1971.†

2135 DAUER, Manning J., and Hans HAMMOND. "John Taylor: Democrat or Aristocrat?" *J Pol,* VI (1944), 381–403.

2136 DENT, Lynwood Miller, Jr. "The Virginia Democratic Party, 1824–1847." Doctoral dissertation, Louisiana State University, 1974.

2137 DODD, William E. "Chief Justice Marshall and Virginia, 1813–1821." *Am Hist Rev,* XII (1907), 776–787.

2138 FISHER, John E. "The Dilemma of a States' Rights Whig: The Congressional Career of R. M. T. Hunter, 1837–1841." *Va Mag Hist Biog,* LXXXI (1973), 387–404.

2139 FISHWICK, Marshall W. *Virginia: A New Look at the Old Dominion.* New York, 1959.

2140 FREEHLING, Alison Harrison Goodyear. "Drift toward Dissolution: The Virginia Slavery Debate of 1831–1832." Doctoral dissertation, University of Michigan, 1974.

2141 GATEWOOD, Joanne L., ed. "Richmond during the Virginia Constitutional Convention of 1829–1830: An Extract from the Diary of Thomas Green, October 1, 1829, to January 31, 1830." *Va Mag Hist Biog,* LXXXIV (1976), 287–332.

2142 GRIGSBY, Hugh Blair. "Sketches of Members of the Constitutional Convention of 1829–1830." *Va Mag Hist Biog,* LXI (1953), 319–332.

2143 GRIGSBY, Hugh Blair. *The Virginia Convention of 1829–30.* Richmond, 1856.

2144 HARRISON, Joseph H., Jr. "Oligarchs and Democrats—The Richmond Junto." *Va Mag Hist Biog,* LXXVIII (1970), 184–198.

2145 HODGES, Wiley E. "The Theoretical Basis of Anti-Governmentalism in Virginia, 1789–1836." *J Pol,* IX (1947), 325–354.

2146 HODGES, Wiley E. "Pro-Governmentalism in Virginia, 1789–1836: A Pragmatic Liberal Pattern in the Political Heritage." *J Pol,* XXV (1963), 333–360.

2147 JORDAN, Daniel Porter. "Virginia Congressmen, 1801–1825." Doctoral dissertation, University of Virginia, 1970.

2148 KURODA, Tadahisa. "The County Court System of Virginia from the Revolution to the Civil War." Doctoral dissertation, Columbia University, 1970.

2149 MCCONNELL, Grant. "John Taylor and the Democratic Tradition." *W Pol Q,* IV (1951), 17–31.

2150 NELSON, Margaret V. "A Study of Judicial Review in Virginia, 1789–1828." Doctoral dissertation, Columbia University, 1946.

2151 OLIVER, George Brown. "A Constitutional History of Virginia, 1776–1860." Doctoral dissertation, Duke University, 1959.

2152 POLE, J. R. "Representation and Authority in Virginia from the Revolution to Reform." *J S Hist,* XXIV (1958), 16–50.

2153 PORTER, Albert Ogden. *County Government in Virginia: A Legislative History, 1607–1904.* New York, 1947.

2154 ROBERT, Joseph Clarke. *The Road from Monticello: A Study of the Virginia Debate of 1832.* Durham, 1941.

2155 SIMMS, Henry H. *The Rise of the Whigs in Virginia, 1824–1840.* Richmond, 1929.

2156 SUTTON, Robert P. "The Virginia Constitutional Convention of 1829–30: A Profile Analysis of Late Jeffersonian Virginia." Doctoral dissertation, University of Virginia, 1967.

2157 SUTTON, Robert P. "Nostalgia, Pessimism, and Malaise: The Doomed Aristocrat in Late-Jeffersonian Virginia." *Va Mag Hist Biog,* LXXVI (1968), 41–55.

2158 SUTTON, Robert P. "Sectionalism and Social Structure: A Case Study of Jeffersonian Democracy." *Va Mag Hist Biog,* LXXX (1972), 70–84.

2159 UPTON, Anthony F. "The Road to Power in Virginia in the Early Nineteenth Century." *Va Mag Hist Biog,* LXII (1954), 259–280.

2160 WHITFIELD, Theodore M. *Slavery Agitation in Virginia, 1829–1832.* Baltimore, 1930.

2161 WILLIAMS, John Alexander. *West Virginia: A Bicentennial History.* New York, 1976.

E. North Carolina

See also 467, 634, 644–646, 782–786, 805, 838–840, 917, 942, 954, 2745, 2747, 2900, 2992, 3047, 3091, 3114, 3150, 3275, 3903, 3945, 4230, 4417, 4480, 4579

2162 BASSETT, John S. "Suffrage in the State of North Carolina (1776–1861). *Ann Rep Am Hist Assn, 1895.* Washington, D.C., 1896, pp. 271–285.

2163 BOYD, William K. *History of North Carolina: The Federal Period, 1783–1860.* Chicago, 1919.

2164 COUNIHAN, Harold Joseph. "The North Carolina Constitutional Convention of 1835: A Study in Jacksonian Democracy." *N C Hist Rev,* XLVI (1969), 335–364.

2165 COUNIHAN, Harold Joseph. "North Carolina, 1815–1836: State and Local Perspectives on the Age of Jackson." Doctoral dissertation, University of North Carolina at Chapel Hill, 1971.

2166 CROSS, Jerry Lee. "Political Metamorphosis: An Historical Profile of the Democratic Party in North Carolina, 1800–1892." Doctoral dissertation, State University of New York at Binghamton, 1976.

2167 GILPATRICK, Delbert Harold. *Jeffersonian Democracy in North Carolina, 1789–1816.* New York, 1931.

2168 HAMILTON, Joseph G. de R. *Party Politics in North Carolina, 1835–1860.* Chapel Hill, 1916.

2169 HOFFMANN, William S. *Andrew Jackson and North Carolina Politics.* Chapel Hill, 1958.

2170 HOFFMAN, William S. "The Downfall of the Democrats: The Reaction of North Carolina to Jacksonian Land Policy." *N C Hist Rev,* XXXIII (1956), 166–180.

2171 HOFFMAN, William S. "The Election of 1836 in North Carolina." *N C Hist Rev,* XXXII (1955), 31–51.

2172 HOFFMAN, William S. "John Branch and the Origins of the Whig Party in North Carolina." *N C Hist Rev,* XXXV (1958), 299–315.

2173 HOYT, Elizabeth Stone. "Reactions in North Carolina to Jackson's Banking Policy, 1829–1832." *N C Hist Rev,* XXV (1948), 167–178.

2174 JEFFREY, Thomas Edward. "The Second Party System in North Carolina, 1836–1860." Doctoral dissertation, Catholic University, 1976.

2175 JOHNSON, Guion G. *Ante-Bellum North Carolina: A Social History.* Chapel Hill, 1937.

2176 LEFLER, Hugh Talmage, and Albert Ray NEWSOME. *The History of a Southern State: North Carolina.* 3d ed. Chapel Hill, 1973.

2177 MCFARLAND, Daniel M. "Rip Van Winkle: Political Evolution in North Carolina, 1815–1835." Doctoral dissertation, University of Pennsylvania, 1954.

2178 NEWSOME, Albert Ray. *The Presidential Election of 1824 in North Carolina.* Chapel Hill, 1939.

2179 NORTON, C. C. *The Democratic Party in Ante-Bellum North Carolina, 1835–1861.* Chapel Hill, 1930.

2180 PEGG, Herbert D. "The Whig Party in North Carolina, 1834–1861." Doctoral dissertation, University of North Carolina at Chapel Hill, 1933.

2181 POLE, J. R. "Election Statistics in North Carolina to 1861." *J S Hist,* XXIV (1958), 225–228.

2182 THORNTON, Mary Lindsay. *A Bibliography of North Carolina, 1589–1956.* Chapel Hill, 1958.

2183 VINSON, John Chalmers. "Electioneering in North Carolina, 1800–1835." *N C Hist Rev,* XXIX (1952), 189–203.

2184 WAGSTAFF, Henry M. *State Rights and Political Parties in North Carolina, 1776–1861.* Baltimore, 1906.

2185 WALLACE, Carolyn Andrews, "David Lowry Swain, The First Whig Governor of North Carolina. *Studies in Southern History.* Ed. J. Carlyle SITTERSON. Chapel Hill, 1957.

2186 WALTON, Brian G. "Elections to the United States Senate in North Carolina, 1835–1861." *N C Hist Rev,* LIII (1976), 168–192.

2187 WILLIAMS, Max R. "The Foundations of the Whig Party in North Carolina: A Synthesis and a Modest Proposal." *N C Hist Rev,* XLVII (1970), 115–129.

F. South Carolina

See also **483–518, 522, 532, 561, 562, 606, 655–656, 660–662, 666, 728–729, 752–753, 764–765, 772, 852–855, 866–869, 900, 932–934, 1048, 1457–1474, 1668, 1683, 2226, 2649, 2750, 2752, 2917, 2980, 3081, 3375, 3912, 3959, 3975, 4212, 4283, 4388, 4428, 4511**

2188 BANNER, James M., Jr. "The Problem of South Carolina." *The Hofstadter Aegis: A Memorial.* Ed. Stanley ELKINS and Eric MCKITRICK. New York, 1974.

2189 BERGERON, Paul H. "The Nullification Controversy Revisited." *Tenn Hist Q,* XXXV (1976), 263–275.

2190 CONGER, John L. "South Carolina and the Early Tariffs." *Miss Val Hist Rev,* V (1919), 415–433.

2191 COUSSONS, John Stanford. "Thirty Years with Calhoun, Rhett, and the Charleston *Mercury:* A Chapter in South Carolina Politics." Doctoral dissertation, Louisiana State University, 1971.

2192 DENNEY, William H. "South Carolina's Conception of the Union in 1832." *S C Hist Mag,* LXXVIII (1977), 171–183.

2193 GREENBERG, Irwin F. "Justice William Johnson: South Carolina Unionist, 1823–1830." *Pa Hist,* XXXVI (1969), 307–334.

2194 GREENBERG, Kenneth S. "Representation and the Isolation of South Carolina, 1776–1860." *J Am Hist,* LXIV (1977), 723–743.

2195 GREENBERG, Kenneth S. "The Second American Revolution: South Carolina Politics, Society, and Secession, 1776–1860." Doctoral dissertation, University of Wisconsin, Madison, 1976.

2196 HARTZ, Louis. "South Carolina vs. the United States." *America in Crisis.* Ed. Daniel AARON, New York, 1952.

2197 HOWE, Daniel Walker. "A Massachusetts Yankee in Senator Calhoun's Court: Samuel Gilman in South Carolina." *N Eng Q,* XLIV (1971), 197–220.

2198 HUFF, A. V., Jr. "The Eagle and the Vulture: Changing Attitudes toward Nationalism in Fourth of July Orations Delivered in Charleston, 1778–1860." *S Atl Q*, LXXIII (1974), 10–22.

2199 JANUARY, Alan Frank. "The First Nullification: The Negro Seamen Acts Controversy in South Carolina, 1822–1860." Doctoral dissertation, University of Iowa, 1976.

2200 "Letters on the Nullification Movement in South Carolina, 1830–1834." *Am Hist Rev*, VI (1901), 736–765, VII (1901), 92–109.

2201 LANDER, Ernest M., Jr. "The Calhoun-Preston Feud, 1836–1842." *S C Hist Mag*, LIX (1958), 24–37.

2202 NORTON, Diane L. Cook. "A Methodological Study of the South Carolina Political Elite of the 1830's." Doctoral dissertation, University of Pennsylvania, 1972.

2203 RAIFORD, Norman Gasque. "South Carolina and the Second Bank of the United States: Conflict in Political Principle or Economic Interest." *S C Hist Mag*, LXXII (1971), 30–43.

2204 RAIFORD, Norman Gasque. "South Carolina and the Issue of Internal Improvements, 1775–1860." Doctoral dissertation, University of Virginia, 1974.

2205 ROGERS, George C., Jr. "South Carolina Federalists and the Origins of the Nullification Movement." *S C Hist Mag*, LXXI (1970), 17–32.

2206 ROLPH, Earl R. "The Economics of the Nullification Movement." *W Econ J*, XI (1963), 381–393.

2207 SCHAPER, W. A. "Sectionalism and Representation in South Carolina." *Ann Rep Am Hist Assn, 1900*. Vol. I, 237–463.

2208 SMITH, Alfred Glaze, Jr. *Economic Readjustment of an Old Cotton State: South Carolina, 1820–1860*. Columbia, 1958.

2209 VAN DEUSEN, John G. *Economic Bases of Disunion in South Carolina*. New York, 1928.

2210 WALLACE, David D. *The History of South Carolina*. 4 vols. New York, 1934.

2211 WEIR, Robert M. "The South Carolinian as Extremist." *S Atl Q*, LXXIV (1975), 86–103.

2212 WELSH, John R. "Washington Allston: Expatriate South Carolinian." *S C Hist Mag*, LXVII (1966), 84–98.

2213 WILD, Philip F. "South Carolina Politics, 1816–1833." Doctoral dissertation, University of Pennsylvania, 1949.

2214 WRIGHT, Louis B. *South Carolina: A Bicentennial History*. New York, 1976.

G. Georgia

See also **453, 565–570, 619, 640, 744, 955, 982–983, 1015, 1425, 1436, 1715, 2761, 2905, 2959, 3034, 3110, 3281, 3695, 3888, 3900, 3981, 4088, 4174, 4195, 4563, 4748**

2215 AVERITT, Jack N. "The Democratic Party in Georgia, 1824–1837." Doctoral dissertation, University of North Carolina at Chapel Hill, 1956.

2216 BOATRIGHT, Eleanor M. "The Political and Civil Status of Women in Georgia, 1783–1860." *Ga Hist Q*, XXV (1941), 301–324.

2217 COULTER, E. Merton. "Presidential Visits to Georgia during Ante-Bellum Times." *Ga Hist Q*, LV (1971), 329–364.

2218 COULTER, E. Merton. *Georgia: A Short History*. Rev. ed. Chapel Hill, 1960.

2219 COULTER, E. Merton. "The Dispute over George R. Gilmer's Election to Congress in 1828." *Ga Hist Q*, LII (1968), 159–186.

2220 COULTER, E. Merton. "The Nullification Movement in Georgia." *Ga Hist Q*, V (1921), 1–39.

2221 DE BATS, Donald Arthur. "Elites and Masses: Political Structure, Communication and Behavior in Ante-Bellum Georgia." Doctoral dissertation, University of Wisconsin, Madison, 1973.

2222 FAIRCLOTH, Ronald Watson. "The Impact of Andrew Jackson in Georgia Politics, 1828–1840." Doctoral dissertation, University of Georgia, 1971.

2223 GREENE, Helen I. "Politics in Georgia, 1830–1854." Doctoral dissertation, University of Chicago, 1946.

2224 HEATH, Milton Sydney. *Constructive Liberalism: The Role of the State in Economic Development in Georgia to 1860.* Cambridge, Mass., 1954.

2225 LEACH, Richard H. "John MacPherson Berrien: A Re-Evaluation." *Ga Rev*, X (1956), 468–475.

2226 MILLER, W. T. "Nullification in Georgia and South Carolina." *Ga Hist Q*, XIV (1930), 286–302.

2227 MURRAY, Paul. "Economic Sectionalism in Georgia Politics, 1825–1835." *J S Hist*, X (1944), 293–307.

2228 MURRAY, Paul. *The Whig Party in Georgia, 1825–1853.* Chapel Hill, 1948.†

2229 PHILLIPS, Ulrich Bonnell. "Georgia and State Rights." *Ann Rep Am Hist Assn, 1901.* Vol. II, 1–224.

2230 ROWLAND, Arthur Ray. *A Bibliography of the Writings on Georgia History.* Hamden, Conn., 1966.

2231 SAYE, Albert B. *A Constitutional History of Georgia, 1732–1945.* Athens, Ga., 1948.

2232 SKELTON, Lynda Worley. "The State Rights Movement in Georgia, 1825–1850." *Ga Hist Q*, L (1966), 391–412.

2233 WARE, Ethel K. *A Constitutional History of Georgia.* New York, 1947.

H. Florida

See also 519, 1185–1194, 1409, 1432–1435, 1438, 1775, 3056, 3369, 3379, 3795, 4062, 4084, 4325, 4358, 4749

2234 CARTER, Clarence Edwin, ed. *The Territorial Papers of the United States.* Vols. XXII–XXVI. *Florida Territory.* Washington, D.C., 1956–1962.

2235 DOHERTY, Herbert J. "Andrew Jackson's Cronies in Florida Territorial Politics." *Fla Hist Q*, XXXIV (1955), 3–29.

2236 DOHERTY, Herbert J. "Political Factions in Territorial Florida." *Fla Hist Q*, XXVIII (1949), 131–142.

2237 DOVELL, J. E. *Florida, Historic, Dramatic, Contemporary.* 4 vols. New York, 1952.

2238 HARRIS, Michael H. *Florida History: A Bibliography.* Metuchen, N.J., 1972.

2239 MARTIN, Sidney Walter. *Florida during the Territorial Days.* Athens, Georgia, 1944.

2240 STANABACK, Richard J. "Postal Operations in Territorial Florida, 1821–1845." *Fla Hist Q,* LII (1973), 157–174.

2241 STANABACK, Richard J. "Florida's Disrupted Mail Service, 1821–1845." *Fla Hist Q,* LII (1974), 66–73.

2242 THOMPSON, Arthur W. *Jacksonian Democracy on the Florida Frontier.* Gainesville, 1961.†

I. Kentucky

See also **389, 422, 454, 463, 533, 540–551, 571, 572, 725–727, 733–735, 757, 876, 1275, 2810, 2865, 2885, 3098, 3829, 3908, 3927, 3995, 4532, 4548, 4585, 4639, 4729, 4730**

2243 BARTON, Tom K. "Politics and Banking in Republican Kentucky, 1805–1824." Doctoral dissertation, University of Wisconsin, Madison, 1968.

2244 BLAKEY, George T. "Rendezvous with Republicanism: John Pope vs. Henry Clay in 1816." *Ind Mag Hist,* LXII (1966), 233–250.

2245 COFFIN, John A. "The History of the Whig Party in Kentucky." Doctoral dissertation, Indiana University, 1933.

2246 COLEMAN, J. Winston, Jr. *A Bibliography of Kentucky History.* Lexington, 1949.

2247 CONGLETON, Betty Carolyn. "The Whig Campaign of 1840: The Editorial Policy of George D. Prentice [of the Louisville *Journal*]." *Ind Mag Hist,* LXIII (1967), 233–246.

2248 CURRY, Leonard P. "Election Year—Kentucky, 1828." *Reg Ky Hist Soc,* LV (1957), 196–212.

2249 DORMON, John Frederick. "Gabriel Slaughter, 1767–1830, Governor of Kentucky, 1816–1820." *Filson Club Hist Q,* XL (1966), 338–356.

2250 FIELDS, Carl R. "Making Kentucky's Third Constitution, 1830–1850." Doctoral dissertation, University of Kentucky, 1951.

2251 IRELAND, Robert M. *The County Courts in Antebellum Kentucky.* Lexington, 1972.

2252 IRELAND, Robert M. "Aristocrats All: The Politics of County Government in Ante-Bellum Kentucky." *Rev Pol,* XXXII (1970), 365–383.

2253 IRELAND, Robert M. "Nullification in Franklin County: Constitutional Problems of Local Government in Ante-Bellum Kentucky." *Filson Club Hist Q,* XLV (1971), 35–48.

2254 IRELAND, Robert M. "The Place of the Justice of the Peace in the Legislature and Party System of Kentucky, 1792–1850." *Am J Leg Hist,* XIII (1969), 202–222.

2255 HARDIN, Billie J. "Amos Kendall and the 1824 Relief Controversy." *Reg Ky Hist Soc,* XLIV (1966), 196–208.

2256 MARSHALL, Lynn L. "The Genesis of Grass-Roots Democracy in Kentucky." *Mid-Am,* XLVII (1965), 269–287.

2257 MATHIAS, Frank F. "The Relief and Court Struggle: Half-Way House to Populism." *Reg Ky Hist Soc,* LXXI (1973), 154–176.

2258 MATHIAS, Frank F. "Slavery, the Solvent of Kentucky's Politics." *Reg Ky Hist Soc,* LXX (1972), 1–16.

2259 MATHIAS, Frank F. "The Turbulent Years of Kentucky Politics, 1820–1850." *Reg Ky Hist Soc,* LXXII (1974), 309–318.

2260 MATHIAS, Frank F. "The Turbulent Years of Kentucky Politics." Doctoral dissertation, University of Kentucky, 1966.

2261 PADGETT, James A., ed. "Correspondence between Governor Joseph Desha and Amos Kendall, 1831–1835." *Reg Ky Hist Soc,* XXXVIII (1940), 5–24.

2262 ROYALTY, Dale Maurice. "Banking, Politics, and the Commonwealth: Kentucky, 1800–1825." Doctoral dissertation, University of Kentucky, 1972.

2263 STICKLES, Arndt M. *The Critical Court Struggle in Kentucky.* Bloomingdale, 1929.

J. Tennessee

See also **439, 440, 521, 573–581, 598, 600, 654, 683, 685–720, 724, 758, 845, 870–874, 1042–1043, 1426, 1784, 2817, 2835, 2837, 3028, 3748, 3780, 3966, 3973**

2264 ABERNETHY, Thomas Perkins. *From Frontier to Plantation in Tennessee: A Study in Frontier Democracy.* Chapel Hill, 1932.

2265 ABERNETHY, Thomas P. "The Origin of the Whig Party in Tennessee." *Miss Val Hist Rev,* XII (1926), 504–522.

2266 ABERNETHY, Thomas P. "Social Relations and Political Control in the Old Southwest." *Miss Val Hist Rev,* XVI (1930), 529–537.

2267 ALEXANDER, Thomas B. "The Presidential Campaign of 1840 in Tennessee." *Tenn Hist Q,* I (1942), 21–43.

2268 BERGERON, Paul H. "The Jackson Party on Trial: Presidential Politics in Tennessee, 1836–1856." Doctoral dissertation, Vanderbilt University, 1965.

2269 BERGERON, Paul H. "Politics and Patronage in Tennessee during the Adams and Jackson Years." *Prologue,* II (1970), 19–24.

2270 BERGERON, Paul H., ed. "A Tennesseean Blasts Calhoun and Nullification." *Tenn Hist Q,* XXVI (1967), 383–386.

2271 BERGERON, Paul H. "Tennessee's Response to the Nullification Crisis." *J S Hist,* XXXIX (1973), 23–44.

2272 BERGERON, Paul H. "A Test for Jacksonians: Sam Houston on Trial [1832]." *E Tenn Hist Soc Pub,* no. 38 (1966), 16–29.

2273 CASSELL, Robert. "Newton Cannon and the Constitutional Convention of 1834." *Tenn Hist Q,* XV (1956), 224–242.

2274 CASSELL, Robert. "Newton Cannon and State Politics, 1835–1839." *Tenn Hist Q,* XV (1956), 306–332.

2275 DYKEMAN, Wilma. *Tennessee: A Bicentennial History.* New York, 1975.

2276 FOLMSBEE, Stanley J.; Robert E. CORLEW; and Enoch L. MITCHELL. *History of Tennessee.* 4 vols. New York, 1960.

2277 FOLMSBEE, Stanley J. *Sectionalism and Internal Improvements in Tennessee, 1796–1845.* Knoxville, 1939.

2278 FOLSOM, Burton W., II. "The Politics of Elites: Prominence and Party in Davidson County, Tennessee, 1835–1861." *J S Hist,* XXXIX (1973), 359–378.

2279 GOODPASTURE, A. V. "John Bell's Political Revolt, and His Vauxhall Garden Speech." *Tenn Hist Mag,* II (1916), 254–263.

2280 GRESHAM, L. Paul. "Hugh Lawson White as a Tennessee Politician and Banker, 1807–1827." *E Tenn Hist Soc Pub,* no. 18 (1946), 25–46.

2281 LACY, Eric Russell. "Crossroads in the Highlands: First District Congressmen and the Age of Jackson." *E Tenn Hist Soc Pub,* no. 37 (1965), 23–30.

2282 LACY, Eric Russell. *Vanquished Volunteers: East Tennessee Sectionalism from Statehood to Secession.* Johnson City, Tenn., 1965.

2283 LOWREY, Frank Mitchell, III. "Tennessee Voters during the Second Two-Party System, 1836–1860: A Study in Voter Constancy and in Socio-Economic and Demographic Distinctions." Doctoral dissertation, University of Alabama, 1973.

2284 MAIDEN, Leota Driver. "Colonel John Williams." *E Tenn Hist Soc Pub,* no. 30 (1958), 7–46.

2285 MOONEY, Chase C. "The Question of Slavery and the Free Negro in the Tennessee Constitutional Convention of 1834." *J S Hist,* XII (1946), 487–509.

2286 MOORE, Powell. "James K. Polk and Tennessee Politics, 1839–1841." *E Tenn Hist Soc Pub,* no. 9 (1937), 31–52.

2287 MOORE, Powell. "The Revolt Against Jackson in Tennessee, 1835–1836." *J S Hist,* II (1936), 335–359.

2288 MURPHY, James Edward. "Jackson and the Tennessee Opposition." *Tenn Hist Q,* XXX (1971), 50–69.

2289 PARKS, Joseph H. "Felix Grundy and the Depression of 1819 in Tennessee." *E Tenn Hist Soc Pub,* no. 10 (1938), 19–43.

2290 SATTERFIELD, R. Beeler. "The Uncertain Trumpet of the Tennessee Jacksonians." *Tenn Hist Q,* XXVI (1967), 79–96.

2291 SELLERS, Charles G., Jr. "Banking and Politics in Jackson's Tennessee, 1817–1827." *Miss Val Hist Rev,* XLI (1954), 61–84.

2292 SIOUSSAT, St. George L. "Some Phases of Tennessee Politics in the Jackson Period." *Am Hist Rev,* XIV (1908), 51–69.

2293 SMITH, Sam B., and Luke H. BANKER, comps. *Tennessee History: A Bibliography.* Knoxville, 1974.

2294 WALKER, Arda S. "John Henry Eaton, Apostate." *E Tenn Hist Soc Pub,* no. 24 (1952), 26–43.

2295 WALKER, William A., Jr. "Tennessee, 1796–1821." Doctoral dissertation, University of Texas at Austin, 1959.

2296 WALTON, Brian G. "A Matter of Timing: Elections to the United States Senate in Tennessee before the Civil War." *Tenn Hist Q,* XXXI (1972), 129–148.

2297 WALTON, Brian G. "The Second Party System in Tennessee." *E Tenn Hist Soc Pub,* no. 43 (1971), 18–33.

2298 WILLIAMS, Frank B., Jr. "Samuel Hervey Laughlin, Polk's Political Handyman." *Tenn Hist Q,* XXIV (1965), 356–392.

K. Alabama

See also **539, 556–558, 745–746, 775–776, 836–837, 856, 955, 1010–1011, 1408, 1427, 1456, 2751, 3127, 3695, 3772, 3909, 3929, 4218, 4436**

2299 ABERNETHY, Thomas P. *The Formative Period in Alabama, 1815–1828.* Montgomery, 1922.

2300 ALEXANDER, Thomas B.; Kit C. CARTER; Jack R. LISTER; Jerry C. OLDSHUE; and Winfred G. SANDLIN. "Who Were the Alabama Whigs?" *Ala Rev,* XVI (1963), 5–19.

2301 ALEXANDER, Thomas B.; Peggy Duckworth ELMORE; Frank M. LOWREY; and Mary Jane Pickens SKINNER. "The Basis of Alabama's Ante-Bellum Two-Party System: A Case Study in Party Alignment and Voter Response in the Traditional Two-Party System of the United States by Quantitative Analysis Methods." *Ala Rev,* XIX (1966), 243–276.

2302 ATKINS, Leah. "The First Legislative Session: The General Assembly of Alabama, Huntsville, 1819." *Ala Rev,* XXIII (1970), 30–44.

2303 BAILEY, Hugh C. "Alabama Political Leaders and the Missouri Compromise." *Ala Rev,* IX (1956), 120–134.

2304 BAILEY, Hugh C. "John W. Walker and the 'Georgia Machine' in Early Alabama Politics." *Ala Rev,* VIII (1955), 179–195.

2305 BIGHAM, Darrel E. "From the Green Mountains to the Tombigbee: Henry Hitchcock in Territorial Alabama, 1817–1819." *Ala Rev,* XXVI (1973), 209–228.

2306 CARTER, Clarence Edwin, ed. *The Territorial Papers of the United States.* Vol. XVIII. *The Territory of Alabama, 1817–1819.* Washington, D.C., 1952.

2307 GOLDEN, B. G. "The Presidential Election of 1840 in Alabama." *Ala Rev,* XXIII (1970), 128–142.

2308 HOWARD, Milo B., Jr. "The General Ticket [1838–1841]." *Ala Rev,* XIX (1966), 164–174.

2309 JACK, Theodore H. *Sectionalism and Party Politics in Alabama, 1819–1842.* Menasha, Wisconsin, 1919.

2310 JACKSON, Carlton Luther. "A History of the Whig Party in Alabama, 1828–1860." Doctoral dissertation, University of Georgia, 1963.

2311 JONES, Allen W. "Party Nominating Machinery in Ante-Bellum Alabama." *Ala Rev,* XX (1967), 34–44.

2312 JORDAN, Weymouth T. *Ante-Bellum Alabama: Town and Country.* Tallahassee, 1957.

2313 MCCORVEY, Thomas C. "The Mission of Francis Scott Key to Alabama in 1833." *Ala Hist Soc Trans,* IV (1904), 141–165.

2314 MCMILLAN, Malcolm Cook. *Constitutional Development in Alabama, 1798–1901: A Study in Politics, the Negro, and Sectionalism.* Chapel Hill, 1955.

2315 MCWHINEY, Grady. "Were the Whigs a Class Party in Alabama?" *J S Hist,* XXIII (1957), 510–522.

2316 MARTIN, John M. "The Early Career of Gabriel Moore." *Ala Hist Q,* XXIX (1967), 89–105.

2317 MOORE, Albert B. *History of Alabama.* University of Alabama, 1934.

2318 NUERMBERGER, Ruth Ketring. "The 'Royal Party' in Early Alabama Politics." *Ala Rev*, VI (1953), 81–98, 198–212.

2319 OWSLEY, Frank L., Jr. "Francis Scott Key's Mission to Alabama in 1833." *Ala Rev*, XXIII (1970), 181–192.

2320 RACHLEFF, Marshall J. "Racial Fear and Political Factionalism: A Study of the Secession Movement in Alabama, 1819–1861." Doctoral dissertation, University of Massachusetts, 1974.

2321 ROBERTS, Frances C. "Politics and Public Land Disposal in Alabama's Formative Period." *Ala Rev*, XXII (1969), 163–174.

2322 THORNTON, Jonathan Mills, III. *Politics and Power in a Slave Society: Alabama, 1806–1860.* Baton Rouge, 1978.

2323 WALTON, Brian G. "Elections to the United States Senate in Alabama before the Civil War." *Ala Rev*, XVII (1974), 3–38.

2324 WILLIAMS, Clanton W. "Conservatism in Old Montgomery, 1817–1861." *Ala Rev*, X (1957), 96–110.

2325 WILLIAMS, Clanton W. "Early Ante-Bellum Montgomery: A Black-Belt Constituency." *J S Hist*, VII (1941), 495–525.

2326 WILLIAMS, Clanton W. "Presidential Election Returns and Related Data for Ante-Bellum Alabama." *Ala Rev*, I (1948), 279–298.

L. Mississippi

See also **537, 617–618, 864–865, 887, 888, 1012–1014, 1414–1417, 1456, 2836, 3072, 3798, 3800, 3936, 3970, 4196, 4586**

2327 BAILEY, Robert J. "The Gubernatorial Administration of George Poindexter, 1820–1822." *J Miss Hist*, XXV (1973), 227–246.

2328 CARTER, Clarence Edwin, ed. *The Territorial Papers of the United States.* Vols. V–VI. *The Territory of Mississippi.* Washington, D.C., 1937–1938.

2329 CLAIBORNE, J. F. H. *Mississippi as a Province, Territory and State.* Jackson, 1880.

2330 COBB, Edwin L. "Powhatan Ellis of Mississippi." *J Miss Hist*, XXX (1968), 91–110.

2331 DRAKE, Winbourne Magruder. "Constitutional Development in Mississippi, 1817–1865." Doctoral dissertation, University of North Carolina at Chapel Hill, 1954.

2332 DRAKE, Winbourne Magruder. "The Framing of Mississippi's First Constitution." *J Miss Hist*, XXIX (1967), 301–327.

2333 DRAKE, Winbourne Magruder. "The Mississippi Constitutional Convention of 1832." *J S Hist*, XXIII (1957), 354–370.

2334 FIKE, Claude E. "The Administration of Walter Leake (1822–1825)." *J Miss Hist*, XXXII (1970), 103–115.

2335 FIKE, Claude E. "The Gubernatorial Administrations of Governor Gerard Chittocque Brandon, 1825–1832." *J Miss Hist*, XXXV (1973), 247–265.

2336 HEARON, Cleo. "Nullification in Mississippi." *Miss Hist Soc Pub*, XII (1912), 37–71.

2337 JORDAN, Daniel P. "Mississippi's Antebellum Congressmen: A Collective Biography." *J Miss Hist,* XXXVIII (1976), 157–182.

2338 MCLEMORE, Richard A., ed. *A History of Mississippi.* 2 vols. Hattiesburg, 1973.

2339 MILES, Edwin A. "Andrew Jackson and Senator George Poindexter." *J S Hist,* XXIV (1958), 51–66.

2340 MILES, Edwin A. *Jacksonian Democracy in Mississippi.* Chapel Hill, 1960.

2341 ROWLAND, Dunbar. *History of Mississippi: The Heart of the South.* 2 vols. Chicago, 1925.

2342 THOMPSON, R. H. "Suffrage in Mississippi." *Miss Hist Soc Pub,* I (1898), 25–49.

2343 WINSTON, James E. "The Mississippi Whigs and the Tariff, 1834–1844." *Miss Val Hist Rev,* XXII (1936), 505–524.

2344 YOUNG, David Nathaniel. "The Mississippi Whigs." Doctoral dissertation, University of Alabama, 1968.

M. Louisiana

See also **468, 478, 761, 770, 877, 1662, 1890, 2352, 2380, 2892, 2978, 2979, 3133, 3180, 3740, 3821, 3833, 3959, 3982, 4020, 4122, 4144, 4332, 4338, 4375, 4453, 4454, 4647, 4648, 4670, 4739, 4741, 4742**

2345 ADAMS, William H. "The Louisiana Whigs," *La Hist,* XV (1974), 213–228.

2346 ADAMS, William H. *The Whig Party of Louisiana.* Lafayette, La., 1973.

2347 HACKETT, D. L. A. "Slavery, Ethnicity, and Sugar: An Analysis of Voting Behaviour in Louisiana, 1828–1844." *La Stud,* XII (1974), 73–118.

2348 HACKETT, D. L. A. "The Social Structure of Jacksonian Louisiana." *La Stud,* XII (1973), 324–353.

2349 HACKETT, D. L. A. " 'Vote Early! Beware of Fraud!' A Note on Voter Turnout in Presidential and Gubernatorial Elections in Louisiana, 1828–1844." *La Stud,* XIV (1975), 179–188.

2350 HOWARD, Perry H. *Political Trends in Louisiana.* Rev. ed. Baton Rouge, 1971.

2351 NORTON, Leslie M. "A History of the Whig Party in Louisiana." Doctoral dissertation, Louisiana State University, 1940.

2352 TAYLOR, Joe Gray. *Louisiana: A Bicentennial History.* New York, 1976.

2353 TREGLE, Joseph G. "Louisiana and the Tariff, 1816–1846." *La Hist Q,* XXV (1942), 24–148.

2354 TREGLE, Joseph G. "Louisiana in the Age of Jackson: A Study in Ego-Politics." Doctoral dissertation, University of Pennsylvania, 1954.

2355 TREGLE, Joseph G. "The Political Apprenticeship of John Slidell." *J S Hist,* XXVI (1960), 57–70.

2356 TREGLE, Joseph G. "Through Friends and Foes with Alexander Porter." *La Hist,* III (1962), 173–191.

N. Arkansas

See also **1144, 3658, 3659, 3723, 4597**

2357 BAIRD, W. David. "Arkansas's Choctaw Boundary: A Study of Justice Delayed." *Ark Hist Q,* XXVIII (1969), 203–222.

2358 BOYETT, Gene W. "Quantitative Differences between the Arkansas Whig and Democratic Parties, 1836–1850." *Ark Hist Q,* XXXIV (1975), 214–226.

2359 BOYETT, Gene W. "The Whigs of Arkansas, 1836–1856." Doctoral dissertation, Louisiana State University, 1972.

2360 CARTER, Clarence Edwin, ed. *The Territorial Papers of the United States.* Vols. XIX–XXI. *The Territory of Arkansas.* Washington, D.C., 1953–1954.

2361 FERGUSON, John L. "William E. Woodruff and the Territory of Arkansas, 1819–1836." Doctoral dissertation, Tulane University, 1960.

2362 MEEK, Melinda. "The Life of Archibald Yell." *Ark Hist Q,* XXVI (1967), 11–23, 162–184, 226–243, 353–378.

2363 MOORE, Waddy William. "Territorial Arkansas, 1819–1836." Doctoral dissertation, University of North Carolina at Chapel Hill, 1963.

2364 SCROGGS, Jack B. "Arkansas Statehood: A Study in State and National Political Schism." *Ark Hist Q,* XX (1961), 227–244.

2365 STOKES, D. Allen, Jr. "First State Elections in Arkansas." *Ark Hist Q,* XX (1961), 126–148.

2366 STOKES, D. Allen, Jr. "Public Affairs in Arkansas, 1836–1850." Doctoral dissertation, University of Texas at Austin, 1966.

2367 WALTON, Brian G. "Ambrose Hundley Sevier in the United States Senate, 1836–1848." *Ark Hist Q,* XXXII (1973), 25–60.

2368 WALTON, Brian G. "The Second Party System in Arkansas, 1836–1848." *Ark Hist Q,* XXXVIII (1969), 120–155.

2369 WHITE, Lonnie J. "Disturbances on the Arkansas-Texas Border, 1827–1831." *Ark Hist Q,* XIX (1960), 95–110.

2370 WHITE, Lonnie J. *Politics on the Southwestern Frontier: Arkansas Territory, 1819–1836.* Memphis, 1964.

2371 WORLEY, Ted R. "Arkansas and the Money Crisis of 1836–1837." *J S Hist,* XV (1949), 178–191.

2372 WORLEY, Ted R. "The Control of the Real Estate Bank of the State of Arkansas, 1836–1855." *Miss Val Hist Rev,* XXXVII (1950), 403–426.

O. Missouri

See also **424, 425, 438, 443–452, 538, 986–987, 1151, 1153, 2904, 2927, 2982, 3799, 3801, 3818, 3823, 3835, 3979, 4156, 4263, 4338, 4576, 4577**

2373 ABRAMOSKI, Donald J. "The Public Lands in Early Missouri Politics." *Mo Hist Rev,* LIII (1959), 295–305.

2374 ANDERSON, Hattie M. "The Evolution of a Frontier Society in Missouri, 1815–1828." *Mo Hist Rev,* XXXII (1938), 298–326, 458–483, XXXIII (1938), 23–44.

2375 ANDERSON, Hattie M. "Frontier Economic Problems in Missouri, 1815–1828." *Mo Hist Rev,* XXXIV (1939–1940), 38–70, 182–203.

2376 ANDERSON, Hattie M. "The Jackson Men in Missouri in 1828." *Mo Hist Rev,* XXXIV (1940), 301–334.

2377 ANDERSON, Hattie M. "Missouri, 1804–1828: Peopling a Frontier State." *Mo Hist Rev,* XXXI (1937), 150–180.

2378 ATHERTON, Lewis E. "Missouri's Society and Economy in 1821." *Mo Hist Rev, LXV (1971), 450–472.*

2379 BREWER, Paul Walter. "The Rise of the Second Party System: Missouri, 1815–1845." Doctoral dissertation, Washington University, 1974.

2380 CARTER, Clarence Edwin, ed. *The Territorial Papers of the United States.* Vol. XV. *The Territory of Louisiana-Missouri, 1815–1821.* Washington, D.C., 1951.

2381 FOLEY, William E. "The Political Philosophy of David Barton." *Mo Hist Rev,* LVIII (1964), 278–289.

2382 FOLEY, William E. "Territorial Politics in Frontier Missouri, 1804–1820." Doctoral dissertation, University of Missouri, Columbia, 1967.

2383 FORDERHASE, Rudolph Eugene. "Jacksonism in Missouri, from Predilection to Party, 1820–1836." Doctoral dissertation, University of Missouri, Columbia, 1968.

2384 HOUF, Walter R. "Organized Labor in Missouri Politics before the Civil War." *Mo Hist Rev,* LVI (1962), 244–254.

2385 MCCANDLESS, Perry. *A History of Missouri: 1820–1860.* Vol. II. Columbia, 1972.

2386 MARCH, David D. "The Admission of Missouri." *Mo Hist Rev,* LXV (1971), 427–449.

2387 MERING, John Vollmer. *The Whig Party in Missouri.* Columbia, 1967.

2388 MOSS, James Earl. "William Henry Ashley: A Jackson Man with Feet of Clay: Missouri's Special Election of 1831." *Mo Hist Rev,* LXI (1966), 1–20.

2389 NEWHARD, Leota. "The Beginning of the Whig Party in Missouri, 1824–1840." *Mo Hist Rev,* XXV (1931), 254–280.

2390 PRIMM, James Neal. *Economic Policy in the Development of a Western State: Missouri, 1820–1860.* Cambridge, Mass., 1954.

2391 REICHARD, Maximilian. "Urban Politics in Jacksonian St. Louis: Traditional Values in Change and Conflict." *Mo Hist Rev,* LXX (1976), 259–271.

2392 SHALHOPE, Robert E. "Jacksonian Politics in Missouri: A Comment on the McCormick Thesis." *C W Hist,* XV (1969), 210–225.

2393 SHARP, James Roger. "Governor Daniel Dunklin's Jacksonian Democracy in Missouri, 1832–1836." *Mo Hist Rev,* LVI (1962), 217–229.

2394 SHOEMAKER, Floyd C. *Missouri's Struggle for Statehood, 1804–1821.* Jefferson City, 1916.

2395 STEFFEN, Jerome O. "William Clark: A New Perspective on Missouri Territorial Politics, 1813–1820." *Mo Hist Rev,* LXVII (1973), 171–197.

2396 WEINER, Alan S. "John Scott, Thomas Hart Benton, David Barton, and the Presidential Election of 1824: A Case Study in Pressure Politics." *Mo Hist Rev,* LX (1966), 460–494.

2397 WISH, Harvey. "The French of Old Missouri (1804–1821): A Study in Assimilation." *Mid-Am,* XXIII (1941), 167–189.

P. Texas

2398 ADAMS, Ephraim Douglass. *British Interests and Activities in Texas, 1838–1846.* Baltimore, 1910.

2399 ASHFORD, Gerald. "Jacksonian Liberalism and Spanish Law in Early Texas." *S W Hist Q,* LVII (1953), 1–37.

2400 BACARISSE, Charles A. "Baron de Bastrop." *S W Hist Q,* LXI (1955), 319–330.

2401 BACARISSE, Charles A. "The Union of Coahuila and Texas." *S W Hist Q,* LXI (1958), 341–349.

2402 BACARISSE, Charles A. "Why Moses Austin Came to Texas." *S W Soc Sci Q,* XL (1959), 16–27.

2403 BARKER, Eugene C. *Mexico and Texas, 1821–1835.* Dallas, 1928.

2404 BARKER, Nancy N. *The French Legation in Texas.* Austin, 1971.

2405 BARTON, Betty Lynn. "Stephen F. Austin's Arrest and Imprisonment in Mexico, 1834–1835." *Tex,* XI (1973), 1–17.

2406 BARTON, Henry W. "The Problem of Command in the Army of the Republic." *S W Hist Q,* LXII (1959), 299–311.

2407 BINKLEY, William C. "The Activities of the Texas Revolutionary Army after San Jacinto." *J S Hist,* VI (1940), 331–346.

2408 BINKLEY, William C. *The Expansionist Movement in Texas, 1836–1850.* Berkeley, 1925.

2409 BINKLEY, William C. *The Texas Revolution.* Baton Rouge, 1952.

2410 BINKLEY, William C., ed. *Official Correspondence of the Texas Revolution, 1835–1836.* 2 vols. New York, 1936.

2411 CONNOR, Seymour V. *Texas: A History.* New York, 1971.

2412 CONNOR, Seymour V., ed. *The Saga of Texas.* 6 vols. Austin, 1965. Vol II, David M. VIGNESS, *The Revolutionary Decades, 1810–1836.* Vol III, Seymour V. CONNOR, *Adventure in Glory, 1836–1849.*

2413 DE LA PENA, José Enrique. *With Santa Anna in Texas: A Personal Narrative of the Revolution.* Trans. and ed. Carmen PERRY. College Station, Texas, 1975.

2414 DOWNS, Fane. "The History of Mexicans in Texas." Doctoral dissertation, Texas Tech University, 1970.

2415 FAULK, Odie B. *The Last Years of Spanish Texas, 1778–1821.* The Hague, 1964.

2416 FRANTZ, Joe B. *Texas: A Bicentennial History.* New York, 1976.

2417 GAMBLE, Steven Grady. "James Pinckney Henderson in Europe: The Diplomacy of the Republic of Texas, 1837–1840." Doctoral dissertation, Texas Tech University, 1976.

2418 GARRISON, George P., ed. *Diplomatic Correspondence of the Republic of Texas.* 3 vols. Washington, D.C., 1908–1911.

2419 HERSHKOWITZ, Leo. " 'The Land of Promise': Samuel Swartwout and Land Speculation in Texas, 1830–1838." *N Y Hist Soc Q,* XLVIII (1964), 307–325.

2420 HICKSON, Charlotte, A. "The Texas Gazette, 1829–1832." *Tex,* XI (1973), 18–29.

2421 HOGAN, William Ransom. *The Texas Republic: A Social and Economic History.* Norman, 1946.†

2422 HOLMES, Robert E. "The Last Days of the Texas Convention of 1836." *Tex,* VIII (1970), 230–255.

2423 HUTCHINSON, C. A. "Mexican Federalists in New Orleans and the Texas Revolution." *La Hist Q,* XXXIX (1950), 1–47.

2424 HUTTON, Margaret "The Houston-Fisher Controversy." *S W Hist Q,* LXXVI (1972), 38–57.

2425 JENKINS, John H., ed. *The Papers of the Texas Revolution, 1835–1836.* 10 vols. Austin, 1973.

2426 LEE, Rebecca Smith. "The Publication of Austin's Louisville Address." *S W Hist Q,* LXX (1967), 424–442.

2427 LUKES, Edward Albert. "The De Witt Colony of Texas, 1825–1836." Doctoral dissertation, Loyola University of Chicago, 1971.

2428 MCLEAN, Malcolm D., ed. *Papers Concerning Robertson's Colony in Texas.* 3 vols to date. Fort Worth, 1974–.

2429 MILLER, Randall M. "After San Jacinto: Santa Anna's Role in Texas Independence." *E Tex Hist J,* IX (1971), 50–59.

2430 MOORE, R. Woods. "The Role of the Baron de Bastrop in the Anglo-American Settlement of the Spanish Southwest." *La Hist Q,* XXXI (1948), 606–681.

2431 MORTON, Ohland. *Terán and Texas: A Chapter in Texas-Mexican Relations.* Austin, 1948.

2432 NACKMAN, Mark E. *A Nation Within a Nation: The Rise of Texas Nationalism.* Port Washington, N.Y., 1975.

2433 NACKMAN, Mark E. "Anglo-American Migrants to the West: Men of Broken Fortunes?: The Case of Texas, 1821–46." *W Hist Q,* V (1974), 441–455.

2434 NANCE, Joseph Milton. *After San Jacinto: The Texas-Mexican Frontier, 1836–1841.* Austin, 1963.

2435 PRESLEY, James. "Santa Anna in Texas: A Mexican Viewpoint." *S W Hist Q,* LXII (1959), 489–512.

2436 RICHARDSON, Rupert N., et al. *Texas: The Lone Star State.* 3d ed. New York, 1969.

2437 SCHMITZ, Joseph W. *Texas Statecraft, 1836–1845.* San Antonio, 1941.

2438 SHUFFLER, R. Henderson. "The Signing of Texas' Declaration of Independence: Myth and Record." *S W Hist Q,* LXV (1962), 310–332.

2439 SHULER, Sam A. "Stephen F. Austin and the City of Austin: An Anomaly." *S W Hist Q,* LXIX (1960), 265–286.

2440 SIBLEY, Marilyn McAdams. "The Texas-Cherokee War of 1839." *E Tex Hist J,* III (1965), 18–33.

2441 SIEGEL, Stanley. *A Political History of the Texas Republic, 1836–1845.* Austin, 1956.

2442 SIEGEL, Stanley. "Santa Anna Goes to Washington." *Tex,* VII (1969), 126–135.

2443 VIGNESS, David M. "A Texas Expedition into Mexico, 1840." *S W Hist Q,* LXII (1958), 18–28.

2444. WINFREY, Dorman H. "Mirabeau B. Lamar and Texas Nationalism." *S W Hist Q,* LIX (1955), 184–205.

The Northwest

A. Regional Studies

See also **1152, 1154, 1175, 1445, 1913, 3387–3455, 3865, 3868, 3951, 4024, 4215, 4374, 4531, 4750, 4763**

2445 BARNHART, John D. *Valley of Democracy: the Frontier versus the Plantation in the Ohio Valley, 1775–1818.* Bloomington, 1953.†

2446 BULEY, R. Carlyle. *The Old Northwest: Pioneer Period, 1815–1840.* 2 vols. Indianapolis, 1950.

2447 ELKINS, Stanley, and Eric MCKITRICK. "A Meaning for Turner's Frontier: Democracy in the Old Northwest." *Pol Sci Q,* LXIX (1954), 321–353.

2448 KINDIG, Everett William II. "Western Opposition to Jackson's 'Democracy': The Ohio Valley as a Case Study, 1827–1836." Doctoral dissertation, Stanford University, 1975.

2449 KOHLMEIER, Albert L. *The Old Northwest as the Keystone of the Arch of the American Federal Union: A Study in Commerce and Politics.* Bloomington, 1938.

2450 MATHEWS, Lois Kimball, *The Expansion of New England: the Spread of New England Settlement and Institutions to the Mississippi River, 1620–1865.* Boston, 1909.

2451 MCCARTY, Dwight G. *The Territorial Governors of the Old Northwest: A Study in Territorial Administration.* Iowa City, 1910.

2452 MILLER, James M. *The Genesis of Western Culture: the Upper Ohio Valley, 1800–1825.* Columbus, 1938.

2453 OGG, Frederic Austin. *The Old Northwest: A Chronicle of the Ohio Valley and Beyond.* New Haven, 1919.

2454 PATTON, James W., ed. "Letters from North Carolina Emigrants in the Old Northwest, 1830–1834." *Miss Val Hist Rev,* XLVII (1960), 263–277.

2455 POWER, Richard Lyle. *Planting Corn Belt Culture: The Impress of the Upland Southerner and Yankee in the Old Northwest.* Indianapolis, 1953.

2456 SHADE, William G. *Banks or No Banks: the Money Issue in Western Politics, 1832–1865.* Detroit, 1972.

2457 STEVENS, Harry R. *The Middle West.* Am Hist Assn Pamphlets. 2d ed. Washington, D.C., 1965.

2458 TUTEROW, Norman E. "Whigs of the Old Northwest and Texas Annexation, 1836–April, 1844." *Ind Mag Hist,* LXVI (1970), 56–69.

2459 WEBSTER, Homer J. "History of Democratic Party Organization in the Northwest, 1820–1840." *Ohio Arch Hist Q,* XXIV (1915), 1–120.

B. Ohio

See also **421, 635, 658, 659, 778, 1046, 1061, 1969, 3103, 3711, 3786, 3791, 3834, 3848, 3902, 3989, 4161, 4393, 4394, 4441, 4463, 4566**

2460 AIELLO, John Douglas. "Ohio's War upon the Bank of the United States: 1817–1824." Doctoral dissertation, Ohio State University, 1972.

2461 DAVIS, Harold E. "Economic Basis of Ohio Politics, 1820–1840." *Ohio Arch Hist Q,* XLVII (1938), 288–318.

2462 FARRELL, Richard Terrence. "Cincinnati in the Early Jackson Era, 1816–1834: An Economic and Political Study." Doctoral dissertation, Indiana University, 1967.

2463 FOX, Stephen Carey. "The Group Bases of Ohio Political Behavior, 1803–1848." Doctoral dissertation, University of Cincinnati, 1973.

2464 FOX, Stephen C. "Politicians, Issues, and Voter Preference in Jacksonian Ohio: A Critique of an Interpretation." *Ohio Hist,* LXXXVI (1977), 155–170.

2465 MCGRANE, Reginald C. "Orator Bob and the Right of Instruction." *Bull Hist Phil Soc Ohio,* XI (1953), 251–273.

2466 NEUENSCHWANDER, John A. "Senator Thomas Morris: Antagonist of the South." *Cincinnati Hist Soc Bull,* XXXII (1974), 123–139.

2467 RATCLIFFE, Donald J. "The Role of Voters and Issues in Party Formation: Ohio, 1824." *J Am Hist,* LIX (1973), 847–870.

2468 ROSEBOOM, Eugene H. "Ohio in the Presidential Election of 1824." *Ohio Arch Hist Q,* XXVI (1917), 153–225.

2469 SCHEIBER, Harry N. *Ohio Canal Era: A Case Study of Government and the Economy, 1820–1861.* Athens, Ohio, 1969.

2470 STEVENS, Harry R. *The Early Jackson Party in Ohio.* Durham, 1957.

2471 STUCKEY, James Herbert. "The Formation of Leadership Groups in a Frontier Town: Canton, Ohio, 1805–1855." Doctoral dissertation, Case Western Reserve University, 1976.

2472 UTTER, William T. "Saint Tammany in Ohio: A Study in Frontier Politics." *Miss Val Hist Rev,* XV (1928), 321–340.

2473 WITTKE, Carl. ed. *History of the State of Ohio.* 6 vols. Columbus, 1941–1944. Vol. II, William T. UTTER, *The Frontier State, 1803–1825.* Vol. III, Francis P. WEISENBERGER, *The Passing of the Frontier, 1825–1850.*

C. Indiana

See also **615, 979, 2781, 2847, 3032, 3846, 4043, 4588**

2474 CARTER, Clarence Edwin, ed. *The Territorial Papers of the United States.* Vol. VIII. *The Territory of Indiana.* Washington, D.C., 1939.

2475 CARTER, Kit Carson, III. "Indiana Voters during the Second American Party System, 1836–1860: A Study in Social, Economic, and Demographic Distinctions in Voter Constancy." Doctoral dissertation, University of Alabama, 1975.

2476 ESAREY, Logan. *A History of Indiana from Its Exploration to 1850.* Indianapolis, 1915.

2477 ESAREY, Logan. *A History of Indiana . . . to 1922.* 3 vols. Dayton, Ohio, 1923.

2478 ESAREY, Logan. "The Organization of the Jacksonian Party in Indiana." *Miss Val Hist Assn Proc,* VII (1914), 220–243.

2479 ESAREY, Logan. "Pioneer Politics in Indiana." *Ind Mag Hist,* XII (1917), 99–127.

2480 GAHL, Daniel R. "Indiana and the Sectional Pattern, 1828–1842." Doctoral dissertation, Northwestern University, 1963.

2481 GUNDERSON, Robert G. "Log-Cabin Canvass [1840]: Hoosier Style." *Ind Mag Hist,* LIII (1957), 245–256.

2482 HILL, Frederick D., ed. "William Hendricks' Political Circulars to His Constituents: Congressional Period, 1816–1822." *Ind Mag Hist,* LXX (1974), 296–344.

2483 HILL, Frederick D., ed. "William Hendricks' Political Circulars to His Constituents: First Senatorial Term, 1826–1831." *Ind Mag Hist,* LXXI (1975), 124–180.

2484 HILL, Frederick D., ed. "William Hendricks' Political Circulars to His Constituents: Second Senatorial Term, 1831–1837." *Ind Mag Hist,* LXXI (1975), 319–374.

2485 HOWARD, Thomas W. "Indiana Newspapers and the Presidential Election of 1824." *Ind Mag Hist,* LXIII (1967), 177–206.

2486 LEONARD, Adam A. "Personal Politics in Indiana, 1816 to 1840." *Ind Mag Hist,* XIX (1923), 1–56, 132–168, 241–281.

2487 RIKER, Dorothy, and Gayle THORNBROUGH, eds. *Messages and Papers Relating to the Administration of James Brown Ray, Governor of Indiana, 1825–1831.* Indianapolis, 1954.

2488 RIKER, Dorothy, and Gayle THORNBROUGH, comps. "Indiana Election Returns." *Ind Hist Coll,* XL (1960).

D. Illinois

See also **559, 604–605, 762–763, 1422, 3062, 3119, 3121, 3169, 3796, 3871, 3899, 4030, 4146, 4329, 4339, 4344, 4411**

2489 ALCORN, Richard S. "Leadership and Stability in Mid-Nineteenth Century America: A Case Study of an Illinois Town [Paris]." *J Am Hist,* LXI (1974), 685–702.

2490 ALVORD, Clarence W. *The Illinois Country, 1673–1818.* Springfield, 1920.

2491 BOGGESS, Arthur Clinton. *The Settlement of Illinois, 1778–1830.* Chicago, 1908.

2492 BROWN, D. Peter. "The Economic Views of Illinois Democrats, 1836–1861." Doctoral dissertation, Boston University, 1960.

2493 BUCK, Solon J. *Illinois in 1818.* Chicago, 1918.

2494 BUCK, Solon J. "The New England Element in Illinois Politics before 1833." *Miss Val Hist Assn Proc,* VI (1912–1913), 49–61.

2495 CARTER, Clarence Edwin, ed. *The Territorial Papers of the United States.* Vols. XVI–XVII. *The Territory of Illinois.* Washington, D.C., 1948–1950.

2496 DAVIDSON, Martha McNiel. "Southern Illinois and Neighboring States at the Whig Convention of 1840." *Ill Hist Soc Trans, 1914,* 150–159.

2497 DAVIS, Rodney O. "Illinois Legislators and Jacksonian Democracy, 1834–1841." Doctoral dissertation, University of Iowa, 1966.

2498 DAVIS, Rodney O. "Partisanship in Jacksonian State Politics: Party Divisions in the Illinois Legislature, 1834–1841. *Quantification in American History: Theory and Research.* Ed. Robert P. SWIERENGA. New York, 1970.

2499 DOYLE, Don Harrison. "Chaos and Community in a Frontier Town: Jacksonville, Illinois, 1825–1860." Doctoral dissertation, Northwestern University, 1973.

2500 HOWARD, Robert P. *Illinois: A History of the Prairie State.* Grand Rapids, 1972.

2501 KELLY, Edith Packard. "Northern Illinois in the Great Whig Convention of 1840." *Ill Hist Soc Trans 1914,* 137–149.

2502 KRENKEL, John H. "Financing the Illinois Internal Improvements." *Mid-Am,* XXIX (1947), 211–244.

2503 KRENKEL, John H. "Internal Improvements in Illinois Politics, 1837–1842." *Mid-Am,* XXXI (1949), 67–91.

2504 MCNULTY, John W. "Sidney Breese: His Early Career in Law and Politics in Illinois." *Ill S Hist J,* LXI (1968), 164–181.

2505 MCNULTY, John W. "Sidney Breese, the Illinois Circuit Judge, 1835–1841." *Ill S Hist J,* LXII (1969), 170–186.

2506 PEASE, Theodore Calvin. *The Frontier State, 1818–1848.* Springfield, 1918.

2507 PEASE, Theodore C., ed. *Illinois Election Returns.* Springfield, 1923.

2508 POOLEY, William V. *Settlement of Illinois from 1830 to 1850.* Madison, 1908.

2509 ROZETT, John Michael. "The Social Bases of Party Conflict in the Age of Jackson: Individual Voting Behavior in Greene County, Illinois, 1838–1848." Doctoral dissertation, University of Michigan, 1974.

2510 SHANKMAN, Arnold. "Partisan Conflicts, 1839–1841, and the Illinois Constitution." *Ill S Hist J,* LXIII (1970), 337–367.

2511 SPENCER, Donald S. "Edward Coles: Virginia Gentleman in Frontier Politics." *Ill S Hist J,* LXI (1968), 150–163.

2512 SUTTON, Robert M. "Illinois' Year of Decision, 1837." *Ill S Hist J,* LVIII (1965), 34–53.

2513 THOMPSON, Charles Manfred. *The Illinois Whigs before 1846.* Urbana, 1915.

2514 THOMPSON, William R. "Illinois Constitutions." Doctoral dissertation, University of Illinois, Urbana-Champaign, 1960.

E. Michigan

See also **529–531, 768, 826–827, 1652, 1653, 3827, 4004, 4005, 4149, 4191**

2515 BLUME, William Wirt, ed. *Transactions of the Supreme Court of the Territory of Michigan, 1805–1836.* 6 vols. Ann Arbor, 1935–1940.

2516 CARTER, Clarence Edwin, ed. *The Territorial Papers of the United States.* Vols. X-XII. *The Territory of Michigan.* Washington, D.C., 1942–1945.

2517 FORMISANO, Ronald P. "A Case Study of Party Formation: Michigan, 1835." *Mid-Am,* L (1968), 83–107.

2518 FORMISANO, Ronald P. *The Birth of Mass Political Parties: Michigan, 1827–1861.* Princeton, 1971.

2519 FULLER, George N. "Settlement of Michigan Territory." *Miss Val Hist Rev,* II (1915), 25–55.

2520 GILPIN, Alec R. *The Territory of Michigan.* East Lansing, 1970.

2521 HALL, Kermit T. "Andrew Jackson and the Judiciary: The Michigan Territorial Judiciary as a Test Case." *Mich Hist,* LIX (1975), 131–151.

2522 HEYDA, Sister Marie. "Justice A. B. Woodward and Michigan Territory." *Mich Hist,* LI (1967), 43–55.

2523 HEYDA, Sister Marie. "The Urban Dimension and the Midwestern Frontier: A Study of Democracy at Ypsilanti, Michigan, 1825–1858." Doctoral dissertation, University of Michigan, 1966.

2524 SHADE, William G. "Banks and Politics in Michigan, 1835–1845: A Reconsideration." *Mich Hist,* LVII (1973), 28–52.

2525 SHERER, Timothy Frederick. "The Role of the Governor and Judges in Michigan Territory, 1805–1823." Doctoral dissertation, Michigan State University, 1976.

2526 STREETER, Floyd Benjamin. *Political Parties in Michigan, 1837–1860: An Historical Study of Political Issues and Parties in Michigan from the Admission of the State to the Civil War.* Lansing, 1918.

2527 TOBIAS, Clifford I. "Henry D. Gilpin: 'Governor in and over the Territory of Michigan.' " *Mich Hist,* LIX (1975), 153–170.

F. Other Territories

2528 BLOOM, John Porter, ed. *The Territorial Papers of the United States.* Vols. XXVII–XXVIII. *The Territory of Wisconsin.* Washington, D.C., 1969–1973.

2529 BOECK, George A. "An Early Iowa Community: Aspects of Economic, Social and Political Development in Burlington, Iowa, 1833–1866." Doctoral dissertation, University of Iowa, 1961.

2530 GATES, Paul W. "Frontier Land Business in Wisconsin." *Wis Mag Hist* LII (1969), 306–327.

2531 HAEGER, John D. "A Time of Change: Green Bay, 1815–1834." *Wis Mag Hist,* LIV (1971), 285–298.

2532 HARRIS, Faye Ermma. "A Frontier Community: The Economic, Social, and Political Development of Keokuk, Iowa, from 1820 to 1866." Doctoral dissertation, University of Iowa, 1965.

The Far West and Expansion

See also **260, 356, 424, 425, 545, 750, 779–781, 1044–1045, 1097, 1098, 1101, 1182, 1184, 1191, 1774, 1780, 1789, 1800, 1813, 1821, 1824, 1866, 1868, 1877, 1890, 1891, 1910, 2430, 2610, 2965**

2533 AMBLER, Charles H. "The Oregon Country, 1810–1830: A Chapter in Territorial Expansion." *Miss Val Hist Rev,* XXX (1943), 3–24.

2534 BAKER, T. Lindsay. "The Survey of the Santa Fe Trail, 1825–1827." *Great Plains J,* XIV (1975), 211–234.

2535 BARTLETT, Richard A. *The New Country: A Social History of the American Frontier, 1776–1890.* New York, 1974.†

2536 BILLINGTON, Ray A. *The Far Western Frontier, 1830–1860.* New York, 1956.†

2537 BILLINGTON, Ray A. *The Frontier Thesis: Valid Interpretation of American History?* New York, 1966.†

2538 BILLINGTON, Ray A. *Westward Expansion: History of the American Frontier.* 4th ed. New York, 1974.

2538A BILLINGTON, Ray A. *The American Frontier Thesis: Attack and Defense.* Am Hist Assn Phamplets. Washington, D.C., 1971.†

2539 CARUTHERS, J. Wade. "The Seaborne Frontier to California, 1796–1850." *Am Neptune,* XXXIX (1969), 81–101.

2540 CHITTENDEN, Hiram M. *The American Fur Trade of the Far West.* 3 vols. New York, 1902.

2541 COUES, Elliott, ed. *The Journal of Jacob Fowler.* Lincoln, 1970.

2542 DONDORE, Dorothy A. *The Prairie and the Making of Middle America.* Cedar Rapids, 1926.

2543 DRURY, Clifford Merrill, ed. *The Diaries and Letters of Henry H. Spalding and Asa Bowen Smith Relating to the Nez Perce Mission, 1838–1842.* Glendale, 1958.

2544 EATON, W. Clement. "Nathaniel Wyeth's Oregon Expeditions." *Pac Hist Rev,* IV (1935), 101–113.

2545 FERRIS, W. A. *Life in the Rocky Mountains: A Diary of Wanderings on the Sources of the Rivers Missouri, Columbia, and Colorado from February, 1830, to November, 1835.* Ed. Paul C. PHILLIPS. Denver, 1940.

2546 FOREMAN, Grant. *Advancing the Frontier, 1830–1860.* Norman, 1933.

2547 FOREMAN, Grant, ed. *A Traveler in Indian Territory: the Journal of Ethan Allen Hitchcock, late Major-General in the United States Army.* Cedar Rapids, 1930.

2548 FRENCH, J. L., ed. *The Pioneer West: Narratives of the Westward March of Empire.* Boston, 1923.

2549 FRITZ, Henry E. "Nationalistic Response to Frontier Expansion." *Mid-Am,* LX (1969), 227–243.

2550 GIBSON, James R. "Russian America in 1821." *Ore Hist Q,* LXXVII (1976), 174–188.

2551 GILBERT, Edmund W. *The Exploration of Western America, 1800–1850: An Historical Geography.* Cambridge, Mass., 1933.

2552 GOETZMANN, William H. *Army Exploration in the American West, 1803–1863.* New Haven, 1959.

2553 GOETZMANN, William H. *Exploration and Empire: The Explorer and the Scientist in the Winning of the American West.* New York, 1966.

2554 GOODWIN, Cardinal. "A Larger View of the Yellowstone Expedition, 1819–1820." *Miss Val Hist Rev,* IV (1917), 299–313.

2555 GOODWIN, Cardinal. *The Trans-Mississippi West (1803–1853): A History of Its Acquisition and Settlement.* New York, 1922.

2556 GREGG, Josiah. *Commerce of the Prairies, or, The Journal of a Santa Fe Trader (1831–39).* 2 vols. New York, 1844.

2557 HANSEN, William A. "Thomas Hart Benton and the Oregon Question." *Mo Hist Rev,* LXIII (1969), 489–497.

2558 HAWGOOD, John A. *America's Western Frontiers: The Exploration and Settlement of the Trans-Mississippi West.* New York, 1967.

2559 HINE, Robert V. *The American West: An Interpretative History.* Boston, 1973.

2560 HOCKETT, Homer C. "The Influence of the West on the Rise and Fall of Political Parties." *Miss Val Hist Rev,* IV (1918), 459–469.

2561 HOCKETT, Homer C., ed. *Western Influence on Political Parties to 1825: An Essay in Historical Interpretation.* Columbus, 1917.

2562 HOLBROOK, Stewart H. *The Yankee Exodus: An Account of Migration from New England.* New York, 1950.†

2563 HULBERT, Archer Butler, ed. *The Call of the Columbia: Iron Men and Saints Take the Oregon Trail.* Denver, 1934.

2564 HULBERT, Archer Butler, ed. *Where Rolls the Oregon: Prophet and Pessimist Look Northwest.* Denver, 1933.

2565 HULBERT, Archer Butler, and Dorothy Printup HULBERT, eds. *The Oregon Crusade: Across Land and Sea to Oregon.* Denver, 1935.

2566 HUSBAND, Michael B. "Senator Lewis F. Linn and the Oregon Question." *Mo Hist Rev,* LXVI (1971), 1–19.

2567 JACOBS, Melvin Clay. *Winning Oregon: A Study of an Expansionist Movement.* Caldwell, 1938.

2568 JENSEN, Richard E., ed. "A Description of the Fur Trade in 1831 by John Dougherty." *Neb Hist,* LVI (1975), 108–120.

2569 KANE, Murray. "Some Considerations on the Safety Valve Doctrine." *Miss Val Hist Rev,* XXIII (1936), 169–188.

2570 KROEBER, Clifton B., ed. "The Route of James O. Pattie on the Colorado in 1826: A Reappraisal by A. L. Kroeber." *Ariz W,* VI (1964), 119–136.

2571 LEWIS, William S., and Paul C. PHILLIPS, eds. *The Journal of John Work, a Chief-Trader of the Hudson's Bay Company, during his Expedition from Vancouver to the Flatheads and Blackfeet of the Pacific Northwest.* Cleveland, 1923.

2572 LINDLEY, Harlow. "Western Travel, 1800–1820." *Miss Val Hist Rev,* VI (1919), 167–191.

2573 LOEWENBERG, Robert J. " 'Not . . . by feeble means': Daniel Lee's Plan to Save Oregon." *Ore Hist Q,* LXXIV (1973), 71–78.

2574 LUCKINGHAM, Bradford F. "[Henry R.] Schoolcraft's Promotion of Scientific Interest in the Frontier, 1818–1820: A Note." *Mid-Am,* LXVII (1965), 139–144.

2575 MATTES, Merrill, J. "Behind the Legend of Colter's Hell: The Early Exploration of Yellowstone National Park." *Miss Val Hist Rev,* XXXVI (1949), 251–282.

2576 MERK, Frederick. "Snake Country Expedition, 1824–25: An Episode of Fur Trade and Empire." *Miss Val Hist Rev,* XXI (1934), 49–62.

2577 MITCHELL, Virgil L. "California and the Transformation of the Mountain Men." *J W,* IX (1970), 413–426.

2578 MORRISON, Raymond Kenneth. "Luis Antonio Arguello: First Mexican Governor of California." *J W,* II (1963), 193–204, 347–361.

2579 NICHOLS, Roger Louis. *Missouri Expedition, 1818–1820: The Journal of Surgeon John Gale With Related Documents.* Norman, 1969.

2580 NUNIS, Doyce B., Jr. "The Fur Men: Key to Westward Expansion, 1822–1830." *Hist,* XXIII (1961), 167–190.

2581 OLIPHANT, J. Orin. "George Simpson and Oregon Missions." *Pac Hist Rev,* VI (1937), 213–248.

2582 PAXSON, Frederick L. *History of the American Frontier, 1763–1893.* Boston, 1924.

2583 PELZER, Louis, ed. "Captain Ford's Journal of an Expedition to the Rocky Mountains." *Miss Val Hist Rev,* XII (1926), 550–579.

2584 PHILBRICK, Francis S. *The Rise of the West, 1754–1830.* New York, 1965.

2585 PEDERSEN, Lyman C., Jr. "Early Penetration of the Uinta Basin." *J W,* XI (1972), 596–615.

2586 POWELL, Fred Wilbur, ed. *Hall J. Kelley on Oregon.* Princeton, 1932.

2587 PRUCHA, Francis Paul, ed. *Army Life on the Western Frontier: Selections from the Official Reports Made between 1826 and 1845 by Colonel George Croghan.* Norman, 1958.

2588 QUAIFE, M. M., ed. "Letters of John Ball, 1832–1833." *Miss Val Hist Rev,* V (1919), 450–468.

2589 ROLLINS, Philip Ashton, ed. *The Discovery of the Oregon Trail: Robert Stuart's Narratives.* New York, 1935.

2590 ROOSEVELT, Theodore. *The Winning of the West.* 6 vols. New York, 1889–1896.

2591 SAYLES, Stephen. "Thomas Hart Benton and the Santa Fe Trail." *Mo Hist Rev,* LXIX (1974), 1–22.

2592 SHAFER, Joseph. "Was the West a Safety Valve for Labor?" *Miss Val Hist Rev,* XXIV (1937), 299–314.

2593 SHUR, Leonid A., and James R. GIBSON. "Russian Travel Notes and Journals as Sources for the History of California, 1800–1850." *Calif Hist Q,* LII (1973), 37–63.

2594 SIMPSON, George. *Fur Trade and Empire: George Simpson's Journal . . . 1824–1825.* Cambridge, Mass., 1932.

2595 SKINNER, Constance L. *Adventurers of Oregon: A Chronicle of the Fur Trade.* New Haven, 1920.

2596 SLOTKIN, Richard. *Regeneration through Violence: The Mythology of the American Frontier, 1600–1860.* Middletown, Conn., 1973.†

2597 SMITH, Alson J. *Men Against the Mountains: Jedediah Smith and the South West Expedition of 1826–1829.* New York, 1965.

2598 SMITH, Henry Nash. *Virgin Land: The American West as Symbol and Myth.* Cambridge, Mass., 1950.†

2599 SMITH, Robert E. "The Wyandot Exploring Expedition of 1839." *Chron Okla,* LV (1977), 282–292.

2600 STUART, Robert. *On the Oregon Trail: Robert Stuart's Journey of Discovery.* Ed. Kenneth A. SPAULDING. Norman, 1953.

2601 TAYLOR, George R. *The Turner Thesis Concerning the Role of the Frontier in American History.* 3d ed. Boston, 1972.†

2602 TURNER, Frederick J. *The Frontier in American History.* New York, 1920.

2603 VAIL, R. W. G. *The Voice of the Old Frontier.* Philadelphia, 1949.

2604 VAN EVERY, Dale. *The Final Challenge: The American Frontier, 1804–1845.* New York, 1964.

2605 WEBER, David J. "Mexico and the Mountain Men." *J W,* VII (1969), 369–378.

2606 WINKS, Robin W. *The Myth of the American Frontier: Its Relevance to America, Canada and Australia.* Leicester, England, 1971.†

2607 WINTHER, Oscar Osburn. *The Old Oregon Country, A History of Frontier Trade, Transportation and Travel.* Stanford, 1950.

2608 WRIGHT, Benjamin, Jr. "American Democracy and the Frontier." *Yale Rev,* XX (1931), 349–365.

2609 WYMAN, Walker D., and Clifton B. KROEBER, eds. *The Frontier in Perspective.* Madison, 1957.†

VII. Intellectual and Social History

1. Intellectual

See also **121, 122, 347, 469–473, 580, 591, 710, 752, 753, 759, 760, 984, 985, 1957, 2019, 2081, 2085, 2086, 2087, 2088, 2096, 2103, 2198, 2598, 3022–3154, 3170, 3201, 3224**

2610 ALFORD, Terry Lee. "Western Desert Images in American Thought, 1800–1860." Doctoral dissertation, Mississippi State University, 1970.

2611 ANDERSON, Paul Russell, and Max Harold FISCH. *Philosophy in America from the Puritans to James.* New York, 1939.

2612 BARKER, Charles A. *American Convictions: Cycles of Public Thought, 1600–1850.* Philadelphia, 1970.

2613 BASSETT, John S. *The Middle Group of American Historians.* New York, 1917.

2614 BOAS, George, ed. *Romanticism in America.* Baltimore, 1940.

2615 BOLLER, Paul F., Jr. *American Transcendentalism, 1830–1860: An Intellectual Inquiry.* New York, 1974.†

2616 BROOKS, Van Wyck. *The Flowering of New England.* Boston, 1936.

2617 BURNS, Rex S. *Success in America: The Yeoman Dream and the Industrial Revolution.* Amherst, Mass., 1976.

2618 CALLCOTT, George H. *History in the United States, 1800–1860: Its Practice and Purpose.* Baltimore, 1970.

2619 CASH, Wilbur J. *The Mind of the South.* New York, 1941.†

2620 CURTI, Merle E. "The Great Mr. Locke: America's Philosopher, 1783–1861." *Hunt Lib Bull,* no. 11 (1937), 107–151.

2621 CURTI, Merle E. *The Growth of American Thought.* New York, 1943.

2622 CURTI, Merle E. *The Roots of American Loyalty.* New York, 1946.†

2623 DAVIS, David Brion. "Some Themes of Counter-Subversion: An Analysis of Anti-Masonic, Anti-Catholic, and Anti-Mormon Literature." *Miss Val Hist Rev,* XLVII (1960), 205–224.

2624 DAVIS, Richard Beale. *Literature and Society in Early Virginia, 1608–1840.* Baton Rouge, 1973.

2625 DAVIS, Richard Beale. *Intellectual Life in Jefferson's Virginia, 1790–1830.* Chapel Hill, 1964.

2626 DODD, William E. "The Social Philosophy of the Old South." *Am J Soc,* XXIII (1918), 735–746.

2627 EATON, Clement. *The Mind of the Old South.* Baton Rouge, 1964.†

2628 EDMONDS, Anthony Owens. "The Image of the Southern Plantation: A Comparison of Recent Historical and Fictional Accounts." Doctoral dissertation, Vanderbilt University, 1970.

2629 EKIRCH, Arthur A., Jr. *The Idea of Progress in America, 1815–1860.* New York, 1944.

2630 FLOAN, Howard R. *The South in Northern Eyes, 1831 to 1861.* Austin, 1958.

2631 FRIEDMAN, Lawrence J. *Inventors of the Promised Land.* New York, 1975.

2632 GABRIEL, Ralph Henry. *The Course of American Democratic Thought: An Intellectual History since 1815.* 2d ed. New York, 1956.

2633 GORDON, G. S. *Anglo-American Literary Relations.* London, 1942.

2634 HANSEN, Klaus J. "The Millennium, the West, and Race in the Antebellum American Mind." *W Hist Q,* III (1972), 373–390.

2635 HOFSTADTER, Richard. *Anti-Intellectualism in American Life.* New York, 1963.†

2636 HOWE, Daniel Walker. *The Unitarian Conscience: Harvard Moral Philosophy, 1805–1861.* Cambridge, Mass., 1970.

2637 HULL, Gary Wayne. "The Prospect for Man in Early American Economic Thought, 1800–1850." Doctoral dissertation, University of Maryland, 1969.

2638 JONES, Howard Mumford. *America and French Culture, 1750–1848.* Chapel Hill, 1927.

2639 JONES, Howard Mumford. *O Strange New World; American Culture: The Formative Years.* New York, 1964.†

2640 JONES, Howard Mumford. *Revolution and Romanticism.* Cambridge, Mass., 1974.

2641 KASSON, John F. *Civilizing the Machine: Technology and Republican Values in American Thought, 1776–1900.* New York, 1974.†

2642 KETCHAM, Ralph. *From Colony to Country: The Revolution in American Thought, 1750–1820.* New York, 1974.

2643 KHER, Inder Nath. "Transcendentalist Aesthetics and Patterns of Consciousness." *Can Rev Am Stud,* VI (1975), 241–309.

2644 KOHN, Hans. *American Nationalism: An Interpretative Essay.* New York, 1957.

2645 KOSTER, Donald N. *Transcendentalism in America.* Boston, 1975.

2646 KUPERSMITH, Abraham. "Montesquieu's Influence on the Quest for the American Character: 1770–1845." Doctoral dissertation, New York University, 1974.

2647 LEMELIN, Robert. *Pathway to the National Character: 1830–1861.* Port Washington, N.Y., 1974.

2648 LONG, Orie William. *Literary Pioneers: Early American Explorers of European Culture.* Cambridge, Mass., 1935.

2649 LONGTON, William Henry. "Some Aspects of Intellectual Activity in Ante-Bellum South Carolina, 1830–1860: An Introductory Study." Doctoral dissertation, University of North Carolina, 1969.

2650 LOVELAND, Anne C. *Emblem of Liberty: The Image of Lafayette in the American Mind.* Baton Rouge, 1971.

2651 LUEDTKE, Luther S. "First Notices of Emerson in England and Germany, 1835–1842." *Notes Qu,* XXII (1975), 106–108.

2652 MARX, Leo. *The Machine in the Garden: Technology and the Pastoral Idea in America.* New York, 1964.†

2653 MCLENNAN, William Gordon Lawson. "Transcendentalism, 1832–1862." Doctoral dissertation, University of Toronto, 1973.

2654 MCWILLIAMS, John P. *Political Justice in a Republic: James Fenimore Cooper's America.* Berkeley 1972.

2655 Meese, Elizabeth A. "Transcendentalism: The Metaphysics of the Theme." *Am Lit,* XLVII (1975), 1–20.

2656 MEYER, Donald H. *The Instructed Conscience: The Shaping of the American National Ethic.* Philadelphia, 1972.

2657 MILES, Edwin A. "The Old South and the Classical World." *N C Hist Rev,* XLVII (1971), 258–275.

2658 MILES, Edwin A. "The Young American Nation and the Classical World." *J Hist Ideas,* XXXV (1974), 259–274.

2659 MILLER, Perry. *The Life of the Mind in America: From the Revolution to the Civil War.* New York, 1965.†

2660 O'BRIEN, Kenneth Paul. "The Savage and the Child in Historical Perspective: Images of Blacks in Southern White Thought, 1830–1915." Doctoral dissertation, Northwestern University, 1974.

2661 OSTERWEIS, Rollin G. *Romanticism and Nationalism in the Old South.* New Haven, 1949.

2662 PARRINGTON, Vernon L. *The Romantic Revolution.* New York, 1927.†

2663 POST, Albert. *Popular Free Thought in America, 1825–1830.* New York, 1943.

2664 RITCHESON, Charles R. "The British Role in American Life, 1800–1850." *Hist Teacher,* VII (1974), 574–596.

2665 ROBINSON, Cecil. "Flag of Illusion: The Texas Revolution Viewed as a Conflict of Culture." *Am W,* V (1968), 10–17.

2666 RONDA, Bruce Allen. "The Transcendental Child Images and Concepts of the Child in American Transcendentalism." Doctoral dissertation, Yale University, 1975.

2667 SAUM, Lewis O. " 'Providence' in the Popular Mind of Pre-Civil War America." *Ind Mag Hist,* LXXII (1976), 315–346.

2668 SCHLOSSMAN, Steven L. "The 'Culture of Poverty' in Ante-Bellum Social Thought." *Soc Sci,* XXXVIII (1974), 150–166.

2669 SCHWARZ, Robert S. "The Image of the American Revolution, 1783–1826." Doctoral dissertation, University of Chicago, 1975.

2670 SHAFER, Boyd C. *Nationalism: Myth and Reality.* New York, 1955.†

2671 SMITH, Duane E. "Romanticism in America: The Transcendentalists." *Rev Pol,* XXXV (1973), 302–325.

2672 SOMKIN, Fred. *Unquiet Eagle: Memory and Desire in the Idea of American Freedom, 1815–1860.* Ithaca, N.Y., 1967.

2673 SWEET, Leonard I. "Black Images of America, 1784–1920." Doctoral dissertation, University of Rochester, 1974.

2674 THORP, Earl E. *Eros and Freedom in Southern Life and Thought.* Durham, N.C., 1967.

2675 TOWNSEND, Harvey G. *Philosophical Ideas in the United States.* New York, 1934.

2676 VESEY, Laurence, ed. *The Perfectionists: Radical Social Thought in the North, 1815–1860.* New York, 1973.

2677 WARD, Robert S. "The American System in Literature." *N Eng Q,* XXXIX (1965), 363–374.

2678 WEDDINGTON, Carolyn Sue. "The Image of the American Revolution in the United States, 1815–1860." Doctoral dissertation, Louisiana State University, 1972.

2679 WELTER, Rush. *The Mind of America, 1820–1860.* New York, 1975.†

2680 WELTER, Rush. "The Frontier as Image of American Society: Conservative Attitudes before the Civil War." *Miss Val Hist Rev,* XLVI (1960), 593–614.

2681 WHICHER, George F., and Gail KENNEDY, eds. *The Transcendalist Revolt.* Boston, 1968.

2682 WHITE, Elizabeth Brett. *American Opinion of France from Lafayette to Poincare.* New York, 1927.

2683 WILSON, Major L. "The Search for Order: The Progress of the Idea of Progress in Two Conservative Thinkers of the National Period." *La Stud,* XI (1972), 295–314.

2684 WILSON, Major L. " 'Paradox Lost: Order and Progress in Evangelical Thought of Mid-Nineteenth Century America." *Church Hist,* XLIV (1975), 352–366.

2685 WILSON, Major L. "An Analysis of the Ideas of Liberty and Union as Used by Members of Congress and the Presidents from 1828 to 1861." See **1685.**

2686 WISH, Harvey. "Aristotle, Plato, and the Mason-Dixon Line." *J Hist Ideas,* X (1949), 254–266.

2687 WRIGHT, Louis B. *Culture on the Moving Frontier.* Bloomington, 1955.

2. Social

See also 367, 1310, 1341, 1579, 1583, 1670, 1806, 1930, 1946, 1953, 1979, 1985, 1987, 2002, 2006, 2089, 2127, 2158, 2195, 2202, 2221, 2266, 2278, 2348, 2374, 2378, 2421, 2471, 2489, 2535, 2668, 2676, 2680, 2754–2848, 2887, 2913, 2992, 2999, 3055, 3101, 3131, 3132, 3155–3203, 4270, 4687, 4770, 4771, 4783

2688 BENDER, Thomas. "The 'Rural' Cemetery Movement: Urban Travail and the Appeal of Nature." *N Eng Q,* XLVII (1974), 196–211.

2689 BERTELSON, David. *The Lazy South.* New York, 1967.

2690 BLUMENTHAL, Henry. *American and French Culture, 1800–1900: Interchange in Art, Science, Literature, and Society.* Baton Rouge, 1975.

2691 BORDIN, Ruth B. "Hofstadter and the Decline of the Gentleman: Fact or Fancy." *Mid-Am,* XLVIII (1966), 119–125.

2692 BOWERS, David F., ed. *Foreign Influences in American Life: Essays and Critical Bibliographies.* Princeton, 1944.

2693 BRANCH, E. Douglas. *The Sentimental Years, 1836–1860.* New York, 1934.

2694 BROWN, Richard Maxwell. *Strain of Violence: Historical Studies of American Violence and Vigilantism.* New York, 1975.†

2695 BUCK, Paul H. "The Poor Whites of the Ante-Bellum South." *Am Hist Rev,* XXXI (1925), 41–54.

2696 BUTLER, Pierce. *The Unhurried Years: Memories of the Old Natchez Region.* Baton Rouge, 1948.

2697 CARDWELL, Guy A. "The Duel in the Old South: Crux of a Concept." *S Atl Q,* LXVI (1967), 40–69.

2698 CUTLER, James E. *Lynch-Law: An Investigation into the History of Lynching in the United States.* New York, 1905.

2699 DICK, Everett. *The Dixie Frontier: A Social History of the Southern Frontier from the First Transmontane Beginnings to the Civil War.* New York, 1948.

2700 DODD, William E. *The Cotton Kingdom: A Chronicle of the Old South.* New Haven, 1919.

2701 ELLIS, David M. *Landlords and Farmers in the Hudson-Mohawk Region, 1790– 1850.* Ithaca, 1946.

2702 ELLSWORTH, Lucius F., ed. *The Americanization of the Gulf Coast, 1803–1850.* Pensacola, 1972.

2703 EVANS, Meryle R. "Knickerbocker Hotels and Restaurants, 1800–1850." *N Y Hist Soc Q,* XXXVI (1952), 377–408.

2704 FARNAM, H. W. *Chapters in the History of Social Legislation in the United States to 1860.* Washington, D.C., 1938.

2705 FRENCH, Stanley. "The Cemetery as Cultural Institution: The Establishment of Mount Auburn and the 'Rural Cemetery' Movement." *Am Q,* XXVI (1974), 37–59.

2706 FRISCH, John Richard. "Youth Culture in America, 1790–1865." Doctoral dissertation, University of Missouri, Columbia, 1970.

2707 GAINES, Francis P. *The Southern Plantation: A Study in the Development and the Accuracy of a Tradition.* New York, 1924.

2708 GREENBERG, Michael S. "Gentlemen Slaveholders: The Social Outlook of the Virginia Planter Class." Doctoral dissertation, Rutgers University, 1972.

2709 GRIMSTED, David. "Rioting in Its Jacksonian Setting." *Am Hist Rev,* LXXVII (1972), 361–397.

2710 GROB, Gerald N., comp. *American Social History before 1860.* Goldentree Bibliographies in American History. Arlington Heights, 1970.†

2711 GROVER, Janice Zita. "Luxury and Leisure in Early Nineteenth-Century America: Saratoga Springs and the Rise of the Resort." Doctoral dissertation, University of California, Davis, 1973.

2712 HAMMETT, Theodore M. "Two Mobs of Jacksonian Boston: Ideology and Interest." *J Am Hist,* LXII (1976), 845–868.

2713 HAREVEN, Tamara K., ed. *Anonymous Americans: Explorations in Nineteenth-Century Social History.* Englewood Cliffs, N.J., 1971.†

2714 HILLIARD, Sam. "Hog Meat and Cornpone: Food Habits in the Ante-bellum South." *Am Phil Soc Proc,* CXIII (1969), 1–13.

2715 HORWITZ, Richard P. "Architecture and Culture: The Meaning of the Lowell Boarding House." *Am Q,* XXV (1973), 64–82.

2716 HUNT, Alfred Nathaniel. "The Influence of Haiti on the Antebellum South, 1791–1865." Doctoral dissertation, University of Texas, Austin, 1975.

2717 JAHER, Frederic Cople. "Nineteenth-Century Elites in Boston and New York." *J Soc Hist,* VI (1972), 32–77.

2718 KING, Doris E. "The First-Class Hotel and the Age of the Common Man." *J S Hist,* XXIII (1957), 173–188.

2719 KNOWLES, Jane Boyle. "Luxury Hotels in American Cities, 1810–1860." Doctoral dissertation, University of Pennsylvania, 1972.

2720 KROUT, John Allen, and Dixon Ryan FOX. *The Completion of Independence, 1790–1830.* New York, 1944.†

2721 KROUT, John A. *Annals of American Sport.* New Haven, 1929.

2722 LAURIE, Bruce. "'Nothing on Impulse': Life Styles of Philadelphia Artisans, 1820–1850." *Labor Hist,* XV (1974), 337–366.

2723 LEONARD, Ira M., and Robert D. PARMET. *American Nativism, 1830–1860.* New York, 1971.†

2724 LIPSON, Dorothy Ann. *Freemasonry in Federalist Connecticut, 1789–1835.* Princeton, 1978.

2725 MACLEOD, Anne Scott. *A Moral Tale: Children's Fiction and American Culture, 1820–1860.* Hamden, Conn., 1975.

2726 MOHL, Raymond A. *Poverty in New York, 1783–1825.* New York, 1971.

2727 MOORE, Arthur K. *The Frontier Mind: A Cultural Analysis of the Kentucky Frontiersman.* Lexington, Ky., 1957.

2728 MOORE, Waddy W. "Some Aspects of Crime and Punishment in Early Arkansas History." *Ark Hist Q,* XXIII (1964), 50–64.

2729 MORAGNÉ, Mary E. *The Neglected Thread: A Journal from the Calhoun Community, 1836–1842.* Columbia, S.C., 1951.

2730 NYE, Russel Blaine. *The Cultural Life of the New Nation, 1776–1830.* New York, 1961.†

2731 NYE, Russel Blaine. *Society and Culture in America, 1830–1860.* New York, 1974.†

2732 PAGE, Thomas N. *Social Life in Old Virginia before the War.* New York, 1897.

2733 PENDLETON, Eldridge Honaker. "The New York Anti-Rent Controversy, 1830–1860." Doctoral dissertation, University of Virginia, 1974.

2734 PERSONS, Stow. *The Decline of American Gentility.* New York, 1973.†

2735 PESSEN, Edward. "A Social and Economic Portrait of Jacksonian Brooklyn: Inequality, Social Immobility, and Class Distinction in the Nation's Seventh City." *N Y Hist Soc Q,* LV (1971), 318–353.

2736 PESSEN, Edward. "Philip Hone's Set: The Social World of the New York City Elite in the 'Age of Egalitarianism'." *N Y Hist Soc Q,* LVI (1972), 285–308.

2737 PESSEN, Edward. "The Marital Theory and Practice of the Antebellum Urban Elite." *N Y Hist,* LIII (1972), 389–410.

2738 PESSEN, Edward. *Riches, Class, and Power Before the Civil War.* Lexington, Mass., 1973.

2739 POSEY, Walter B. "The Public Manners of Ante-Bellum Southerners." *J Miss Hist,* XIX (1957), 219–233.

2740 PRIES, Nancy Ruth. "Patterns of Value Emphasis in the Antebellum North." Doctoral dissertation, University of Pennsylvania, 1972.

2741 ROTUNDO, Barbara. "The Rural Cemetery Movement." *Essex Inst Hist Coll,* CIX (1973), 231–240.

2742 SCHLESINGER, Arthur M., Sr. *Learning How to Behave, A Historical Study of American Etiquette Books.* New York, 1946.

2743 SCHNEIDER, John Charles. "Mob Violence and Public Order in the American City, 1830–1865." Doctoral dissertation, University of Minnesota, 1971.

2744 SELDES, Gilbert. *The Stammering Century.* New York, 1928.

2745 SIMPSON, George Lee, Jr. *The Cokers of Carolina: A Social Biography of a Family.* Chapel Hill, 1956.

2746 THORPE, Earl E. *The Old South: A Psychohistory.* Durham, 1972.

2747 WATSON, Elgiva Dundas. "The Pursuit of Pride: Cultural Attitudes in North Carolina, 1830–1861." Doctoral dissertation, University of North Carolina at Chapel Hill, 1972.

2748 WEINBAUM, Paul Owen. "Mobs and Demagogues: The Response to Collective Violence in New York City in the Early Nineteenth Century." Doctoral dissertation, University of Rochester, 1977.

2749 WERNER, John Melvin. "Race Riots in the United States during the Age of Jackson: 1829–1849." Doctoral dissertation, Indiana University, 1972.

2750 WILLIAMS, Jack Kenny. "The Code of Honor in Ante-Bellum South Carolina." *S C Hist Mag,* LIV (1953), 113–128.

2751 WILLIAMS, Jack K. "Crime and Punishment in Alabama, 1819–1840." *Ala Rev,* VI (1953), 14–30.

2752 WILLIAMS, Jack K. *Vogues in Villainy, Crime and Retribution in Ante-Bellum South Carolina.* Columbia, S.C., 1959.

2753 YODER, Paton. "Private Hospitality in the South, 1775–1850." *Miss Val Hist Rev,* XLVII (1960), 419–433.

3. Reform

See also 642, 676–679, 721, 846–847, 897, 936, 943, 1667, 1806, 1953, 2069, 2116, 2152, 2855, 3182, 3185, 4270, 4732

2754 BAGHDADI, Maria Kleinburd. "Protestants, Poverty and Urban Growth: A Study of the Organization of Charity in Boston and New York, 1820–1865." Doctoral dissertation, Brown University, 1975.

2755 BARNES, Harry E. *The Evolution of Penology in Pennsylvania: A Study in American Social History.* Indianapolis, 1927.

2756 BARNETT, Redmond J. "From Philanthropy to Reform: Poverty, Drunkenness, and the Social Order in Massachusetts, 1780–1825." Doctoral dissertation, Harvard University, 1973.

2757 BELL, Howard H. "The American Moral Reform Society, 1836–1841." *J Neg Educ,* XXVII (1958), 34–40.

2758 BESTOR, Arthur Eugene. *Backwoods Utopias: The Sectarian and Owenite Phases of Communitarian Socialism in America: 1663–1829.* Philadelphia, 1950.†

2759 BESTOR, Arthur Eugene, ed. "Education and Reform at New Harmony." *Ind Hist Soc Pub,* XV (1948), 285–417.

2760 BONELLI, Vincent Francis. "The Response of Public and Private Philanthropy to the Panic of 1819 in New York City." Doctoral dissertation, Fordham University, 1976.

2761 BONNER, James C. "The Georgia Penitentiary at Milledgeville, 1817–1874." *Ga Hist Q,* LV (1971), 303–328.

2762 CHERRINGTON, Ernest H. *The Evolution of Prohibition in the United States of America.* Westerville, 1920.

2763 COLL, Blanche D. "The Baltimore Society for the Prevention of Pauperism, 1820–1822." *Am Hist Rev,* LXI (1955), 77–87.

2764 CURTI, Merle E. *The American Peace Crusade, 1815–1860.* Durham, 1929.

2765 CURTI, Merle E. *Peace or War: The American Struggle, 1636–1936.*

2766 CUTLER, William W., III. "Status, Values and Education of the Poor: The Trustees of the New York Public School Society, 1805–1853." *Am Q,* XXIV (1972), 69–85.

2767 DANN, John Christie. "Humanitarian Reform and Organized Benevolence in the Southern United States, 1780–1830." Doctoral dissertation, College of William and Mary, 1975.

2768 DAVIS, David Brion, ed. *Ante-Bellum Reform.* New York, 1967.†

2769 DAVIS, David Brion. "The Movement to Abolish Capital Punishment in America, 1787–1861." *Am Hist Rev,* LXIII (1957), 23–46.

2770 DE PUY, Le Roy B. "The Triumph of the 'Pennsylvania System' at the States Penitentiaries." *Pa Hist,* XXI (1954), 128–144.

2771 DOLL, Eugene E. "Trial and Error at Allegheny: The Western State Penitentiary, 1818–1838." *Pa Mag Hist Biog,* LXXXI (1957), 3–27.

2772 DORCHESTER, Daniel. *The Liquor Problem in All Ages.* New York, 1884.

2773 EGBERT, Donald D., and Stow PERSONS, eds. *Socialism and American Life.* 2 vols. Princeton, 1952.

2774 EMERSON, O. B. "Frances Wright and Her Nashoba Experiment." *Tenn Hist Q,* VI (1947), 291–314.

2775 FRANCIS, Richard. "Circumstances and Salvation: The Ideology of the Fruitlands Utopia." *Am Q,* XXV (1973), 202–234.

2776 GALPIN, W. Freeman. *Pioneering for Peace: A Study of American Peace Efforts to 1846.* Syracuse, 1933.

2777 GETTLEMAN, Marvin E. "The Maryland Penitentiary in the Age of Tocqueville, 1828–1842." *Md Hist Mag,* LVI (1961), 269–290.

2778 GRIBBIN, William. "Republicanism, Reform, and the Sense of Sin in Ante-Bellum America." *Cithara,* XIV (1974), 25–42.

2779 GRIFFIN, Clifford S. *The Ferment of Reform, 1830–1860.* New York, 1967.†

2780 GROB, Gerald N. *Mental Institutions in America: Social Policy to 1875.* New York, 1973.

2781 HANEY, George William. "Capital Punishment in the State of Indiana, 1816–1971." Doctoral dissertation, Ball State University, 1975.

2782 HARRIS, David. *Socialist Origins in the United States: American Forerunners of Marx, 1817–1832.* Assen, 1966.

2783 HAWKS, Joanne Varner. "Social Reform in the Cotton Kingdom, 1830–1860." Doctoral dissertation, University of Mississippi, 1970.

2784 HEALE, M. J. "Humanitarianism in the Early Republic: The Moral Reforms of New York, 1776–1826." *J Am Stud,* II (1968), 161–176.

2785 HEALE, M. J. "Patterns of Benevolence: Charity and Morality in Rural and Urban New York, 1783–1830." *Soc,* III (1973), 337–359.

2786 HEALE, M. J. "The New York Society for the Prevention of Pauperism, 1817–1823." *N Y Hist Soc Q,* LV (1971), 153–176.

2787 HILDRETH, Flora Bassett. "The Howard Association of New Orleans, 1837–1838." Doctoral dissertation, University of California, Los Angeles, 1975.

2788 HINDS, William A. *American Communities and Co-operative Colonies.* 2d rev. Chicago, 1908.

2789 HOLBROOK, Stewart H. *Dreamers of the American Dream.* Garden City, New York, 1957.

2790 HUGINS, Walter E., comp. *The Reform Impulse, 1825–1850.* Columbia, S.C., 1972.†

2791 KELSO, Robert W. *The History of Public Poor Relief in Massachusetts, 1620–1920.* Boston, 1922.

2792 KLEBANER, Benjamin J. "Poverty and Its Relief in American Thought, 1815–1861." *Soc Sci Rev,* XXXVIII (1964), 382–399.

2793 KLEBANER, Benjamin J. "The Home Relief Controversy in Philadelphia, 1782–1861." *Pa Mag Hist Biog,* LXXVIII (1954), 413–423.

2794 KLEIN, Philip. *Prison Methods in New York State: A Contribution to the Study of the Theory and Practice of Correctional Institutions in New York State.* New York, 1920.

2795 KROUT, John A. *The Origins of Prohibition.* New York, 1925.

2796 LAWSON, David Clifton. "Swords into Plowshares, Spears into Pruninghooks: The Intellectual Foundations of the First American Peace Movement, 1815–1865. Doctoral dissertation, University of New Mexico, 1975.

2797 LEWIS, Orlando F. *The Development of American Prisons and Prison Customs, 1776–1845.* Albany, 1922.

2798 LEWIS, W. David. *From Newgate to Dannemora: The Rise of the Penitentiary in New York, 1796–1848.* Ithaca, 1965.

2799 LEWIS, W. David. "Newgate of New York: A Case History (1796–1828) of Early American Prison Reform." *N Y Hist Soc Q,* XLVII (1963), 137–171.

2800 LEWIS, W. David. "The Reformer as Conservative: Protestant Counter-Subversion in the Early Republic." *The Development of an American Culture.* Ed. Stanley COBEN and Lorman RATNER. Englewood Cliffs, N.J., 1970.

2801 LOCKWOOD, George B. *The New Harmony Movement.* New York, 1905.

2802 LUTZKER, Michael A. "Abolition of Imprisonment for Debt in New Jersey." *Proc N J Hist Soc,* LXXXIV (1966), 1–29.

2803 MACDONALD, Clyde Winfield. "The Massachusetts Peace Society, 1815–1828: A Study in Evangelical Reform." Doctoral dissertation, University of Maine, 1973.

2804 MCCOLGAN, Daniel T. *Joseph Tuckerman: Pioneer in American Social Work.* Washington, D.C., 1940.

2805 MCELROY, James Logan. "Social Reform in the Burned-Over District: Rochester, New York, as a Test Case, 1830–1854." Doctoral dissertation, State University of New York at Binghamton, 1974.

2806 MCKELVEY, Blake. *American Prisons: A Study in American Social History Prior to 1915.* Chicago, 1936.

2807 MACKEY, Philip English. " 'The Result May be Glorious'—Anti-Gallows Movement in Rhode Island, 1838–1852." *R I Hist,* XXXIII (1974), 19–31.

2808 MACKEY, Philip English. "Edward Livingston and the Origins of the Movement to Abolish Capital Punishment in America." *La Hist,* XVI (1975), 145–166.

2809 MEYER, Paul Rudolph, Jr. "The Transformation of American Temperance: The Popularization and Radicalization of a Reform Movement, 1813–1860." Doctoral dissertation, State University of Iowa, 1976.

2810 MITTLEBEELER, Emmet V. "The Decline of Imprisonment for Debt in Kentucky." *Filson Club Hist Q,* XLIX (1975), 169–189.

2811 MOHL, Raymond A. "Humanitarianism in the Preindustrial City: The New York Society for the Prevention of Pauperism, 1817–1823." *J Am Hist,* LVII (1970), 576–599.

2812 MOHL, Raymond A. "The Humane Society and Urban Reform in Early New York, 1787–1831." *N Y Hist Soc Q,* LIV (1970), 30–52.

2813 MUNCY, Raymond Lee. *Sex and Marriage in Utopian Communities: 19th Century America.* Bloomington, Indiana, 1973.

2814 NESHEIM, William C. "The Early Years of the Missouri State Penitentiary, 1833 to 1853." *Mo Hist Soc Bull,* XXVIII (1972), 246–263.

2815 NOYES, John H. *History of American Socialisms.* Philadelphia, 1870.

2816 PEARSON, C. C., and J. Edwin HENDRICKS. *Liquor and Anti-Liquor in Virginia, 1619–1919.* Durham, 1967.

2817 PEASE, William H., and Jane H. PEASE. "A New View of Nashoba." *Tenn Hist Q,* XIX (1960), 99–109.

2818 PHELPS, Christina. *The Anglo-American Peace Movement in the Mid-Nineteenth Century.* New York, 1930.

2819 PICKETT, Robert S. *House of Refuge: Origins of Juvenile Reform in New York State, 1815–1857.* Syracuse, 1969.

2820 RANDALL, Edwin T. "Imprisonment for Debt in America: Fact and Fiction." *Miss Val Hist Rev,* XXXIX (1952), 89–102.

2821 RATNER, Lorman, ed. *Pre-Civil War Reform: The Variety of Principles and Programs.* Englewood Cliffs, 1967.

2822 RORABAUGH, William J. "The Alcoholic Republic, America 1790–1840." Doctoral dissertation, University of California, Berkeley, 1976.

2823 ROTHMAN, David J. *The Discovery of the Asylum: Social Order and Disorder in the New Republic.* Boston, 1971.†

2824 SCHLESINGER, Arthur M., Sr. *The American as Reformer.* Cambridge, Mass., 1951.†

2825 SCHNEIDER, David M. *The History of Public Welfare in New York State.* 2 vols. Chicago, 1938.

2826 SELLING, Lowell S. *Men Against Madness.* New York, 1940.

2827 SHAMBAUGH, Bertha M. H. *Amana That Was and the Amana That is.* Iowa City, 1932.

2828 SHAW, Albert. *Icaria, a Chapter in the History of Communism.* New York, 1884.

2829 SPONHOLTZ, Lloyd L. "Pittsburgh and Temperance, 1830–1854." *W Pa Hist Mag,* XLVI (1963), 347–379.

2830 SPRUNGER, Keith L. "Cold Water Congressmen: The Congressional Temperance Society Before the Civil War." *Hist,* XXXVIII (1965), 498–515.

2831 SULLIVAN, David K. "Behind Prison Walls: The Operation of the District Penitentiary, 1831–1862." *Rec Col Hist Soc,* XLVIII (1973), 243–266.

2832 SULLIVAN, David K. "The District of Columbia Penal System, 1825 to 1875." Doctoral dissertation, Georgetown University, 1973.

2833 TEETERS, Negley K. "The Early Days of the Eastern State Penitentiary at Philadelphia." *Pa Hist,* XVI (1949), 261–302.

2834 THOMAS, John L. "Romantic Reform in America, 1815–1865." *Am Q,* XVII (1965), 656–681.

2835 THOMPSON, E. Bruce. "Reforms in the Care of the Insane in Tennessee, 1830–1850." *Tenn Hist Q,* III (1944), 319–334.

2836 THOMPSON, E. Bruce. "Reforms in the Penal System of Mississippi, 1820–1850." *J Miss Hist,* VII (1945), 51–74.

2837 THOMPSON, E. Bruce. "Reforms in the Penal System of Tennessee, 1820–1850." *Tenn Hist Q*, I (1942), 291–308.

2838 THOMPSON, T. I. *Penal Reform in Illinois*. New York, 1934.

2839 TOCQUEVILLE, Alexis de, and Gustave de BEAUMONT. *On the Penitentiary System in the United States, and Its Application in France*. Philadelphia, 1833.

2840 TYLER, Alice Felt. *Freedom's Ferment*. Minneapolis, 1944.†

2841 TYRELL, Ian Robert. "Drink and the Process of Social Reform: From Temperance to Prohibition in Ante-Bellum America, 1813–1860." Doctoral dissertation, Duke University, 1974.

2842 VIGILANTE, Emil Christopher. "The Temperance Reform in New York State, 1829–1851. Doctoral dissertation, New York University, 1964.

2843 WARE, Henry. *Memoirs of the Rev. Noah Worcester*. New York, 1972.

2844 WEBBER, Everett. *Escape to Utopia: The Communal Movement in America*. New York, 1959.

2845 WELLMAN, Judith M. "The Burned-Over District Revisited: Benevolent Reform and Abolitionism in Mexico, Paris and Ithaca, New York, 1825–1852. Doctoral dissertation, University of Virginia, 1974.

2846 WHITNEY, Edson L. *American Peace Society; A Centennial History*. Washington, D.C., 1928.

2847 WILSON, William E. *The Angel and the Serpent: The Story of New Harmony*. Bloomington, 1964.

2848 WINES, Frederick Howard. *Punishment and Reformation; a Study of the Penitentiary System*. New York, 1919.

4. Religion

See also 471, 1267, 1308, 1447, 1922, 1974, 2636, 3104, 3115, 3348–3357, 3661, 3708, 3712, 4131, 4139, 4706

2849 ADDISON, James T. *The Episcopal Church in the United States, 1789–1931*. New York, 1951.

2850 AHLSTROM, Sydney E. *A Religious History of the American People*. New Haven, 1972.†

2851 ANDREWS, John A., III. *Rebuilding the Christian Commonwealth: New England Congregationalists and Foreign Missions, 1800–1830*. Lexington, 1976.

2852 ARRINGTON, Leonard J. *Great Basin Kingdom: An Economic History of the Latter-Day Saints, 1830–1900*. Cambridge, Mass., 1958.†

2853 ATKINS, Gaius Glenn, and Frederick L. FAGLEY. *History of American Congregationalism*. Boston, 1942.

2854 BANNER, Lois W. "Religion and Reform in the Early Republic: The Role of Youth." *Am Q*, XXIII (1971), 677–695.

2855 BANNER, Lois W. "Religious Benevolence as Social Control: A Critique of an Interpretation." *J Am Hist*, LX (1973), 23–41.

2856 BANNER, Lois W. "The Protestant Crusade: Religious Missions, Benevolence, and Reform in the United States, 1790–1840." Doctoral dissertation, Columbia University, 1970.

2857 BARCLAY, Wade Crawford. *Early American Methodism.* New York, 1950.

2858 BARNETT, Suzanne W. "Silent Evangelism: Presbyterians and the Mission Press in China, 1807–1860." *J Presby Hist Soc,* XLIX (1971), 287–302.

2859 BEAM, Christopher Merriman. "Millennialism in American Thought, 1740–1840." Doctoral dissertation, University of Illinois, Urbana-Champaign, 1976.

2860 BILLINGTON, Ray Allen. *The Protestant Crusade, 1800–1860: A Study of the Origins of American Nativism.* New York, 1938.†

2861 BIRDSALL, Richard D. "The Second Great Awakening and the New England Social Order." *Church Hist,* XXXIX (1970), 345–371.

2862 BLANKS, W. D. "Corrective Church Discipline in the Presbyterian Churches of the Nineteenth Century South." *J Presby Hist Soc,* XLIV (1966), 89–105.

2862A BLAU, Joseph L. *Judaism in America: From Curiosity to Third Faith.* Chicago, 1978.

2863 BLAUVELT, Martha T. "Society, Religion, and Revivalism: The Second Great Awakening in New Jersey, 1780–1830." Doctoral dissertation, Princeton University, 1975.

2864 BODO, John R. *The Protestant Clergy and Public Issues, 1812–1848.* Princeton, 1954.

2865 BOLES, John B. *Religion in Antebellum Kentucky.* Lexington, 1976.

2866 BONKOWSKY, Elizabeth Leitch. "The Church and the City: Protestant Concern for Urban Problems, 1800–1840." Doctoral dissertation, Boston University, 1973.

2867 BOYLAN, Anne Mary. " 'The Nursery of the Church': Protestant Sunday Schools, 1820–1880." Doctoral dissertation, University of Wisconsin, Madison, 1973.

2868 BOZEMAN, Theodore Dwight. "Inductive and Deductive Politics: Science and Society in Antebellum Presbyterian Thought." *J Am Hist,* LXIV (1977), 704–722.

2869 BOZEMAN, Theodore Dwight. "Baconism and the Bible: The Baconian Ideal in Ante-Bellum American Presbyterian Thought." Doctoral dissertation, Duke University, 1974.

2870 BRANNAN, Emora Thomas. "The Presiding Elder Question: Its Critical Nature in American Methodism, 1820–1824 and Its Impact upon Ecclesiastical Institutions." Doctoral dissertation, Duke University, 1974.

2871 BRODIE, Fawn M. *No Man Knows My History: The Life of Joseph Smith.* New York, 1945.

2872 BROWN, Lawrence L. "1835 and All That: Domestic and Foreign Missionary Society Membership and the Missionary Spirit." *Hist Mag P E Ch,* XL (1971), 399–405.

2873 BRUCE, Dickson D. *And They All Sang Hallelujah: Plain-Folk Camp-Meeting Religion, 1800–1845.* Knoxville, 1974.

2874 BRUCE, Dickson D. "Religion, Society and Culture in the Old South: A Comparative View." *Am Q,* XXVI (1974), 399–416.

2875 BUCKE, Emory Stevens, et al., eds. *The History of American Methodism.* 3 vols. New York, 1964.

2876 BUELL, Lawrence. "The Unitarian Movement and the Art of Preaching in the 19th Century America." *Am Q,* XXIV (1972), 166–190.

2877 BURR, Nelson R., comp. *Religion in American Life.* Goldentree Bibliographies in American History. Arlington Heights, 1971.†

2878 BUSHKO, Andrew Alan. "Religious Revivals in American Colleges, 1783–1860." Doctoral dissertation, Columbia University, 1974.

2879 CARWARDINE, Richard. "The Second Great Awakening in the Urban Centers: An Examination of Methodism and the 'New Measures'." *J Am Hist,* LIX (1972), 327–340.

2880 CHADWICK, John W. *William Ellery Channing, Minister of Religion.* Boston, 1903.

2881 COLE, Charles C., Jr. *The Social Ideas of the Northern Evangelists, 1826–1860.* New York, 1954.

2882 COOKE, George W. *Unitarianism in America: A History of Its Origin and Development.* Boston, 1902.

2883 CORY, Earl Wallace, Jr. "The Unitarians and Universalists of the Southeastern United States during the Nineteenth Century." Doctoral dissertation, University of Georgia, 1970.

2884 CROSS, Whitney R. *The Burned-Over District: The Social and Intellectual History of Enthusiastic Religion in Western New York, 1800–1850.* Ithaca, 1950.†

2885 CURRAN, Francis X. "The Jesuits in Kentucky, 1831–1846." *Mid-Am,* XXXV (1953), 223–246.

2886 DESCHAMPS, Margaret Burr. "Union or Division? South Atlantic Presbyterians and Southern Nationalism, 1820–1861." *J S Hist,* XX (1954), 484–498.

2887 DOHERTY, Robert W. "Social Bases for the Presbyterian Schism of 1837–1838." *J Soc Hist,* II (1968), 69–79.

2888 DOHERTY, Robert W. "A Response to Orthodoxy: The Hicksite Movement in the Society of Friends." *Pa Mag Hist Biog,* XC (1966), 233–246.

2889 DOHERTY, Robert W. "Non-Urban Friends and the Hicksite Separation." *Pa Hist,* XXXIII (1966), 432–445.

2890 DOLAN, Jay P. *The Immigrant Church: New York's Irish and German Catholics, 1815–1865.* Baltimore, 1975.

2891 DRAKE, Thomas E. *Quakers and Slavery in America.* New Haven, 1950.

2892 DUFFY, John, ed. *Parson Clapp of the Strangers' Church of New Orleans.* Baton Rouge, 1957.

2893 EDDY, Richard. *Universalism in America, a History.* 2 vols. Boston, 1884–1886.

2894 ELLIS, John T. *American Catholicism.* 2d ed. Chicago, 1969.†

2895 ELLIS, John T. *A Guide to American Catholic History.* Milwaukee, 1959.

2896 EVANS, John H. *Joseph Smith, An American Prophet.* New York, 1933.

2897 FINNEY, Charles G. *Memoirs of Rev. Charles G. Finney.* New York, 1876.

2898 FOSTER, Charles I. *An Errand of Mercy: The Evangelical United Front, 1790–1837.* Chapel Hill, 1960.

2899 FOSTER, William Lawrence. "Between Two Worlds: The Origins of Shaker Celibacy, Oneida Community Complex Marriage, and Mormon Polygamy." Doctoral dissertation, University of Chicago, 1976.

2900 FRIES, Adelaide L. *Records of the Moravians in North Carolina.* 7 vols. Raleigh, 1922–1947.

2901 GARRISON, Winfred Ernest, and Alfred T. DE GROOT. *The Disciples of Christ, a History.* St. Louis, 1948.

2902 GAUSTAD, Edwin Scott. *American Religious History.* Am Hist Assn Service Center for Teachers Publication. Washington, D.C., 1967.†

2903 GEDDES, Joseph A. *The United Order Among the Mormons.* Salt Lake City, 1924.

2904 GENTRY, Leland Homer. "A History of the Latter-Day Saints in Northern Missouri from 1836 to 1839." Doctoral dissertation, Brigham Young University, 1965.

2905 GIBSON, George H. "Unitarian Congregations in Ante-Bellum Georgia." *Ga Hist Q,* LIV (1970), 147–168.

2906 GLANZ, Rudolf. "The Spread of Jewish Communities Through America Before the Civil War." *Yivo Ann Jew Soc Sci,* XV (1974), 7–45.

2907 GLAZER, Nathan. *American Judaism.* Rev. ed. Chicago, 1972.†

2908 GOODHEART, Lawrence B., and Richard O. CURRY, eds. " 'A Plea for the West': Elizur Wright, Jr. and the American Tract Society in Western Pennsylvania, 1828–1829." *Pa Hist,* XLIV (1977), 249–266.

2909 GRANT, Dorothy Fremont. *John England: American Christopher.* Milwaukee, 1949.

2910 GRIBBIN, William. "Vermont's Universalist Controversy of 1824." *Vt Hist,* XXXI (1973), 82–94.

2911 GRIBBIN, William. "Republican Religion and the American Churches in the Early National Period." *Hist,* XXXV (1972), 61–74.

2912 GRIBBIN, William. "Antimasonry, Religious Radicalism, and the Paranoid Style of the 1820s." *Hist Teacher,* VII (1974), 239–254.

2913 GRIFFIN, Clifford S. "Religious Benevolence as Social Control, 1815–1860." *Miss Val Hist Rev,* XLIV (1957), 423–444.

2914 GRIFFIN, Clifford S. "Converting the Catholics: American Benevolent Societies and the Ante-Bellum Crusade against the Church." *Cath Hist Rev,* XLVII (1961), 325–341.

2915 GRIFFIN, Clifford S. *Their Brother's Keeper: Moral Stewardship in the United States, 1800–1865.* New Brunswick, 1960.

2916 GUERRIERI, Mother Dora A. "Catholic Thought in the Age of Jackson." Doctoral dissertation, Boston College, 1960.

2917 GUILDAY, Peter. *Life and Times of John England, First Bishop of Charleston, 1786–1842.* New York, 1927.

2918 HARRELL, David Edwin. *A Social History of the Disciples of Christ.* Volume I. *Quest for a Christian America: The Disciples of Christ and American Society to 1866.* Nashville, 1966.

2919 HARWOOD, Thomas F. "British Evangelical Abolitionism and American Churches in the 1830's." *J S Hist,* XXVIII (1962), 287–306.

2920 HENRY, Stuart C. "The Lane Rebels: A Twentieth Century Look." *J Presby Hist Soc*, XLIX (1971), 1–14.

2921 HILL, Marvin S. "Secular or Sectarian History? A Critique of *No Man Knows My History.*" *Church Hist*, XLIII (1974), 78–96.

2922 HUCH, Ronald K. "James Gillespie Birney and the New England Friends." *Reg Ky Hist Soc*, LXVII (1969), 350–359.

2923 HUDSON, Winthrop S. *American Protestantism.* Chicago, 1961.†

2924 HUDSON, Winthrop S. *Religion in America.* 2d ed. New York, 1973.†

2925 JENNINGS, Warren Abner. "Zion is Fled: The Expulsion of the Mormons from Jackson County, Missouri." Doctoral dissertation, University of Florida, 1962.

2926 JENNINGS, Warren Abner. "Isaac McCoy and the Mormons." *Mo Hist Rev*, LXI (1960), 62–82.

2927 JENNINGS, Warren Abner. "The Expulsion of the Mormons from Jackson County, Missouri." *Mo Hist Rev*, LXIV (1969), 41–63.

2928 JICK, Leon A. *The Americanization of the Synagogue, 1820–1870.* Hanover, N.H., 1976.

2929 JOHNSON, Charles A. *The Frontier Camp Meeting: Religion's Harvest Time.* Dallas, 1955.

2930 JOHNSON, Charles D. *Higher Education of Southern Baptists: An Institutional History, 1826–1954.* Waco, 1955.

2931 JOHNSON, Dale A. "Between Evangelicalism and a Social Gospel: The Case of Joseph Rayner Stephens." *Church Hist*, XLII (1973), 229–242.

2932 JOHNSON, James E. "Charles G. Finney and Oberlin Perfectionism." *J Presby Hist Soc*, XLVI (1968), 42–57, 128–138.

2933 JOHNSON, James E. "Charles G. Finney and a Theology of Revivalism." *Church Hist*, XXXVIII (1969), 338–358.

2934 LANNIE, Vincent P., and Bernard C. DIETHORN. "For the Honor and Glory of God: The Philadelphia Bible Riots of 1840." *Hist Educ Q*, VIII (1968), 44–106.

2935 LA RUE, William E. *The Foundations of Mormonism.* New York, 1919.

2936 LEBUFFE, Leon Adolphe. "Tension in American Catholicism, 1820–1870: An Intellectual History." Doctoral dissertation, Catholic University, 1973.

2937 LOETSCHER, Lefferts A. "The Problem of Christian Unity in Early Nineteenth Century America." *Church Hist*, XXXII (1963), 3–16.

2938 LOWE, Jay R. "A Study of the General Conferences of the Church of Jesus Christ of Latter-Day Saints, 1830–1901." Doctoral dissertation, Bringham Young University, 1972.

2939 MCALLISTER, Lester G., and William E. TUCKER. *Journey in Faith: A History of the Christian Church.* St. Louis, 1975.

2940 MCAVOY, Thomas T. "The Formation of the Catholic Minority in the United States, 1820–1860." *Rev Pol*, X (1948), 13–34.

2941 MCBRIDE, Robert R. "An Account of the Great 'Two-Lines' Controversy." *W Pa Hist Mag*, LV (1972), 160–184.

2942 MCCORMAC, Earl R. "Missions and the Presbyterian Schism of 1837." *Church Hist*, XXXII (1963), 32–45.

2943 MCCORMAC, Earl R. "The Development of Presbyterian Missionary Organizations: 1790–1870." *J Presby Hist Soc,* XLIII (1965), 149–173.

2944 MCLOUGHLIN, William G. *New England Dissent, 1630–1833: The Baptists and the Separation of Church and State.* Cambridge, Mass., 1971.

2945 MCLOUGHLIN, William G. *Modern Revivalism: Charles Grandison Finney to Billy Graham.* New York, 1959.

2946 MANFRA, Jo Ann. "The Catholic Episcopacy in America, 1789–1852." Doctoral dissertation, State University of Iowa, 1975.

2947 MANROSS, William W. *A History of the American Episcopal Church.* 3d ed. New York, 1959.

2948 MANROSS, William W. *Episcopal Church in the United States, 1800–1840: A Study in Church Life.* New York, 1950.

2949 MATHEWS, Donald G. *Slavery and Methodism: A Chapter in American Morality, 1780–1845.* Princeton, 1965.

2950 MATHEWS, Donald G. *Religion in the Old South.* Chicago, 1977.

2951 MATHEWS, Donald G. "Religion in the Old South: Speculation on Methodology" *S Atl Q,* LXXIII (1974), 34–52.

2952 MATTSON, John Stanley. "Charles Grandison Finney and the Emerging Tradition of 'New Measure' Revivalism." Doctoral dissertation, University of North Carolina at Chapel Hill, 1970.

2953 MAYNARD, Theodore. *The Story of American Catholicism.* New York, 1941.

2954 MELCHER, Marguerite. *The Shaker Adventure.* Princeton, 1941.†

2955 MIYAKAWA, Tetsuo Scott. *Protestants and Pioneers: Individualism and Conformity on the American Frontier.* Chicago, 1964.

2956 MODE, Peter G. *Source Book and Bibliographical Guide for American Church History.* Menasha, Wis., 1921.

2957 MORRISON, John L. "A Rational Voice [Alexander Campbell] in an Emotional Wilderness." *W Va Hist,* XXXIV (1973), 125–140.

2958 MORRISON, Michael Gordon. "Conceptions of Sin in American Evangelical Thought in the Early Nineteenth Century." Doctoral dissertation, University of Wisconsin, Madison, 1971.

2959 MOSELEY, J. Edward. *Disciples of Christ in Georgia.* St. Louis, 1954.

2960 MUELDER, Hermann R. "Jacksonian Democracy in Religious Organizations." Doctoral dissertation, University of Minnesota, 1933.

2961 MURRAY, Andrew E. *Presbyterians and the Negro: A History.* Philadelphia, 1966.

2962 O'DAY, Thomas F. *The Mormons.* New York, 1957.

2963 OLMSTEAD, Clifton E. *History of Religion in the United States.* Englewood Cliffs, N. J., 1960.

2964 PEARSON, Samuel C., Jr. "From Church to Denomination: American Congregationalism in the Nineteenth Century." *Church Hist,* XXXVIII (1969), 67–87.

2965 PETERS, Robert Norton. "From Sect to Church: A Study in the Permutation of Methodism on the Oregon Frontier." Doctoral dissertation, University of Washington, 1973.

2966 PHILLIPS, Clifton Jackson. *Protestant American and the Pagan World: The First Half Century of the American Board of Commissioners for Foreign Missions, 1810–1860.* Cambridge, Mass., 1969.

2967 POSEY, Walter Brownlow. "The Baptist Church in the Lower Mississippi Valley." *J Neg Hist,* XLI (1956), 117–130.

2968 POSEY, Walter Brownlow. *The Baptist Church in the Lower Mississippi Valley, 1776–1845.* Lexington, 1957.

2969 POSEY, Walter Brownlow. *Frontier Mission: A History of Religion West of the Southern Appalachians to 1861.* Lexington, 1966.

2970 POSEY, Walter Brownlow. *The Presbyterian Church in the Old Southwest,* 1778–1838. Richmond, 1952.

2971 POSEY, Walter Brownlow. "The Protestant Episcopal Church: An American Adaptation." *J S Hist,* XXV (1959), 3–30.

2972 POSEY, Walter Brownlow. "The Slavery Question in the Presbyterian Church in the Old Southwest." *J S Hist,* XV (1949), 311–324.

2973 POSEY, Walter Brownlow. *Religious Strife on the Southern Frontier.* Baton Rouge, 1965.

2974 QUAIFE, Milo M. *Kingdom of St. James: A Narrative of the Mormons.* New Haven, 1930.

2975 RAWLEY, James A. "Joseph John Gurney's Mission to America, 1837–1840." *Miss Val Hist Rev,* XLIX (1963), 653–674.

2976 REARDON, John J. "Religious and Other Factors in the Defeat of the 'Standing Order' in Connecticut, 1800–1818." *Hist Mag P E Ch,* XXX (1961), 93–110.

2977 REILLY, Duncan Alexander. "William Capers: An Evaluation of His Life and Thought." Doctoral dissertation, Emory University, 1972.

2978 REILLY, Timothy F. "Heterodox New Orleans and the Protestant South." *La Stud,* XII (1973), 533–551.

2979 REILLY, Timothy F. "Religious Leaders and Social Criticism in New Orleans, 1800–1861." Doctoral dissertation, University of Missouri, 1972.

2980 REZNIKOFF, Charles. *The Jews of Charleston: A History of An American Jewish Community.* Philadelphia, 1950.

2981 RICHARDSON, Robert. *Memoirs of Alexander Campbell, Embracing a view of the Origin, Progress and Principles of the Religions Reformation Which He Advocated.* 2 vols. Philadelphia, 1868–1870.

2982 ROBERTSON, R. J., Jr. "The Mormon Experience in Missouri, 1830–1839." *Mo Hist Rev,* LXVIII (1974), 280–298, 393–415.

2983 ROSELL, Garth Mervin. "Charles Grandison Finney and the Rise of the Benevolence Empire." Doctoral dissertation, University of Minnesota, 1971.

2984 ROSENBERG, Carroll Smith. *Religion and the Rise of the American City: The New York City Mission Movement, 1812–1870.* Ithaca, 1971.

2985 ROWE, David Leslie. "Thunder and Trumpets: The Millerite Movement and Apocalyptic Thought in Upstate New York, 1800–1845." Doctoral dissertation, University of Virginia, 1974.

2986 ROWE, Henry K. *The History of Religion in the United States.* New York, 1924.

2987 SALOUTOS, Theodore. "American Missionaries in Greece, 1820–1869." *Church Hist,* XXIV (1955), 152–174.

2988 SANDEEN, Ernest R. *The Roots of Fundamentalism: British and American Millenarianism, 1800–1930.* Chicago, 1970.

2989 SELLERS, Charles C. *Lorenzo Dow, the Bearer of the Word.* New York, 1928.

2990 SHEA, John D. G. *A History of the Catholic Church within the Limits of the United States, from the First Attempted Colonization to the Present Time.* 4 vols. New York, 1886–1892.

2991 SHIELDS, James LeRoy, Jr. "Alexander Campbell: A Synthesis of Faith and Reason." Doctoral dissertation, Syracuse University, 1974.

2992 SMITH, Cortland Victor. "Church Organization as an Agency of Social Control: Church Discipline in North Carolina, 1800–1860." Doctoral dissertation, University of North Carolina at Chapel Hill, 1967.

2993 SMITH, Elwyn A. *Religious Liberty in the United States: The Development of Church-State Thought Since the Revolutionary Era.* Philadelphia, 1972.

2994 SMITH, Elwyn A. "The Role of the South in the Presbyterian Schism of 1837–1838." *Church Hist,* XXIX (1960), 44–63.

2995 SMITH, James Ward, and Albert Leland JAMISON, eds. *Religion in American Life.* 4 vols. Princeton, 1961.

2996 SMITH, H. Shelton. *In His Image, but . . .: Racism in Southern Religion, 1780–1910.* Durham, N.C., 1972.

2997 SMITH, Ralph Ruggles, Jr. " 'In Every Destitute Place': The Mission Program of the American Sunday School Union, 1817–1834." Doctoral dissertation, University of Southern California, 1973.

2998 SMITH, Timothy L. "Protestant Schooling and American Nationality, 1800–1850." *J Am Hist,* LIII (1967), 679–695.

2999 SMITH, Timothy L. *Revivalism and Social Reform in Mid-Nineteenth Century America.* New York, 1957.

3000 SOKOLOW, J. A. "Revivalism and Radicalism: William Lloyd Garrison, Henry Clarke Wright and the Ideology of Nonresistance." Doctoral dissertation, New York University, 1972.

3001 STAIGER, C. Bruce. "Abolitionism and the Presbyterian Schism of 1837–1838." *Miss Val Hist Rev,* XXXVI (1949), 391–414.

3002 STROUPE, Henry Smith. *The Religious Press in the South Atlantic States, 1802–1865: An Annotated Bibliography with Historical Introduction and Notes.* Durham, 1956.

3003 SWANSON, Michael Richard Hans. "Robert Baird and the Evangelical Crusade in America, 1820–1860." Doctoral dissertation, Case Western Reserve University, 1971.

3004 SWEET, William W. *Methodism in American History.* Rev. Ed. Nashville, 1954.

3005 SWEET, William W. *Religion in the Development of American Culture, 1765–1840.* New York, 1952.

3006 SWEET, William W. *The Story of Religion in America.* 2d rev. ed. New York, 1950.

3007 SWEET, William W., ed. *Religion on the American Frontier.* 4 vols. New York, 1931–1946.

3008 THOMAS, Allen C. *A History of the Friends in America.* 6th ed. Philadelphia, 1930.

3009 THOMPSON, Ernest Trice. *Presbyterians in the South, 1607–1972.* 3 vols. Richmond, 1963–1973.

3010 TORBET, Robert G. *A History of the Baptists.* Rev ed. Valley Forge, 1973.

3011 TWADDELL, Elizabeth. "The American Tract Society, 1814–1860." *Church Hist,* XV (1940), 116–132.

3012 UPTON, James. "The Shakers as Pacifists in the Period Between 1812 and the Civil War." *Filson Club Hist Q,* XLVII (1973), 267–283.

3013 VAN DE BURG, William Lloyd. "Rejected of Men: The Changing Religious Views of William Lloyd Garrison and Frederick Douglass." Doctoral dissertation, Michigan State University, 1973.

3014 VERNON, Walter N. "Beginnings of Methodism in Arkansas." *Ark Hist Q,* XXXI (1972), 356–372.

3015 WAYLAND, Francis. *Memoir of the Life and Labors of the Rev. Adoniram Judson.* 2 vols. Boston, 1853.

3016 WEISBERGER, Bernard A. *They Gathered at the River: The Story of the Great Revivalists and Their Impact upon Religion in America.* Boston, 1958.†

3017 WENTZ, Adbel R. *A Basic History of Lutheranism in America.* Rev. ed. Philadelphia, 1964.

3018 WEST, Earl Irvin. "Early Cincinnati's 'Unprecedented Spectacle'." *Ohio Hist,* LXXIX (1970), 5–17.

3019 WEST, Earl Irvin. "Religion and Politics in the Jacksonian Era." Doctoral dissertation, Indiana University, 1968.

3020 WHALEN, Robert Kieran. "Millenarianism and Millennialism in America, 1790–1880." Doctoral dissertation, State University of New York at Stony Brook, 1972.

3021 WYATT-BROWN, Bertram. "The Antimission Movement in the Jacksonian South: A Study in Regional Folk Culture." *J S Hist,* XXXVI (1970), 501–529.

5. Education

See also **592, 806, 2055, 2070, 2465, 2759, 2766, 2878, 2930, 2998, 3166, 3168, 4269, 4557, 4700**

3022 ADAMS, Herbert Baxter. *The Life and Writings of Jared Sparks.* 2 vols. Boston, 1893.

3023 ALLMENDINGER, David F., Jr. "The Dangers of Ante-Bellum Student Life." *J Soc Hist,* VII (1973), 75–83.

3024 ALLMENDINGER, David F., Jr. *Paupers and Scholars: The Transformation of Student Life in Nineteenth-Century New England.* New York, 1975.

3025 ALLMENDINGER, David F., Jr. "The Strangeness of the American Education Society: Indigent Students and the New Charity, 1815–1840." *Hist Educ Q,* XI (1971), 3–22.

3026 BARNARD, Henry, ed. *Educational Biography.* New York, 1859.

3027 BATTLE, Kemp P. *History of the University of North Carolina.* 2 vols. Raleigh, 1907–1912.

3028 BAUGH, Milton L. "An Early Experiment in Adult Education: The Nashville Lyceum, 1830–1832." *Tenn Hist Q,* XI (1952), 235–245.

3029 BENNETT, Charles A. *History of Manual and Industrial Education Up to 1870.* Peoria, 1926.

3030 BIDWELL, Charles E. "The Moral Significance of the Common School: A Sociological Study of Local Patterns of School Control and Moral Education in Massachusetts and New York, 1837–1840." *Hist Educ Q,* VI (1966), 52–91.

3031 BINDER, Frederick Melvin. *The Age of the Common School, 1830–1865.* New York, 1974.

3032 BOONE, Richard G. *A History of Education in Indiana.* New York, 1892.

3033 BRADEN, Waldo W. "The Beginnings of the Lyceum, 1826–1840." *S Sp J,* XX (1954), 125–135.

3034 BROOKS, Robert Preston. *The University of Georgia under Sixteen Administrations, 1785–1955.* Athens, 1956.

3035 BROWN, Elmer E. *The Making of Our Middle Schools: An Account of the Development of Secondary Education in the United States.* New York, 1907.

3036 BRUBACHER, John S., and Willis RUDY. *Higher Education in Transition: A History of American Colleges and Universities, 1636–1976.* 3d rev. ed. New York, 1976.

3037 BRUCE, Philip A. *History of the University of Virginia 1819–1919: The Lengthened Shadow of One Man.* 5 vols. New York, 1920–22.

3038 BURKE, Colin Bradley. "The Quiet Influence: The American Colleges and their Students, 1800–1860." Doctoral dissertation, Washington University, 1973.

3039 BURNS, James A. *The Growth and Development of the Catholic School System in the United States.* Cincinnati, 1912.

3040 BUTTS, R. Freeman, and Lawrence A. CREMIN. *A History of Education in American Culture.* New York, 1953.

3041 CALHOUN, Daniel. *The Intelligence of a People.* Princeton, N.J., 1973.†

3042 CALLCOTT, George H. *A History of the University of Maryland.* Baltimore, 1966.

3043 CARLTON, F. T. *Economic Influences Upon Educational Progress in the United States, 1820–1850.* Madison, 1908.

3044 CHEYNEY, Edward P. *History of the University of Pennsylvania, 1790–1940.* Philadelphia, 1940.

3045 CHURCH, Robert L., and Michael W. SEDLAK. *Education in the United States: An Interpretative History.* New York, 1976.

3046 COBUN, Frank E. "The Educational Level of the Jacksonians." *Hist Educ Q,* VII (1967), 515–520.

3047 COON, Charles L., ed. *The Beginnings of Public Education in North Carolina: A Documentary History, 1790–1840.* 2 vols. Raleigh, 1908.

3048 COPELAND, J. Isaac. "The Tutor in the Ante-Bellum South." *S C Hist Assn Proc* (1965), 36–47.

3049 COULTER, E. Merton. *College Life in the Old South.* New York, 1928.

3050 CRANE, Theodore Rawson, ed. *The Colleges and the Public, 1787–1862.* New York, 1963.

3051 CRANE, Theodore Rawson, ed. "Francis Wayland: Political Economist as Educator." *R I Hist,* XXI (1962), 65–90, 105–124.

3052 CREMIN, Lawrence A. *The American Common School.* New York, 1951.

3053 CUBBERLEY, Ellwood P. *Public Education in the United States: A Study and Interpretation of American Educational History.* Boston, 1934.

3054 CULVER, Raymond B. *Horace Mann and Religion in the Massachusetts Public Schools.* New Haven, 1929.

3055 CURTI, Merle. *The Social Ideas of American Educators.* New York, 1935.†

3056 CUTHBERT, Norma, ed. "Yankee Preacher-Teacher in Florida, 1838." *Hunt Lib Q,* VIII (1944), 95–104.

3057 EDWARDS, Newton, and Herman G. RICHEY. *The School in the American Social Order.* Boston, 1947.

3058 FAHERTY, William Barnaley. "Nativism and Midwestern Education: The Experience of Saint Louis University, 1832–1856." *Hist Educ Q,* VIII (1948), 447–458.

3059 FLETCHER, Robert S. *A History of Oberlin College from Its Foundation Through the Civil War.* Oberlin, 1943.

3060 FREIDEL, Frank. "A Plan for Modern Education in Early Philadelphia." *Pa Hist,* XIV (1947), 175–184.

3061 GARA, Larry, ed. "A New Englander's View of Plantation Life: Letters of Edwin Hall [tutor] to Cyrus Woodman, 1837." *J S Hist,* XVIII (1952), 343–354.

3062 GEHLMANN, Robert. "Education in Illinois before 1857." *Ill St Hist J,* L (1957), 119–140.

3063 GODBOLD, Albea. *The Church College of the Old South.* Durham, 1944.

3064 GOODMAN, David Michael. "The American Institute of Instruction and the Contours of Educational Association and Reform in New England, 1830–1918." Doctoral dissertation, Clark University, 1972.

3065 GORDON, Mary McDougall. "Union with the Virtuous Past: The Development of School Reform in Massachusetts, 1789–1837." Doctoral dissertation, University of Pittsburgh, 1974.

3066 GORDY, John P. *Rise and Growth of the Normal-School Idea in the United States.* Washington, D.C., 1891.

3067 GRIZZELL, Emit D. *Origin and Development of the High School in New England before 1865.* New York, 1923.

3068 GURALNIK, Stanley M. *Science and the Ante-Bellum American College.* Philadelphia, 1975.†

3069 HANSEN, Allen O. *Early Educational Leadership in the Ohio Valley: A Study of Educational Reconstruction Through the Western Literary Institute and College of Professional Teachers, 1829–1841.* New York, 1923.

3070 HALSEY, LeRoy J., ed. *The Works of Philip Lindsley.* 3 vols. Philadelphia, 1866.

3071 HARDING, Thomas S. *College Literary Societies: Their Contribution to Higher Education in the United States, 1815–1876.* New York, 1971.

3072 HARRELL, Laura D. S. "The Development of the Lyceum Movement in Mississippi." *J Miss Hist,* XXXI (1969), 187–201.

3073 HAUNTON, Richard H. "Education and Democracy: The Views of Philip Lindsley." *Tenn Hist Q,* XXI (1962), 131–139.

3074 HAYES, Cecil B. *The American Lyceum: Its History and Contribution to Education.* Washington, D.C., 1932.

3075 HENDERSON, Archibald. *The Campus of the First State University.* Chapel Hill, 1949.

3076 HERBST, Jurgen, comp. *The History of American Education.* Goldentree Bibliographies in American History. Arlington Heights, 1973.†

3077 HINSDALE, Burke A. *Horace Mann and the Common School Revival in the United States.* New York, 1898.

3078 HOFSTADTER, Richard, and Wilson SMITH, eds. *American Higher Education: A Documentary History.* Chicago, 1961.†

3079 HOFSTADTER, Richard. *Academic Freedom in the Age of the College,* New York, 1961.†

3080 HOGELAND, Ronald W. "Coeducation of the Sexes at Oberlin College: A Study of Social Ideas in Mid-Nineteenth Century America." *J Soc Hist,* VI (1972), 160–177.

3081 HOLLIS, Daniel Walker. *University of South Carolina.* 2 vols. Columbia, S.C., 1951.

3082 HUEHNER, David Robert. "Reform and the Pre-Civil War American Colleges." Doctoral dissertation, University of Illinois, Urbana-Champaign, 1972.

3083 JACKSON, Sidney L. *America's Struggle for Free Schools: Social Tension and Education in New England and New York, 1827–42.* Washington, D.C., 1941.

3084 JENNINGS, Walter Wilson. *Transylvania: Pioneer University of the West.* New York, 1955.

3085 KAESTLE, Carl F. *The Evolution of an Urban School System: New York City, 1750–1850.* Cambridge, Mass., 1973.

3086 KATZ, Michael B. *The Irony of Early School Reform: Educational Innovation in Mid-Nineteenth Century Massachusetts.* Cambridge, Mass., 1968.†

3087 KELLY, Robert L. *The American Colleges and the Social Order.* New York, 1940.

3088 KNIGHT, Edgar W. *Education in the United States.* 3d rev. ed. Boston, 1951.

3089 KNIGHT, Edgar W. *A Documentary History of Education in the South before 1860.* 5 vols. Chapel Hill, 1949–1953.

3090 KNIGHT, Edgar W. *Public Education in the South.* Boston, 1922.

3091 KORNEGAY, William Gordon. "The North Carolina Institute of Education, 1831–1834." *N C Hist Rev,* XXXVI (1959), 141–152.

3092 KRUMPELMANN, John T. *Southern Scholars in Goethe's Germany.* Chapel Hill, 1965.

3093 LANNIE, Vincent Peter. "William Seward and the New York School Controversy, 1840–1842: A Problem in Historical Motivation." *Hist Educ Q,* VI (1966), 52–71.

3094 LANNIE, Vincent Peter. "William Seward and Common School Education." *Hist Educ Q,* IV (1964), 181–192.

3095 MCCADDEN, Joseph J. *Education in Pennsylvania, 1801–1835, and its Debt to Robert Vaux.* Philadelphia, 1937.

3096 MCLEAN, Robert Colin, ed. "A Yankee Tutor [Samuel H. Perkins] in the Old South." *N C Hist Rev,* XLVII (1970), 51–85.

3097 MACLEOD, Anne Scott. "Education for Freedom: Children's Fiction in Jacksonian America." *Har Ed Rev,* XLVI (1976), 425–435.

3098 MCVEY, Frank L. *The Gates Open Slowly: A History of Education in Kentucky.* Lexington, 1949.

3099 MADSEN, David. *Early National Education, 1776–1830.* New York, 1974.†

3100 MANGUN, Vernon L. *The American Normal School: Its Rise and Development in Massachusetts.* Baltimore, 1928.

3101 MATTINGLY, Paul. *The Classless Profession: American Schoolmen of the Nineteenth Century.* New York, 1975.†

3102 MILLER, Edward A. *The History of Educational Legislation in Ohio from 1803 to 1850.* Chicago, 1920.

3103 MILLER, George F. *The Academy System of the State of New York.* Albany, 1922.

3104 MILLER, Howard. *The Revolutionary College: American Presbyterian Higher Education, 1707–1837.* New York, 1976.

3105 MOHL, Raymond A. "Education as Social Control in New York City, 1784–1825." *N Y Hist,* LI (1970), 219–237.

3106 MONROE, Paul. *Founding of the American Public School System: A History of Education in the United States from the Early Settlements to the Close of the Civil War Period.* New York, 1940.

3107 MONROE, Will S. *The Educational Labors of Henry Barnard: A Study in the History of American Pedagogy.* Syracuse, 1893.

3108 MORISON, Samuel E. *Three Centuries of Harvard, 1636–1936.* Cambridge, Mass., 1936.

3109 NAYLOR, Natalie A. "The Ante-Bellum College Movement: A Reappraisal of Tewksbury's *Founding of American Colleges and Universities.*" *Hist Educ Q,* XIII (1973), 261–274.

3110 ORR, Dorothy. *A History of Education in Georgia.* Chapel Hill, 1950.

3111 PAULSTON, Roland G. "French Influence in American Institutions of Higher Learning, 1784–1825." *Hist Educ Q,* VIII (1968), 229–245.

3112 PAWA, Jay M. "Workingmen and Free Schools in the Nineteenth Century: A Comment on the Labor-Education Thesis." *Hist Educ Q,* XI (1971), 287–302.

3113 PETERSON, Charles E. "The *Common School* Advocate: Moulders of the Public Mind." *Ill St Hist J,* LVII (1964), 261–269.

3114 POPE, Christie Franham. "Preparation for Pedestals: North Carolina Antebellum Female Seminaries." Doctoral dissertation, University of Chicago, 1977.

3115 POTTS, David B. "Baptist Colleges in the Development of American Society, 1812–1861." Doctoral dissertation, Harvard University, 1967.

3116 POTTS, David B. "American Colleges in the Nineteenth Century: From Localism to Denominationalism." *Hist Educ Q,* XI (1971), 363–380.

3117 PRATT, John W. "Governor Seward and New York City School Controversy, 1840–1842." *N Y Hist,* XLII (1961), 351–364.

3118 PRATT, John W. "Religious Conflict in the Development of the New York City Public School System." *Hist Educ Q,* V (1965), 110–120.

3119 PULLIAM, John. "Changing Attitudes toward Free Public Schools in Illinois, 1825–1860." *Hist Educ Q,* VII (1967), 191–208.

3120 RAINSFORD, George N. *Congress and Higher Education in the Nineteenth Century.* Knoxville, Tenn., 1972.

3121 RAMMELKAMP, Charles H. *Illinois College: A Centennial History, 1829–1929.* New Haven, 1928.

3122 RUDOLPH, Frederick. *The American College and University: A History.* New York, 1962.†

3123 RYON, Roderick N. "Public Sponsorship of Special Education in Pennsylvania from 1818 to 1834." *Pa Hist,* XXXIV (1967), 240–249.

3124 SACK, Saul. *History of Higher Education in Pennsylvania.* Harrisburg, 1963.

3125 SCHMIDT, George P. *The Liberal Arts College: A Chapter in American Cultural History.* New Brunswick, 1957.

3126 SCHULTZ, Stanley K. *The Culture Factory: Boston Public Schools, 1789–1860.* New York, 1973.

3127 SELLERS, James B. *History of the University of Alabama.* Vol. I, 1818–1902. University of Alabama, 1953.

3128 SHOEMAKER, Ervin C. *Noah Webster, Pioneer of Learning.* New York, 1936.

3129 SLOSSON, Edwin E. *The American Spirit in Education: A Chronicle of Great Teachers.* New Haven, 1921.

3130 SMITH, Sherman M. *The Relation of the State to Religious Education in Massachusetts.* Syracuse, 1926.

3131 STORY, Ronald. "Harvard and the Boston Brahmins: A Study in Institutional and Class Development, 1800–1865." *J Soc Hist,* VIII (1975), 94–121.

3132 STORY, Ronald. "Harvard Students, the Boston Elite and the New England Preparatory System, 1800–1870." *Hist Educ Q,* XV (1975), 281–298.

3133 SUAREZ, Raleigh A. "Chronicle of a Failure: Public Education in Antebellum Louisiana." *La Hist,* XII (1971), 109–122.

3134 SWIFT, David E. "Yankee in Virginia: James Marsh at Hampden-Sydney, 1823–1826." *Va Mag Hist Biog,* LXXX (1972), 312–332.

3135 SWIFT, David E. "Thomas Jefferson, John Holt Rice and Education in Virginia, 1815–1825." *J Presby Hist,* XLIX (1971), 32–58.

3136 TAYLOR, James M. *Before Vassar Opened: A Contribution to the History of Higher Education of Women in America.* Boston, 1914.

3137 TEWKSBURY, Donald G. *The Founding of American Colleges and Universities before the Civil War, with Particular Reference to the Religious Influences Bearing upon the College Movement.* New York, 1922.

3138 THWING, Charles F. *A History of Higher Education in America.* New York, 1906.

3139 TREON, Selwyn K. "Popular Education in Nineteenth Century St. Louis." *Hist Educ Q,* XIII (1973), 23–40.

3140 UROFSKY, Melvin I. "Reforms and Response: The Yale Report of 1828." *Hist Educ Q*, V (1965), 53–67.

3141 VAN DEUSEN, Glyndon G. "Seward and the School Question Reconsidered." *J Am Hist*, LII (1965), 313–319.

3142 VINOVSKIS, Maris A. "Trends in Massachusetts Education, 1826–1860." *Hist Educ Q*, XII (1972), 501–529.

3143 WARFEL, Harry R. *Noah Webster, Schoolmaster to America*. New York, 1936.

3144 WELTER, Rush. *Popular Education and Democratic Thought in America*. New York, 1962.†

3145 WERTENBAKER, Thomas J. *Princeton, 1746–1896*. Princeton, 1946.

3146 WHITE, Arthur O. "Salem's Antebellum Black Community: Seedbed of the School Integration Movement." *Essex Inst Hist Coll*, CVIII (1972), 99–118.

3147 WHITEHEAD, John S. *The Separation of College and State: Columbia, Dartmouth, Harvard, and Yale, 1776–1876*. New Haven, Conn., 1973.

3148 WICKERSHAM, James P. *A History of Education in Pennsylvania, Private and Public, Elementary and Higher*. Lancaster, 1886.

3149 WOODSON, Carter G. *The Education of the Negro Prior to 1861: A History of the Education of the Colored People of the United States from the Beginning of Slavery to the Civil War*. New York, 1915.

3150 WILLIAMS, E. I. F. *Horace Mann: Educational Statesman*. New York, 1937.

3151 WOODY, Thomas. *A History of Women's Education in the United States*. 2 vols. New York, 1929.

3152 WOOLVERTON, John F. "Philip Lindsley and the Cause of Education in the Old Southwest." *Tenn Hist Q*, XIX (1960), 3–22.

3153 WRIGHT, John D., Jr. *Transylvania: Tutor to the West*. Lexington, 1975.

3154 YAKELEY, Leon. "The Development of Higher Education in the Jacksonian Period, 1825–1840." *Hist*, III (1940), 37–51.

6. Family

See also **1667, 1948, 2660, 2666, 2725, 2813, 2819, 2856, 2899, 3097, 3228, 4554**

3155 BREMNER, Robert H.; John BARNARD; Tamara K. HAREVEN; and Robert M. MENNEL, eds. *Children and Youth in America: A Documentary History*. 2 vols. Cambridge, Mass., 1970–1971.†

3156 CALHOUN, Arthur W. *A Social History of the American Family from Colonial Times to the Present*. 3 vols. Cleveland, 1917–19.

3157 COCKS, Edmund. "The Malthusian Theory in Pre-Civil War America: An Original Relation to the Universe." *Popl Stud*, XX (1967), 343–363.

3158 GREVEN, Philip J., comp. *Child-Rearing Concepts, 1628–1861*. Itasca, Ill., 1973.

3159 HAWES, Joseph M. *Children in Urban Society: Juvenile Delinquence in Nineteenth-Century America*. New York, 1971.

3160 MCGLONE, Robert Elno. "Suffer the Children: The Emergence of Modern Middle-Class Family Life in America, 1820–1870." Doctoral dissertation, University of California, Los Angeles, 1971.

3161 MCLOUGHLIN, William G. "Evangelical Child-Rearing in the Age of Jackson: Francis Wayland's View of When and How to Subdue the Willfulness of Children." *J Soc Hist,* IX (1975), 21–43.

3162 MILDEN, James Wallace. "The Sacred Sanctuary: Family Life in Nineteenth-Century America." Doctoral dissertation, University of Maryland, 1974.

3163 REED, James. *The Birth Control Movement and American Society Since 1830.* New York, 1978.

3164 SMITH, Daniel Scott. "Population, Family and Society in Hingham, Massachusetts, 1635–1880." Doctoral dissertation, University of California, Berkeley, 1973.

3165 WALTERS, Ronald G. "The Family and Ante-Bellum Reform: An Interpretation." *Soc,* III (1973), 221–232.

7. Women

See also **588, 589, 648–653, 2216, 3114, 3136, 3151, 3257, 4247, 4302**

3165A BERG, Barbara J. *The Remembered Gate: Origins of American Feminism: The Woman and the City, 1800–1860.* New York, 1978.

3166 BRENZEL, Barbara. "Lancaster Industrial School for Girls: A Social Portrait of a Nineteenth Century Reform School for Girls." *Fem Stud,* III (1975), 40–53.

3167 BUNKLE, Phillida. "Sentimental Womanhood and Domestic Education, 1830–1870." *Hist Educ Q,* XIV (1974), 13–30.

3168 BURSTYN, Joan N. "Catherine Beecher and the Education of American Women." *N Eng Q,* XLVII (1974), 386–403.

3169 CLINTON, Katherine. "Pioneer Women in Chicago, 1833–1837." *J W,* XII (1973), 317–324.

3170 CONRAD, Susan Phinney. *Perish the Thought: Intellectual Women in Romantic America, 1830–1860.* New York, 1976.

3170A COTT, Nancy F. *The Bonds of Womanhood: 'Women's Sphere' in New England, 1780–1835.* New Haven, 1977.

3171 COTT, Nancy F., comp. *Root of Bitterness: Documents of the Social History of American Women.* New York, 1972.†

3171A DOUGLAS, Ann. *The Feminization of American Culture.* New York, 1977.

3172 DUBLIN, Thomas Louis. "Women at Work: The Transformation of Work and Community in Lowell, Massachusetts, 1826–1860." Doctoral dissertation, Columbia University, 1975.

3173 DUBLIN, Thomas Louis. "Women, Work, and the Family: Female Operatives in the Lowell Mills, 1830–1860." *Fem Stud,* III (1975), 30–39.

3174 DUBLIN, Thomas Louis. "Women, Work, and Protest in the Early Lowell Mills: 'The Oppressing Hand of Avarice Would Enslave Us.' " *Labor Hist,* XVI (1975), 99–116.

3175 FLEXNER, Eleanor. *Century of Struggle: the Women's Rights Movement in the United States.* Cambridge, Mass., 1959.†

3176 JAMES, Janet Wilson. "Changing Ideas about Women in the United States, 1776–1825." Doctoral dissertation, Harvard University, 1954.

3177 KELLEY, Mary Bremer. "The Unconscious Rebel: Studies in Feminine Fiction, 1820–1880." Doctoral dissertation, State University of Iowa, 1974.

3178 KENDALL, Kathleen Edgerton, and Jeanne Y. FISHER. "Francis Wright on Women's Rights: Eloquence versus Ethos." *Q J Sp,* LX (1974), 58–68.

3179 KRADITOR, Aileen S., ed. *Up From the Pedestal: Selected Writings in the History of American Feminism.* Chicago, 1970.†

3180 LABBÉ, Dolores Egger. "Women in Early Nineteenth-Century Louisiana." Doctoral dissertation, University of Delaware, 1975.

3181 LERNER, Gerda. "The Lady and the Mill Girl: Changes in the Status of Women in the Age of Jackson." *Mid-Am,* X (1969), 5–15.

3182 LEWIS, W. David. "The Female Criminal and the Prisons of New York, 1825–1845." *N Y Hist,* XLII (1961), 215–236.

3183 LUTZ, Alma. *Emma Willard, Daughter of Democracy.* New York, 1929.

3184 MELDER, Keith. "Ladies Bountiful: Organized Women's Benevolence in Early 19th Century America." *N Y Hist,* XLVIII (1967), 231–254.

3185 MELDER, Keith E. *Beginnings of Sisterhood: The American Women's Rights Movement, 1800–1850.* New York, 1978.

3186 MOHR, James C. *Abortion in America: The Origins and Evolution of a National Policy, 1800–1900.* New York, 1978.

3187 NISSENBAUM, Stephen W. "Careful Love: Sylvester Graham and the Emergence of Victorian Sexual Theory in America, 1830–1840." Doctoral dissertation, University of Wisconsin, Madison, 1968.

3188 OSTROGORSKI, M. *The Rights of Women: A Comparative Study in History and Legislation.* New York, 1893.

3189 PIEL, Ethel. "The Atrophied Rib: Urban Middle-Class Women in Jacksonian America." Doctoral dissertation, University of Pittsburgh, 1970.

3190 RICCIOTTI, Dominic. "Popular Art in Godey's Lady's Book: An Image of the American Woman, 1830–1860." *Hist N H,* XXVII (1972), 3–26.

3191 RILEY, Glenda Lou Gates. "Changing Image of the American Woman, 1828–1848." Doctoral dissertation, Ohio State University, 1967.

3192 ROSENBERG, Carroll Smith. "Beauty, the Beast, and the Militant Woman: A Case Study in Sex Roles and Social Stress in Jacksonian America." *Am Q,* XXIII (1971), 562–584.

3193 ROSENBERG, Carroll Smith, and Charles ROSENBERG. "The Female Animal: Medical and Biological Views of Woman and Her Role in Nineteenth-Century America." *J Am Hist,* LX (1973), 332–356.

3194 ROSENBERG, Charles E. "Sexuality, Class and Role in 19th-Century America." *Am Q,* XXV (1973), 131–153.

3195 ROWBOTHAM, Sheila. *Women, Resistance, and Revolution: A History of Women and Revolution in the Modern World.* New York, 1972.†

3196 RYAN, Mary Patricia. "American Society and the Cult of Domesticity, 1830–1860." Doctoral dissertation, University of California, Santa Barbara, 1971.

3197 RUOFF, John C. "Frivolity to Consumption: Or, Southern Womanhood in Antebellum Literature." *C W Hist*, XVIII (1972), 213–229.

3198 SCOTT, Anne Firor. *The Southern Lady: From Pedestal to Politics, 1830–1930.* Chicago, 1970.†

3199 SMITH, Page. *Daughters of the Promised Land: Women in American History.* Boston, 1970.†

3200 STRONG, Floyd Bryan. "Sex, Character, and Reform in America, 1830–1920." Doctoral dissertation, Stanford University, 1972.

3201 WELTER, Barbara. "Anti-Intellectualism and the American Woman." *Mid-Am,* XLVIII (1966), 258–270.

3202 WELTER, Barbara. *Dimity Convictions: The American Woman in the Nineteenth Century.* Athens, Ohio, 1976.†

3203 WELTER, Barbara. "The Cult of True Womanhood, 1820–1860." *Am Q,* XVIII (1966), 151–174.

VIII. Blacks and Slavery

1. General Works

See also **458–460, 627–633, 634–637, 648–653, 762, 763, 766, 767, 936, 1040, 1136, 1138, 1147, 1148, 1728, 2160, 2660, 2673, 2749, 2891, 2948, 2969, 2973, 3149, 3678, 3700, 3701, 3719, 3746, 3917, 3918, 4273, 4764, 4768**

3204 BINDER, Frederick Melvin. *The Color Problem in Early National America as Viewed by John Adams, Jefferson, and Jackson.* The Hague, 1968.

3205 BLASSINGAME, John W. *The Slave Community; Plantation Life in the Antebellum South.* New York, 1972.†

3206 CATTERALL, Helen T., ed. *Judicial Cases Concerning American Slavery and the Negro.* 5 vols. Washington, D.C., 1926–1937.

3207 CRAVEN, Avery O. "Poor Whites and Negroes in the Ante-Bellum South." *J Neg Hist,* XV (1930), 14–25.

3208 DAVIS, David Brion. *The Problem of Slavery in the Age of Revolution: 1770–1823.* Ithaca, 1975.†

3209 DAVIS, David Brion. "Slavery and the Post-World War II Historians." *Daed,* CIII (1974), 1–16.

3210 DEGLER, Carl N. *Neither Black Nor White: Slavery and Race Relations in Brazil and the United States.* New York, 1971.†

3211 DOYLE, Bertram W. *The Etiquette of Race Relations in the South.* Chicago, 1937.†

3212 EBLIN, Jack E. "Growth of the Black Population in *ante bellum* America, 1820–1860." *Popl Stud,* XXVI (1972), 273–287.

3213 ELKINS, Stanley M. *Slavery: A Problem in American Institutional and Intellectual Life.* 3d ed. Chicago, 1976.†

3214 ENGERMAN, Stanley L., and Eugene D. GENOVESE, eds. *Race and Slavery in the Western Hemisphere: Quantitative Studies.* Princeton, 1975.

3215 FELDSTEIN, Stanley. *Once a Slave: The Slaves' View of Slavery.* New York, 1971.†

3216 FINKELMAN, Paul. "A More Perfect Union? Slavery, Comity, and Federalism: 1787–1861." Doctoral dissertation, University of Chicago, 1976.

3217 FLANIGAN, Daniel John. "The Criminal Law of Slavery and Freedom, 1800–1868." Doctoral dissertation, Rice University, 1973.

3218 FLANIGAN, Daniel J. "Criminal Procedure in Slave Trials in the Antebellum South." *J S Hist,* XL (1974), 537–564.

3219 FRANKLIN, John Hope. *From Slavery to Freedom: A History of Negro Americans.* 4th ed. New York, 1974.†

3220 FRANKLIN, Vincent P. "Slavery, Personality, and Black Culture—Some Theoretical Issues." *Phylon,* XXXV (1974), 54–63.

3221 FRAZIER, E. Franklin. *The Free Negro Family: A Study of Family Origins before the Civil War.* Nashville, 1932.

3222 FRAZIER, E. Franklin. *The Negro Family in the United States.* Rev. ed. Chicago, 1966.†

3223 FRAZIER, E. Franklin. *The Negro in the United States.* Rev. ed. New York, 1957.

3224 FREDERICKSON, George M. *The Black Image in the White Mind: The Debate on Afro-American Character and Destiny, 1817–1914.* New York, 1971.†

3225 GENOVESE, Eugene D. *The World the Slaveholders Made.* New York, 1969.

3226 GENOVESE, Eugene D. *Roll, Jordan, Roll: The World the Slaves Made.* New York, 1974.†

3227 GOLDIN, Claudia Dale. *Urban Slavery in the American South, 1820–1860: A Quantitative Study.* Chicago, 1976.

3228 GUTMAN, Herbert G. *The Black Family in Slavery and Freedom, 1750–1925.* New York, 1976.†

3229 HARLAN, Louis R. *The Negro in American History.* Am Hist Assn Pamphlets. Washington, D.C., 1965.

3230 HUGGINS, Nathan I. *Black Odyssey: The Afro-American Ordeal in Slavery.* New York, 1978.

3231 HURD, John C. *The Law of Freedom and Bondage in the United States.* 2 vols. Boston, 1862.

3232 IRWIN, Leonard B., comp. *Black Studies: A Bibliography.* Brooklawn, N.J., 1973.

3233 JONES, Bobby Frank. "A Cultural Middle Passage: Slave Marriage and Family in the Ante-Bellum South." Doctoral dissertation, University of North Carolina at Chapel Hill, 1965.

3234 KLEIN, Herbert S. *Slavery in the Americas: A Comparative Study of Virginia and Cuba.* Chicago, 1967.

3235 KUGLER, Ruben F. "U. B. Phillips' Use of Sources." *J Neg Hist,* XLVII (1962), 153–168.

3236 LABINJOK, Justin. "The Sexual Life of the Oppressed: An Examination of the Family Life of Ante-Bellum Slaves." *Phylon,* XXXV (1974), 375–397.

3237 LACK, Paul Dean. "Urban Slavery in the Southwest." Doctoral dissertation, Texas Tech University, 1973.

3238 LANE, Ann J., ed. *The Debate over Slavery: Stanley Elkins and His Critics.* Urbana, 1971.†

3239 LEWIS, Mary Agnes. "Slavery and Personality: A Further Comment." *Am Q,* XIX (1967), 114–121.

3240 LYND, Staughton. "On Turner, Beard and Slavery." *J Neg Hist,* XLVIII (1963), 235–250.

3241 MCKENZIE, Edna Chappell. "Self-Hire among Slaves, 1820–1860: Institutional Variation or Aberration?" Doctoral dissertation, University of Pittsburgh, 1973.

3242 MCPHERSON, James M. "Slavery and Race." *Perspectives Am Hist,* III (1969), 460–473.

3243 MCPHERSON, James M.; Laurence B. HOLLAND; James M. BANNER, Jr.; Nancy J. WEISS; and Michael D. BELL. *Blacks in America: Bibliographical Essays.* Garden City, 1971.

3244 MEIER, August, and Elliott M. RUDWICK. *From Plantation to Ghetto: An Interpretive History of American Negroes.* 3d ed. New York, 1976.†

3245 MILLER, Elinor, and Eugene D. GENOVESE, eds. *Plantation, Town, and Country: Essays on the Local History of American Slave Society.* Urbana, 1974.†

3246 MILLER, Elizabeth W., and Mary L. FISHER, eds. *The Negro in America: A Bibliography.* 2d ed. Cambridge, Mass., 1970.†

3247 MILLER, Wayne Charles, and Faye Nell VOWELL, comps. *A Comprehensive Bibliography for the Study of American Minorities.* 2 vols. New York, 1976.

3248 MORRIS, Richard B. "The Measure of Bondage in the Slave States." *Miss Val Hist Rev,* XLI (1954), 219–240.

3249 OWENS, Harry P., ed. *Perspectives and Irony in American Slavery.* Jackson, 1976.†

3250 OWENS, Leslie Howard. *This Species of Property: Slave Life and Culture in the Old South.* New York, 1976.†

3251 PHILLIPS, Ulrich B. *American Negro Slavery.* New York, 1918.†

3252 PHILLIPS, Ulrich B. *Life and Labor in the Old South.* Boston, 1929.†

3253 RAWICK, George P., ed. *The American Slave: A Composite Autobiography.* 19 vols. Westport, 1972. Vol. I: *From Sundown to Sunup: The Making of the Black Community.* †

3254 RICE, C. Duncan. *The Rise and Fall of Black Slavery.* New York, 1975.†

3255 ROSE, Willie Lee, ed. *A Documentary History of Slavery in North America.* New York, 1976.†

3256 SALEM, Sam E. "U. B. Phillips and the Scientific Tradition." *Ga Hist Q,* XLIV (1960), 172–185.

3257 SIDES, Sudie Duncan. "Women and Slaves: An Interpretation Based on the Writings of Southern Women." Doctoral dissertation, University of North Carolina at Chapel Hill, 1969.

3258 SIO, Arnold A. "Interpretations of Slavery: The Slave Status in the Americas." *Comp Stud Soc Hist,* VII (1965), 298–308.

3259 SMITH, Burton M. "A Study of American Historians and their Interpretation of Negro Slavery in the United States." Doctoral dissertation, Washington State University, 1970.

3260 SMITH, Dwight L., ed. *Afro-American History: A Bibliography.* Santa Barbara, 1974.

3261 SMITH, John David. "The Formative Period of American Slave Historiography, 1890–1920." Doctoral dissertation, University of Kentucky, 1977.

3262 STAMPP, Kenneth M. "The Historian and Southern Negro Slavery." *Am Hist Rev,* LVII (1952), 613–624.

3263 STAMPP, Kenneth M. *The Peculiar Institution: Slavery in the ante-Bellum South.* New York, 1956.†

3264 STAMPP, Kenneth M. "Rebels and Sambos: The Search for the Negro's Personality in Slavery." *J S Hist,* XXXVII (1971), 367–392.

3265 STAROBIN, Robert S. *Industrial Slavery in the Old South.* New York, 1970.†

3266 STAROBIN, Robert S., ed. *Blacks in Bondage: Letters of American Slaves.* New York, 1974.†

3267 STONE, James Herbert. "Black Leadership in the Old South: The Slave Drivers of the Rice Kingdom." Doctoral dissertation, Florida State University, 1976.

3268 WADE, Richard C. *Slavery in the Cities: The South, 1820–1860.* New York, 1964.†

3269 WALL, Bennett H. "African Slavery." *Writing Southern History: Essays in Historiography in Honor of Fletcher M. Green.* Ed. Arthur S. LINK and Rembert W. PATRICK. Baton Rouge, 1965.

3270 WEBBER, Thomas L. *Deep Like the Rivers: Education in the Slave Quarter Community, 1831–1865.* New York, 1978.

3271 WINSELL, Keith Andrew. "Black Identity: The Southern Negro, 1830–1895." Doctoral dissertation, University of California, Los Angeles, 1971.

3272 WISH, Harvey. *Slavery in the South: First-Hand Accounts of the Ante-Bellum American Southland.* New York, 1964.†

3273 YOUNGER, Richard D. "Southern Grand Juries and Slavery." *J Neg Hist,* XL (1955), 166–178.

2. Slavery: State and Local Studies

See also **1438, 2140, 2160, 2258, 2285, 2347, 3146**

3274 BALLAGH, James Curtis. *A History of Slavery in Virginia.* Baltimore, 1902.

3275 BASSETT, John S. *Slavery in the State of North Carolina.* Baltimore, 1899.

3276 BOGGER, Tommy Lee. "The Slave and Free Black Community in Norfolk, 1775–1865." Doctoral dissertation, University of Virginia, 1976.

3277 BRACKETT, Jeffrey R. *The Negro in Maryland: A Study of the Institution of Slavery.* Baltimore, 1889.

3278 COLEMAN, J. Winston. *Slavery Times in Kentucky.* Chapel Hill, 1940.

3279 DORSETT, Lyle Wesley. "Slaveholding in Jackson County, Missouri." *Mo Hist Soc Bull,* XX (1963), 25–37.

3280 DUFFNER, Robert William. "Slavery in Missouri River Counties, 1820–1865." Doctoral dissertation, University of Missouri, Columbia, 1974.

3281 FLANDERS, Ralph B. *Plantation Slavery in Georgia.* Chapel Hill, 1933.

3282 HINDUS, Michael S. "Black Justice under White Law: Criminal Prosecutions of Blacks in Antebellum South Carolina." *J Am Hist,* LXIII (1976), 575–599.

3283 HOLT, Bryce R. *The Supreme Court of North Carolina and Slavery.* Durham, 1927.

3284 HUNTER, Lloyd A. "Slavery in St. Louis, 1804–1860." *Mo Hist Soc Bull,* XXX (1974), 233–263.

3285 JAMESON, J. Franklin, ed. "Autobiography of Omar ibn Said, Slave in North Carolina, 1831." *Am Hist Rev,* XXX (1925), 787–795.

3286 JOHNSTON, James Hugo. *Race Relations in Virginia & Miscegenation in the South, 1776–1860.* Amherst, 1970.

3287 LEWIS, Ronald Loran. "Slavery in the Chesapeake Iron Industry, 1716–1865." Doctoral dissertation, Akron University, 1974.

3288 MATHIAS, Frank F. "John Randolph's Freedmen: The Thwarting of a Will." *J S Hist,* XXXIX (1973), 263–272.

3289 MOHR, Clarence L. "Slavery in Oglethorpe County, Georgia, 1773–1865." *Phylon,* XXXIII (1972), 4–21.

3290 MOODY, V. Alton. "Slavery on Louisiana Sugar Plantations." *La Hist Q,* VII (1924), 191–301.

3291 MOONEY, Chase C. *Slavery in Tennessee.* Bloomington, 1957.

3292 MUNFORD, Beverley B. *Virginia's Attitude toward Slavery and Secession.* New York, 1909.

3293 OPPER, Peter Kent. "North Carolina Quakers: Reluctant Slaveholders." *N C Hist Rev,* LII (1975), 37–58.

3294 PHIFER, Edward W. "Slavery in Microcosm: Burke County, North Carolina." *J S Hist,* XXVIII (1962), 137–165.

3295 RICHTER, William L. "Slavery in Baton Rouge, 1820–1860." *La Hist,* X (1969), 125–146.

3296 SAVITT, Todd L. *Medicine and Slavery: The Health Care of Blacks in Antebellum Virginia.* Urbana, Ill., 1978.

3297 SELLERS, James Benson. *Slavery in Alabama.* University, Ala., 1950.

3298 SMITH, Julia Floyd. *Slavery and Plantation Growth in Antebellum Florida, 1821–1860.* Gainesville, 1973.

3299 STEALEY, John Edmund, III. "Slavery and the Western Virginia Salt Industry." *J Neg Hist,* LIX (1974), 105–131.

3300 STEEL, Edward M., Jr. "Black Monongalians: A Judicial View of Slavery and the Negro in Monongalia County, 1776–1865." *W Va Hist,* XXXIX (1973), 331–359.

3301 STRICKLAND, Arvarh E. "Aspects of Slavery in Missouri, 1821." *Mo Hist Rev,* LXV (1971), 505–526.

3302 SYDNOR, Charles S. *Slavery in Mississippi.* New York, 1933.

3303 TAYLOR, Joe Gray. *Negro Slavery in Louisiana.* Baton Rouge, 1963.

3304 TAYLOR, Orville W. *Negro Slavery in Arkansas.* Durham, 1958.

3305 TAYLOR, Rosser H. *Slaveholding in North Carolina: An Economic View.* Chapel Hill, 1926.

3306 TREMAIN, Mary. *Slavery in the District of Columbia: The Policy of Congress and the Struggle for Abolition.* New York, 1892.

3307 TREXLER, Harrison A. *Slavery in Missouri, 1804–1865.* Baltimore, 1914.

3308 WILLIAMS, E. Russ, Jr., ed. "Slave Patrol Ordinances of St. Tammany Parish, Louisiana, 1835–1838." *La Hist,* XIII (1972), 399–412.

3. The Slave Trade

See also **1827, 1860, 1864, 1865, 1869**

3309 BANCROFT, Frederic. *Slave Trading in the Old South.* Baltimore, 1931.†

3310 CABLE, Mary. *Black Odyssey: The Case of the Slave Ship Amistad.* New York, 1971.†

3311 CALDERHEAD, William. "The Role of the Professional Slave Trader in a Slave Economy: Austin Woolfolk, A Case Study." *C W Hist,* XXIII (1977), 195–211.

3312 COLLINS, Winfred H. *The Domestic Slave Trade of the Southern States.* New York, 1904.

3313 CURTIN, Philip D. *The Atlantic Slave Trade: A Census.* Madison, 1969.†

3314 DU BOIS, W. E. B. *The Suppression of the African Slave Trade to the United States of America, 1638–1870.* New York, 1896.†

3315 HOWELL, Isabel. "John Armfield, Slave-Trader." *Tenn Hist Q,* II (1943), 3–29.

3316 LAPRADE, William T. "The Domestic Slave Trade in the District of Columbia." *J Neg Hist,* XI (1926), 17–34.

3317 MCNEILLY, Earl E. "The United States Navy and the Suppression of the West African Slave Trade, 1819–1862." Doctoral dissertation, Case Western Reserve University, 1973.

3318 MANNIX, Daniel P., and Malcolm COWLEY. *Black Cargoes: A History of the Atlantic Slave Trade, 1518–1865.* New York, 1962.

3319 MILLER, William L. "A Note on the Importance of the Interstate Slave Trade of the Ante-Bellum South." *J Pol Econ,* LXXIII (1965), 181–187.

3320 NOONAN, John T., Jr. *The Antelope: The Ordeal of the Recaptured Africans in the Administrations of James Monroe and J. Q. Adams.* Berkeley, 1977.

3321 SHINGLETON, Royce Gordon. "David Brydie Mitchell and the African Importation Case of 1820." *J Neg Hist,* LVIII (1973), 327–340.

3322 STAFFORD, Frances J. "Illegal Importations: Enforcement of the Slave Trade Laws along the Florida Coast, 1810–1828." *Fla Hist Q,* XLVI (1967), 124–133.

3323 STEPHENSON, Wendell Holmes. *Isaac Franklin, Slave Trader and Planter of the Old South.* Baton Rouge, 1938.

3324 WHITTEN, David O. "Slave Buying in 1835 Virginia as Revealed by Letters of a Louisiana Negro Sugar Planter." *La Hist,* XI (1970), 231–244.

4. The Economics of Slavery

3325 AITKEN, Hugh G. J., ed. *Did Slavery Pay? Readings in the Economics of Black Slavery in the United States.* Boston, 1971.†

3326 AUFHAUSER, R. Keith. "Slavery and Scientific Management." *J Econ Hist,* XXXIII (1973), 811–824.

3327 CONRAD, Alfred H., and John R. MEYER. "The Economics of Slavery in the Ante-Bellum South." *J Pol Econ,* LXVI (1958), 95–130.

3328 CONRAD, Alfred H., and John R. MEYER. *The Economics of Slavery: And Other Studies in Econometric History.* Chicago, 1964.

3329 DAVID, Paul A.; Herbert G. GUTMAN; Richard SUTCH; Peter TEMIN; and Gavin WRIGHT. *Reckoning with Slavery: A Critical Study in the Quantitative History of American Negro Slavery.* New York, 1976.†

3330 DOWD, Douglas F. "The Economics of Slavery in the Ante-Bellum South: A Comment." *J Pol Econ,* LXVI (1958), 440–442.

3331 ENGERMAN, Stanley L. "The Effects of Slavery upon the Southern Economy: A Review of the Recent Debate." *Explo Entrep Hist,* 2d series, IV (1967), 71–97.

3332 EVANS, Robert, Jr. "The Economics of American Negro Slavery, 1830–1860." *Aspects of Labor Economics.* National Bureau of Economic Research. Princeton, 1962, pp. 185–243.

3333 FOGEL, Robert W. "Cliometrics and Culture: Some Recent Developments in the Historiography of Slavery." *J Soc Hist,* XI (1977), 34–51.

3334 FOGEL, Robert W., and Stanley L. ENGERMAN. *Time on the Cross: The Economics of American Negro Slavery.* 2 vols. Boston, 1974.†

3335 GENOVESE, Eugene D. *The Political Economy of Slavery: Studies in the Economy & Society of the Slave South.* New York, 1965.†

3336 MOES, John E. "The Absorption of Capital in Slave Labor in the Ante-Bellum South and Economic Growth." *Am J Econ Soc,* XX (1961), 535–541.

3337 SARAYDAR, Edward. "A Note on the Profitability of Ante-Bellum Slavery." *S Econ J,* XXX (1964), 325–332.

3338 "Slavery as an Obstacle to Economic Growth in the United States: A Panel Discussion." *J Econ Hist,* XXVII (1967), 518–560.

3339 STAROBIN, Robert S. "The Economics of Industrial Slavery in the Old South." *Bus Hist Rev,* XLIV (1970), 131–174.

3340 SUTCH, Richard. "The Profitability of Ante-Bellum Slavery—Revisited." *S Econ J,* XXXI (1965), 365–377.

3341 WOODMAN, Harold D. "The Profitability of Slavery: A Historical Perennial." *J S Hist,* XXIX (1963), 303–325.

3342 WOOLFOLK, George R. "Cotton Capitalism and Slave Labor in Texas." *S W Soc Sci Q,* XXXVII (1956), 43–52.

3343 WOOLFOLK, George R. "Planter Capitalism and Slavery: The Labor Thesis." *J Neg Hist,* XLI (1956), 103–116.

3344 WOOLFOLK, George R. "Taxes and Slavery in the Ante-Bellum South." *J S Hist,* XXVI (1960), 180–200.

3345 WRIGHT, Gavin. "New and Old Views on the Economics of Slavery." *J Econ Hist,* XXXIII (1973), 452–466.

3346 YARBROUGH, William H. *Economic Aspects of Slavery in Relation to Southern and Southwestern Migration.* Nashville, 1932.

3347 YASUBA, Yasukichi. "The Profitability and Viability of Plantation Slavery in the United States." *Econ Stud Q,* XII (1961), 60–67.

5. The Religion of Afro-Americans

3348 ADEFILA, Johnson Ajibade. "Slave Religion in the Antebellum South: A Study of the Role of Africanisms in the Black Response to Christianity." Doctoral dissertation, Brandeis University, 1975.

3349 ALHO, Olli. *The Religion of the Slaves: A Study of the Religious Tradition and Behaviour of Plantation Slaves in the United States, 1830–1865.* Helsinki, 1976.

3350 BAILEY, Kenneth K. "Protestantism and Afro-Americans in the Old South: Another Look." *J S Hist,* XLI (1975), 451–472.

3351 CORNELIUS, Janet Duitsman. "God's Schoolmasters: Southern Evangelists to the Slaves, 1830–1860." Doctoral dissertation, University of Illinois, Urbana-Champaign, 1977.

3352 DANIEL, W. Harrison. "Virginia Baptists and the Negro in the Antebellum Era." *J Neg Hist,* LVI (1971), 1–16.

3353 FORDHAM, Monroe. *Major Themes in Northern Black Religious Thought, 1800–1860.* Hicksville, N.Y., 1975.

3354 MATHEWS, Donald G. "The Methodist Mission to the Slaves, 1829–1844." *J Am Hist,* LI (1965), 615–631.

3355 SERNETT, Milton C. *Black Religion and American Evangelicalism: White Protestants, Plantation Missions, and the Flowering of Negro Christianity, 1787–1865.* Metuchen, N.J., 1975.

3356 TOUCHSTONE, Donald Blake. "Planters and Slave Religion in the Deep South." Doctoral dissertation, Tulane University, 1973.

3357 TOUCHSTONE, Donald Blake. "Voodoo in New Orleans." *La Hist,* XIII (1972), 371–386.

6. Slave Unrest and Rebellion

See also **1194, 1438, 1594**

3358 APTHEKER, Herbert. *American Negro Slave Revolts.* New York, 1943.†

3359 APTHEKER, Herbert. *Nat Turner's Slave Rebellion, Together with the Full Text of the So-Called "Confessions" of Nat Turner Made in Prison in 1831.* New York, 1966.

3360 BERLIN, Ira, ed. "After Nat Turner: A Letter from the North." *J Neg Hist,* LV (1970), 144–151.

3361 CARROLL, Joseph C. *Slave Insurrections in the United States, 1800–1865.* Boston, 1938.

3362 DREWRY, William S. *Slave Insurrections in Virginia.* Washington, 1900.

3363 DUFF, John B., and Peter M. MITCHELL, eds. *The Nat Turner Rebellion: The Historical Event and the Modern Controversy.* New York, 1971.

3364 EATON, Clement. "A Dangerous Pamphlet in the Old South." *J S Hist,* II (1936), 323–334.

3365 ELLIOTT, Robert N., Jr. "The Nat Turner Insurrection as Reported in the North Carolina Press." *N C Hist Rev,* XXXVIII (1961), 1–18.

3366 FONER, Eric, ed. *Nat Turner.* Englewood Cliffs, 1971.†

3367 FREDRICKSON, George M., and Christopher LASCH. "Resistance to Slavery." *C W Hist,* XIII (1967), 315–329.

3368 GENOVESE, Eugene D. "Rebelliousness and Docility in the Negro Slave: A Critique of the Elkins Thesis." *C W Hist,* XIII (1967), 293–314.

3369 GRANADE, Ray. "Slave Unrest in Florida." *Fla Hist Q,* LV (1976), 18–36.

3370 GROSS, Seymour L., and Eileen BENDER. "History, Politics and Literature: The Myth of Nat Turner." *Am Q,* XXIII (1971), 487–518.

3371 HALASZ, Nicholas. *The Rattling Chains: Slave Unrest and Revolt in the Antebellum South.* New York, 1966.

3372 JOHNSON, F. Roy. *The Nat Turner Insurrection.* Murfreesboro, N.C., 1966.

3373 KILLENS, John Oliver, ed. *The Trial Record of Denmark Vesey.* Boston, 1970.

3374 KLEINMAN, Max L. "The Denmark Vesey Conspiracy." *Neg Hist Bull,* XXXVII (1974), 225–229.

3375 LOFTON, John M., Jr. "Denmark Vesey's Call to Arms." *J Neg Hist,* XXXIII (1948), 395–417.

3376 LOFTON, John. *Insurrection in South Carolina: The Turbulent World of Denmark Vesey.* Yellow Springs, Ohio, 1964.

3377 MCKIBBEN, Davidson Burns. "Negro Slave Insurrections in Mississippi, 1800–1865." *J Neg Hist,* XXXIV (1949), 73–90.

3378 MILES, Edwin A. "The Mississippi Slave Insurrection Scare of 1835." *J Neg Hist,* XLII (1957), 48–60.

3379 MILLIGAN, John D. "Slave Rebelliousness and the Florida Maroon." *Prologue,* VI (1974), 5–18.

3380 OATES, Stephen B. *The Fires of Jubilee: Nat Turner's Fierce Rebellion.* New York, 1974.†

3381 PEASE, William H., and Jane H. Pease. "Walker's Appeal Comes to Charleston: A Note and Documents." *J Neg Hist,* LIX (1974), 287–292.

3382 STAROBIN, Robert S., ed. *Denmark Vesey: The Slave Conspiracy of 1822.* Engle-wood Cliffs, 1970.†

3383 TRAGLE, Henry Irving, comp. *The Southampton Slave Revolt of 1831.* Amherst, 1971.

3384 WADE, Richard C. "The Vesey Plot: A Reconsideration." *J S Hist,* XXX (1964), 143–161.

3385 WISH, Harvey, "American Slave Insurrections before 1861." *J Neg Hist,* XXII (1937), 299–320.

7. The Free Negro

See also **1438, 1862**

3386 ADAMS, James T. "Disfranchisement of Negroes in New England." *Am Hist Rev,* XXX (1925), 543–547.

3387 BELLAMY, Donnie D. "Free Blacks in Antebellum Missouri, 1820–1860." *Mo Hist Rev,* LXVII (1973), 198–226.

3388 BELLAMY, Donnie D. "The Education of Blacks in Missouri Prior to 1861." *J Neg Hist,* LIX (1974), 143–157.

3389 BERLIN, Ira. *Slaves Without Masters: The Free Negro in the Antebellum South.* New York, 1974.†

3390 BERLIN, Ira. "The Structure of the Free Negro Caste in the Antebellum United States." *J Soc Hist,* IX (1976), 297–318.

3391 BISSON, Wilfred Joseph. "Some Conditions for Collective Violence: The Charles-town Convent Riot of 1834." Doctoral dissertation, Michigan State University, 1974.

3392 BONACICH, Edna. "Abolition, the Extension of Slavery, and the Position of Free Blacks: A Study of Split Labor Markets in the United States, 1830–1863. *Am J Soc,* LXXXI (1975), 601–628.

3393 BROWN, Letitia Woods. *Free Negroes in the District of Columbia, 1790–1846.* New York, 1972.

3394 CALLIGARO, Lee. "The Negro's Legal Status in Pre-Civil War New Jersey." *N J Hist,* LXXXV (1967), 167–180.

3395 CHILD, Alfred Thurston, Jr. "Prudence Crandall and the Canterbury Experi-ment." *Bull Friends Hist Assn,* XXII (1933), 35–55.

3396 COHEN, David W., and Jack P. GREENE, eds. *Neither Slave Nor Free: The Freedman of African Descent in the Slave Societies of the New World.* Baltimore, 1972.†

3397 COOPER, Frederick. "Elevating the Race: The Social Thought of Black Leaders, 1827–1850." *Am Q,* XXIV (1972), 604–625.

3398 DAVIS, Edwin Adams, and William Ransom HOGAN. *The Barber of Natchez* [William Johnson]. Baton Rouge, 1954.†

3399 DICK, Robert C. *Black Protest: Issues and Tactics.* Westport, 1974.†

3400 DU BOIS, W. E. B. *The Philadelphia Negro.* Philadelphia, 1899.

3401 DU BOIS, W. E. B., and Augustus G. DILL. *The Negro American Artisan.* Atlanta, 1912.†

3402 ENGLAND, J. Merton. "The Free Negro in Ante-Bellum Tennessee." *J S Hist,* IX (1943), 37–59.

3403 ERICKSON, Leonard. "Politics and the Repeal of Ohio's Black Laws, 1837–1849." *Ohio Hist,* LXXXII (1973), 154–175.

3404 FISCHER, Roger A. "Racial Segregation in Ante-Bellum New Orleans." *Am Hist Rev,* LXXIV (1969), 926–937.

3405 FLANDERS, Ralph B. "The Free Negro in Ante-Bellum Georgia." *N C Hist Rev,* IX (1932), 250–272.

3406 FORMISANO, Ronald P. "The Edge of Caste: Colored Suffrage in Michigan, 1827–1861." *Mich Hist,* LVI (1972), 19–41.

3407 FOX, Dixon Ryan. "The Negro Vote in Old New York." *Pol Sci Q,* XXXII (1917), 252–275.

3408 FRANKLIN, John Hope. *The Free Negro in North Carolina, 1790–1860.* Chapel Hill, 1943.†

3409 FREEMAN, Rhoda G. "The Free Negro in New York City in the Era before the Civil War." Doctoral dissertation, Columbia University, 1966.

3410 FRIEDMAN, Lawrence J. "Racism and Sexism in Ante-Bellum America: the Prudence Crandall Episode Reconsidered." *Soc,* IV (1974), 211–278.

3411 FULLER, Edmund. *Prudence Crandall: An Incident in Nineteenth Century Connecticut.* Middletown, 1971.

3412 GARVIN, Russell. "The Free Negro in Florida before the Civil War." *Fla Hist Q,* XLVI (1967), 1–18.

3413 GREEN, Alan Wilbert Currie. "Legacy of Illusion: The Image of the Negro in the Pre-Civil War North, 1787–1857." Doctoral dissertation, Claremont University, 1968.

3414 HANCOCK, Harold B. "Not Quite Men: The Free Negroes in Delaware in the 1830's." *C W Hist,* XVII (1971), 320–331.

3415 HARRIS, N. Dwight. *The History of Negro Servitude in Illinois, and of the Slavery Agitation in that State, 1719–1864.* Chicago, 1904.

3416 HARRIS, Robert L., Jr. "The Free Black Response to American Racism, 1790–1863." Doctoral dissertation, Northwestern University, 1974.

3417 HERSHBERG, Theodore. "Free Blacks in Antebellum Philadelphia: A Study of Ex-Slaves, Freeborn, and Socioeconomic Decline." *J Soc Hist,* V (1971–1972), 183–209.

3418 HICKOK, Charles T. *The Negro in Ohio, 1802–1870.* Cleveland, 1896.

3419 HIRSCH, Leo H., Jr. "The Negro and New York, 1783 to 1865." *J Neg Hist,* XVI (1931), 382–473.

3420 HOGAN, William Ransom, and Edwin Adams DAVIS, eds. *William Johnson's Natchez: The Ante-Bellum Diary of a Free Negro.* Baton Rouge, 1951.

3421 HORTON, James Oliver. "Black Activism in Boston, 1830–1860." Doctoral dissertation, Brandeis University, 1973.

3422 HORTON, James Oliver. "Generations of Protest: Black Families and Social Reform in Ante-Bellum Bostom." *N Eng Q,* XLIX (1976), 242–256.

BLACKS AND SLAVERY

3423 JACOBS, Donald Martin. "A History of the Boston Negro from the Revolution to the Civil War." Doctoral dissertation, Boston University, 1968.

3424 JACOBS, Donald M. "David Walker: Boston Race Leader, 1825–1830." *Essex Inst Hist Coll,* CVII (1971), 94–107.

3425 JACOBS, Donald M. "William Lloyd Garrison's Liberator and Boston Blacks, 1830–1865." *N Eng Q,* XLIV (1971), 259–277.

3426 JOHNSON, Whittington Bernard. "Negro Laboring Classes in Early America, 1750–1820." Doctoral dissertation, University of Georgia, 1970.

3427 LANG, William Louis. "Black Bootstraps: The Abolitionist Educators' Ideology and the Education of the Northern Free Negro, 1828–1860." Doctoral dissertation, University of Delaware, 1974.

3428 LEVESQUE, George A. "Black Abolitionists in the Age of Jackson: Catalysts in the Radicalization of American Abolitionism." *J Black Stud,* I (1970), 187–201.

3429 LITWACK, Leon F. *North of Slavery: The Negro in the Free States, 1790–1860.* Chicago, 1961.†

3430 MATISON, Sumner Eliot. "Manumission by Purchase." *J Neg Hist,* XXXIII (1948), 146–167.

3431 MOORE, N. Webster. "John Berry Meachum (1789–1854): St. Louis Pioneer, Black Abolitionist, Educator, and Preacher." *Mo Hist Soc Bull,* XXIX (1973), 96–103.

3432 PEASE, Jane H., and William H. PEASE. "Black Power—The Debate in 1840." *Phylon,* XXIX (1968), 19–26.

3433 PEASE, William H., and Jane H. PEASE. *Black Utopia: Negro Communal Experiments in America.* Madison, 1972.†

3434 PERLMAN, Daniel. "Organizations of the Free Negro in New York City, 1800–1860." *J Neg Hist,* LVI (1971), 181–197.

3435 PIH, Richard W. "Negro Self-Improvement Efforts in Ante-Bellum Cincinnati." *Ohio Hist,* LXXVIII (1969), 179–187.

3436 PINGEON, Frances D. "Dissenting Attitudes toward the Negro in New Jersey —1837." *N J Hist,* LXXXIX (1971), 197–220.

3437 PRICE, Edward J., Jr. "Let the Law Be Just: The Quest for Racial Equality in Pennsylvania, 1780–1915." Doctoral dissertation, Pennsylvania State University, 1973.

3438 PROVINE, Dorothy. "The Economic Position of Free Blacks in the District of Columbia, 1800–1860." *J Neg Hist,* LVIII (1973), 61–72.

3439 ROBINSON, Henry S. "Some Aspects of the Free Negro Population of Washington, D.C., 1800–1862." *Md Hist Mag,* LXIV (1969), 43–64.

3440 RUNCIE, John. " 'Hunting the Nigs' in Philadelphia: The Race Riot of August 1834." *Pa Hist,* XXXIX (1972), 187–218.

3441 SILCOX, Harry C. "Delay and Neglect: Negro Public Education in Antebellum Philadelphia, 1800–1860." *Pa Mag Hist Biog,* XCVII (1973), 444–464.

3442 SMALL, Edwin W., and Miriam R. SMALL. "Prudence Crandall, Champion of Negro Education." *N Eng Q,* XVII (1944), 506–529.

3443 STAHL, Annie Lee West. "The Free Negro in Ante-Bellum Louisiana." *La Hist Q,* XXV (1942), 201–396.

194

3444 STERKX, H. E. *The Free Negro in Ante-Bellum Louisiana.* Rutherford, 1972.

3445 SWEET, Leonard I. *Black Images of America, 1784–1870.* New York, 1976.†

3446 SYDNOR, Charles S. "The Free Negro in Mississippi before the Civil War." *Am Hist Rev,* XXXII (1927), 769–788.

3447 TURNER, Edward R. *The Negro in Pennsylvania; Slavery—Servitude—Freedom, 1639–1861.* Washington, D.C., 1911

3448 VAN DYKE, Roger Raymond. "The Free Negro in Tennessee, 1790–1860." Doctoral dissertation, Florida State University, 1972.

3449 WHITTEN, David O. "A Black Entrepreneur [Andrew Durnford] in Antebellum Louisiana." *Bus Hist Rev,* XLV (1971), 201–219.

3450 WIKRAMANAYAKE, Marina. *A World in Shadow: The Free Black in Antebellum South Carolina.* Columbia, 1973.

3451 WOODSON, Carter G., ed. "Free Negro Owners of Slaves in the United States in 1830." *J Neg Hist,* IX (1924), 41–85.

3452 WOOLFOLK, George Ruble. *The Free Negro in Texas, 1800–1860: A Study in Cultural Compromise.* Ann Arbor, 1976.

3453 WORMLEY, G. Smith. "Prudence Crandall." *J Neg Hist,* VIII (1923), 72–80.

3454 WRIGHT, James M. *The Free Negro in Maryland, 1634–1860.* New York, 1921.

3455 ZUCKER, Charles Noye. "The Free Negro Question: Race Relations in Ante-Bellum Illinois, 1801–1860." Doctoral dissertation, Northwestern University, 1972.

IX. Slavery on the Defensive

1. The African Colonization Movement

3456 ALLEN, Jeffrey Brooke. "Did Southern Colonizationists Oppose Slavery? Kentucky, 1816–1850, as a Test Case." *Reg Ky Hist Soc,* LXXV (1977), 92–111.

3457 CAMPBELL, Penelope. *Maryland in Africa: The Maryland State Colonization Society, 1831–1857.* Urbana, 1971.

3458 CARTER, Ralph Donald. "Black American or African: The Response of New York City Blacks to African Colonization, 1817–1841." Doctoral dissertation, Clark University, 1974.

3459 CASSELL, C. A. *Liberia: A History of the First African Republic.* New York, 1970.

3460 FOSTER, Charles I. "The Colonization of Free Negroes in Liberia, 1816–1835." *J Neg Hist,* XXXVIII (1953), 41–66.

3461 FOX, Early Lee. *The American Colonization Society, 1817–1840.* Baltimore, 1919.

3462 FRANKLIN, Vincent P. "Education for Colonization: Attempts to Educate Free Blacks in the United States for Emigration to Africa, 1823–1833." *J Neg Ed,* XLIII (1974), 91–103.

3463 FRENCH, David. "Elizur Wright, Jr. and the Emergence of Anti-Colonization Sentiments on the Connecticut Western Reserve." *Ohio Hist,* LXXV (1976), 49–66.

3464 FRIEDMAN, Lawrence J. "Purifying the White Man's Country: The American Colonization Society Reconsidered, 1816–40." *Soc,* VI (1976), 1–24.

3465 HUBERICH, Charles H. *The Political and Legislative History of Liberia.* 2 vols. New York, 1947.

3466 MILLER, Floyd J. *The Search for a Black Nationality: Black Emigration and Colonization, 1787–1863.* Urbana, 1975.

3467 OPPER, Peter Kent. "The Mind of the White Participant in the African Colonization Movement, 1816–1840." Doctoral dissertation, University of North Carolina at Chapel Hill, 1972.

3468 POE, William A. "Lott Cary: Man of Purchased Freedom." *Church Hist,* XXXIX (1970), 49–61.

3469 POE, William A. "Georgia Influence in the Development of Liberia." *Ga Hist Q,* LVII (1973), 1–16.

3470 ROSEN, Bruce. "Abolition and Colonization, the Years of Conflict: 1829–1834." *Phylon,* XXXIII (1972), 177–192.

3471 SEIFMAN, Eli. "A History of the New York State Colonization Society." Doctoral dissertation, New York University, 1965.

3472 SIGLER, Phil S. "The Attitudes of Free Blacks towards Emigration to Liberia." Doctoral dissertation, Boston University, 1969.

3473 STANGE, Douglas C. "Lutheran Involvement in the American Colonization Society." *Mid-Am,* XLIX (1967), 140–151.

3474 STAUDENRAUS, P. J., *The African Colonization Movement, 1816–1865.* New York, 1961.

3475 STOPAK, Aaron. "The Maryland State Colonization Society." *Md Hist Mag,* LXIII (1968), 275–298.

3476 STUCKEY, Ples Sterling. "The Spell of Africa: The Development of Black Nationalist Theory, 1829–1945." Doctoral dissertation, Northwestern University, 1973.

3477 WANDER, Philip C. "Salvation Through Separation: The Image of the Negro in the American Colonization Society." *Q J Sp,* LVII (1971), 57–67.

3478 WEEKS, Louis, III. "John Holt Rice and the American Colonization Society." *J Presby Hist,* XLVI (1968), 26–41.

3479 WICKSTROM, Werner Theodor. "The American Colonization Society and Liberia (An Historical Study in Religious Motivation and Achievement), 1817–1867." Doctoral dissertation, Hartford Seminary Foundation, 1958.

3480 WILSON, Charles M. *Liberia: Black Africa in Microcosm.* New York, 1970.

2. The Antislavery Movement

See also **458–460, 627–633, 635–637, 648–653, 762–763, 766, 767, 898, 936, 967–968, 1040, 1355, 1594, 1601, 1604, 1994, 2160, 2919, 2922, 3000, 3001, 3710, 4270, 4272**

3481 ABZUG, Robert B. "The Influence of Garrisonian Abolitionists' Fears of Slave Violence on the Antislavery Argument, 1829–1840." *J Neg Hist,* LV (1970), 15–28.

3482 ADAMS, Alice Dana. *The Neglected Period of Anti-Slavery in America (1808–1831).* Boston, 1908.

3483 ALLEN, Jeffrey Brooke. "The Debate over Slavery and Race in Ante-Bellum Kentucky: 1792–1850." Doctoral dissertation, Northwestern University, 1973.

3484 BANNINGA, Jerald L. "John Quincy Adams on the Right of a Slave to Petition Congress." *S Sp Com J,* XXXVIII (1972), 151–163.

3485 BARNES, Gilbert Hobbs. *The Antislavery Impulse, 1830–1844.* New York, 1933.

3486 BASSETT, John S. *Anti-Slavery Leaders of North Carolina.* Baltimore, 1898.

3487 BATES, Jack W. "John Quincy Adams and the Antislavery Movement." Doctoral dissertation, University of Southern California, 1953.

3488 BERWANGER, Eugene H. *The Frontier Against Slavery: Western Anti-Negro Prejudice and the Slavery Extension Controversy.* Urbana, 1967.†

3489 BERWANGER, Eugene H. "Negrophobia in Northern Proslavery and Antislavery Thought." *Phylon,* XXXIII (1972), 266–275.

3490 BLUESTONE, Donald Martin. " 'Steamboats, Sewing Machines and Bibles'— The Roots of Antislaveryism in Illinois and the Old Northwest." Doctoral dissertation, University of Wisconsin, 1973.

3491 BRETZ, Julian P. "The Economic Background of the Liberty Party." *Am Hist Rev,* XXXIV (1929), 250–264.

3492 CARTER, George Edward. "The Use of the Doctrine of Higher Law in the American Anti-Slavery Crusade, 1830–1860." Doctoral dissertation, University of Oregon, 1970.

3493 CAVE, Alfred A. "The Case of Calvin Colton: White Racism in Northern Antislavery Thought." *N Y Hist Soc Q,* LIII (1969), 215–229.

3494 COVER, Robert M. *Justice Accused: Antislavery and the Judicial Process.* New Haven, 1975.

3495 CURRY, Richard O., ed. *The Abolitionists.* Rev. ed. Hinsdale, Ill., 1973.

3496 DAVIS, David Brion. "The Emergence of Immediatism in British and American Antislavery Thought." *Miss Val Hist Rev,* XLIX (1962), 209–230.

3497 DEMOS, John. "The Antislavery Movement and the Problem of Violent Means." *N Eng Q,* XXXVII (1964), 501–526.

3498 DILLON, Merton L. *The Abolitionists: The Growth of a Dissenting Minority.* DeKalb, 1974.†

3499 DILLON, Merton L. "The Antislavery Movement in Illinois: 1824–1835." *Ill St Hist J,* XLVII (1954), 149–166.

3500 DILLON, Merton L. "Sources of Early Antislavery Thought in Illinois." *Ill St Hist J,* L(1957), 36–50.

3501 DILLON, Merton L. "The Failure of the American Abolitionists." *J S Hist,* XXV (1959), 159–177.

3502 DILLON, Merton L. "Abolitionism Comes to Illinois." *Ill St Hist J,* LIII (1960), 389–403.

3503 DILLON, Merton L. "Three Southern Antislavery Editors: The Myth of the Southern Antislavery Movement." *E Tenn Hist Soc Pub,* no. 42 (1970), 47–56.

3504 DONALD, David H. "Toward a Reconsideration of the Abolitionists." *Lincoln Reconsidered.* New York, 1956.

3505 DUBERMAN, Martin B. "The Abolitionists and Psychology." *J Neg Hist,* XLVII (1962), 183–192.

3506 DUBERMAN, Martin B., ed. *The Antislavery Vanguard: New Essays on the Abolitionists.* Princeton, 1965.†

3507 DUMOND, Dwight L. *Antislavery Origins of the Civil War in the United States.* Ann Arbor, 1939.†

3508 DUMOND, Dwight L. *Antislavery: The Crusade for Freedom in America.* Ann Arbor, 1961.†

3509 DUMOND, Dwight L. *A Bibliography of Antislavery in America.* Ann Arbor, 1961.

3510 EBERLY, Wayne J. "The Pennsylvania Abolition Society, 1775–1830." Doctoral dissertation, Pennsylvania State University, 1973.

3511 FILLER, Louis. *The Crusade against Slavery, 1830–1860.* New York, 1960.†

3512 FILLER, Louis, ed. *Abolition and Social Justice in the Era of Reform.* New York, 1972.†

3513 FINNIE, Gordon E. "The Antislavery Movement in the Upper South before 1840." *J S Hist,* XXXV (1969), 319–342.

3514 FLADELAND, Betty L. *Men and Brothers: Anglo-American Antislavery Cooperation.* Urbana, 1972.

3515 FLADELAND, Betty L. "Who Were the Abolitionists?" *J Neg Hist,* XLIX (1964), 99–115.

3516 FLADELAND, Betty L. "Compensated Emancipation: A Rejected Alternative." *J S Hist,* XLII (1976), 169–186.

3517 FREEHLING, Alison Harrison. "Drift toward Dissolution: The Virginia Slavery Debate of 1831–1832." Doctoral dissertation, University of Michigan, 1974.

3518 FRENCH, David Charles. "The Conversion of an American Radical: Elizur Wright, Jr., and the Abolitionist Committment." Doctoral dissertation, Case Western Reserve University, 1970.

3519 GAMBLE, Douglas Andrew. "Moral Suasion in the West: Garrisonian Abolitionism, 1831–1861." Doctoral dissertation, Ohio State University, 1973.

3520 GAMBLE, Douglas A. "Garrisonian Abolitionists in the West: Some Suggestions for Study." *C W Hist,* XXIII (1977), 52–68.

3521 GRIFFIN, Clifford S. "The Abolitionists and the Benevolent Societies, 1831–1861." *J Neg Hist,* XLIV (1959), 195–216.

3522 HACKETT, Derek. "The Days of this Republic Will be Numbered: Abolition, Slavery, and the Presidential Election of 1836." *La Stud,* XV (1976), 131–160.

3523 HAMMOND, John L. "Revival Religion and Anti-Slavery Politics." *Am Soc Rev,* XXXIX (1975), 175–185.

3524 HART, Albert B. *Slavery and Abolition, 1831–1841.* New York, 1906.

3525 HARWOOD, Thomas F. "Great Britain and American Antislavery." Doctoral dissertation, University of Texas at Austin, 1959.

3526 HAWKINS, Hugh, ed. *The Abolitionists: Means, Ends, and Motivations.* 2d ed. Lexington, Mass., 1972.†

3527 HENDERSON, Alice Hatcher. "The History of the New York State Anti-Slavery Society." Doctoral dissertation, University of Michigan, 1963.

3528 HENIG, Gerald S. "The Jacksonian Attitude toward Abolitionism in the 1830's." *Tenn Hist Q,* XXVIII (1969), 42–56.

3529 HERSH, Blanche Glassman. " 'The Slavery of Sex': Feminist-Abolitionists in Nineteenth-Century America." Doctoral dissertation, University of Illinois, Chicago Circle, 1975.

3530 HICKIN, Patricia Elizabeth Prickett. "Antislavery in Virginia, 1831–1861." Doctoral dissertation, University of Virginia, 1968.

3531 HICKIN, Patricia. " 'Situation Ethics' and Antislavery Attitudes in the Virginia Churches." *America, The Middle Period: Essays in Honor of Bernard Mayo.* Ed. John B. BOLES. Charlottesville, 1973.

3532 HOWARD, Victor B. "The Anti-Slavery Movement in the Presbyterian Church, 1835–1861." Doctoral dissertation, Ohio State University, 1961.

3533 HUME, John Ferguson. *The Abolitionists, Together with Personal Memories of the Struggle for Human Rights, 1830–1864.* New York, 1905.

3534 JARVIS, Charles Austin. "John Greenleaf Whittier and the Anti-Slavery Movement, 1828–1860." Doctoral dissertation, University of Missouri, Columbia, 1970.

3535 KERBER, Linda K. "Abolitionists and Amalgamators: The New York City Race Riots of 1834." *N Y Hist,* XLVIII (1967), 28–39.

3536 KRADITOR, Aileen S. *Means and Ends in American Abolitionism: Garrison and His Critics on Strategy and Tactics, 1834–1850.* New York, 1969.

3537 KRADITOR, Aileen S. "A Note on Elkins and the Abolitionists." *C W Hist,* XIII (1967), 330–339.

3538 LADER, Lawrence. *The Bold Brahmins: New England's War against Slavery, 1831–1863.* New York, 1961.

3539 LESLIE, William R. "The Pennsylvania Fugitive Slave Act of 1826." *J S Hist,* XVIII (1952), 429–445.

3540 LEVY, Leonard W. "The 'Abolition Riot': Boston's First Slave Rescue." *N Eng Q,* XXV (1952), 85–92.

3541 LITWACK, Leon. "The Abolitionist Dilemma: The Antislavery Movement and the Northern Negro." *N Eng Q,* XXXIV (1961), 50–73.

3542 LLOYD, Arthur Y. *The Slavery Controversy, 1831–1860.* Chapel Hill, 1939.

3543 LOVELAND, Anne C. "Evangelicalism and 'Immediate Emancipation' in American Antislavery Thought." *J S Hist,* XXXII (1966), 172–188.

3544 LUDLUM, Robert P. "The Antislavery 'Gag Rule': History and Argument." *J Neg Hist,* XXVI (1941), 203–243.

3545 LUMPKINS, Josephine. "Antislavery Opposition to the Annexation of Texas, with Special Reference to John Quincy Adams." Doctoral dissertation, Cornell University, 1941.

3546 LUTZ, Alma. *Crusade for Freedom: Women of the Antislavery Movement.* Boston, 1968.

3547 LYND, Staughton. "Rethinking Slavery and Reconstruction." *J Neg Hist,* L (1965), 198–209.

3548 MABEE, Carleton. *Black Freedom: The Nonviolent Abolitionists from 1830 through the Civil War.* New York, 1970.

3549 MCDONALD, Lawrence Herbert. "Prelude to Emancipation: The Failure of the Great Reaction in Maryland, 1831–1850." Doctoral dissertation, University of Maryland, 1974.

3550 MCFAUL, John M. "Expedience vs. Morality: Jacksonian Politics and Slavery." *J Am Hist,* LXII (1975), 24–39.

3551 MCPHERSON, James M. "The Fight against the Gag Rule: Joshua Leavitt and Antislavery Insurgency in the Whig Party, 1839–1842." *J Neg Hist,* XLVIII (1963), 177–195.

3552 MACY, Jesse. *The Anti-Slavery Crusade.* New Haven, 1919.

3553 MARTIN, Asa Earl. *The Anti-Slavery Movement in Kentucky Prior to 1850.* Louisville, 1918.

3554 MARTIN, Asa E. "Pioneer Anti-Slavery Press." *Miss Val Hist Rev,* II (1916), 509–528.

3555 MARTIN, Asa E. "The Anti-Slavery Societies of Tennessee." *Tenn Hist Mag,* I (1915), 261–281.

3556 MATHEWS, Donald G., ed. *Agitation for Freedom: The Abolitionist Movement.* New York, 1972.

3557 MATHEWS, Donald G. "The Abolitionists on Slavery: The Critique behind the Social Movement." *J S Hist,* XXXIII (1967), 163–182.

3558 MAXWELL, John F. "The Charismatic Origins of the Christian Anti-Slavery Movement in North America." *Quaker Hist,* LXIII (1974), 108–116.

3559 MAYNARD, Douglas H. "The World's Anti-Slavery Convention of 1840." *Miss Val Hist Rev,* XLVII (1960), 452–471.

3560 MOONEY, James Eugene. "Antislavery in Worcester County, Massachusetts: A Case Study." Doctoral dissertation, Clark University, 1971.

3561 MORRIS, Thomas D. *Free Men All: The Personal Liberty Laws of the North, 1780–1861.* Baltimore, 1974.

3562 MOSELEY, Thomas Robert. "A History of the New York Manumission Society, 1785–1849." Doctoral dissertation, New York University, 1963.

3563 MUELDER, Hermann R. *Fighters for Freedom: The History of Anti-Slavery Activities of Men and Women Associated with Knox College.* New York, 1959.

3564 MYERS, John L. "The Beginning of Anti-Slavery Agencies in New York State, 1833–1836." *N Y Hist,* XLIII (1962), 149–181.

3565 MYERS, John L. "Antislavery Activities of Five Lane Seminary Boys in 1835–1836." *Bull Hist Phil Soc Ohio,* XXI (1963), 95–111.

3566 MYERS, John L. "The Early Antislavery Agency System in Pennsylvania, 1833–1837." *Pa Hist,* XXXI (1964), 62–80.

3567 MYERS, John L. "The Major Effort of National Anti-Slavery Agents in New York State." *N Y Hist,* XLVI (1965), 162–186.

3568 MYERS, John L. "Organization of 'the Seventy': To Arouse the North against Slavery." *Mid-Am,* XLVIII (1966), 29–46.

3569 MYERS, John L. "American Antislavery Society Agents and the Free Negro, 1833–1838. *J Neg Hist,* LII (1967), 200–219.

3570 MYERS, John L. "The Beginning of Antislavery Agencies in Vermont, 1832–1836." *Vt Hist,* XXXVI (1968), 126–141.

3571 MYERS, John L. "The Major Efforts of Anti-Slavery Agents in Vermont, 1836–1838.' *Vt Hist,* XXXVI (1968), 214–229.

3572 MYERS, John L. "The Beginning of Antislavery Agencies in New Hampshire, 1832–1835. *Hist N H,* XXV (Fall 1970), 3–25.

3573 MYERS, John L. "Antislavery Agencies in Rhode Island, 1832–1835." *R I Hist,* XXIX (1970), 82–93.

3574 MYERS, John L. "Antislavery Agents in Rhode Island, 1835–1837." *R I Hist,* XXX (1971), 21–33.

3575 MYERS, John L. "The Major Efforts of Antislavery Agents in New Hampshire, 1835–1837." *Hist N H,* XXVI (Fall 1971), 3–27.

3576 NELSON, Truman, ed. *Documents of Upheaval: Selections from William Lloyd Garrison's* The Liberator, *1831–1865.* New York, 1966.

3577 NUERMBERGER, Ruth Ketring. *The Free Produce Movement: A Quaker Protest against Slavery.* Durham, 1942.

3578 NYE, Russel B. *Fettered Freedom: Civil Liberties and the Slavery Controversy, 1830–1860.* East Lansing, 1949.†

3579 PARKER, Russell Dean. " 'Higher Law': Its Development and Application to the American Antislavery Controversy." Doctoral dissertation, University of Tennessee, 1966.

3580 PARKER, Russell D. "The Philosophy of Charles G. Finney: Higher Law and Revivalism." *Ohio Hist,* LXXXII (1973), 142–153.

3581 PEASE, William H., and Jane H. PEASE, eds. *The Antislavery Argument.* New York, 1965.

3582 PEASE, William H., and Jane H. PEASE. "Antislavery Ambivalence: Immediatism, Expediency, Race." *Am Q,* XVII (1965), 682–695.

3583 PEASE, Jane H., and William H. PEASE. *Bound with Them in Chains: A Biographical History of the Antislavery Movement.* Westport, 1972.

3584 PEASE, Jane H., and William H. PEASE. *They Who Would Be Free: Blacks' Search for Freedom, 1830–1861.* New York, 1974.

3585 PERRY, Lewis. *Radical Abolitionism: Anarchy and the Government of God in Antislavery Thought.* Ithaca, 1973.

3586 PERRY, Lewis. "Versions of Anarchism in the Antislavery Movement." *Am Q,* XX (1968), 768–782.

3587 QUARLES, Benjamin. *Black Abolitionists.* New York, 1969.†

3588 RABLE, George C. "Slavery, Politics and the South: The Gag Rule as a Case Study." *Cap Stud,* III (1975), 69–88.

3589 RATCLIFFE, Donald J. "Captain James Riley and Antislavery Sentiment in Ohio, 1819–1824." *Ohio Hist,* LXXXI (1972), 76–94.

3590 RATNER, Lorman. "Northern Concern for Social Order as Cause for Rejecting Anti-Slavery." *Hist,* XXVIII (1965), 1–18.

3591 RATNER, Lorman. *Powder Keg: Northern Opposition to the Antislavery Movement, 1831–1840.* New York, 1968.

3592 RICE, C. Duncan. "The Anti-Slavery Mission of George Thompson to the United States, 1834–1835." *J Am Stud,* II (1968), 13–32.

3593 RICHARDS, Leonard L. *"Gentlemen of Property and Standing": Anti-Abolition Mobs in Jacksonian America.* New York, 1970.†

3594 ROSENBLATT, Armin Stanton. "Antiabolitionism in New York State, 1830–1839. Doctoral dissertation, St. John's University, 1974.

3595 RUCHAMES, Louis, ed. *The Abolitionists.* New York, 1963.

3596 SAVAGE, W. Sherman. *The Controversy over the Distribution of Abolition Literature, 1830–1860.* Washington, D.C., 1938.

3597 SCARBOROUGH, Ruth. *The Opposition to Slavery in Georgia Prior to 1860.* Nashville, 1933.

3598 SCHLOBOHM, Dietrich Hans. "The Declaration of Independence and Negro Slavery: 1776–1876." Doctoral dissertation, Michigan State University, 1970.

3599 SCHRIVER, Edward Oswald. "The Antislavery Impulse in Maine, 1833–1855." Doctoral dissertation, University of Maine, 1967.

3600 SENIOR, Robert C. "New England Congregationalists and the Anti-Slavery Movement, 1830–1860." Doctoral dissertation, Yale University, 1954.

3601 SEVITCH, Benjamin. "The Well-Planned Riot of October 21, 1835: Utica's Answer to Abolitionism." *N Y Hist,* L (1969), 251–263.

3602 SEWELL, Richard H. *Ballots for Freedom: Antislavery Politics in the United States, 1837–1860.* New York, 1976.

3603 SHAY, John Michael. "The Antislavery Movement in North Carolina." Doctoral dissertation, Princeton University, 1971.

3604 SIMMS, Henry H. *Emotion at High Tide: Abolition as a Controversial Factor, 1830–1845.* Richmond, 1960.

3605 SKOTHEIM, Robert Allen. "A Note on Historical Method: David Donald's 'Toward a Reconsideration of Abolitionists.'" *J S Hist,* XXV (1959), 356–365.

3606 SMITH, Theodore C. *The Liberty and Free Soil Parties in the Northwest.* New York, 1897.

3607 SOUTHALL, Eugene Portlette. "Arthur Tappan and the Anti-Slavery Movement." *J Neg Hist,* XV (1930), 162–197.

3608 SOKOLOW, J. A. "Revivalism and Radicalism: William Lloyd Garrison, Henry Clarke Wright and the Ideology of Nonresistance." Doctoral dissertation, New York University, 1972.

3609 SORIN, Gerald. *Abolitionism: A New Perspective.* New York, 1972.†

3610 SORIN, Gerald. *The New York Abolitionists: A Case Study of Political Radicalism.* Westport, 1970.

3611 SOWLE, Patrick. "The North Carolina Manumission Society, 1816–1834." *N C Hist Rev,* XLII (1965), 47–69.

3612 STAMPP, Kenneth M. "The Fate of the Southern Antislavery Movement." *J Neg Hist,* XXVIII (1943), 10–22.

3613 STAMPP, Kenneth M. "The Southern Refutation of the Proslavery Argument." *N C Hist Rev,* XXI (1944), 35–45.

3614 STEWART, James Brewer. *Holy Warriors: The Abolitionists and American Slavery.* New York, 1976.

3615 STEWART, James Brewer. "Evangelicalism and the Radical Strain in Southern Antislavery Thought during the 1820's." *J S Hist,* XXXIX (1973), 379–396.

3616 SULLIVAN, David K. "William Lloyd Garrison in Baltimore, 1829–1830." *Md Hist Mag,* LXVIII (1973), 64–79.

3617 SUN, Tung-hsun. "Some Interpretations of the Abolition Movement." Doctoral dissertation, Michigan State University, 1972.

3618 SZASZ, Ferenc M. "Antebellum Appeals to the 'Higher Law,' 1830–1860." *Essex Inst Hist Coll,* CX (1974), 33–48.

3619 TAYLOR, Clare, ed. *British and American Abolitionists: An Episode in Transatlantic Understanding.* Edinburgh, 1974.

3620 THOMPSON, J. Earl, Jr. "Lyman Beecher's Long Road to Conservative Abolitionism." *Church Hist,* XLII (1973), 89–109.

3621 THOMPSON, J. Earl, Jr. "Abolitionism and Theological Education at Andover." *N Eng Q,* XLVII (1974), 238–261.

3622 THORNBROUGH, Emma Lou. "Indiana and Fugitive Slave Legislation." *Ind Mag Hist,* L (1954), 201–228.

3623 TRENDEL, Robert. "The Expurgation of Antislavery Materials by American Presses." *J Neg Hist,* LVIII (1973), 271–290.

3624 USREY, Miriam L. "Charles Lenox Remond, 'Garrison's Ebony Echo': World Anti-Slavery Convention, 1840." *Essex Inst Hist Coll,* CVI (1970), 112–125.

3625 VAN DEBURG, William L. "Henry Clay, the Right of Petition, and Slavery in the Nation's Capital." *Reg Ky Hist Soc,* LXVIII (1970), 132–146.

3626 WALTERS, Ronald G. "The Erotic South: Civilization and Sexuality in American Abolitionism." *Am Q,* XXV (1973), 177–201.

3627 WALTERS, Ronald G. *The Antislavery Appeal: American Abolitionism after 1830.* Baltimore, 1977.

3628 WEEKS, Stephen B. *Southern Quakers and Slavery.* Baltimore, 1896.

3629 WEEKS, Stephen B. "Anti-Slavery Sentiment in the South." *S Hist Assn Pub,* II (1898), 87–130.

3630 WEIMER, Gordon M. "Pennsylvania Congressmen and the 1836 Gag Rule: A Quantitative Note." *Pa Hist,* XXXVI (1969), 335–340.

3631 WEISBERGER, Bernard A., ed. *Abolitionism: Disrupter of the Democratic System or Agent of Progress?* Chicago, 1963.

3632 WIECEK, William M. *The Sources of Antislavery Constitutionalism in America, 1760–1848.* Ithaca, 1977.

3633 WILLIAMS, David Alan. "William Lloyd Garrison, the Historians, and the Abolitionist Movement." *Essex Inst Hist Coll,* XCVIII (1962), 84–99.

3634 WOLF, Hazel Catherine. *On Freedom's Altar: The Martyr Complex in the Abolition Movement.* Madison, 1952.

3635 WYATT-BROWN, Bertram. "The Abolitionists' Postal Campaign of 1835." *J Neg Hist,* L (1965), 227–238.

3636 WYATT-BROWN, Bertram. "New Leftists and Abolitionists: A Comparison of American Radical Styles." *Wis Mag Hist,* LIII (1970), 256–268.

3637 WYATT-BROWN, Bertram. "Stanley Elkins' *Slavery:* The Antislavery Interpretation Reexamined." *Am Q,* XXV (1973), 154–176.

3638 ZORN, Roman J. "The New England Anti-Slavery Society: Pioneer Abolition Organization." *J Neg Hist,* XLII (1957), 157–176.

3. The Southern Response to the Antislavery Movement

See also **860, 969**

3639 DONALD, David. "The Proslavery Argument Reconsidered." *J S Hist,* XXXVII (1971), 3–18.

3640 EATON, Clement. "Mob Violence in the Old South." *Miss Val Hist Rev,* XXIX (1942), 351–370.

3641 EATON, Clement. "Censorship of the Southern Mails." *Am Hist Rev,* XLVIII (1943), 266–280.

3642 GATELL, Frank O., ed. "Postmaster Huger and the Incendiary Publications." *S C Hist Mag,* LXIV (1963), 193–201.

3643 GAY, Dorothy Ann. "The Tangled Skein of Romanticism and Violence in the Old South: the Southern Response to Abolitionism and Feminism, 1830–1861." Doctoral dissertation, University of North Carolina at Chapel Hill, 1975.

3644 GREENBERG, Kenneth S. "Revolutionary Ideology and the Proslavery Argument; the Abolition of Slavery in Antebellum South Carolina." *J S Hist,* XLII (1976), 365–384.

3645 GUJER, Bruno. *Free Trade and Slavery: Calhoun's Defense of Southern Interests against British Interference, 1811–1848.* Zurich, 1971.

3646 HESSELTINE, William B. "Some New Aspects of the Pro-Slavery Argument." *J Neg Hist,* XXI (1936), 1–15.

3647 JENKINS, William S. *Pro-Slavery Thought in the Old South.* Chapel Hill, 1935.

3648 MORRISON, Larry Robert. "The Proslavery Argument in the Early Republic, 1790–1830." Doctoral dissertation, University of Virginia, 1975.

3649 MORROW, Ralph E. "The Proslavery Argument Revisited." *Miss Val Hist Rev,* XLVIII (1961), 79–94.

3650 SELLERS, Charles G. "The Travail of Slavery." *The Southerner as American.* Ed. Charles G. Sellers. Chapel Hill, 1960.

3651 SHALHOPE, Robert E. "Race, Class, Slavery, and the Antebellum Southern Mind." *J S Hist,* XXXVII (1971), 557–574.

3652 THATCHER, Harold W. "Calhoun and Federal Reinforcement of State Laws." *Am Pol Sci Rev,* XXXVI (1942), 873–880.

3653 TISE, Larry Edward. "Proslavery Ideology: A Social and Intellectual History of the Defense of Slavery in America, 1790–1840." Doctoral dissertation, University of North Carolina at Chapel Hill, 1975.

X. Indians

See also **461, 462, 706, 769, 773–774, 860, 911–912, 1059, 1060, 1406–1456, 1793, 1802, 1907, 2357, 2440, 2543, 2547, 4084, 4354**

3654 ABEL, Anne Heloise. *The History of Events Resulting in Indian Consolidation West of the Mississippi.* Washington, D.C., 1908.

3655 BAIRD, W. David. "The Reduction of a People: The Quapaw Removal, 1824–1834." *Red River Val Hist Rev,* I (1974), 21–36.

3656 BAIRD, W. David. "Fort Smith and the Red Man." *Ark Hist Q,* XXX (1971), 337–348.

3657 BALLENGER, T. L. "The Death and Burial of Major Ridge." *Chron Okla,* LI (1973), 100–105.

3658 BEARSS, Edwin C. "The Arkansas Whiskey War: A Fort Smith Case Study." *J W,* VII (1968), 143–172.

3659 BEARSS, Edwin C. "Fort Smith as the Agency for the Western Choctaws." *Ark Hist Q,* XXVII (1968), 40–58.

3660 BENSON, Maxine. "[Henry Rowe] Schoolcraft, [Edwin] James, and the 'White Indian' [John Tanner]." *Mich Hist,* LIV (1970), 311–328.

3661 BERKHOFER, Robert F., Jr. *Salvation and the Savage: An Analysis of Protestant Missions and American Indian Response, 1787–1862.* Lexington, 1965.†

3662 BERLANDIER, Jean Louis. *The Indians of Texas in 1830.* Ed. John C. EWERS, and trans. Patricia Reading LECLERQ. Washington, D.C., 1969.

3663 BLACKBURN, George M. "George Johnston and the Sioux-Chippewa Boundary Survey." *Mich Hist,* LI (1967), 313–322.

3664 BLACKBURN, George M. "Foredoomed to Failure: The Manistee Indian Station." *Mich Hist,* LIII (1969), 37–50.

3665 BOYD, Joel D. "Creek Indian Agents, 1834–1874." *Chron Okla,* LI (1973), 37–58.

3666 BRAY, Martha Coleman, ed. *The Journals of Joseph N. Nicollet; a Scientist on the Mississippi Headwaters With Notes on Indian Life, 1836–37.* Trans. Andre FERTEY. St. Paul, 1970.

3667 BROEMELING, Carol B. "Cherokee Indian Agents, 1830–1874." *Chron Okla,* L (1972), 437–457.

3668 CHALOU, George. "Massacre on Fall Creek." *Prologue,* IV (1972), 109–114.

3669 CLARK, Thomas D. "The Jackson Purchase: A Dramatic Chapter in Southern Indian Policy and Relations." *Filson Club Hist Q,* L (1976), 302–320.

3670 CLARKE, Mary Whatley. *Chief Bowles and the Texas Cherokees.* Norman, Okla., 1971.

3671 COTTERILL, Robert S. "Federal Indian Management in the South, 1789–1825." *Miss Val Hist Rev,* XX (1933–1934), 333–352.

3672 COTTERILL, Robert S. *The Southern Indians: The Story of the Civilized Tribes before Removal.* Norman, 1954.†

3673 DALE, Edward Everett, and Gaston LITTON, eds. *Cherokee Cavaliers: Forty Years of Cherokee History as told in the Correspondence of the Ridge-Watie-Boudinot Family,* Norman, 1939.

3674 DEBO, Angie. *A History of the Indians of the United States.* Norman, 1970.

3675 DEBO, Angie. *The Road to Disappearance.* Norman, 1941.

3676 DEBO, Angie. *The Rise and Fall of the Choctaw Republic.* 2d ed. Norman, 1961.†

3677 DEROSIER, Arthur H. "John C. Calhoun and the Removal of the Choctaw Indians." *S C Hist Assn Proc,* (1957), 33–45.

3678 DEROSIER, Arthur H. "Pioneers with Conflicting Ideals: Christianity and Slavery in the Choctaw Nation." *J Miss Hist,* XXI (1959), 174–189.

3679 DOLLAR, Clyde D. "The High Plains Smallpox Epidemic of 1837–1838." *W Hist Q,* VIII (1977), 15–38.

3680 DRIVER, Harold E. *Indians of North America.* 2d ed. Chicago, 1969.†

3681 ENGLUND, Donald Ralph. "A Demographic Study of the Cherokee Nation." Doctoral dissertation, University of Oklahoma, 1974.

3682 FENTON, William N., et al. *American Indian and White Relations to 1830: Needs and Opportunities for Study.* Chapel Hill, 1957.

3683 FISHER, Robert L. "The Treaties of Portage des Sioux." *Miss Val Hist Rev,* XIX (1933), 495–508.

3684 FOREMAN, Grant. *Sequoyah.* Norman, 1938.†

3685 FOREMAN, Grant, ed. "John Howard Payne and the Cherokees." *Am Hist Rev,* XXXVII (1932), 723–730.

3686 FOREMAN, Grant. *Indians and Pioneers: the Story of the American Southwest before 1830.* New Haven, 1930.†

3687 FOREMAN, Grant. *The Five Civilized Tribes.* Norman, 1934.†

3688 FOREMAN, Grant. *The Last Trek of the Indians.* Chicago, 1946.

3689 FRANKS, Kenny Arthur. "Political Intrigue in the Cherokee Nation, 1839." *J W,* XIII (1974), 17–25.

3690 FRANKS, Kenny Arthur. "Stand Watie and the Agony of the Cherokee Nation." Doctoral dissertation, Oklahoma State University, 1973.

3691 GABRIEL, Ralph Henry. *Elias Boudinot, Cherokee, and His America.* Norman, 1941.

3692 GIBSON, Arrel M. *The Chickasaws.* Norman, 1971.†

3693 GOODYKOONTZ, Colin B. *Home Missions on the American Frontier.* Caldwell, 1939.

3694 GREEN, Michael D. "The Sac-Fox Annuity Crisis of 1840 in Iowa Territory." *Ariz W,* XVI (1974), 141–156.

3695 GREEN, Michael David. "Federal-State Conflict in the Administration of Indian Policy: Georgia, Alabama and the Creeks, 1824–1834." Doctoral dissertation, State University of Iowa, 1973.

3696 GRINDLE, Donald, Jr. "Cherokee Removal and American Politics." *Ind Hist,* VIII (1975), 33–42, 56.

3697 HAGAN, William T. *The Sac and Fox Indians.* Norman, 1958.

3698 HAGAN, William T. *American Indians.* Chicago, 1961.†

INDIANS

3699 HAGAN, William T. *The Indians in American History. Am Hist Assn Pamphlets.* Washington, D.C., 1968.†

3700 HALLIBURTON, R., Jr. "Origins of Black Slavery among the Cherokees." *Chron Okla,* LII (1974–1975), 483–496.

3701 HALLIBURTON, R., Jr. *Red Over Black: Black Slavery among the Cherokee Indians.* Westport, Conn., 1977.

3702 HARMON, George Dewey. *Sixty Years of Indian Affairs: Political, Economic, and Diplomatic, 1789–1850.* Chapel Hill, 1941.

3703 HARTLEY, William, and Ellen HARTLEY. *Osceola: The Unconquered Indian.* New York, 1973.

3704 HASDORFF, James Curtis. "Four Indian Tribes in Texas, 1758–1858: A Reevaluation of Historical Sources." Doctoral dissertation, University of New Mexico, 1971.

3705 HORAN, James D. *The McKenney-Hall Portrait Gallery of American Indians.* New York, 1972.

3706 HRYNIEWICKI, Richard J. "The Creek Treaty of Washington, 1826." *Ga Hist Q,* XLVIII (1964), 425–441.

3707 HUDSON, Charles. *The Southeastern Indians.* Knoxville, 1976.

3708 JESSETT, Thomas E. "Christian Missions to the Indians of Oregon." *Church Hist,* XXVIII (1959), 147–156.

3709 KAPPLER, Charles J. *Indian Affairs, Laws and Treaties.* 3 vols. Washington, D.C., 1892–1913.

3710 KERBER, Linda K. "The Abolitionist Perception of the Indian." *J Am Hist,* LXII (1975), 271–296.

3711 KLOPFENSTEIN, Carl G. "The Removal of the Indians from Ohio, 1820–1843." Doctoral dissertation, Western Reserve University, 1956.

3712 LEWIT, Robert T. "Indian Missions and Antislavery Sentiment: A Conflict of Evangelical and Humanitarian Ideals." *Miss Val Hist Rev,* L (1963), 39–55.

3713 LITTLEFIELD, Daniel F., Jr., and Lonnie E. UNDERHILL. "The Cherokee Agency Reserve, 1828–1886." *Ark Hist Q,* XXXI (1972), 166–180.

3714 LOLLAR, Wayne B. "Seminole-United States Financial Relations, 1823–1866." *Chron Okla,* L (1972), 190–198.

3715 MCCLUGGAGE, Robert W. "The Senate and Indian Land Titles, 1800–1825." *W Hist Q,* I (1970), 415–425.

3716 MCKENNEY, Thomas L. *Sketches of a Tour to the Lakes, of the Character and Customs of the Chippeway Indians, and of Incidents Connected with the Treaty of Fond du Lac.* Barre, Mass., 1972.

3717 MCLOUGHLIN, William G. "Civil Disobedience and Evangelism among the Missionaries to the Cherokees, 1829–1839." *J Presby Hist,* LI (1973), 116–139.

3718 MCLOUGHLIN, William G., and Walter H. CONSER, Jr. "The Cherokees in Transition: A Statistical Analysis of the Federal Cherokee Census of 1835." *J Am Hist,* LXIV (1977), 678–703.

3719 MCLOUGHLIN, William G. "Red Indians, Black Slavery and White Racism: America's Slaveholding Indians." *Am Q,* XXVI (1974), 367–385.

3720 MCREYNOLDS, Edwin C. *The Seminoles.* Norman, 1957.†

INDIANS

3721 MALONE, Henry Thompson. *Cherokees of the Old South: A People in Transition.* Athens, 1956.

3722 MARDOCK, Robert W. "The Anti-Slavery Humanitarians and Indian Policy Reform." *W Hum Rev,* XII (1958), 131–146.

3723 MARKMAN, Robert Paul. "The Arkansas Cherokees: 1817–1828." Doctoral dissertation, University of Oklahoma, 1972.

3724 METCALF, P. Richard. "Who Should Rule at Home? Native American Politics and Indian-White Relations." *J Am Hist,* LXI (1974), 651–665.

3725 MILES, William. " 'Enamoured with Colonization': Isaac McCoy's Plan of Indian Reform." *Kan Hist Q,* XXXVIII (1972), 268–286.

3726 MONAHAN, Forrest D., Jr. "The Kiawas and New Mexico, 1800–1845." *J W,* VIII (1969), 67–75.

3727 MOONEY, James. *Historical Sketch of the Cherokee.* Chicago, 1975.†

3728 MORRIS, Cheryl Haun. "Choctaw and Chickasaw Indian Agents, 1831–1874." *Chron Okla,* L (1972), 415–436.

3729 NICHOLS, Roger L. "The Army and the Indians, 1800–1830—A Reappraisal: the Missouri Valley Example." *Pac Hist Rev,* XLI (1972), 151–168.

3730 PARKER, Thomas V. *The Cherokee Indians.* New York, 1907.

3731 PARSONS, John E., ed. "Letters on the Chickasaw Removal of 1837." *N Y Hist Soc Q,* XXXVII (1953), 273–283.

3732 PARSONS, Lynn Hudson. " 'A Perpetual Harrow Upon My Feelings': John Quincy Adams and the American Indian." *N Eng Q,* XLVI (1973), 339–379.

3733 PAULSON, Howard W. "Federal Indian Policy and the Dakota Indians: 1800–1840." *S D Hist,* III (1973), 285–309.

3734 PEAKE, Ora Brooks. *A History of the United States Indian Factory System, 1795–1822.* Denver, 1954.

3735 PRUCHA, Francis Paul. *Amerian Indian Policy in the Formative Years: The Indian Trade and Intercourse Acts, 1790–1834.* Cambridge, Mass., 1962.†

3736 PRUCHA, Francis Paul. *A Bibliographical Guide to the History of Indian-White Relations in the United States.* Chicago, 1977.†

3737 PRUCHA, Francis Paul. "Indian Removal and the Great American Desert." *Ind Mag Hist,* LIX (1963), 299–322.

3738 PRUCHA, Francis Paul, et al. *American Indian Policy.* Indianapolis, 1971.†

3739 PRUCHA, Francis Paul. *United States Indian Policy: A Critical Bibliography.* Bloomington, 1977.

3740 PURSER, Joyce. "The Administration of Indian Affairs in Louisiana, 1803–1820." *La Hist,* V (1964), 401–419.

3741 RAY, Florence R. *Chieftain Greenwood Leflore and the Choctaw Indians of the Mississippi Valley.* Memphis, 1938.

3742 REED, Gerald A. "Financial Controversy in the Cherokee Nation, 1839–1846." *Chron Okla,* LII (1974), 82–98.

3743 REESE, Calvin Lee. "The United States Army and the Indian: Low Plains Area, 1815–1854." Doctoral dissertation, University of Southern California, 1963.

3744 REID, Phillip. *A Law of Blood: The Primitive Law of the Cherokee Nation.* New York, 1970.

3745 RILEY, Sam G. "The Cherokee Phoenix: The Short, Unhappy Life of the First Indian Newspapers." *Jour Q,* LIII (1976), 666–671.

3746 ROETHLER, Michael Donald. "Negro Slavery among the Cherokee Indians, 1540–1866." Doctoral dissertation, Fordham University, 1964.

3747 ROYCE, Charles C. *The Cherokee Nation of Indians.* Chicago, 1975.†

3748 SATZ, Ronald N. *Tennessee's Indian Peoples from White Contact to Removal, 1540–1840.* Knoxville, 1977.†

3749 SCHMECKEBIER, Laurence F. *The Office of Indian Affairs: Its History, Activities, and Organizations.* Baltimore, 1927.

3750 SCHUSKY, Ernest L. "The Upper Missouri Indian Agency, 1819–1868." *Mo Hist Rev,* LXV (1971), 249–269.

3751 SHEEHAN, Bernard W. *Seeds of Extinction: Jeffersonian Philanthropy and the American Indian.* Chapel Hill, 1973.†

3752 STARKEY, Marion L. *The Cherokee Nation.* New York, 1946.

3753 STEIN, Gary Carl. "Federal Indian Policy as Seen by British Travelers in America, 1783–1860." Doctoral dissertation, University of New Mexico, 1975.

3754 STEIN, Gary Carl. "A Fearful Drunkenness: The Liquor Trade to the Western Indians as Seen by European Travelers in America, 1800–1860." *Red River Val Hist Rev,* I (1974), 109–121.

3755 STONE, William L. *Life and Times of Red-Jacket, or Sa-go-ye-wat-ha.* New York, 1941.

3756 STRICKLAND, Rennard. *Fire and the Spirits: Cherokee Law from Clan to Court.* Norman, 1975.

3757 STRICKLAND, Rennard. "From Clan to Court: Development of Cherokee Law." *Tenn Hist Q,* XXXI (1972), 316–327.

3758 SWANTON, John R. *Early History of the Creek Indians and Their Neighbors.* Washington, D.C., 1922.

3759 TURNER, Alvin O. "Financial Relations between the United States and Cherokee Nation, 1830–1870." *J W,* XII (1973), 372–385.

3760 UNGER, Robert W. "Lewis Cass, Indian Superintendent of the Michigan Territory, 1813–1831." Doctoral dissertation, Ball State University, 1967.

3761 UNRAU, William E. "United States 'Diplomacy' with the Dhegiha-Siouan Kansa, 1815–1825." *Kan Hist Q,* III (1971), 39–46.

3762 VIOLA, Herman J. "Invitation to Washington—A Bid for Peace [1821]." *Am W,* IX (January, 1972), 18–31.

3763 WASHBURN, Wilcomb E., comp. *The Indian and the White Man.* Garden City, N.Y., 1964.

3764 WASHBURN, Wilcomb E. *Red Man's Land—White Man's Law: A Study of the Past and Present Status of the American Indian.* New York, 1971.

3765 WASHBURN, Wilcomb E. *The Indian in America.* New York, 1975.†

3766 WAY, Royal B. "The United States Factory System for Trading with the Indians, 1796–1822." *Miss Val Hist Rev,* VI (1919), 220–235.

3767 WILKINS, Thurman. *Cherokee Tragedy: The Story of the Ridge Family and the Decimation of a People.* New York, 1970.

3768 WILSON, Elinor. *Jim Beckwourth: Black Mountain Man and War Chief of the Crows.* Norman, 1972.

3769 WINSOR, Henry M. "Chickasaw-Choctaw Financial Relations with the United States, 1830–1880." *J W,* XII (1973), 356–371.

3770 WOODWARD, Grace Steele. *The Cherokees.* Norman, 1963.

3771 WRIGHT, Muriel H. "Notes on Events Leading to the Chickasaw Treaties of Franklin and Pontotoc, 1830 and 1832." *Chron Okla,* XXXIV (1956–1957), 465–483.

XI. Urban and Economic History

1. Urban

See also 2043, 2111–2113, 2122, 2125, 2391, 2462, 2523, 2688, 2717, 2722, 2735–2738, 2743, 2748, 2754, 2763, 2786, 2787, 2812, 2845, 2866, 2879, 2890, 2984, 3018, 3105, 3126, 3139, 3227 3237, 3268, 3848, 3849, 3871, 4020, 4050, 4061, 4067, 4081, 4122, 4126, 4132, 4143, 4144, 4249, 4263, 4270, 4271, 4275, 4403, 4454, 4456, 4511, 4545, 4573, 4720, 4755

3772 AMOS, Harriet Elizabeth. "Social Life in an Antebellum Cotton Port: Mobile, Alabama, 1820–1860." Doctoral dissertation, Emory University, 1976.

3773 ARMSTRONG, Thomas Field. "Urban Vision in Virginia: A Comparative Study of Ante-Bellum Fredricksburg, Lynchburg, and Staunton." Doctoral dissertation, University of Virginia, 1974.

3774 BENDER, Thomas. *Toward an Urban Vision: Ideas and Institutions in Nineteenth Century America.* Lexington, 1975.

3775 BLUMIN, Stuart M. *The Urban Threshold: Growth and Change in a Nineteenth Century American Community* [Kingston, N.Y.]. Chicago, 1976.

3776 BLUMIN, Stuart M. "Mobility in a 19th Century American City: Philadelphia, 1820–1860." Doctoral dissertation, University of Pennsylvania, 1968.

3777 BLUMIN, Stuart. "Mobility and Change in Ante-Bellum Philadelphia." *Nineteenth-Century Cities: Essays in the New Urban History.* Ed. Stephan THERNSTROM and Richard SENNETT. New Haven, Conn., 1969.†

3778 BROWN, Richard D. "The Emergence of Urban Society in Rural Massachusetts, 1760–1820." *J Am Hist,* LXI (1974), 29–51.

3779 BROWNE, Gary Lawson. "Baltimore in the Nation, 1789–1861: A Social Economy in Industrial Revolution." Doctoral dissertation, Wayne State, 1973.

3780 CAPERS, Gerald M. *Biography of a River Town, Memphis: Its Heroic Age.* Chapel Hill, 1939.

3781 CARTER, Edward C., III. "Benjamin Henry Latrobe and the Growth and Development of Washington." *Rec Col Hist Soc,* LXXI-LXXII (1971), 128–149.

3782 CEI, Louis Bernard. "Law Enforcement in Richmond: A History of Police-Community Relations, 1737–1974." Doctoral dissertation, Florida State University, 1975.

3783 CROWTHER, Simeon J. "Urban Growth in the Mid-Atlantic States, 1785–1850." *J Econ Hist,* XXXVI (1976), 624–644.

3784 CURRY, Leonard P. "Urbanization and Urbanism in the Old South: A Comparative View." *J S Hist,* XL (1974), 43–60.

3785 DORSETT, Lyle W., and Arthur H. SHAFFER. "Was the Antebellum South Antiurban? A Suggestion." *J S Hist,* XXXVIII (1972), 93–100.

3786 FARRELL, Richard T. "Cincinnati, 1800–1830: Economic Development Through Trade and Industry." *Ohio Hist,* LXXVII (1968), 111–129.

3787 GILCHRIST, David T., ed. *The Growth of the Seaport Cities, 1790–1825.* Charlottesville, 1967.

3788 GILPIN, Henry D. "Washington in 1825: Observations by Henry D. Gilpin." Ed. Ralph D. GRAY. *Del Hist,* XI (1965), 240–250.

3789 GINSBERG, Stephen F. "Above the Law: Volunteer Firemen in the New York City, 1836–1837." *N Y Hist,* L (1969), 165–186.

3790 GLAAB, Charles N., and A. Theodore BROWN. *A History of Urban America.* 2d ed. New York, 1976.†

3791 GLAZER, Walter Stix. "Cincinnati in 1840: A Community Profile." Doctoral dissertation, University of Michigan, 1968.

3792 GREEN, Constance McLaughlin. *Holyoke, Massachusetts: A Case Study of the Industrial Revolution in America.* New Haven, 1939.

3793 GREEN, Constance McLaughlin. *History of Naugatuck, Connecticut.* New Haven, 1948.

3794 GRIFFIN, Clyde. "Public Opinion in Urban History." *J Interdis Hist,* IV (1974), 469–474.

3795 GROENE, Bertram Hawthorne. "Ante-Bellum Tallahassee: It was a Gay Time Then." Doctoral dissertation, Florida State University, 1967.

3796 HAEGER, John Denis. "Eastern Money and the Urban Frontier: Chicago, 1833–1842." *Ill St Hist J,* XLIV (1971), 267–284.

3797 HAEGER, John D. "The American Fur Company and the Chicago of 1812–1835." *Ill St Hist J,* LXI (1968), 117–139.

3798 HEARN, Walter Carey. "Towns in Antebellum Mississippi." Doctoral dissertation, University of Mississippi, 1969.

3799 HOLT, Glen Edward. "The Shaping of St. Louis, 1763–1860." Doctoral dissertation, University of Chicago, 1975.

3800 JAMES, D. Clayton. *Antebellum Natchez.* Baton Rouge, 1968.

3801 KELLNER, George Helmuth. "The German Element on the Urban Frontier: St. Louis, 1830–1860." Doctoral dissertation, University of Missouri, 1973.

3802 KNIGHTS, Peter R. *The Plain People of Boston, 1830–1860.* New York, 1971.†

3803 LANE, Roger. *Policing in the City: Boston, 1822–1885.* Cambridge, Mass., 1967.

3804 LIVINGOOD, James W. *The Philadelphia-Baltimore Trade Rivalry, 1780–1860.* Harrisburg, 1947.

3805 LOCKWOOD, Charles. "The Bond Street Area." *N Y Hist Soc Q,* LVI (1972), 309–320.

3806 MCCAUGHEY, Robert A. "From Town to City: Boston in the 1820s." *Pol Sci Q,* LXXXVIII (1973), 191–213.

3807 MCKELVEY, Blake. *Rochester, The Water-Power City, 1812–1854.* Cambridge, Mass., 1945.

3808 MCKELVEY, Blake, comp. *The City in American History.* New York, 1969.

3809 MCLEAR, Patrick E. " '. . . And Still They Come . . .' Chicago from 1832–1836." *J W,* VII (1968), 397–404.

3810 MANN, Arthur et al. *History and the Role of the City in American Life.* Indianapolis, 1972.

3811 NODYAR, Kenneth R. "The Role of DeWitt Clinton and the Municipal Government in the Development of Cultural Organizations in New York City, 1803–1817. Doctoral dissertation, New York University, 1969.

3812 PESSEN, Edward. "The Social Configuration of the Antebellum City: A Historical and Theoretical Inquiry." *J Urban Hist,* II (1976), 267–306.

3813 PESSEN, Edward. "The Wealthiest New Yorkers of the Jacksonian Era: A New List." *N Y Hist Soc Q,* LIV (1970), 145–172.

3814 PESSEN, Edward. "Who Governed the Nation's Cities in the 'Era of the Common Man'." *Pol Sci Q,* LXXXVII (1972), 591–614.

3815 PESSEN, Edward. "Who Has Power in the Democratic Capitalistic Community? Relfections on Antebellum New York City." *N Y Hist,* LVIII (1977), 129–155.

3816 PESSEN, Edward. "Did Fortunes Rise and Fall Mercurially in Antebellum America? The Tale of Two Cities: Boston and New York." *J Soc Hist,* IV (1971), 339–357.

3817 PESSEN, Edward. "The Lifestyle of the Antebellum Urban Elite." *Mid-Am,* LV (1973), 163–183.

3818 PHELAN, Doris Ann. "Boosterism in St. Louis, 1810–1860." Doctoral dissertation, University of St. Louis, 1970.

3819 PIERCE, Bessie L. *A History of Chicago.* 3 vols. New York, 1937–1957.

3820 PRED, Allan R. *Urban Growth and the Circulation of Information: The United States System of Cities, 1790–1840.* Cambridge, Mass., 1973.

3821 PROCTOR, Samuel. "Jewish Life in New Orleans, 1718–1860." *La Hist Q,* XL (1957), 110–132.

3822 REED, Thomas H. *Municipal Government in the United States.* New York, 1934.

3823 REICHARD, Maximilian. "Black and White on the Urban Frontier: the St. Louis Community in Transition, 1800–1820." *Mo Hist Soc Bull,* XXXIII (1976), 3–17.

3824 REISER, Catherine Elizabeth. *Pittsburgh's Commercial Development, 1800–1850.* Harrisburg, 1951.

3825 RICH, Robert Stanley. "Politics and Pedigrees: The Wealthy Men of Boston, 1798–1852." Doctoral dissertation, University of California, Los Angeles, 1975.

3826 RICHARDSON, James F. *The New York Police: Colonial Times to 1901.* New York, 1970.

3827 SCHNEIDER, John C. "Urbanization and the Maintenance of Order: Detroit, 1824–1847." *Mich Hist,* LX (1976), 260–281.

3828 SIMON, Donald E. "The Public Park Movement in Brooklyn, 1824–1873." Doctoral dissertation, New York University, 1972.

3829 SPRAGUE, Stuart S. "Town Making in the Era of Good Feelings: Kentucky, 1814–1820." *Reg Ky Hist Soc,* LXXII (1974), 337–341.

3830 STILL, Bayrd. "New York City in 1824: A Newly Discovered Description." *N Y Hist Soc Q,* XLVI (1962), 137–169.

3831 THERNSTROM, Stephan, and Richard SENNETT, eds. *Nineteenth-Century Cities.* New Haven, 1969.†

3832 THERNSTROM, Stephan, and Peter R. KNIGHTS. "Men in Motion: Some Data and Speculations about Urban Population Mobility in Nineteenth-Century America." *J Interdis Hist,* I (1970), 7–35.

3833 TREGLE, Joseph G., Jr. "Early New Orleans Society: A Reappraisal." *J S Hist,* XVIII (1952), 20–36.

3834 TUCKER, Louis Leonard. "Cincinnati: Athens of the West, 1830–1861." *Ohio Hist,* LXXV (1966), 10–25.

3835 VOSS, Stuart F. "Town Growth in Central Missouri, 1815–1880: An Urban Chaparral." *Mo Hist Rev,* LXIV (1969), 64–80, 197–217, 322–350.

3836 WADE, Richard C. *The Urban Frontier: The Rise of Western Cities, 1790–1830.* Cambridge, Mass., 1959.†

3837 WADE, Richard C. "Urban Life in Western America, 1790–1830." *Am Hist Rev,* LXIV (1958), 14–30.

3838 WALL, Alexander, Jr. "The Great Fire of 1835." *N Y Hist Soc Q,* XX (1936), 3–22.

3839 WARNER, Sam Bass, Jr. *The Urban Wilderness: A History of the American City.* New York, 1972.†

3840 WEAVER, Herbert. "Foreigners in Ante-Bellum Towns of the Lower South." *J S Hist,* XIII (1947), 62–73.

3841 WEBER, Adna F. *The Growth of Cities in the Nineteenth Century.* New York, 1899.†

3842 WHEELER, Kenneth. *To Wear a City's Crown: The Beginnings of Urban Growth in Texas, 1836–1865.* Cambridge, Mass., 1968.

3843 WILLIAMSON, Jeffrey G. "Ante-Bellum Urbanization in the American Northeast." *J Econ Hist,* XXV (1965), 592–608.

3844 WILLIAMSON, Jeffrey G., and Joseph A. SWANSON. "The Growth of Cities in the American Northeast, 1820–1870." *Explo Entrep Hist,* IV (1966), 3–101.

3845 ZACHARY, Alan M. "Social Thought in the Philadelphia Leadership Community, 1800–1840." Doctoral dissertation, Northwestern University, 1974.

3846 ZIMMER, Donald Thomas. "Madison, Indiana, 1811–1860: A Study in the Process of City Building." Doctoral dissertation, Indiana University, 1974.

2. Economic Thought and Growth

See also **2013, 2051, 2206, 2209, 2224, 2227, 2375, 2390, 2421, 2461, 2492, 2637, 2852, 3043, 3209–3347**

3847 ALDRICH, Mark. "Earnings of American Civil Engineers, 1820–1859." *J Econ Hist,* XXXI (1971), 407–419.

3848 BERRY, Thomas Senior. *Western Prices before 1861: A Study of the Cincinnati Market.* Cambridge, Mass., 1943.

3849 BEZANSON, Anne, et al. *Wholesale Prices in Philadelphia, 1784–1861.* Philadelphia, 1936.

3850 BRISTED, John. *The Resources of the United States of America.* New York, 1818.

3851 BRUCHEY, Stuart. *The Roots of American Economic Growth, 1601–1801.* New York, 1965.†

3852 CALLENDER, Guy Stevens, ed. *Selections from the Economic History of the United States, 1765–1860.* Boston, 1909.

3853 COCHRAN, Thomas C., and William MILLER. *The Age of Enterprise.* New York, 1942.†

3854 COLE, Arthur H. *Wholesale Commodity Prices in the United States, 1700–1861.* Cambridge, Mass., 1938.

3855 COLEMAN, Peter J. *Debtors and Creditors in American: Insolvency, Imprisonment for Debt, and Bankruptcy, 1607–1900.* Madison, 1974.

3856 COXE, Tench. *A Study in American Economic Development.* Baltimore, 1938.

3857 DAVID, Paul A. "The Growth of Real Product in the United States before 1840: New Evidence, Controlled Conjectures." *J Econ Hist,* XXVII (1967), 151–197.

3858 DORFMAN, Joseph. *The Economic Mind in American Civilization.* 5 vols. New York, 1946–1959.

3859 FORSTER, Colin, and G. S. L. TUCKER. *Economic Opportunity and White American Fertility Ratios, 1800–1860.* New Haven, 1972.

3860 GOODRICH, Carter. "Recent Contributions to Economic History: The United States, 1789–1860." *J Econ Hist,* XIX (1959), 25–43.

3861 GOODRICH, Carter, ed. *The Government and the Economy.* Indianapolis, 1967.

3862 GOODRICH, Carter. "The Virginia System of Mixed Enterprise." *Pol Sci Q,* LXIV (1949), 355–387.

3863 HITE, James C., and Ellen J. HALL. "The Reactionary Evolution of Economic Thought in Antebellum Virginia." *Va Mag Hist Biog,* LXXX (1972), 476–488.

3864 HUGHES, J. R. T., and Nathan ROSENBERG. "The United States Business Cycles before 1860: Some Problems of Interpretation." *Econ Hist Rev,* 2d ser., XV (1963), 476–493.

3865 HUNTER, Louis C. *Studies in the Economic History of the Ohio Valley.* Northampton, Mass., 1934.

3866 JACOBSEN, Diane Lindstrom. "Demand, Markets and Eastern Economic Development: Philadelphia, 1815–1840." Doctoral dissertation, University of Delaware, 1974.

3867 KIRKLAND, Edward C. *A History of American Economic Life.* 4th ed. New York, 1969.†

214

3868 KLINGAMAN, David C., and Richard K. VEDDER, eds. *Essays in Nineteenth Century Economic History: The Old Northwest.* Athens, Ohio, 1975.

3869 KUZNETS, Simon. "National Income Estimates for the United States Prior to 1870." *J Econ Hist,* XII (1952), 115–130.

3870 LEBERGOTT, Stanley. *Manpower in Economic Growth: The American Record Since 1800.* New York, 1964.

3871 LIVELY, Robert A. "The American System, A Review Article." *Bus Hist Rev,* XXIX (1955), 81–96.

3872 MCGRANE, Reginald C. *Foreign Bondholders and American State Debts.* New York, 1935.

3873 MCLEAR, Patrick E. "Speculation, Promotion, and the Panic of 1837 in Chicago." *Ill St Hist J,* LXII (1969), 135–146.

3874 NORTH, Douglass C. *Economic Growth in the United States, 1790–1860.* New York, 1961.†

3875 NORTH, Douglass C. International Capital Flows and the Development of the American West." *J Econ Hist,* XVI (1956), 493–505.

3876 NORTH, Douglass C. "The United States Balance of Payments, 1790–1860." *Trends in the American Economy in the Nineteenth Century: Studies in Income and Wealth.* Vol. XXIV, pp. 573–627. Princeton, 1960.

3877 NORTH, Douglass C. "Capital Formation in the United States during the Early Period of Industrialization: A Reexamination of the Issues." *The Reinterpretation of American Economic History.* Ed. Robert W. FOGEL and Stanley L. ENGERMAN. New York, 1971.

3878 NORTH, Douglass C., and Robert Paul THOMAS, eds. *The Growth of the American Economy to 1860.* New York, 1968.

3879 ORSAGH, Thomas, et al., eds. *The Economic History of the United States Prior to 1860: An Annotated Bibliography.* Santa Barbara, Calif., 1975.

3880 PORTER, Glenn, and Harold C. LIVESAY. *Merchants and Manufacturers: Studies in the Changing Structure of Nineteenth-Century Marketing.* Baltimore, 1971.

3881 POULSON, Barry Warren. *Value Added in Manufacturing, Mining and Agriculture in the American Economy from 1809 to 1839.* New York, 1975.

3882 RATCHFORD, Benjamin U. *American State Debts.* Durham, 1941.

3883 ROTHSTEIN, Morton. "The Antebellum South as a Dual Economy: A Tentative Hypothesis." *Ag Hist,* XLI (1967), 373–382.

3884 SCHUMPETER, J. A. *Business Cycles.* 2 vols. New York, 1939.

3885 SEYBERT, Adam. *Statistical Annals . . . of the United States, 1789–1818.* Philadelphia, 1818.

3886 SMITH, Norman W. "A Mature Frontier: The New Hampshire Economy, 1790–1850." *Hist N H,* XXIV (Fall, 1969), 3–19.

3887 SOLTOW, Lee. "Economic Inequality in the United States in the Period from 1790 to 1860." *J Econ Hist,* XXXI (1971), 822–839.

3888 STONE, James H. "Economic Conditions in Macon, Georgia in the 1830s." *Ga Hist Q,* LIV (1970), 209–225.

3889 TAYLOR, George Rogers, comp. *American Economic History Before 1860.* Goldentree Bibliographies in American History. Arlington Heights, 1969.†

3890 TAYLOR, George Rogers. "American Economic Growth before 1840: An Exploratory Essay." *J Econ Hist,* XXIV (1964), 427–444.

3891 TEMIN, Peter. "The Anglo-American Business Cycle, 1820–1860." *Econ Hist Rev,* 2d ser., XXVII (1974), 207–221.

3892 USELDING, Paul "Conjectural Estimates of Gross Human Capital Inflows to the American Economy: 1790–1860." *Explo Econ Hist,* IX (1971), 49–61.

3893 WILLIAMSON, Jeffrey G. *American Growth and the Balance of Payments, 1820–1913, A Study of the Long Swing.* Chapel Hill, 1964.

A. Agriculture

See also **464, 916, 935, 1874, 2208, 2347, 2455, 2715, 3204–3653, 3772, 3881, 4372**

3894 ABBOTT, Richard H. "The Agricultural Press Views the Yeoman: 1819–1859." *Ag Hist,* XLII (1968), 35–48.

3895 BASSETT, John Spencer, ed. *The Southern Plantation Overseer as Revealed in His Letters.* Northampton, Mass., 1925.

3896 BIDWELL, Percy W. "The Agricultural Revolution in New England." *Am Hist Rev,* XXVI (1921), 683–702.

3897 BIDWELL, Percy W., and John I. FALCONER. *History of Agriculture in the Northern United States, 1620–1860.* Washington, D.C., 1941.

3898 BOGART, Ernest L. *Economic History of American Agriculture.* New York, 1923.

3899 BOGUE, Allan G. *From Prairie to Corn Belt: Farming on the Illinois and Iowa Prairies in the Nineteenth Century.* Chicago, 1963.

3900 BONNER, James C. *A History of Georgia Agriculture, 1732–1860.* Athens, Ga., 1964.

3901 BRUCHEY, Stuart, ed. *Cotton and the Growth of the American Economy, 1790–1860.* New York, 1967.

3902 BURKETT, Charles W. *History of Ohio Agriculture.* Concord, 1900.

3903 CATHEY, Cornelius O. *Agriculture Developments in North Carolina, 1783–1860.* Chapel Hill, 1957.

3904 CLIFTON, James M. "Golden Grains of White: Rice Planters on the Lower Cape Fear." *N C Hist Rev,* L (1973), 365–393.

3905 COHN, David L. *The Life and Times of King Cotton.* New York, 1956.

3906 COOPER, William J., Jr. "The Cotton Crisis in the Antebellum South: Another Look." *Ag Hist,* XLIX (1975), 381–391.

3907 CRAVEN, Avery O. *Soil Exhaustion as a Factor in the Agricultural History of Virginia and Maryland, 1606–1860.* Urbana, Ill., 1926.

3908 CROWGEY, Henry G. *Kentucky Bourbon: The Early Years of Whiskey-making.* Lexington, 1971.

3909 DAVIS, Charles S. *The Cotton Kingdom in Alabama.* Montgomery, 1939.

3910 DAY, Clarence A. *A History of Maine Agriculture, 1604–1860.* Orono, Me., 1954.

3911 DEMAREE, A. L. *The American Agricultural Press, 1819–1860.* New York, 1941.

3912 EASTERBY, James H., ed. *The South Carolina Rice Plantation as Revealed in the Papers of Robert F. W. Allston.* Chicago, 1945.

3913 EDGAR, William C. *The Story of a Grain of Wheat.* New York, 1903.

3914 EDWARDS, Everett E. *A Bibliography of the History of Agriculture in the United States.* Washington, D.C., 1930.

3915 FLETCHER, S. W. *Pennsylvania Agricultural and Country Life, 1640–1840.* Harrisburg, 1950.

3916 GATES, Paul W. *The Farmer's Age: Agriculture, 1815–1850.* New York, 1960.†

3917 GENOVESE, Eugene D. "Livestock in the Slave Economy of the Old South— A Revised View." *Ag Hist,* XXXVI (1962), 143–149.

3918 GENOVESE, Eugene D. "Yeomen Farmers in Slaveholders' Democracy." *Ag Hist,* XLIX (1975), 331–334.

3919 GIBSON, James R. "Food for the Fur Traders: The First Farmers in the Pacific Northwest, 1805–1846." *J W,* VII (1968), 18–30.

3920 GRAY, Lewis C. *History of Agriculture in the Southern United States, to 1860.* 2 vols. Washington, D.C., 1933.

3921 HAMMOND, Matthew B. *The Cotton Industry.* New York, 1897.

3922 HASKINS, Ralph W. "Planter and Cotton Factor in the Old South: Some Areas of Friction." *Ag Hist,* XXIX (1955), 1–14.

3923 HEDRICK, Ulysses P. *A History of Horticulture in America to 1860.* New York, 1950.

3924 HENLEIN, Paul C. *The Cattle Kingdom in the Ohio Valley, 1783–1860.* Lexington, 1959.

3925 HILLIARD, Sam. "Hog Meat and Cornpone: Food Habits in the Antebellum South." *Am Phil Soc Proc,* CXIII (1969), 1–13.

3926 HOLBROOK, Abigail Curlee. "Cotton Marketing in Antebellum Texas." *S W Hist Q,* LXXIII (1970), 431–455.

3927 HOPKINS, James F. *A History of the Hemp Industry in Kentucky.* Lexington, 1951.

3928 HUTCHINSON, William K., and Samuel H. WILLIAMSON. "The Self-Sufficiency of the Antebellum South: Estimates of the Food Supply." *J Econ Hist,* XXXI (1971), 591–612.

3929 JORDAN, Weymouth T. *Hugh Davis and His Alabama Plantation.* University of Alabama, 1948.

3930 KELLAR, Herbert A., ed. *Solon Robinson: Pioneer and Agriculturist.* 2 vols. Indianapolis, 1936.

3931 KELSEY, Darwin P., ed. "American Agriculture, 1790–1840: A Symposium." *Ag Hist,* XLVI (1972), 1–233.

3932 MARKWALDER, Donald. "The Ante-Bellum South as A Market for Food: Myth or Reality?" *Ga Hist Q,* LIV (1970), 408–418.

3933 MARTI, Donald B. "The Purposes of Agricultural Education: Ideas and Projects in New York State, 1819–1865." *Ag Hist,* XLV (1971), 271–283.

3934 MCDONALD, Forrest, and Grady MCWHINEY. "The Antebellum Southern Herdsman: A Reinterpretation." *J S Hist,* XLI (1975), 147–166.

3935 MCNALL, Neil Adams. *An Agricultural History of the Genesee Valley, 1790–1860.* Philadelphia, 1952.

3936 MOORE, John Hebron. *Agriculture in Ante-Bellum Mississippi.* New York, 1958.

3937 NICHOLS, Roger L. "Soldiers as Farmers: Army Agriculture in the Missouri Valley, 1818–1827." *Ag Hist,* XLIV (1970), 213–222.

3938 OLMSTEAD, Alan L. "The Mechanization of Reaping and Mowing in American Agriculture, 1833–1870." *J Econ Hist,* XXXV (1975), 327–352.

3939 PARKER, William N., ed. "The Structure of the Cotton Economy of the Antebellum South." *Ag Hist,* XLIV (1970), 1–165.

3940 PASSELL, Peter. "The Impact of Cotton Land Distribution on the Antebellum Economy." *J Econ Hist,* XXXI (1971), 917–937.

3941 PAUL, Rodman W. "The Beginnings of Agriculture in California: Innovation vs. Continuity." *Calif Hist Soc Q,* LII (1973), 16–27.

3942 PINKETT, Harold T. "The American Farmer, a Pioneer Agricultural Journal, 1819–1834." *Ag Hist,* XXXIV (1950), 146–151.

3943 PUFFER, Raymond La Bounty. "The Michigan Agricultural Frontier: Southeastern Region, 1820–1860." Doctoral dissertation, University of New Mexico, 1976.

3944 ROBERT, Joseph C. *The Story of Tobacco in America.* New York, 1949.†

3945 ROBERT, Joseph C. *The Tobacco Kingdom: Plantation, Market and Factory in Virginia and North Carolina, 1800–1860.* Durham, 1938.

3946 SCARBOROUGH, William Kauffman. *The Overseer: Plantation Management in the Old South.* Baton Rouge, 1966.

3947 SCHAFER, Joseph. *The Social History of American Agriculture.* New York, 1936.

3948 SCHLEBECKER, John T., comp. *Bibliography of Books and Pamphlets on the History of Agriculture in the United States, 1607–1967.* Santa Barbara, Calif., 1969.

3949 SCHMIDT, Louis B. *Topical Studies and References on the History of American Agriculture.* Ames, 1940.

3950 SCHOB, David E. *Hired Hands and Plowboys: Farm Labor in the Midwest, 1815–1860.* Urbana, Ill., 1975.

3951 SCHOB, David E. "Sodbusting on the Upper Midwestern Frontier, 1820–1860." *Ag Hist,* XLVII (1973), 47–56.

3952 SITTERSON, J. Carlyle. *Sugar Country: The Cane Sugar Industry in the South, 1753–1950.* Lexington, 1953.

3953 STONE, Alfred H. "The Cotton Factorage System of the Southern States." *Am Hist Rev,* XX (1915), 557–565.

3954 TEMIN, Peter. "The Causes of Cotton-Price Fluctuations in the 1830s." *Rev Econ Stat,* XLIX (1967), 463–470.

3955 TURNER, Charles W. "Virginia State Agricultural Societies, 1811–1860." *Ag Hist,* XXXVIII (1964), 167–177.

3956 TURNER, Charles W. "Virginia Agricultural Reform, 1815–1860." *Ag Hist,* XXVI (1952), 80–89.

3957 WEATHERWAX, Paul. *The Story of the Maize Plant.* Chicago, 1923.

3958 WHITTEN, David O. "Tariff and Profit: The Antebellum Louisiana Sugar Industry." *Bus Hist Rev,* XLIV (1970), 226–233.

3959 WHITTEN, David O. "Antebellum Sugar and Rice Plantations, Louisiana and South Carolina: A Profitability Study." Doctoral dissertation, Tulane University, 1970.

3960 WISHART, David. "Agriculture at the Trading Posts on the Upper Missouri Prior to 1843." *Ag Hist,* XLVII (1973), 57–62.

3961 WOODMAN, Harold D. "Itinerant Cotton Merchants of the Antebellum South." *Ag Hist,* (1966), 79–90.

3962 WOODMAN, Harold D. *King Cotton and His Retainers; Financing and Marketing the Cotton Crop of the South, 1800–1925.* Lexington, 1967.

3963 WOODWARD, Carl R. *The Development of Agriculture in New Jersey, 1640–1880.* New Brunswick, N.J., 1927.

3964 WRIGHT, Gavin. "An Econometric Study of Cotton Production and Trade, 1830–1860." *Rev Econ Stat,* LIII (1971), 111–120.

3965 WRIGHT, Gavin. *The Political Economy of the Cotton South: Households, Markets, and Wealth in the Nineteenth Century.* New York, 1978.†

B. Banking

See also **455–456, 564, 731, 1049, 1067, 1075, 1077, 1157, 1175, 1475–1519, 2070, 2203, 2243, 2262, 2291, 2372, 2456, 2524**

3966 ABERNETHY, Thomas P. "The Early Development of Banking in Tennessee." *Miss Val Hist Rev,* XIV (1927), 311–325.

3967 ADAMS, Donald R., Jr. "The Bank of Stephen Girard, 1812–1831." *J Econ Hist,* XXXII (1972), 841–868.

3968 AITKEN, Hugh G. J. "Yates and McIntyre: Lottery Managers." *J Econ Hist,* XIII (1953), 36–57.

3969 BAUGHMAN, James P. "Early American Checks: Forms and Functions." *Bus Hist Rev,* XLI (1967), 421–435.

3970 BENTLEY, Marvin. "Incorporated Banks and the Economic Development of Mississippi, 1829–1837." *J Miss Hist,* XXXV (1973), 381–401.

3971 BRANTLEY, William H. *Banking in Alabama, 1816–1860.* Birmingham, 1961.

3972 BROWN, John C. *A Hundred Years of Merchant Banking.* New York, 1909.

3973 CAMPBELL, Claude A. "Banking and Finances in Tennessee During the Depression of 1837." *E Tenn Hist Soc Pub,* IX (1937), 19–30.

3974 CHADDOCK, Robert E. *The Safety Fund Banking System in New York, 1829–1866.* Washington, D.C., 1910.

3975 CLARK, Washington Augustus. *The History of the Banking Institutions Organized in South Carolina, Prior to 1860.* Columbia, S.C., 1922.

3976 DEWEY, Davis R. *State Banking before the Civil War.* Washington, D.C., 1910.

3977 ELAZAR, Daniel J. "Banking and Federalism in the Early American Republic." *Hunt Lib Q,* XXXVIII (1965), 301–320.

3978 ERICKSON, Erling A. *Banking in Frontier Iowa, 1836–1865.* Ames, Ia., 1971.

3979 GLEICH, Harry S. "Banking in Early Missouri." *Mo Hist Rev,* LXI (1967), 427–443, LXII (1967), 30–44.

3980 GOLEMBE, Carter H. "State Banks and the Economic Development of the West, 1830–1844." Doctoral dissertation, Columbia University, 1952.

3981 GOVAN, Thomas P. "Banking and the Credit System in Georgia, 1810–1860." *J S Hist,* IV (1938), 164–184.

3982 GREEN, George D. *Finance and Economic Development in the Old South: Louisiana Banking, 1804–1861.* Stanford, 1972.

3983 HAMMOND, Bray. "Banking in the Early West: Monopoly, Prohibition and Laissez Faire." *J Econ Hist,* VIII (1948), 1–25.

3984 HAMMOND, Bray. "The Chestnut Street Raid on Wall Street, 1839." *Q J Econ,* LXI (1947), 605–618.

3985 HERBERT, William Charles. "Jackson, the Bank, and the Press." Doctoral dissertation, University of Missouri, 1975.

3986 HIDY, Ralph W. "The Organization and Functions of Anglo-American Merchant Bankers, 1815–1860." *J Econ Hist,* I (1941), 53–66.

3987 HIDY, Ralph W. *The House of Baring in American Trade and Finance: English Merchant Bankers at Work, 1763–1861.* Cambridge, Mass., 1949.

3988 HOLDSWORTH, J. T., and D. R. DEWEY. *The First and Second Banks of the United States.* Chicago, 1903.

3989 HUNTINGTON, Charles Clifford. *A History of Banking and Currency in Ohio before the Civil War.* Columbus, 1915.

3990 KEYES, Robert William III. "The Formation of the Second Bank of the United States, 1811–1817." Doctoral dissertation, University of Delaware, 1975.

3991 LAFORCE, J. Clayburn. "Gresham's Law and the Suffolk System: A Misapplied Epigram." *Bus Hist Rev,* XL (1966), 149–166.

3992 LAKE, Wilfred S. "The End of the Suffolk System." *J Econ Hist,* VII (1947), 183–207.

3993 LESESNE, J. Mauldin. *The Bank of the State of South Carolina: A General and Political History.* Columbia, 1970.

3994 LUCE, W. Ray. "The Cohen Brothers of Baltimore: From Lotteries to Banking." *Md Hist Mag,* LXVIII (1973), 288–308.

3995 MALLALIEU, William C., and Sabri M. AKURAL. "Kentucky Banks in the Crisis Decade." *Reg Ky Hist Soc,* LXV (1970), 294–303.

3996 MILLER, Harry E. *Banking Theories in the United States before 1860.* Cambridge, Mass., 1927.

3997 MYERS, Margaret G. *The New York Money Market: Origins and Development.* New York, 1931.

3998 OLMSTEAD, Alan L. "Investment Constraints and New York City Mutual Savings Bank Financing of Antebellum Development." *J Econ Hist,* XXXII (1972), 811–840.

3999 OLMSTEAD, Alan L. *New York City Mutual Savings Banks, 1819–1861.* Chapel Hill, 1976.

4000 REDLICH, Fritz, and Webster M. CHRISTMAN. "Early American Checks and an Example of Their Use." *Bus Hist Rev,* XLI (1967), 285–302.

4001 REDLICH, Fritz. *The Moulding of American Banking: Men and Ideas, Part I.* New York, 1947.

4002 REDLICH, Fritz. "American Banking and Growth in the Nineteenth Century: Epistemological Reflections." *Explo Econ Hist,* X (1973), 305–314. See also Richard SYLLA, "Economic History 'von unten nach oben' and 'von oben nach unten': A Reply to Fritz Redlich,' " ibid., 315–318.

4003 SCHEIBER, Harry N. "Public Canal Finance and State Banking in Ohio, 1825–1837." *Ind Mag Hist,* LXV (1969), 119–132.

4004 SCHEIBER, Harry N. "George Bancroft and the Bank of Michigan, 1837–1841. *Mich Hist,* XLIV (1960), 82–90.

4005 SCHEIBER, Harry N. "The Commercial Bank of Lake Erie, 1831–1843." *Bus Hist Rev,* XL (1966), 47–65.

4006 SHADE, William G. "The Background of the Michigan Free Banking Law." *Mich Hist,* LII (1968), 229–244.

4007 STEVENS, Harry R. "Bank Enterprisers in a Western Town, 1815–1822." *Bus Hist Rev,* XXIX (1955), 139–156.

4008 SUMNER, William Graham. *A History of Banking in the United States.* New York, 1896.

4009 SYLLA, Richard. "American Banking and Growth in the Nineteenth Century: A Partial View of the Terrain." *Explo Entrep Hist,* IX (1971), 197–228.

4010 SYLLA, Richard. "Forgotten Men of Money: Private Bankers in Early U.S. History." *J Econ Hist,* XXXVI (1976), 84–99.

4011 TAUS, Esther R. *Central Banking Functions of the United States Treasury, 1789–1941.* New York, 1943.

4012 TIMBERLAKE, Richard H. *Money, Banking, and Central Banking.* New York, 1965.

4013 VAN FENSTERMAKER, Joseph. *The Development of American Commercial Banking: 1782–1837.* Kent, Ohio, 1965.

4014 WARBURTON, Clark. "Variations in Economic Growth and Banking Developments in the United States from 1835 to 1885." *J Econ Hist,* XVIII (1958), 283–297.

4015 WORLEY, Ted R. "The Arkansas State Bank: Ante-Bellum Period." *Ark Hist Q,* XXIII (1964), 65–73.

4016 WRIGHT, David McCord. "Langdon Cheves and Nicholas Biddle: New Data for a New Interpretation. *J Econ Hist,* XIII (1953), 305–319.

C. Business

See also **564, 667–668, 1151–1157, 1570–1583, 1850, 1946, 2024, 2289, 2580**

4017 ATHERTON, Lewis E. "Itinerant Merchandising in the Ante-Bellum South." *Bus Hist Soc Bull,* XIX (1945), 35–59.

4018 ATHERTON, Lewis E. *The Pioneer Merchant in Mid-America.* Columbia, 1939.

4019 ATHERTON, Lewis E. *The Southern Country Store, 1800–1860.* Baton Rouge, 1949.

4020 BOYLE, James E. *Cotton and the New Orleans Cotton Exchange: A Century of Commercial Evolution.* Garden City, N.Y., 1934.

4021 BROWNE, Gary L. "Business Innovation and Social Change: The Career of Alexander Brown after the War of 1812." *Md Hist Mag,* LXIX (1974), 243–255.

4022 CARSON, Gerald. *The Old Country Store.* New York, 1954.

4023 COCHRAN, Thomas C. *Business in American Life: A History.* New York, 1972.†

4023A COCHRAN, Thomas C. *200 Years of American Business.* New York, 1977.

4024 CORNET, Florence Doll. "The Experiences of a Midwest Salesman in 1836." *Mo Hist Soc Bull,* XXIX (1973), 227–235.

4025 DANIELLS, Lorna M. *Studies in Enterprise: A Selected Bibliography of American and Canadian Company Histories and Biographies of Businessmen.* Cambridge, Mass., 1957.

4026 DAVIS, John P. *Corporations: A Study of the Origin and Development of Great Business Combinations and their Relation to the Authority of the State.* 2 vols. New York, 1905.

4027 DAVIS, Joseph S. *Essays in the Earlier History of American Corporations.* 2 vols. Cambridge, Mass., 1917.

4028 DODD, Edwin Merrick. *American Business Corporations until 1860, with Special Reference to Massachusetts.* Cambridge, Mass., 1954.

4029 DOUGLASS, Elisha P. *The Coming of Age of American Business: Three Centuries of Enterprise, 1600–1900.* Chapel Hill, N.C., 1971.

4030 EILERT, John W. "Illinois Business Incorporations, 1816–1869." *Bus Hist Rev,* XXXVII (1963), 169–180.

4031 EVANS, George H., Jr. *Business Incorporations in the United States, 1800–1943.* New York, 1948.

4032 FRANTZ, Joe B. "The Mercantile House of McKinney & Williams, Underwriters of the Texas Revolution." *Bus Hist Soc Bull,* XXVI (1952), 1–18.

4033 GRAY, Edward. *William Gray of Salem, Merchant.* Boston, 1884.

4034 HANDLIN, Oscar, and Mary Handlin. "Origins of the American Business Corporation." *J Econ Hist,* V (1945), 1–23.

4035 HUNT, Freeman. *Lives of American Merchants.* 2 vols. New York, 1858.

4036 HURST, James Willard. *The Legitimacy of the Business Corporation in the Law of the United States, 1780–1970.* Charlottesville, 1970.

4037 JAHER, Frederic C. "Businessmen and Gentlemen: Nathan and Thomas Gold Appleton—An Exploration in Intergenerational History." *Explo Entrep Hist,* IV (1966), 17–39.

4038 JENKS, L. H. *The Migration of British Capital to 1875.* New York, 1927.

4039 KILLICK, John R. "The Cotton Operations of Alexander Brown and Sons in the Deep South." *J S Hist,* XLIII (1977), 169–194.

4040 KNIGHT, Charles K. *The History of Life Insurance in the United States to 1870.* Philadelphia, 1920.

4041 LARSON, Henrietta M. *Guide to Business History.* Cambridge, Mass., 1948.

4042 LAWRENCE, William R., ed. *Extracts from the Diary and Correspondence of the Late Amos Lawrence.* Boston, 1859.

4043 MADISON, James Henry. "Businessmen and the Business Community in Indianapolis, 1820–1860." Doctoral dissertation, Indiana University, 1918.

4044 MCMASTER, John Bach. *The Life and Times of Stephen Girard, Mariner and Merchant.* 2 vols. Philadelphia, 1918.

4045 PARTON, James. *Life of John Jacob Astor.* New York, 1865.

4046 PORTER, Kenneth W. *John Jacob Astor, Business Man.* 2 vols. Cambridge, Mass., 1931.

4047 PORTER, Kenneth W. *The Jacksons and the Lees.* Cambridge, Mass., 1937.

4048 SMITH, Walter B., and Arthur H. COLE. *Fluctuations in American Business, 1790–1860.* Cambridge, Mass., 1935.

4049 THOMPSON, Robert T. *Colonel James Neilson: A Businessman of the Early Machine Age in New Jersey, 1784–1862.* New Brunswick, N.J., 1940.

4050 TOOKER, Elva. *Nathan Trotter, Philadelphia Merchant, 1787–1853.* Cambridge, Mass., 1955.

4051 USELDING, Paul J. "Peddling in the Antebellum Economy." *Am J Econ Soc,* XXXIV (1975), 55–66.

D. Commerce

See also **851, 1199, 1838, 1980, 1981, 2556**

4052 ALBION, Robert G. *The Rise of New York Port, 1815–1860.* New York, 1939.

4053 BERMAN, Edward H. "Salem and Zanzibar, 1825–1850: Twenty-five Years of Commercial Relations." *Essex Inst Hist Coll,* CV (1969), 338–362.

4054 BERRY, Don. *A Majority of Scoundrels: An Informal History of the Rocky Mountain Fur Company.* New York, 1961.

4055 BORST, William Adam. "The American Merchant and the Genesis of Japanese-American Commercial Relations, 1790–1858." Doctoral dissertation, St. Louis University, 1972.

4056 BROWN, Thomas Andrew. "An Episode in United States Foreign Trade: Silver and Gold, Santa Fe and St. Louis (1820–1840)." Doctoral dissertation, Ball State University, 1974.

4057 BUCK, Norman Sydney. *The Development of the Organization of Anglo-American Trade.* New Haven, 1925.

4058 DE PEW, Chauncey M., ed. *1795–1895. One Hundred Years of American Commerce.* 2 vols. New York, 1895.

4059 DOWNS, Jacques M. "American Merchants and the China Opium Trade, 1800–1840." *Bus Hist Rev,* XLII (1968), 418–442.

4060 DUNCAN, Bingham. "Diplomatic Support of the American Rice Trade, 1835–1845." *Ag Hist,* XXIII (1949), 92–96.

4061 EISTERHOLD, John A. "Lumber and Trade in the Lower Mississippi Valley and New Orleans, 1800–1860." *La Hist,* XIII (1972), 71–91.

4062 EISTERHOLD, John A. "Lumber and Trade in Pensacola and West Florida, 1800–1860." *Fla Hist Q,* LI (1973), 267–280.

4063 EISTERHOLD, John Anthony. "Lumber and Trade in the Seaboard Cities of the Old South, 1607–1860." Doctoral dissertation, University of Mississippi, 1970.

4064 EISTERHOLD, John A. "Charleston: Lumber and Trade in a Declining Southern Port." *S C Hist Mag,* LXXIV (1973), 61–72.

4065 GOEBEL, Dorothy Burne. "British Trade to the Spanish Colonies, 1796–1823." *Am Hist Rev,* XLIII (1938), 288–320.

4066 GOEBEL, Dorothy Burne. "British-American Rivalry in the Chilean Trade, 1817–1820." *J Econ Hist,* II (1942), 190–202.

4067 HIGGINBOTHAM, Sanford W. "Philadelphia Commerce with Latin America, 1820–1830." *Pa Hist,* IX (1942), 252–266.

4068 HUNTER, William C. The *"Fan Kwae" at Canton before Treaty Days, 1823–1824.* London, 1882.

4069 JOHNSON, Emory R., et al. *History of Domestic and Foreign Commerce of the United States.* 2 vols. Washington, D.C., 1915.

4070 JONES, Fred M. *Middlemen in the Domestic Trade of the United States, 1800–1860.* Urbana, 1937.

4071 LAVENDER, David. "Some Characteristics of the American Fur Company, 1808–1834." *Minn Hist,* XL (1966), 178–187.

4072 LOGAN, Frenise A. "A British East India Company Agent in the United States, 1839–1840." *Ag Hist,* XLVIII (1974), 267–276.

4073 MAK, James, "Intraregional Trade in the Antebellum West: Ohio, A Case Study." *Ag Hist,* IV (1972), 489–497.

4074 MILLER, Stuart C. "The American Trader's Image of China, 1785–1840." *Pac Hist Rev,* XXXVI (1967), 375–395.

4075 MILLS, James Cooke. *Our Inland Seas: Their Shipping and Commerce for Three Centuries.* Chicago, 1910.

4076 OGDEN, Adele. *The California Sea Otter Trade, 1784–1848.* Berkeley, 1941.

4077 PERKINS, Edwin J. *Financing Anglo-American Trade: The House of Brown, 1800–1880.* Cambridge, Mass., 1975.

4078 PHILLIPS, Paul C. *The Fur Trade.* Norman, 1961.

4079 PRUCHA, Francis Paul. "Army Sutlers and the American Fur Company." *Minn Hist,* XL (1966), 22–31.

4080 PUTNEY, Martha S. "Black Merchant Seamen of Newport, 1803–1865: A Case Study in Foreign Commerce." *J Neg Hist,* LVII (1972), 156–168.

4081 RUTTER, Frank R. *South American Trade of Baltimore.* Baltimore, 1897.

4082 SAUL, Normal E. "Beverley C. Sanders and the Expansion of American Trade with Russia, 1833–1855." *Md Hist Mag,* LXVI (1972), 156–171.

4083 SETSER, Vernon G. *The Commercial Reciprocity Policy of the United States, 1774–1829.* Philadelphia, 1937.

4084 WHITE, David H. "The John Forbes Company: Heir to the Florida Indian Trade, 1801–1819." Doctoral dissertation, University of Alabama, 1973.

4085 WILLIAMSON, Jeffrey G. "International Trade and United States Economic Development, 1827–1843." *J Econ Hist,* XXI (1961), 372–383.

4086 WILLIAMSON, Jeffrey G. "The Long Swing: Comparisons and Interactions Between British and American Balance of Payments, 1820–1913." *J Econ Hist,* XXII (1962), 21–46.

4087 WRIGHT, Homer Edward. "Diplomacy of Trade on the Southern Frontier: A Case Study of the Influence of William Panton and John Forbes, 1784–1817." Doctoral dissertation, University of Georgia, 1972.

4088 YATES, Bowling C. "Macon, Georgia, Inland Trading Center, 1826–1836." *Ga Hist Q,* LV (1971), 365–377.

E. Currency and Finance

See also **626, 1570–1583, 2371, 2502, 3759, 3796, 4483**

4089 BOGART, Ernest L. *Financial History of Ohio.* Urbana, Ill., 1912.

4090 BOLLES, Albert S. *The Financial History of the United States from 1789 to 1860.* 4th ed. New York, 1894.

4091 BULLOCK, Charles J. *Historical Sketch of the Finances and Financial Policy of Massachusetts from 1780–1905.* New York, 1907.

4092 DEWEY, Davis Rich. *Financial History of the United States.* 12th ed. New York, 1934.

4093 DORFMAN, Joseph. "A Note on the Interpretation of Anglo-American Finance, 1837–1841." *J Econ Hist,* XI (1951), 140–147.

4094 DUNBAR, Charles Franklin, comp. *Laws of the United States Relating to Currency, Finance, and Banking from 1789 to 1891.* Boston, 1891.

4095 HILDRETH, Richard. *Banks, Banking, and Paper Currencies.* Boston, 1840.

4096 HURST, James Willard. *A Legal History of Money in the United States, 1774–1970.* Lincoln, Neb., 1973.

4097 HUSE, Charles P. *The Financial History of Boston from May 1, 1822 to January 31, 1909.* New York, 1916.

4098 JEWETT, Fred E. *A Financial History of Maine.* New York, 1937.

4099 KIMMEL, Lewis H. *Federal Budget and Fiscal Policy, 1789–1958.* Washington, D.C., 1959.

4100 LAUGHLIN, James Laurence. *The History of Bimetallism in the United States.* New York, 1897.

4101 MACESICH, George. "Sources of Monetary Disturbances in the United States, 1834–1845." *J Econ Hist,* XX (1960), 407–434.

4102 MARTIN, David A. "Bimetallism in the United States before 1850." *J Pol Econ,* LXXVI (1968), 428–442.

4103 MARTIN, David A. "Metallism, Small Notes, and Jackson's War with the B. U. S." *Explo Entrep Hist,* XI (1974), 227–247.

4104 MYERS, Margaret G. *A Financial History of the United States.* New York, 1970.†

4105 NUSSBAUM, Arthur. *A History of the Dollar.* New York, 1957.

4106 O'LEARY, Paul M. "The Coinage Legislation of 1834." *J Pol Econ,* XLV (1937), 80–94.

4107 RATNER, Sidney. *American Taxation: Its History as a Social Force in Democracy.* New York, 1942.

4108 SHULTZ, William J., and M. R. CAINE. *Financial Development of the United States.* New York, 1937.

4109 STUDENSKI, Paul, and Herman E. KROOSS. *Financial History of the United States.* 2d ed. New York, 1963.

4110 SUMNER, William G. *A History of American Currency.* New York, 1874.

4111 SUSHKA, Marie Elizabeth. "The Antebellum Money Market and the Economic Impact of the Bank War." *J Econ Hist,* XXXVI (1976), 809–835.

4112 TRESCOTT, Paul B. "Federal-State Financial Relations, 1790–1860." *J Econ Hist,* XV (1955), 227–245.

4113 WILLETT, Thomas D. "International Specie Flows and American Monetary Stability, 1834–1860." *J Econ Hist,* XXVIII (1968), 28–50.

4114 ZABLER, Jeffrey F. "Further Evidence on American Wage Differentials, 1800–1830." *Explo Econ Hist,* X (1972), 109–117.

F. Immigration and Ethnicity

See also **1931, 2433, 2450, 2454, 2562, 2890, 3801**

4115 ABBOTT, Edith. *Historical Aspects of the Immigration Problem: Selected Documents.* Chicago, 1926.

4116 ABBOTT, Edith. *Immigration: Select Documents and Case Records.* Chicago, 1924.

4117 ADAMS, William Forbes. *Ireland and Irish Emigration to the New World from 1815 to the Famine.* New Haven, 1932.

4118 ANDERSON, Rasmus B. *The First Chapter of Norwegian Immigration (1821–1840). Its Causes and Results.* Madison, 1896.

4119 BABCOCK, Kendric C. *The Scandanavian Element in the United States.* Urbana, Ill., 1914.

4120 BERTHOFF, Rowland T. *British Immigrants in Industrial America, 1790–1950.* Cambridge, Mass., 1953.

4121 BLEGEN, T. C. *Norwegian Migration to America.* 2 vols. Northfield, Minn., 1931–1940.

4122 CONWAY, Alan. "New Orleans as a Port of Immigration, 1820–1860." *La Stud,* I (1962), 1–22.

4123 CONWAY, Alan, ed. *The Welsh in America: Letters from the Immigrants.* Minneapolis, 1961.

4124 COPSON-NIECKO, Maria J. E. "Orthography and Polish Emigrants from Trieste, 1834–1835." *Polish Am Stud,* XXXI (1974), 20–29.

4125 CURRAN, Thomas J. *Xenophobia and Immigration, 1820–1930.* Boston, 1975.

4126 ERNST, Robert. *Immigrant Life in New York City, 1825–1863.* New York, 1949.

4127 ERICKSON, Charlotte. *Invisible Immigrants: the Adaptation of English and Scottish Immigrants in Nineteenth-Century America.* Coral Gables, 1972.

4128 FAUST, Albert B. *The German Element in the United States.* 2 vols. Boston, 1909.

4129 FLEMING, Donald, and Bernard BAILYN, eds. *Dislocation and Emigration: The Social Background of American Immigration.* Perspectives in American History, VII. Philadelphia, 1973.

4130 FRANKLIN, Frank George. *The Legislative History of Naturalization in the United States from the Revolutionary War to 1861.* Chicago, 1906.

4131 GLANZ, Rudolph. "The German Jewish Mass Emigration: 1820–1880." *Am Jew Archiv,* XXII (1970), 49–66.

4132 HANDLIN, Oscar. *Boston's Immigrants, 1790–1880: A Study in Acculturation.* Rev. ed. Cambridge, Mass., 1959.†

4133 HANDLIN, Oscar. *The Uprooted: The Epic Story of the Great Migrations that Made the American People.* Boston, 1951.†

4134 HANSEN, Marcus L. *The Atlantic Migration, 1607–1860.* Cambridge, Mass., 1940.

4135 HANSEN, Marcus L. *The Immigrant in American History.* Cambridge, Mass., 1940.†

4136 HAWGOOD, J. A. *The Tragedy of German-America: The Germans in the United States of America during the Nineteenth Century—and After.* New York, 1940.

4137 JONES, Maldwyn A. *American Immigration.* Chicago, 1960.†

4138 KAPP, Fredrick. *Immigration, and the Commissioners of Emigration of the State of New York.* New York, 1870.

4139 KELLY, Sister Mary G. *Catholic Immigrant Colonization Projects in the United States, 1815–1860.* New York, 1939.

4140 KNOBEL, Dale Thomas. "Paddy and the Republic: Popular Images of the American Irish, 1820–1860." Doctoral dissertation, Northwestern University, 1976.

4141 LINDBERG, John S. *The Background of Swedish Emigration to the United States.* Minneapolis, 1930.

4142 LUCAS, Henry S. *Netherlanders in America: Dutch Immigration to the United States and Canada, 1789–1950.* Ann Arbor, 1955.

4143 MARRARO, Howard R. "Italians in New York during the First Half of the Nineteenth Century." *N Y Hist,* XXVI (1945), 278–306.

4144 NIEHAUS, Earl F. *The Irish in New Orleans, 1800–1860.* Baton Rouge, 1965.

4145 QUALEY, Carlton C. *Norwegian Settlement in the United States.* Northfield, Minn., 1938.

4146 RADMON, Jane. "The English Settlement in Southern Illinois, 1815–1825." *Ind Mag Hist,* XLIII (1947), 329–362.

4147 SEMMINGSEN, Ingrid. "A Shipload of German Emigrants and Their Significance for the Norwegian Emigration of 1825." *Swed Pioneer Hist Q,* XXV (1974), 183–193.

4148 SHOOK, Robert W. "German Migration to Texas, 1830–1850." *Tex,* X (1972), 226–241.

4149 STACK, Robert Edward. "The McCleers and the Birneys—Irish Immigrant Families—Into Michigan and the California Gold Fields, 1820–1893." Doctoral dissertation, St. Louis University, 1972.

4150 STEPHENSON, George M. *A History of American Immigration, 1820–1924.* Boston, 1925.

4151 TABACHNIK, Leonard. "Political Patronage and Ethnic Groups: Foreign-born in the United States Customhouse Service, 1821–1860." *C W Hist,* XVII (1971), 222–231.

4152 WITTKE, Carl F. *We Who Built America: The Saga of the Immigrant.* Rev. ed. Cleveland, 1964.

4153 WITTKE, Carl F. *The Irish in America.* Baton Rouge, 1956.†

4154 YEARLEY, Clifton K. *Britons in American Labor: A History of the Influence of the United Kingdom Immigrants on American Labor, 1820–1914.* Baltimore, 1957.

G. Manufactures and Industrialization

See also **599, 2054, 2617, 3881**

4155 ABBOTT, Collamer M. "Isaac Tyson, Jr., Pioneer Industrialist." *Bus Hist Rev,* XLII (1968), 67–83.

4156 ABRAMOSKE, Donald J. "The Federal Lead Leasing System in Missouri." *Mo His Rev,* LIV (1959), 27–38.

4157 APPLETON, Nathan. *The Introduction of the Power Loom and Origin of Lowell.* Lowell, 1858.

4158 ASHER, Ephraim. "Industrial Efficiency and Biased Technical Change in American and British Manufacturing: The Case of Textiles in the Nineteenth Century." *J Econ Hist,* XXXII (1972), 431–442.

4159 BATCHELDER, Samuel. *Introduction and Early Progress of the Cotton Manufacture in the United States.* Boston, 1863.

4160 BATEMAN, Fred, and Thomas WEISS. "Market Structure before the Age of Big Business: Concentration and Profit in Early Southern Manufacturing." *Bus Hist Rev,* XLIX (1975), 312–336.

4161 BECKER, Carl M. "Mill, Shop, and Factory: The Industrial Life of Dayton, Ohio, 1830–1900." Doctoral dissertation, University of Cincinnati, 1971.

4162 BERRY, Thomas S. "The Rise of Flour Milling in Richmond." *Va Mag Hist Biog,* LXXVIII (1970), 387–408.

4163 BINDER, Frederick Moore. *Coal Age Empire: Pennsylvania Coal and Its Utilization to 1860.* Harrisburg, 1974.

4164 BISHOP, John Leander. *A History of American Manufactures from 1608 to 1860.* 3 vols. Philadelphia, 1861–1868.

4165 BRUCE, Kathleen. *Virginia Iron Manufacture in the Slave Era.* New York, 1930.

4166 CAPPON, Lester J. "Trend of the Southern Iron Industry under the Plantation System." *J Econ Bus Hist,* II (1930), 353–381.

4167 CHANDLER, Alfred D., Jr. "Anthracite Coal and the Beginnings of the Industrial Revolution in the United States." *Bus Hist Rev,* XLVI (1972), 141–181.

4168 CLARK, Victor S. *History of Manufactures in the United States, 1607–1860.* 3 vols. Washington, D.C., 1916.

4169 CLARK, Victor S. "The Influence of Manufactures upon Political Sentiment in the United States from 1820 to 1860." *Am Hist Rev,* XXII (1916), 58–64.

4170 COLE, Arthur H. *The American Wool Manufacture.* 2 vols. Cambridge, Mass., 1926.

4171 COLE, Arthur H., and Harold F. WILLIAMSON. *The American Carpet Manufacture.* Cambridge, Mass., 1941.

4172 COMMONS, John R., et al. *A Documentary History of American Industrial Society.* Cleveland, 1910.

4173 CONRAD, James Lawson, Jr. "The Evolution of Industrial Capitalism in Rhode Island, 1790–1830: Almy, the Browns and the Slaters." Doctoral dissertation, University of Connecticut, 1973.

4174 COULTER, E. Merton. *Auraria: The Story of a Georgia Gold-Mining Town.* Athens, Ga., 1956.

4175 CUMMINGS, Richard O. *American Ice Harvests: A Historical Study in Technology, 1800–1918.* Berkeley 1949.

4176 DAVID, Paul A. "Learning by Doing and Tariff Protection: A Reconsideration of the Case of the Ante-Bellum United States Cotton Textile Industry." *J Econ Hist,* XXX (1970), 521–601.

4177 DAVID, Paul A. "The 'Horndal Effect' in Lowell, 1834–1856: A Short-Run Learning Curve for Integrated Cotton Textile Mills." *Explo Econ Hist,* X (1973), 131–150.

4178 DAVIS, Lance E., and H. Louis STETTLER, III. "The New England Textile Industry, 1825–1860: Trends and Fluctuations." Conference on Research in Income and Wealth. *Output, Employment, and Productivity in the United States after 1800.* New York, 1966.

4179 DAVIS, Pearce. *The Development of the American Glass Industry.* Cambridge, Mass., 1949.

4180 DAVIS, Stephen Robert. "From Plowshares to Spindles: Dedham, Massachusetts, 1790–1840." Doctoral dissertation, University of Wisconsin, Madison, 1973.

4181 DAY, Clive. "The Early Development of American Cotton Manufactures." *Q J Econ,* XXXIX (1925), 450–468.

4182 DEFEBAUGH, James E. *History of the Lumber Industry of America.* 2 vols. Chicago, 1906–07.

4183 DEYRUP, Felicia Johnson. *Arms Makers of the Connecticut Valley, A Regional Study of the Economic Development of the Small Arms Industry, 1798–1870.* Northampton, Mass., 1948.

4184 DICKMAN, Howard. "Technological Innovation in the Woolen Industry: The Middletown Manufacturing Company." *Conn Hist Soc Bull,* XXXVIII (1972), 52–58.

4185 DUTTON, William Sherman. *Du Pont: One Hundred and Forty Years.* 3d ed. New York, 1951.

4186 EAVENSON, Howard N. *The First Century and a Quarter of American Coal Industry.* Pittsburgh, 1942.

4187 FALER, Paul. "Cultural Aspects of the Industrial Revolution: Lynn, Massachusetts Shoemakers and Industrial Morality, 1826–1860." *Labor Hist,* XV (1974), 367–394.

4188 FISHER, Marvin. *Workshops in the Wilderness: The European Response to American Industrialization, 1830–1860.* New York, 1967.

4189 FOX, William F. *A History of the Lumber Industry in the State of New York.* Washington, 1902.

4190 FRIES, Robert F. *Empire in Pine, The Story of Lumbering in Wisconsin, 1830–1900.* Madison, 1951.

4191 GATES, William B., Jr. *Michigan Copper and Boston Dollars: An Economic History of the Michigan Copper Mining Industry.* Cambridge, Mass., 1951.

4192 GIBB, George S. *The Saco-Lowell Shops: Textile Machinery Building in New England, 1813–1949.* Cambridge, Mass., 1950.

4193 GIBSON, George H. "The Mississippi Market for Woolen Goods: An 1822 Analysis." *J S Hist,* XXXI (1965), 80–90.

4194 GIBSON, George H. "The Delaware Woolen Industry." *Del Hist,* XII (1966), 83–120.

4195 GRIFFIN, Richard W. "The Origins of the Industrial Revolution in Georgia: Cotton Textiles, 1810–1865." *Ga Hist Q,* XLII (1958), 355–375.

4196 GRIFFIN, Richard W. "Manufacturing Interests of Mississippi Planters, 1810–1832." *J Miss Hist,* XXII (1960), 110–122.

4197 GRIFFIN, Richard W. "An Origin of the Industrial Revolution in Maryland: The Textile Industry, 1789–1826." *Md Hist Mag,* LXI (1966), 24–36.

4198 HABAKKUK, H. J. *American and British Technology in the Nineteenth Century.* Cambridge, Mass., 1962.†

4199 HARVEY, Katherine A. "Building a Frontier Ironworks: Problems of Transport and Supply, 1837–1840." *Md Hist Mag,* LXX (1975), 149–166.

4200 HAZARD, Blanche Evans. *The Organization of the Boot and Shoe Industry in Massachusetts before 1875.* Cambridge, Mass., 1921.

4201 HEMPSTEAD, Alfred G. *The Penobscot Boom and the Development of the West Branch of the Penobscot River for Log Driving.* Orono, Me, 1931.

4202 HILL, Hamilton A. *Memoir of Abbott Lawrence.* Boston, 1884.

4203 HOAR, Charles. "Legislative Regulation of New York Industrial Corporations, 1800–1850." *N Y Hist,* XXII (1941), 191–207.

4204 HUNTER, Louis C. "Influence of the Market upon Techniques in the Iron Industry of Western Pennsylvania to 1860." *J Econ Bus Hist,* I (1929), 241–281.

4205 HUNTER, Louis C. "Financial Problems of the Early Pittsburgh Iron Manufactures." *J Econ Bus Hist,* II (1930), 520–544.

4206 INGALLS, Walter R. *Lead and Zinc in the United States.* New York, 1908.

4207 JEREMY, David J. "British Textile Technology Transmission to the United States: the Philadelphia Region Experience, 1770–1820." *Bus Hist Rev,* XLVII (1973), 24–52.

4208 JONES, Eliot. *The Anthracite Coal Combination in the United States.* Cambridge, Mass., 1914.

4209 LANDER, E. M., Jr. "South Carolina Textile Industry before 1845." *S C Hist Assn Proc,* 1961, 19–28.

4210 LANDER, Ernest M., Jr. "The Iron Industry in Ante-Bellum South Carolina." *J S Hist,* XX (1954), 337–355.

4211 LANDER, Ernest M., Jr. "Manufacturing in South Carolina, 1815–1860." *Bus Hist Rev,* XXVIII (1954), 59–66.

4212 LANDER, Ernest M., Jr. *The Textile Industry in Antebellum South Carolina.* Baton Rouge, 1969.

4213 LATHROP, William G. *The Brass Industry in Connecticut.* Shelton, Conn., 1909.

4214 LEWIS, W. David. "The Early History of the Lackawanna Iron and Coal Company: A Study in Technological Adaptation." *Pa Mag Hist Biog,* XCVI (1972), 424–468.

4215 LIPPINCOTT, Isaac. *A History of Manufactures in the Ohio Valley to the Year 1860.* New York, 1914.

4216 LIVESAY, Harold C. "Marketing Patterns in the Antebellum American Iron Industry." *Bus Hist Rev,* XLV (1971), 269–295.

4217 LIVESAY, Harold C., and Glenn PORTER. "The Financial Role of Merchants in the Development of U.S. Manufacturing, 1815–1860." *Explo Econ Hist,* IX (1971), 63–87.

4218 MILLER, Randall Martin. "The Cotton Mill Movement in Antebellum Alabama." Doctoral dissertation, Ohio State University, 1971.

4219 MITCHELL, Broadus. *William Gregg, Factory Master of the Old South.* Chapel Hill, 1928.

4220 MITCHELL, Broadus. *The Rise of Cotton Mills in the South.* Baltimore, 1921.

4221 MOORE, John Hebron. *Andrew Brown and Cypress Lumbering in the Old Southwest.* Baton Rouge, 1967.

4222 NAVIN, Thomas R. *The Whitin Machine Works Since 1831: A Textile Machine Company in an Industrial Village.* Cambridge, Mass., 1950.

4223 NORRIS, James D. *Frontier Iron: The Maracec Iron Works, 1826–1876.* Madison, 1964.

4224 PASSELL, Peter, and Maria SCHMUNDT. "Pre-Civil War Land Policy and the Growth of Manufacturing." *Explo Econ Hist,* IX (1971), 35–48.

4225 PORTER, Glenn, and Harold C. LIVESAY. *Merchants and Manufacturers: Studies in the Changing Structure of Nineteenth-Century Marketing.* Baltimore, 1971.

4226 PREYER, Norris W. "Why Did Industrialization Lay in the Old South?" *Ga Hist Q,* LV (1971), 378–396.

4227 REZNECK, Samuel. "The Rise and Early Development of Industrial Consciousness in the United States, 1760–1830." *J Econ Bus Hist,* IV (1932), 784–811.

4228 RICKARD, Thomas A. *A History of American Mining.* New York, 1932.

4229 SHLAKMAN, Vera. *Economic History of a Factory Town: A Study of Chicopee, Massachusetts.* Northampton, Mass., 1935.

4230 STANDARD, Diffee W., and Richard GRIFFIN. "The Cotton Textile Industry in Ante-Bellum North Carolina." *N C Hist Rev,* XXXIV (1957), 15–35, 131–164.

4231 STEALEY, John Edmund III. "The Salt Industry of the Great Kanawha Valley of Virginia: A Study in Ante-Bellum Internal Commerce." Doctoral dissertation, University of West Virginia, 1970.

4232 TEMIN, Peter. *Iron and Steel in Nineteenth-Century America, An Economic Inquiry.* Cambridge, Mass., 1964.

4233 TEMIN, Peter. "Steam and Waterpower in the Early Nineteenth Century." *J Econ Hist,* XXVI (1966), 187–205.

4234 TOWLES, John K. *Factory Legislation of Rhode Island.* Princeton, 1908.

4235 TRYON, Rolla M. *Household Manufactures in the United States, 1640–1860.* Chicago, 1917.

4236 TSUNEO, Ishikawa. "Conceptualization of Learning by Doing: A Note on Paul David's 'Learning by Doing and . . . the Ante-Bellum United States Cotton Textile Industry." *J Econ Hist,* XXXIII (1973), 851–861.

4237 TUCKER, Barbara May. "Samuel Slater and Sons: The Emergence of an American Factory System, 1790–1860." Doctoral dissertation, University of California, Davis, 1975.

4238 USELDING, Paul. "A Note on the Inter-Regional Trade in Manufacturers in 1840." *J Econ Hist,* XXXVI (1976), 428–435.

4239 USELDING, Paul J. "Technical Progress at the Springfield Armory, 1820–1850." *Explo Econ Hist,* IX (1972), 291–316.

4240 WALSH, Margaret. *The Manufacturing Frontier: Pioneer Industry in Ante-bellum Wisconsin, 1830–1860.* Madison, 1972.

4241 WARE, Caroline F. *The Early New England Cotton Manufactures.* Boston, 1931.

4242 WILLIAMSON, Jeffrey G. "Embodiment, Disembodiment, Learning by Doing, and Returns to Scale in Nineteenth-Century Cotton Textiles." *J Econ Hist,* XXXII (1972), 691–705.

4243 WISH, Judith Barry. "From Yeoman Farmer to Industrious Producer: The Relationship between Classical Republicanism and the Development of Manufacturing in America from the Revolution to 1850." Doctoral dissertation, Washington University, 1976.

4244 WOOD, Richard G. *A History of Lumbering in Maine, 1820–1861.* Orono, Me., 1935.

4245 YATES, W. Ross. "Discovery of the Process for Making Anthracite Iron." *Pa Mag Hist Biog,* XCVIII (1974), 206–223.

4246 ZEVIN, Robert Brooke. "The Growth of Cotton Textile Production after 1815." *The Reinterpretation of American Economic History.* Ed. Robert W. FOGEL and Stanley L. ENGERMAN. New York, 1971.

H. Labor

See also **835, 1934, 1938, 1944, 1950, 1958, 1976, 1989, 1999, 2037, 2045, 2062, 2384, 2592, 3112, 3172–3174, 3181, 3847, 4114, 4154, 4187, 4355**

4247 ABBOTT, Edith. *Women in Industry: A Study in American Economic History.* New York, 1910.

4248 ADAMS, Donald R. "Some Evidence on English and American Wage Rates, 1790–1830." *J Econ Hist,* XXX (1970), 499–520.

4249 ADAMS, Donald R. "Wage Rates in the Early National Period: Philadelphia, 1785–1830." *J Econ Hist,* XXVIII (1968), 404–426.

4250 ANDERSON, Ralph V. "Labor Utilization and Productivity, Diversification and Self Sufficiency: Southern Plantations, 1800–1840." Doctoral dissertation, University of North Carolina at Chapel Hill, 1974.

4251 BAIRD, W. David. "Violence along the Chesapeake and Ohio Canal: 1839." *Md Hist Mag,* LXVI (1971), 121–134.

4252 BEARD, Mary R. *The American Labor Movement: A Short History.* New York, 1931.

4253 BLOOMBERG, Susan Eleanor Hirsch. "Industrialization and Skilled Workers: Newark, 1826–1860." Doctoral dissertation, University of Michigan, 1974.

4254 BRITO, D. L., and Jeffrey G. Williamson. "Skilled Labor and Nineteenth Century Anglo-American Managerial Behavior." *Explo Econ Hist,* X (1973), 235–251.

4255 BURNS, Rex S. "The Yeoman Mechanic: 'Venturous Conservative'." *Roc Mt Soc Sci J,* IV (1967), 9–21.

4256 CARLTON, Frank Tracy. *Organized Labor in American History.* New York, 1920.

4257 COMMONS, John R., et al. *History of Labour in the United States.* 4 vols. New York, 1918–1935.

4258 DORFMAN, Joseph. "The Jackson Wage-Earner Thesis." *Am Hist Rev,* LIV (1948), 296–306.

4259 DULLES, Foster R. *Labor in America: A History.* 2d ed. New York, 1960.†

4260 EDWARDS, Alba M. *The Labor Legislation of Connecticut.* New York, 1907.

4261 ELY, Richard T. *The Labor Movement in the United States.* New York, 1905.

4262 FALER, Paul Gustaf. "Workingmen, Mechanics and Social Change: Lynn, Massachusetts, 1800–1860." Doctoral dissertation, University of Wisconsin, Madison, 1971.

4263 FINK, Gary M. "The Paradoxical Experiences of St. Louis Labor during the Depression of 1837." *Mo Hist Soc Bull,* XXVI (1969), 53–63.

4264 FONER, Philip S. *History of the Labor Movement in the United States.* 4 vols. New York, 1947.†

4265 GEIS, Robert. "Liberty, Equality, Fraternity: The Ideology of the American Labor Movement from 1828 to 1848." Doctoral dissertation, University of Minnesota, 1971.

4266 GOODRICH, Carter, and Sol DAVIDSON. "The Wage Earner in the Westward Movement." *Pol Sci Q,* L (1935), 161–185.

4267 GRIFFIN, Richard W. "Poor White Laborers in Southern Cotton Factories, 1789–1865." *S C Hist Mag,* LXI (1960), 26–40.

4268 GUTMAN, Herbert G. "Work, Culture, and Society in Industrializing America, 1815–1919." *Am Hist Rev,* LXXVIII (1973), 531–588.

4269 JACKSON, Sidney. "Labor, Education and Politics in the 1830s." *Pa Mag Hist Biog,* LXVI (1942), 279–293.

4270 JENTZ, John Barkley. "Artisans, Evangelicals, and the City: A Social History of Abolition and Labor Reform in Jacksonian New York." Doctoral dissertation, City University of New York, 1977.

4271 LAURIE, Bruce Gordon. "The Working People of Philadelphia, 1827–1853." Doctoral dissertation, University of Pittsburgh, 1971.

4272 LOFTON, Williston H. "Abolition and Labor." *J Neg Hist,* XXXIII (1948), 249–283.

4273 MANDEL, Bernard. *Labor: Free and Slave; Workingmen and the Antislavery Movement in the United States.* New York, 1955.

4274 MCBREARTY, James C., comp. *American Labor History and Comparative Labor Movements: A Selected Bibliography.* Tucson, 1973.

4275 MCLEOD, Richard Alan. "The Philadelphia Artisan, 1828–1850." Doctoral dissertation, University of Missouri, Columbia, 1971.

4276 MCMASTER, John B. *The Acquisition of Political, Social, and Industrial Rights of Man in America.* Cleveland, 1903.

4277 MCPHERSON, Donald S. "Mechanics' Institutes and the Pittsburgh Workingmen, 1830–1840." *W Pa Hist Mag,* LVI (1973), 155–169.

4278 MONTGOMERY, David. "The Working Class of the Pre-Industrial American City, 1780–1830." *Labor Hist,* IX (1968), 3–22.

4279 MORRIS, Richard B. "American Labor History Prior to the Civil War: Sources and Opportunities for Research." *Labor Hist,* I (1960), 308–318.

4280 MORRIS, Richard B. "Andrew Jackson, Strikebreaker." *Am Hist Rev,* LV (1949), 54–68.

4281 MORRIS, Richard B. "Labor Controls in Maryland in the Nineteenth Century." *J S Hist,* XIV (1948), 385–400

4282 MORRIS, Richard B. "White Bondage in Ante-Bellum South Carolina." *S C Hist Gen Mag,* XLIX (1948), 191–207.

4283 MORRIS, Richard B. "The Course of Peonage in a Slave State [Delaware]." *Pol Sci Q,* LXV (1950), 238–263.

4284 NEUFELD, Maurice F. *A Representative Bibliography of American Labor History.* Ithaca, N.Y., 1964.†

4285 NEUFELD, Maurice F. "Realms of Thought and Organized Labor in the Age of Jackson." *Labor Hist,* X (1969), 5–43.

4286 PERLMAN, Selig. *A History of Trade Unionism in the United States.* New York, 1922.

4287 PESSEN, Edward. "Should Labor Have Supported Jackson? Or Questions the Quantitative Studies Do Not Answer." *Labor Hist,* XIII (1972), 427–437.

4288 PESSEN, Edward. "The Workingmen's Movement of the Jacksonian Era." *Miss Val Hist Rev,* XLIII (1956), 428–443.

4289 PESSEN, Edward. *Most Uncommon Jacksonians: The Radical Leaders of the Early Labor Movement.* Albany, N.Y., 1967.

4290 PESSEN, Edward. "The Working Men's Party Revisited." *Labor Hist,* IV (1963), 203–226.

4291 PESSEN, Edward. "Thomas Skidmore, Agrarian Reformer in the Early American Labor Movement." *N Y Hist,* XXXV (1954), 280–296.

4292 RAYBACK, Joseph G. *A History of American Labor.* New York, 1959.†

4293 ROSE, F. D. *American Labor In Journals of History: A Bibliography.* Champaign, Ill., 1962.

4294 ROSENBERG, Nathan. "Anglo-American Wage Differences in the 1820s." *J Econ Hist,* XXVII (1967), 221–229.

4295 STEWART, Ethelbert. *A Documentary History of the Early Organizations of Printers.* Indianapolis, 1907.

4296 STROUD, Gene S., and Gilbert E. DONAHUE, comps. *Labor History in the United States: A General Bibliography.* Urbana, Ill., 1961.

4297 SULLIVAN, William A. "A Decade of Labor Strife." *Pa Hist,* XVII (1950), 23–38.

4298 SULLIVAN, William A. "Philadelphia Labor During the Jackson Era." *Pa Hist,* XV (1948), 305–320.

4299 SULLIVAN, William A. "Did Labor Support Jackson?" *Pol Sci Q,* LXII (1947), 569–580.

4300 SULLIVAN, William A. *The Industrial Worker in Pennsylvania, 1800–1840.* Harrisburg, 1955.

4301 WHITMAN, Alden. *Labor Parties, 1827–1834.* New York, 1943.

4302 WRIGHT, Helena. "The Uncommon Mill Girls of Lowell." *Hist Today,* XXIII (1973), 10–19.

4303 ZAHLER, Helene Sara. *Eastern Workingmen and National Land Policy, 1829–1862.* New York, 1941.

I. Maritime

See also **1179, 1817, 1843, 1849**

4304 ACKERMAN, Edward A. *New England's Fishing Industry.* Chicago, 1941.

4305 ALBION, Robert G. *Square-Riggers on Schedule.* Cambridge, Mass. 1949.

4306 BATES, William Wallace. *American Navigation: The Political History of Its Rise and Ruin and the Proper Means for its Encouragement.* Boston, 1902.

4307 BAUGHMAN, James P. *The Mallorys of Mystic: Six Generations in American Maritime Enterprise.* Middletown, Conn., 1972.

4308 CHAPELLE, Howard I. *The History of American Sailing Ships.* New York, 1935.

4309 CUTLER, Carl C. *Greyhounds of the Sea: the Story of the American Clipper Ship.* New York, 1930.

4310 CUTLER, Carl C. *Queens of the Western Ocean: the Story of America's Mail and Passenger Sailing Lines.* Annapolis, 1961.

4311 GOODE, George B., et al. *The Fisheries and Fishery Industries of the United States.* 7 vols. Washington, D.C., 1884–1887.

4312 HAMMOND, E. A. "The Spanish Fisheries of Charlotte Harbor." *Fla Hist Q,* LI (1973), 355–380.

4313 HOFMAN, Elmo P. *The American Whaleman: A Study of Life and Labor in the Whaling Industry.* New York, 1928.

4314 HUTCHINS, John G. B. *The American Maritime Industries and Public Policy, 1789–1914, and Economic History.* Cambridge, Mass., 1941.

4315 INNIS, Harold A. *The Cod Fisheries, the History of an International Economy.* New Haven, 1940.

4316 KUSHNER, Howard I. "Hellships: Yankee Whaling along the Coasts of Russian America, 1835–1852." *N Eng Q,* XLV (1972), 81–95.

4317 MARVIN, Winthrop L. *The American Merchant Marine: Its History and Romance from 1620 to 1902.* New York, 1902.

4318 MCFARLAND, Raymond. *A History of the New England Fisheries.* Philadelphia, 1911.

4319 MORISON, Samuel Eliot. *The Maritime History of Massachusetts, 1783–1860.* Boston, 1921.

4320 MURDOCK, Richard K. "Cod or Mackeral: Bounty Payment Disputes, 1829–1832." *Essex Inst Hist Coll,* CV (1969), 306–337.

4321 SINCLAIR, Bruce. "Treasures from the Vasty Deep: The Wilmington Whaling Company, 1833–1846." *Del Hist,* XII (1966), 6–24.

4322 SPEARS, John R. *The Story of the American Merchant Marine.* Rev. ed. New York, 1915.

4323 STACKPOLE, Edouard A. *The Sea-Hunters: the New England Whalemen during Two Centuries, 1635–1835.* Westport, Conn., 1972.

4324 STARBUCK, Alexander. *History of the American Whale Fishery From Its Earliest Inception to the Year 1876.* Waltham, Mass., 1878.

4325 THURSTON, William Nathaniel. "A Study of Maritime Activity in Florida in the Nineteenth Century." Doctoral dissertation, Florida State University, 1972.

4326 TOWER, Walter S. *A History of the American Whale Fishery.* Philadelphia, 1907.

4327 VERRILL, Alpheus H. *The Real Story of the Whaler.* New York, 1916.

J. Public Lands

See also **557, 558, 1514, 1515, 2170, 2373, 2419, 2530, 3715, 4224**

4328 BOGUE, Allan and Margaret B. BOGUE. " 'Profits' and the Frontier Land Speculators." *J Econ Hist,* XVII (1957), 1–24.

4329 CARLSON, Theodore L. *The Illinois Military Tract: A Study of Land Occupation, Utilization and Tenure.* Urbana, Ill., 1951.

4330 CHAPPELL, Gordon T. "Some Patterns of Land Speculation in the Old Southwest." *J S Hist,* XV (1949), 463–477.

4331 COLE, Arthur H. "Cyclical and Sectional Variations in the Sale of Public Lands, 1816–1860." *Rev Econ Stat,* IX (1927), 41–53.

4332 COLES, Harry L., Jr. "A History of the Administration of Federal Land Policies and Land Tenure in Louisiana, 1803–1860." Doctoral dissertation, Vanderbilt University, 1949.

4333 DONALDSON, Thomas. *The Public Domain, Its History, with Statistics.* Washington, D.C., 1884.

4334 EAST, Dennis. "The New York and Mississippi Land Company and the Panic of 1837." *J Miss Hist,* XXXIII (1971), 299–332.

4335 EICHERT, Magdalen. "Daniel Webster's Western Land Investments." *Hist N H,* XXVI (Fall, 1971), 29–35.

4336 EICHERT, Magdalen. "Henry Clay's Policy of Distribution of the Proceeds from Public Land Sales." *Reg Ky Hist Soc,* LII (1950), 138–157.

4337 EICHERT, Magdalen. "John C. Calhoun's Land Policy of Cession." *S C Hist Mag,* LV (1954), 198–209.

4338 FARNAM, William Thomas. "Land Claims Problems and the Federal Land System in the Louisiana-Missouri Territory." Doctoral dissertation, St. Louis University, 1971.

4339 GARA, Larry. "Yankee Land Agent [Cyrus Woodman] in Illinois." *Ill St Hist J,* XLIV (1951), 120–141.

4340 GATES, Paul W. "Tenants of the Log Cabin." *Miss Val Hist Rev,* XLIX (1962), 3–31.

4341 GATES, Paul W. "Land Policy and Tenancy in the Prairie States." *J Econ Hist,* I (1941), 60–82.

4342 GATES, Paul W. "The Role of the Land Speculator in Western Development." *Pa Mag Hist Biog,* LXVI (1942), 314–333.

4343 HIBBARD, Benjamin Horace. *A History of the Public Land Policies.* New York, 1924.†

4344 MCCAMPBELL, Coleman. "H. L. Kinney and Daniel Webster in Illinois in the 1830s." *Ill St Hist J,* XLVII (1954), 35–44.

4345 MILLER, Zane L. "Senator Nathaniel Macon and the Public Domain, 1815–1828." *N C Hist Rev,* XXXVIII (1961), 483–499.

4346 NESBIT, Robert. "The Federal Government as Townsite Speculator." *Explo Econ Hist,* VII (1970), 293–312.

4347 PETERS, Bernard C. "Early Town-Site Speculation in Kalamazoo County." *Mich Hist,* LVI (1972), 201–215.

4348 PICHT, Douglas R. "The American Squatter and Federal land Policy." *J W,* XIV (1975), 72–83.

4349 ROBBINS, Roy M. *Our Landed Heritage: The Public Domain, 1776–1936.* Princeton, 1942.†

4350 ROBBINS, Roy M. "Preemption—A Frontier Triumph." *Miss Val Hist Rev,* XVIII (1931), 331–349.

4351 ROHRBOUGH, Malcolm. *The Land Office Business: The Settlement and Administration of American Public Lands, 1789–1837.* New York, 1968.

4352 SATO, Shoshuke. *History of the Land Question in the United States.* Baltimore, 1886.

4353 SCHEIBER, Harry N. "State Policy and the Public Domain." *J Econ Hist,* XXV (1965), 86–113.

4354 SILVER, James W. "Land Speculation Profits in the Chickasaw Cession." *J S Hist,* X (1944), 84–92.

4355 STEVENS, Harry R. "Did Industrial Labor Influence Jacksonian Land Policy?" *Ind Mag Hist,* XLIII (1947), 159–167.

4356 TREAT, Payson J. *The National Land System, 1785–1820.* New York, 1967.

4357 WELLINGTON, Raynor G. *The Political and Sectional Influence of the Public Lands, 1828–1842.* Cambridge, Mass., 1914.

4358 WHATLEY, George C., and Sylvia COOK. "The East Florida Land Commission: A Study in Frustration." *Fla Hist Q,* L (1971), 39–52.

K. Tariff

See also **1073, 1095, 1284, 1467–1470, 2082, 2343, 2353, 3958, 4176**

4359 BAACK, Bennett D., and Edward J. RAY. "Tariff Policy and Income Distribution: The Case of the U.S. 1830–1860." *Explo Econ Hist,* XI (1973), 103–121.

4360 EDWARDS, Richard C. "Economic Sophistication in Nineteenth Century Congressional Tariff Debates." *J Econ Hist,* XXX (1970), 802–838.

4361 EISELEN, Malcolm R. *The Rise of Pennsylvania Protectionism.* Philadelphia, 1932.

4362 ELLIOTT, Orrin L. *The Tariff Controversy in the United States, 1789–1833.* Palo Alto, 1892.

4363 KAISER, Carl William. *History of the Academic Protectionist-Free Trade Controversy in America before 1860.* Philadelphia, 1939.

4364 PINCUS, Jonathan James. "A Positive Theory of Tariff Formation Applied to Nineteenth Century United States." Doctoral dissertation, Stanford University, 1972.

4364A PINCUS, Jonathan James. *Pressure Groups and Politics in Antebellum Tariffs.* New York, 1977.

4365 POPE, Clayne. "The Impact of the Ante-Bellum Tariff on Income Distribution." *Explo Econ Hist,* IX (1972), 375–422.

4366 RATNER, Sidney. *The Tariff in American History.* New York, 1972.

4367 STANWOOD, Edward. *American Tariff Controversies in the Nineteenth Century.* 2 vols. Boston, 1903.

4368 TAUSSIG, Frank W., comp. *State Papers and Speeches on the Tariff.* Cambridge, Mass., 1893.

4369 TAUSSIG, Frank W. *The Tariff History of the United States.* 8th ed. New York, 1931.

4370 VIPPERMAN, Carl J. "William Lowndes and the Tariff: Common-Sense Nationalism." *America, The Middle Period: Essays in Honor of Bernard Mayo.* Ed. John B. BOLES. Charlottesville, Va., 1973.

4371 WELLINGTON, Raynor G. "The Tariff and Public Lands from 1828 to 1833." *Ann Rep Am Hist Assn, 1911.* I, 177–185.

4372 WRIGHT, Chester Whitney. *Wood-Growing and the Tariff: A Study in the Economic History of the United States.* Boston, 1910.

L. Transportation and Internal Improvements

See also **1368, 2204, 2277, 2502, 2503, 4251**

4373 ALVAREZ, Eugene. *Travel on Southern Antebellum Railroads, 1828–1860.* University of Alabama, 1975.

4374 AMBLER, Charles H. *A History of Transportation in the Ohio Valley.* Glendale, 1932.

4375 ANDREASEN, Johann Christian Ludwig. "Internal Improvements in Louisiana, 1824–1837." *La Hist Q,* XXX (1947), 5–119.

4376 BALDWIN, Leland D. *The Keelboat Age on Western Water.* Pittsburgh, 1941.

4377 BINDER, Frederick Moore. "Pennsylvania Coal and the Beginnings of American Steam Navigation." *Pa Mag Hist Biog,* LXXXIII (1959), 420–445.

4378 BISHOP, Avard L. *The State Works of Pennsylvania.* New Haven, 1907.

4379 BROWN, William H. *The History of the First Locomotives in America.* New York, 1874.

4380 CALLENDER, G. S. "Early Transportation and Banking Enterprises of the States in Relation to the Growth of Corporations." *Q J Econ,* XVII (1902), 111–162.

4381 CAMPBELL, E. G. "Railroads in National Defense, 1829–1848." *Miss Val Hist Rev,* XXVII (1940), 361–378.

4382 CARLSON, Robert E. "The Pennsylvania Improvement Society and Its Promotion of Canals and Railroads, 1824–1826." *Pa Hist,* XXXI (1964), 295–310.

4383 CHANDLER, Alfred D., Jr. "Patterns of American Railroad Finance, 1830–1850." *Bus Hist Rev,* XXVIII (1954), 248–263.

4384 CLARK, Malcolm C. "The Birth of an Enterprise: Baldwin Locomotive, 1831–1842." *Pa Mag Hist Biog,* XC (1966), 423–444.

4385 CRANMER, H. Jerome. "Canal Investment, 1815–1860." *Trends in the American Economy in the Nineteenth Century.* Ed. William N. PARKER. Princeton, 1960.

4386 CRANMER, H. Jerome. "Internal Improvements in New Jersey: Planning the Morris Canal." *Proc N J Hist Soc,* LXIX (1951), 324–341.

4387 CRANMER, H. Jerome. "The New Jersey Canals, A Study of the Role of Government in Economic Development." Doctoral dissertation, Columbia University, 1955.

4388 DERRICK, Samuel M. *Centennial History of South Carolina Railroad.* Columbia, 1930.

4389 DOZIER, Howard D. *History of Atlantic Coast Line Railroad.* Boston, 1920.

4390 DUNAWAY, Wayland F. *History of James River and Kanawha Company.* New York, 1922.

4391 DUNBAR, Seymour. *A History of Travel in America.* 4 vols. Indianapolis, 1915.

4392 DURRENBERGER, Joseph A. *Turnpikes: A Study of the Toll Road Movement in the Middle Atlantic States and Maryland.* Valdosta, Ga., 1931.

4393 FARRELL, Richard T. "Internal-Improvement Projects in Southwestern Ohio, 1815–1834." *Ohio Hist,* LXXX (1971), 4–23.

4394 FATOUT, Paul. "Canal Agitation at Ohio Falls." *Ind Mag Hist,* LVII (1960), 279–309.

4395 FILANTE, Ronald W. "A Note on the Economic Viability of the Erie Canal, 1825–1860." *Bus Hist Rev,* LXXX (1971), 4–23.

4396 FISHLOW, Albert. *American Railroads and the Transformation of the Ante-Bellum Economy.* Cambridge, Mass., 1965.

4397 FOGEL, Robert W. *Railroads and American Economic Growth: Essays in Econometric History.* Baltimore, 1964.†

4398 GOODRICH, Carter. "American Development Policy: The Case of Internal Improvements." *J Econ Hist,* XVI (1956), 449–460.

4399 GOODRICH, Carter. *Government Promotion of American Canals and Railroads, 1800–1900.* New York, 1960.

4400 GOODRICH, Carter. "Internal Improvements Reconsidered." *J Econ Hist,* XXX (1970), 289–311.

4401 GOODRICH, Carter, et al. *Canals and American Economic Development.* New York, 1961.

4402 GOODRICH, Carter. "National Planning of Internal Improvements." *Pol Sci Q,* LXIII (1948), 16–44.

4403 GOODRICH, Carter, and Harvey H. SEGAL. "Baltimore's Aid to Railroads: A Study in the Municipal Planning of Internal Improvements." *J Econ Hist* XIII (1953), 2–35.

4404 GRAY, Ralph D. "Transportation and Brandywine Industries, 1800–1840." *Del Hist,* IX (1961), 303–325.

4405 GRAY, Ralph D. "The Early History of the Chesapeake and Delaware Canal." *Del Hist;* VIII (1958), 207–264, 354–397, IX (1960), 66–98.

4406 GRAY, Ralph D. *The National Waterway: A History of the Chesapeake and Delaware Canal, 1769–1965.* Urbana, Ill., 1967.

4407 HAITES, Erik F., and James MAK. "Steamboating on the Mississippi, 1810–1860: A Purely Competitive Industry." *Bus Hist Rev,* XLV (1971), 52–78.

4408 HAITES, Erik F., and James MAK. "The Decline of Steamboaters on the Ante-Bellum Western Rivers: Some New Evidence and an Alternative Hypothesis." *Explo Entrep Hist,* XI (1973), 25–36.

4409 HAITES, Erik F., and James MAK. "Ohio and Mississippi River Transportation, 1810–1860." *Explor Entrep Hist,* VIII (1970–1971), 153–180.

4410 HAITES, Erik F.; James MAK; and Gary M. WALTON. *Western River Transportation: The Era of Early Internal Development, 1810–1860.* Baltimore, 1975.

4411 HARDIN, Thomas L. "The National Road in Illinois." *Ill St Hist J,* LX (1967), 5–22.

4412 HARLOW, Alvin F. *Old Towpaths: the Story of the American Canal Era.* New York, 1926.

4413 HEATH, Milton S. "Public Railroad Construction and the Development of Private Enterprise in the South before 1861." *J Econ Hist,* X (1950), 40–53.

4414 HEINE, Cornelius W. "The Washington City Canal." *Rec Col Hist Soc,* LIII-LVI (1953–1956), 1–27.

4415 HIJIYA, James A. "Making a Railroad: The Political Economy of the Ithaca and Owego, 1828–1842." *N Y Hist,* LIV (1973), 145–173.

4416 HILL, Forest G. *Roads, Rails and Waterways: The Army Engineers and Early Transportation.* Norman, Okla., 1957.

4417 HINSHAW, Clifford Reginald, Jr. "North Carolina Canals before 1860." *Va Mag Hist Biog,* XLIX (1961), 278–289.

4418 HOLMES, William F. "The New Castle and Frenchtown Turnpike and Railroad Company, 1809–1830." *Del Hist,* X (1962), 71–114, 152–180, 235–271.

4419 HULBERT, Archer Butler. *The Cumberland Road.* Cleveland, 1904.

4420 HULBERT, Archer B. *The Paths of Inland Commerce; a Chronicle of Trail, Road, and Waterway.* New Haven, 1920.

4421 HUNGERFORD, Edward. *Men and Iron: The History of New York Central.* New York, 1938.

4422 HUNGERFORD, Edward. *The Story of the Baltimore and Ohio Railroad, 1827–1927.* 2 vols. New York, 1928.

4423 HUNTER, Louis C. *Steamboats on the Western Rivers: An Economic and Technological History.* Cambridge, Mass., 1949.

4424 HUNTER, Robert F. "The Turnpike Movement in Virginia, 1816–1860." *Va Mag Hist Biog,* XLIX (1961), 278–289.

4425 JONES, Chester L. *The Economic History of the Anthracite-Tidewater Canals.* Philadelphia, 1908.

4426 JORDAN, Philip D. *The National Road.* Indianapolis, 1948.

4427 KIRKLAND, Edward Charles. *Men, Cities, and Transportation, A Study in New England History, 1820–1900.* Cambridge, Mass., 1948.

4428 KOHN, David, ed. and comp. *Internal Improvements in South Carolina, 1817–1828.* Washington, D.C., 1938.

4429 KRENKEL, John H. "Financing the Illinois Internal Improvements." *Mid-Am,* XXIX (1947), 211–244.

4430 LANE, Wheaton J. *Commodore Vanderbilt: An Epic of the Steam Age.* New York, 1942.

4431 LANE, Wheaton J. *From Indian Trail to Iron Horse: Travel and Transportation in New Jersey, 1620–1860.* Princeton, 1939.

4432 MACGILL, Caroline E., et al. *History of Transportation in the United States before 1860.* New York, 1948.

4433 MCKELVEY, Blake. "Erie Canal: Mother of Cities." *N Y Hist Soc Q,* XXXV (1951), 55–71.

4434 MAK, James, and Gary M. WALTON. "Steamboats and the Great Productivity Surge in River Transportation." *J Econ Hist,* XXXII (1972), 619–640.

4435 MAK, James, and Gary M. WALTON. "The Persistence of Old Technologies: The Case of Flatboats." *J Econ Hist,* XXXIII (1973), 444–451.

4436 MARTIN, William E. *Internal Improvements in Alabama.* Baltimore, 1902.

4437 MEYER, Balthasar H., et al. *History of Transportation in the United States before 1860.* Washington, D.C., 1917.

4438 MILLER, Nathan. *The Enterprise of a Free People: Aspects of Economic Development in New York State during the Canal Period, 1792–1838.* Ithaca, 1962.

4439 MITCHELL, Samuel A. *Mitchell's Compendium of the Internal Improvements of the United States.* Philadelphia, 1835.

4440 NICHOLS, Roger L. "Army Contributions to River Transportation, 1818–1825." *Mil Aff,* XXXIII (1969), 242–249.

4441 NORRIS, Charles N. "Internal Improvements in Ohio, 1825–1850." *Am Hist Assn Papers,* III (1888), 351–380.

4442 PAXSON, Frederick L. "The Railroads of the Old Northwest before the Civil War." *Wis Acad Sci Trans,* XVII (1911), 243–274.

4443 PETERSEN, William J. *Steamboating on the Upper Mississippi.* Iowa City, 1937.

4444 PHILLIPS, Ulrich Bonnell. *A History of Transportation in the Eastern Cotton Belt to 1860.* New York, 1908.

4445 PIERCE, Harry H. *The Railroads of New York, A Study of Government Aid, 1826–1875.* Cambridge, Mass., 1953.

4446 POOR, Henry V. *History of the Railroads and Canals of the United States.* New York, 1860.

4447 POWELL, H. Benjamin. "Coal and Pennsylvania's Transportation Policy." *Pa Hist,* XXXVIII (1971), 134–151.

4448 PUTNAM, James W. *The Illinois and Michigan Canal; A Study in Economic History.* Chicago, 1918.

4449 RAE, John Bell. "Federal Land Grants in Aid of Canals." *J Econ Hist,* IV (1944), 167–177.

4450 RANSOM, Roger L. "A Closer Look at Canals and Western Manufacturing in the Canal Era." *Explo Entrep Hist,* VIII (1971), 501–510.

4451 RANSOM, Roger L. "Interregional Canals and Economic Specialization in the Antebellum United States." *Explo Entrep Hist,* V (1967), 12–35.

4452 RANSOM, Roger L. "Canals and Development: A Discussion of the Issues." *Am Econ Rev,* LIV (1964), 365–376.

4453 REED, Merl E. "Government Investment and Economic Growth: Louisiana's Ante Bellum Railroads." *J S Hist,* XXVIII (1962), 183–201.

4454 REED, Merl E. *New Orleans and the Railroads: The Struggle for Commerical Empire, 1830–1860.* Baton Rouge, 1966.

4455 RHOADS, Willard R. "The Pennsylvania Canal." *W Pa Hist Mag,* XLIII (1960), 203–238.

4456 RUBIN, Julius. *Canal or Railroad? Imitation and Innovation in the Response to the Erie Canal in Philadelphia, Baltimore and Boston.* Philadelphia, 1961.

4457 SADOVE, Abraham H. "Transport Improvement and the Appalachian Barrier: A Case Study in Economic Innovation." Doctoral dissertation, Harvard University, 1950.

4458 SALSBURY, Stephen. *The State, the Investor, and the Railroad: The Boston and Albany, 1825–1867.* Cambridge, Mass., 1967.

4459 SANDERLIN, Walter S. *The Great National Project: A History of the Chesapeake and Ohio Canal.* Baltimore, 1946.

4460 SANDERLIN, Walter S. "The Maryland Canal Project: An Episode in the History of Maryland's Internal Improvements. " *Md Hist Mag,* XLI (1946), 51–65.

4461 SCHEIBER, Harry N., and Stephen SALSBURY. "Reflections on George Rogers Taylor's *The Transportation Revolution, 1815–1860:* A Twenty-Five Year Retrospect." *Bus Hist Rev,* LI (1977), 77–80.

4462 SCHNEIDER, Norris F. "The National Road: Main Street of America." *Ohio Hist,* LXXXIII (1974), 114–144.

4463 SEGAL, Harvey H. "Canal Cycles, 1834–1861: Public Construction Experience in New York, Pennsylvania and Ohio." Doctoral dissertation, Columbia University, 1956.

4464 SHAW, Ronald E. *Erie Water West: A History of the Erie Canal, 1792–1854.* Lexington, 1966.

4465 SHINGLETON, Royce Gordon. "Stages, Steamers, and Stations in the Ante-Bellum South: A British View." *Ga Hist Q,* LVI (1972), 243–258.

4466 STEVENSON, David. *Sketch of the Civil Engineering of North America.* London, 1838.

4467 STEWART, Peter C. "Railroads and Urban Rivalries in Antebellum Eastern Virginia." *Va Mag Hist Biog,* LXXXI (1973), 3–22.

4468 STIMSON, Alexander L. *History of the Express Business, Including the Origin of the Railway System in America.* New York, 1881.

4469 STOVER, John F. *American Railroads.* Chicago, 1961.†

4470 TAYLOR, George Rogers. *The Transporation Revolution, 1815–1860.* New York, 1951.†

4471 TRESCOTT, Paul B. "The Louisville and Portland Canal Company, 1825–1874." *Miss Val Hist Rev,* XLIV (1958), 686–708.

4472 TURNER, Charles W. "Railroad Service to Virginia Farmers, 1828–1860." *Ag Hist,* XXII (1948), 239–248.

4473/4 TURNER, Charles W. "Early Virginia Railroad Entrepreneurs and Personnel." *Va Mag Hist Biog,* LVIII (1950), 325–334.

4475 WAGGONER, Madeline Sadler. *The Long Haul West: The Great Canal Era, 1817–1850.* New York, 1958.

4476 WALLNER, Peter Andrew. "Politics and Public Works: A Study of the Pennsylvania Canal System, 1825–1857." Doctoral dissertation, Pennsylvania State University, 1973.

4477 WARD, James A. "A New Look at Antebellum Southern Railroad Development." *J S Hist,* XXXIX (1973), 409–420.

4478 WATKINS, John E. *The Development of the American Rail and Track.* Washington, D.C., 1891.

4479 WAY, R. B. "The Mississippi Valley and Internal Improvements, 1825–1850." *Miss Val Hist Assn Proc,* IV (1910–1911), 153–180.

4480 WEAVER, Charles Clinton. *Internal Improvements in North Carolina Previous to 1860.* Baltimore, 1903.

4481 WHITFORD, Noble E. *History of the Canal System of the State of New York.* 2 vols. Albany, 1906.

4482 WINTHER, Oscar Osburn. *The Old Oregon Country, A History of Frontier Trade, Transportation and Travel.* Stanford, 1950.

4483 YOUNG, Jeremiah S. *A Political and Constitutional Study of the Cumberland Road.* Chicago, 1904.

XII. Scientific and Cultural History

1. Art

See also **2690**

4484 BARKER, Virgil. *American Painting, History and Interpretation.* New York, 1950.

4485 BRAZER, Esther. *Early American Decoration.* Springfield, Mass., 1947.

4486 BURROUGHS, Alan. *Limners and Likenesses: Three Centuries of American Painting.* Cambridge, Mass., 1936.

4487 CAFFIN, Charles H. *The Story of American Painting: The Evolution of Painting in America from Colonial Times to the Present.* New York, 1907.

4488 CAHILL, Holger, and Alfred H. BARR, eds. *Art in America; A Complete Survey.* New York, 1935.

4489 DUNLAP, William. *History of the Rise and Progress of the Arts of Design in the United States.* New ed. by Frank W. BAYLEY and Charles GOODSPEED. 3 vols. New York, 1965.

4490 FEHL, Philipp. "The Account Book of Thomas Appleton of Livorno: A Document in the History of American Art, 1802–1825." *Winterthur Port,* IX (1974), 123–151.

4491 FLEXNER, James Thomas. *The Light of Distant Skies, American Painting, 1760–1835.* New York, 1954.†

4492 FOWBLE, E. McSherry. "Without a Blush: The Movement toward Acceptance of the Nude as an Art Form in America, 1800–1825." *Winterthur Port,* IX (1974), 103–121.

4493 FRESE, Joseph R. "Federal Patronage of Paintings to 1860." *Cap Stud,* II (1974), 71–82.

4494 GARDNER, Albert Ten Eyck. *Yankee Stonecutters; the First American School of Sculpture, 1800–1850.* New York, 1945.

4495 GERDTS, William H. *American Neo-Classical Sculpture: The Marble Resurrection.* New York, 1973.

4496 HARRIS, Neil. *The Artist in American Society: The Formative Years, 1790–1860.* New York, 1966.†

4497 ISHAM, Samuel. *The History of American Painting.* New York, 1927.

4498 LAFOLLETTE, Suzanne. *Art in America.* New York, 1929.

4499 LARKIN, Oliver W. *Samuel F. B. Morse and American Democratic Art.* Boston, 1954.

4500 LARKIN, Oliver W. *Art and Life in America.* New ed. New York, 1960.

4501 MATHER, Frank J., et al. *The American Spirit in Art.* New Haven, 1927.

4502 MENDELOWITZ, Daniel M. *A History of American Art.* New York, 1960.†

4503 MILLER, Lillian B. "Paintings, Sculpture, and the National Character, 1815–1860." *J Am Hist,* LIII (1967), 696–707.

4504 MILLER, Lillian B. *Patrons and Patriotism: The Encouragement of the Fine Arts in the United States: 1790–1860.* Chicago, 1966.†

4505 NIELSEN, George R. "Painting and Politics in Jacksonian America." *Cap Stud,* I (1972), 87–92.

4506 PURCELL, Ralph. *Government and Art, A Study of the American Experience.* Washington, D.C., 1956.

4507 RICHARDSON, Edgar P. *American Romantic Painting.* New York, 1944.

4508 RICHARDSON, Edgar P. *Washington Allston, A Study of the Romantic Artist in America.* Chicago, 1948.†

4509 RICHARDSON, Egar P. *Painting in America; From 1502 to the Present.* New York, 1965.†

4510 ROGERS, Meyric R. *American Interior Design; the Traditions and Development of Domestic Design from Colonial Times to the Present.* New York, 1947.

4511 RUTLEDGE, Anna Wells. *Artists in the Life of Charleston: Through Colony and State from Restoration to Reconstruction.* Philadelphia, 1949.

4512 SIZER, Theodore, ed. *The Autobiography of Colonel John Trumbull, Patriot-Artist, 1756–1843.* New Haven, 1953.

4513 TAFT, Lorado. *The History of American Sculpture.* New York, 1930.

4514 WEITENKAMPF, Frank. *American Graphic Art.* New York, 1924.

4515 WILLIAMS, Sarah Elizabeth. "William Dunlap and the Professionalization of the Arts in the Early Republic." Doctoral dissertation, Brown University, 1974.

4516 WILLOUGHBY, John C. " 'The Old Manse' Revisited: Some Analogues for Art." *N Eng Q,* XLVI (1973), 45–61.

4517 WRIGHT, Nathalia. *Horatio Greenough, the First American Sculptor.* Philadelphia, 1963.

2. Architecture

See also **2715**

4518 ANDREWS, Wayne. *Architecture, Ambition and Americans; A History of American Architecture.* New York, 1955.†

4519 BURCHARD, John E., and Albert BUSH-BROWN. *The Architecture of America: A Social and Cultural History.* Boston, 1961.†

4520 COHEN, Hennig, ed. "The Journal of Robert Mills, 1828–1830." *S C Hist Mag,* LII (1951), 133–139, 218–224; LIII (1952), 31–36, 90–100.

4521 FORMAN, Henry Chandlee. *The Architecture of the Old South: The Medieval Style, 1585–1850.* Cambridge, Mass., 1948.

4522 GALLAGHER, H. M. Pierce. *Robert Mills, Architect of the Washington Monument, 1781–1855.* New York, 1935.

4523 GOWANS, Alan. *Images of American Living: Four Centuries of Architecture and Furniture as Cultural Expression.* Philadelphia, 1964.†

4524 HAMLIN, Talbot F. *The American Spirit in Architecture.* New Haven, 1926.

4525 HAMLIN, Talbot F. *Greek Revival Architecture in America.* New York, 1944.†

4526 HAMLIN, Talbot F. *Benjamin Henry Latrobe.* New York, 1955.

4527 HORWITZ, Richard P. "Architecture and Culture: The Meaning of the Lowell Boarding House." *Am Q,* XXV (1973), 64–82.

4528 KIMBALL, Fiske. *Domestic Architecture of the American Colonies and of the Early Republic.* New York, 1922.

4529 MORRISON, Hugh S. *Early American Architecture, From the First Colonial Settlements to the National Period.* New York, 1952.

4530 MUMFORD, Lewis. *Sticks and Stones: A Study of American Architecture and Civilization.* 2d ed. New York, 1955.†

4531 NEWCOMB, Rexford. *Architecture of the Old Northwest Territory.* Chicago, 1950.

4532 NEWCOMB, Rexford. *Architecture in Old Kentucky.* Urbana, 1952.

4533 PLACE, Charles A. *Charles Bullfinch, Architect and Citizen.* Boston, 1925.

4534 TALLMADGE, Thomas E. *The Story of Architecture in America.* Rev. ed. New York, 1936.

4535 WILSON, Charles C. *Robert Mills, Architect.* Columbia, S.C., 1919.

3. Books, Magazines, Newspapers, and Libraries

See also **441, 442, 463, 621, 647, 658–659, 733A, 754–756, 841–843, 901–902, 913–915, 935, 1016, 1161, 1171, 1176, 1274, 1291, 1364, 1377–1379, 1481, 1523, 1539, 1553, 1600, 2191, 2247, 2420, 2485, 3745, 3911, 3985, 4632, 4706, 4759**

4536 AMES, William Eugene. *A History of the National Intelligencer.* Chapel Hill, 1972.

4537 AMES, William E. "Federal Patronage and the Washington, D.C., Press." *Jour Q,* XLIX (1972), 22–30.

4538 BACARISSE, Charles A. "Texas Gazette, 1829–1831." *S W Hist Q,* LVI (1952), 239–253.

4539 BELL, Earl L., and Kenneth C. CRABBE. *The Augusta Chronicle: Indomitable Voice of Dixie, 1785–1960.* Athens, Ga., 1960.

4540 BLAND, Richard Adrian. "Politics, Propaganda, and the Public Printing: The Administration Organs, 1829–1849." Doctoral dissertation, University of Kentucky, 1975.

4541 BLEYER, Willard G. *Main Currents in the History of American Journalism.* Boston, 1927.

4542 BOYNTON, Henry Walcott. *Annals of American Bookselling, 1638–1850.* New York, 1932.

4543 BRIGHAM, Clarence S. *History and Bibliography of American Newspapers, 1690–1820.* 2 vols. Worcester, 1947.

4544 CAPPON, Lester J. *Virginia Newspapers, 1821–1935.* New York, 1936.

4545 CHAMBERLIN, Joseph Edgar. *The Boston Transcript, A History of Its First Hundred Years.* Boston, 1930.

4546 CLEMONS, Harry. *The University of Virginia Library, 1825–1950: Story of a Jeffersonian Foundation.* Charlottesville, 1954.

4547 CONGLETON, Betty Carolyn. "George D. Prentice and His Editorial Policy in National Politics, 1830–1861" Doctoral dissertation, University of Kentucky, 1962.

4548 CONGLETON, Betty Carolyn. "The *Louisville Journal:* Its Origins and Early Years." *Reg Ky Hist Soc,* LXII (1964), 87–107.

4549 CONGLETON, Betty Carolyn. "George D. Prentice: Nineteenth Century Southern Editor." *Reg Ky Hist Soc,* LXV (1967), 94–119.

4550 CRAMTON, Willa G. "Selleck Osborn: A Republican Editor in Wilmington, Delaware, 1816–1822." *Del Hist,* XII (1967), 198–217.

4551 CROUTHAMEL, James L. "James Watson Webb, Mercantile Editor." *N Y Hist,* XLI (1960), 400–422.

4552 CROUTHAMEL, James L. "The Newspaper Revolution in New York, 1830–1860." *N Y Hist,* XLV (1964), 91–113.

4553 CROUTHAMEL, James L. "James Gordon Bennett, the New York *Herald,* and the Development of Newspaper Sensationalism." *N Y Hist,* LIV (1973), 294–316.

4554 CRUME, John B. "Children's Magazines, 1826–1857." *J Pop Cult,* VI (1973), 698–706.

4555 DABNEY, Thomas Ewing. *One Hundred Great Years: the Story of the Times-Picayune from Its Founding to 1940.* Baton Rouge, 1944.

4556 ELLIOTT, Robert Neal, Jr. *The Raleigh Register, 1799–1863.* Chapel Hill, 1955.

4557 ELSON, Ruth Miller. "American Schoolbooks and 'Culture' in the Nineteenth Century." *Miss Val Hist Rev,* XLVI (1959), 411–434.

4558 EMERY, Edwin. *The Press and America, an Interpretative History of Journalism.* 2d ed. Englewood Cliffs, N.J., 1962.

4559 EMERY, Fred A. "Washington Newspaper Correspondents." *Rec Col Hist Soc,* XXV (1935), 247–288.

4560 EXMAN, Eugene. *The Brothers Harper: A Unique Publishing Partnership and Its Impact upon the Cultural Life of America from 1817 to 1853.* New York, 1965.

4561 FINLEY, Ruth E. *The Lady of Godey's, Sara Josepha Hale.* Philadelphia, 1931.

4562 FORSYTH, David P. *The Business Press in America, 1750–1865.* Philadelphia, 1964.

4563 GRIFFITH, Louis Turner, and John Erwin TALMADGE. *Georgia Journalism, 1763–1950.* Athens, Ga., 1951.

4564 HAMILTON, Milton W., comp. "Anti-Masonic Newspapers, 1826–1834." *Bibliog Soc Am Pap,* XXXII (1938), 71–97.

4565 HARPER, J. Henry. *The House of Harper: A Century of Publishing in Franklin Square.* New York, 1912.

4566 HOOPER, Osman Castle. *History of Ohio Journalism, 1793–1933.* Columbus, Ohio, 1933.

4567 HORWOOD, Donald D., and William W. ROGERS. "The American Press and the Death of Napoleon." *Jour Q*, XLIII (1966), 715–721.

4568 HUDSON, Frederic. *Journalism in the U.S. from 1690 to 1872*. New York, 1873.

4569 KASER, David. *Messrs. Carey & Lea of Philadelphia: A Study in the History of the Booktrade*. Philadelphia, 1957.

4570 LEE, Alfred M. *The Daily Newspaper in America: The Evolution of a Social Instrument*. New York, 1937.

4571 LEE, James M. *History of American Journalism*. New York, 1923.

4572 LEHMAN-HAUPT, Hellmut. *The Book in America: A History of the Making and Selling of Books in America*. 2d ed. New York, 1951.

4573 LEVERMORE, Charles H. "The Rise of Metropolitan Journalism, 1800–1840." *Am Hist Rev*, VI (1901), 446–465.

4574 LUXON, Norval Neil. "H. Niles, the Man and the Editor." *Miss Val Hist Rev*, XXVIII (1941), 27–40.

4575 LUXON, Norval Neil. *Niles' Weekly Register: News Magazine of the Nineteenth Century*. Baton Rouge, 1947.

4576 LYON, William H. "Joseph Charless, Father of Missouri Journalism." *Mo Hist Soc Bull*, XVIII (1961), 133–145.

4577 LYON, William H. *The Pioneer Editor in Missouri, 1808–1860*. Columbia, Mo., 1965.

4578 MCDONOUGH, John. "John Silva Meehan: A Gentleman of Amiable Manners." *Q J Lib Cong*, XXXIII (1976), 3–28.

4579 MCFARLAND, Daniel Miles. "North Carolina Newspapers, Editors, and Journalistic Politics, 1815–1835." *N C Hist Rev*, XXX (1953), 376–414.

4580 MARBUT, Frederick B. "The United States Senate and the Press, 1838–1841." *Jour Q*, XXVIII (1951), 342–350.

4581 MARBUT, Frederick B. *News from the Capital: The Story of Washington Reporting*. Carbondale, Ill., 1971.

4582 MATHESON, William. "George Watterston: Advocate of the National Library. *Q J Lib Cong*, XXXII (1975), 371–388.

4583 MAYO, Edward Lawrence. "The *National Intelligencer* and Jacksonian Democracy: A Whig Persuasion." Doctoral dissertation, Claremont Graduate School, 1970.

4584 MEARNS, David C. *The Story Up To Now: The Library of Congress, 1800–1946*. Washington, D.C., 1947.

4585 MIKKELSON, Dwight Lawrence. "*Kentucky Gazette*, 1787–1848: 'The Herald of a Noisy World.' " Doctoral dissertation, University of Kentucky, 1963.

4586 MILES, Edwin A. "The Mississippi Press in the Jackson Era, 1824–1841." *J Miss Hist*, XIX (1957), 1–20.

4587 MILLER, Alan R. "America's First Political Satirist: Seba Smith of Maine." *Jour Q*, XLVII (1970), 488–492.

4588 MILLER, John William. "The Pioneer Newspapers of Indiana, 1804–1850." Doctoral dissertation, Purdue University, 1975.

4589 MINOR, Benjamin, B. *The Southern Literary Messenger, 1834–1864*. New York, 1905.

4590 MOTT, Frank Luther. *A History of American Magazines, 1741–1850.* Cambridge, Mass., 1930.

4591 MOTT, Frank Luther. *American Journalism: A History, 1690–1960.* 3d ed. New York, 1962.†

4592 NEVINS, Allan. *The Evening Post: A Century of Journalism.* New York, 1922.

4593 O'BRIEN, Frank M. *The Story of the Sun, 1833–1928.* Rev. ed. New York, 1928.

4594 ROGERS, Tommy W. "Libraries in the Ante-Bellum South." *Ala Hist Q,* XXX (1968), 15–26.

4595 ROSENBERG, Norman L. "The Law of Libel and Freedom of Press: Criticism of Public Officials and Candidates, 1800–1917." Doctoral dissertation, State University of New York at Stony Brook, 1972.

4596 ROSENBERG, Norman L. "The Law of Political Libel and Freedom of Press in Nineteenth Century America: An Interpretation." *Am J Leg Hist,* XVII (1973), 336–352.

4597 ROSS, Margaret. *Arkansas Gazette: The Early Years, 1819–1866.* Little Rock, 1969.

4598 RUTLAND, Robert A. *The Newsmongers: Journalism in the Life of the Nation, 1690–1972.* New York, 1973.

4599 SHERA, Jesse H. *Foundations of the Public Library: The Origins of the Public Library Movement in New England, 1629–1855.* Chicago, 1949.

4600 SILVER, Rollo G. *Typefounding in America, 1787–1825.* Charlottesville, Va., 1965.

4601 SMITH, Culver H. *The Press, Politics, & Patronage: The American Government's Use of Newspapers, 1789–1875.* Athens, Ga., 1977.

4602 SMITH, Henry Ladd. "The Two Major Downings: Rivalry in Political Satire." *Jour Q,* XLI (1964), 74–78, 127.

4603 SMITH, James Eugene. *One Hundred Years of Hartford's Courant, from Colonial Times through the Civil War.* New Haven, 1949.

4604 SMYTH, Albert H. *The Philadelphia Magazines and their Contributors, 1741–1850.* Philadelphia, 1892.

4604A TEBBEL, John W. *The Compact History of the American Newspaper.* New York, 1963.

4605 TEBBEL, John W. *A History of Book Publishing in the United States.* New York, 1972.

4606 THOMPSON, Charles Seymour. *Evolution of the American Public Library, 1653–1876.* Washington, D.C., 1952.

4607 TOMLINSON, Robert Hume. "The Origins and Editorial Policies of the *Richmond Whig and Public Advertiser,* 1824–1865." Doctoral dissertation, Michigan State University, 1971.

4608 WEISBERGER, Bernard A. *The American Newspaperman.* Chicago, 1961.

4609 WELSH, Peter C. "Henry R. Robinson: Printmaker to the Whig Party." *N Y Hist,* LIII (1972), 25–53.

4610 WYMAN, Mary A. *Two American Pioneers, Seba Smith and Elizabeth Oakes Smith.* New York, 1927.

4. Music, Literature, and the Theater

See also 736–738, 741, 848–850, 932–934, 986–987, 2081, 2452, 2616, 2624, 2633, 2648, 2662, 2677, 2690, 3177, 3190

4611 ALLEN, Hervey. *Israfel: The Life and Times of Edgar Allan Poe.* 2 vols. New York, 1926.

4612 BARNES, James J. *Authors, Publishers and Politicians: The Quest for an Anglo-American Copyright Agreement, 1815–1854.* Columbus, Ohio, 1974.

4613 BARNETT, Louise K. *The Ignoble Savage: American Literary Racism, 1790–1890.* Westport, Conn., 1975.

4614 BITTNER, William R. *Poe: A Biography.* Boston, 1962.†

4615 BLAIR, Walter. *Native American Humor, 1800–1900.* New York, 1931.†

4616 BROOKS, Van Wyck. *Makers and Finders: A History of the Writer in America, 1800–1915.* 5 vols. New York, 1936–1952.

4617 BROOKS, Van Wyck. *The Dream of Arcadia: American Writers and Artists in Italy, 1760–1915.* New York, 1958.

4618 BROWN, Charles H. *William Cullen Bryant.* New York, 1971.

4619 BROWN, Herbert R. *The Sentimental Novel in America, 1789–1860.* Durham, 1940.

4620 BROWN, Thomas A. *A History of the New York Stage from the First Performance in 1732 to 1901.* 3 vols. New York, 1903.

4621 BUELL, Lawrence. *Literary Transcendentalism: Style and Vision in the American Renaissance.* Ithaca, N.Y., 1973.†

4622 CHASE, Gilbert. *America's Music, from the Pilgrims to the Present.* Rev. ed. New York, 1966.

4623 CLARK, Harry Hayden, ed. *Transitions in American Literary History.* Durham, 1953.

4624 COAD, Oral S., and Edwin MIMS, Jr. *The American Stage.* New Haven, 1939.

4625 CRANE, Fred Arthur. "The Noble Savage in America, 1815–1860." Doctoral dissertation, Yale University, 1952.

4626 CRAWFORD, Mary C. *The Romance of the American Theatre.* Boston, 1925.

4627 DAVIS, Curtis Carroll. *Chronicler of the Cavaliers: A Life of the Virginia Novelist Dr. William A. Caruthers.* Richmond, 1953.

4628 DAVIS, David Brion. *Homicide in American Fiction, 1798–1860: A Study in Social Values.* Ithaca, N.Y., 1957.†

4629 DORMON, James H., Jr. *Theater in the Ante-Bellum South, 1815–1861.* Chapel Hill, 1967.

4630 DORMON, James H., Jr. "The Strange Career of Jim Crow Rice (with Apologies to Professor Woodward)." *J Soc Hist,* III (1969–1970), 109–122.

4631 ELSON, Louis C. *The History of American Music.* Rev. ed. New York, 1925.

4632 FIRDA, Richard Arthur. "German Philosophy of History and Literature in the *North American Review:* 1815–1860." *J Hist Ideas,* XXXII (1971), 133–142.

4633 FOSTER, Edward Halsey. *The Civilized Wilderness: Backgrounds to American Romantic Literature.* New York, 1975.

4634 FREDERICK, John T. "American Literary Nationalism: The Process of Definition, 1825–1850." *Rev Pol,* XXI (1959), 224–238.

4635 FROTHINGHAM, Octavius Brooks. *Transcendentalism in New England; A History.* New York, 1876.†

4636 GRIMSTED, David. *Melodrama Unveiled: American Theatre and Culture, 1800–1850.* Chicago, 1968.

4637 HAVENS, Daniel F. *The Columbian Muse of Comedy: The Development of a Native Tradition in Early American Social Comedy, 1787–1845.* Carbondale, Ill., 1973.

4638 HEDGE, William L. *Washington Irving: An American Study, 1802–1832.* Baltimore, 1965.

4639 HILL, West T., Jr. *The Theatre in Early Kentucky, 1790–1820.* Lexington, 1971.

4640 HODGE, Francis. *Yankee Theatre: The Image of America on the Stage, 1825–1850.* Austin, 1964.

4641 HORNBLOW, Arthur. *A History of the Theatre in America, from Its Beginning to the Present Time.* 2 vols. Philadelphia, 1919.

4642 HOWARD, John T. *Our American Music; A Comprehensive History from 1620 to the Present.* 4th ed. New York, 1965.

4643 HUBBELL, Jay B. *The South in American Literature, 1607–1900.* Durham, 1954.

4644 HUGHES, Glenn. *A History of the American Theatre, 1700–1950.* New York, 1951.

4645 HUNTER, Doreen May. "Richard Henry Dana, Sr: An American Romanticist." Doctoral dissertation, University of California, Berkeley, 1969.

4646 JONES, Howard Mumford. *History and the Contemporary: Essays in Nineteenth-Century Literature.* Madison, 1964.

4647 KENDALL, John S. *The Golden Age of the New Orleans Theatre.* Baton Rouge, 1952.

4648 KMEN, Henry A. *Music in New Orleans: The Formative Years, 1791–1841.* Baton Rouge, 1966.

4649 LAHEE, Henry C. *Annals of Music in America.* Boston, 1922.

4650 MCCLOSKEY, John C. "Jacksonian Democracy in Mrs. Kirkland's *A New Home—Who'll Follow?* [1839]." *Mich Hist,* XLV (1961), 347–352.

4651 MCLEAN, Albert F. *William Cullen Bryant.* New York, 1964.†

4652 MATTHIESSEN, Francis O. *American Renaissance; Art and Expression in the Age of Emerson and Whitman.* New York, 1941.†

4653 METCALF, Frank J. *American Writers and Compilers of Sacred Music.* New York, 1925.

4654 MILLER, Perry, ed. *The Transcendentalists, an Anthology.* Cambridge, Mass., 1950.†

4655 MOODY, Richard. *Edwin Forrest: First Star of the American Stage.* New York, 1960.

4656 NICHOLS, Harold J. "The Prejudice against Native American Drama from 1778 to 1830." *Q J Speech,* LX (1974), 279–288.

4657 ODELL, George C. D. *Annals of the New York Stage.* 15 vols. New York, 1927–1949.

4658 PATTEE, Fred Lewis. *The First Century of American Literature, 1770–1870.* New York, 1935.

4659 PECKHAM, Harry H. *Gotham Yankee: A Biography of William Cullen Bryant.* New York, 1950.

4660 QUINN, Arthur H. *American Fiction.* New York, 1936.

4661 QUINN, Arthur H. *Edgar Allan Poe: A Critical Biography.* New York, 1941.

4662 QUINN, Arthur H. *A History of the American Drama, from the Beginning to the Civil War.* 2d ed. New York, 1943.

4663 ROURKE, Constance M. *American Humor: A Study of the National Character.* New York, 1931.†

4664 RUBIN, Louis D., Jr., ed. *A Bibliographical Guide to the Study of Southern Literature.* Baton Rouge, 1969.

4665 RUSK, Ralph L. *The Literature of the Middle Western Frontier.* New York, 1925.

4666 RUSK, Ralph L. *The Life of Ralph Waldo Emerson.* New York, 1949.

4667 SAXTON, Alexander. "Blackface Minstrelsy and Jacksonian Ideology." *Am Q,* XXVII (1975), 3–28.

4668 SCHMITZ, Neil. "Tall Tale, Tall Talk: Pursuing the Lie in Jacksonian Literature." *Am Lit,* XLVIII (1977), 471–491.

4669 SIMPSON, Lewis P. *The Dispossessed Garden: Pastoral and History in Southern Literature.* Athens, Ga., 1975.

4670 SMITHER, Nelle. "A History of the English Theatre at New Orleans, 1806–1842." *La Hist Q,* XXXVIII (1945), 85–276, 361–572.

4671 SPAETH, Sigmund G. *A History of Popular Music in America.* New York, 1948.

4672 SPENCER, Benjamin T. *The Quest for Nationality: An American Literary Campaign.* Syracuse, 1957.

4673 SPILLER, Robert E. *Fenimore Cooper, Critic of His Time.* New York, 1931.

4674 SPILLER, Robert E., ed. *The American Literary Revolution, 1783–1837.* New York, 1967.

4675 TANDY, Jennette R. *Crackerbox Philosophers in American Humor and Satire.* New York, 1925.

4676 TAYLOR, William R. *Cavalier and Yankee: The Old South and American National Character.* New York, 1961.†

4677 THOMPSON, Ralph. *American Literary Annuals and Gift Books, 1825–1865.* New York, 1936.

4678 TOLL, Robert C. *Blacking Up: The Minstrel Show in Nineteenth-Century America.* New York, 1974.†

4679 VAN DOREN, Carl. *The American Novel, 1789–1939.* Rev. ed. New York, 1940.

4680 WADE, John D. *Augustus Baldwin Longstreet; A Study of the Development of Culture in the South.* New York, 1924.

4681 WAGGONER, Hyatt H. *American Poetry from the Puritans to the Present.* Boston, 1968.

4682 WALHOUT, Clarence P. "John Pendleton Kennedy: Late Disciple of the Enlightenment." *J S Hist,* XXXII (1966), 358–367.

4683 WILLIAMS, Stanley T. *The Life of Washington Irving.* 2 vols. New York, 1935.

4684 WITTKE, Carl. *Tambo and Bones: A History of the American Minstrel Stage.* Durham, 1930.

5. Science and Technology

See also **955, 1787, 1808, 1810, 1998, 2552, 2574, 2579, 2641, 2652, 2690, 2868, 3068, 3679**

4685 ADAMS, Alexander B. *John James Audubon, a Biography.* New York, 1966.

4686 BATES, Ralph S. *Scientific Societies in the United States.* New York, 1946.

4687 BURLINGAME, Roger. *March of the Iron Men, A Social History of Union through Invention.* New York, 1938.

4688 CLARK, Albert Elliott. "The American Scientist, 1800–1863; His origins, Career and Interests." Doctoral dissertation, Case Western Reserve University, 1970.

4689 CLARK, Paul F. *Pioneer Microbiologists of America.* Madison, 1961.

4690 COULSON, Thomas. *Joseph Henry, His Life and Work.* Princeton, 1950.

4691 DANIELS, George H. *American Science in the Age of Jackson.* New York 1968.

4692 DUPREE, A Hunter. *Science in the Federal Government, A History of Policies and Activities to 1940.* Cambridge, Mass., 1957.

4693 ELLIOTT, Arlene Ann. "The Development of the Mechanics' Institutes and Their Influence upon the Field of Engineering: Pennsylvania, A Case Study, 1824–1860." Doctoral dissertation, University of Southern California, 1972.

4694 FORD, Alice E. *John James Audubon.* Norman, 1964.†

4695 FRASER, Chelsea C. *The Story of Engineering in America.* New York, 1928.

4696 FULTON, John F., and Elizabeth H. THOMPSON. *Benjamin Silliman, 1779–1864, Pathfinder in American Science.* New York, 1947.

4697 GEISER, Samuel W. *Naturalists of the Frontier.* Dallas, 1937.

4698 GRAUSTEIN, Jeannette E. *Thomas Nuttall, Naturalist: Explorations in America, 1808–1841.* Cambridge, Mass., 1967.

4699 GREENE, John C. "American Science Comes of Age, 1780–1820." *J Am Hist,* LV (1968), 22–41.

4700 GURALNICK, Stanley M. "Sources of Misconception on the Role of Science in the Nineteenth-Century American College." *Isis,* LXV (1974), 352–366.

4701 HARRIS, Jonathan. "De Witt Clinton as Naturalist." *N Y Hist Soc Q,* LVI (1972), 265–284.

4702 HERRICK, Francis H. *Audubon the Naturalist, a History of His Life and Time.* 2d ed. New York, 1938.

4703 JAFFE, Bernard. *Men of Science in America.* Rev. ed. New York, 1958.

4704 JOHNSON, Thomas C. *Scientific Interests in the Old South.* New York, 1936.

4705 KAEMPFFERT, Walter B., ed. *A Popular History of American Invention.* 2 vols. New York, 1924.

4706 MCELLIGOTT, John Francis. "Before Darwin: Religion and Science as Presented in American Magazines, 1830–1860." Doctoral dissertation, New York University, 1973.

4707 MEIER, Hugo A. "Technology and Democracy, 1800–1860." *Miss Val Hist Rev,* XLIII (1957), 618–640.

4708 MEISEL, Max. *A Bibliography of American Natural History, the Pioneer Century, 1769–1865.* 3 vols. New York, 1924–1929.

4709 MERRILL, George P. *The First Hundred Years of American Geology.* New Haven, 1924.

4710 MORISON, Elting E. *From Know-How to Nowhere: The Development of American Technology.* New York, 1975.

4711 NICOLLET, Joseph N. *The Journal of Joseph N. Nicollet: A Scientist on the Mississippi Headwaters with Notes on Indian Life, 1836–37.* Ed. Martha Coleman BRAY, and trans. Andre FERTEY. St. Paul, 1970.

4712 OLIVER, John W. *History of American Technology.* New York, 1956.

4713 RAFINESQUE, Constantine S. *A Life of Travels and Researches in North America and South Europe.* Philadelphia, 1836.

4714 REINGOLD, Nathan, ed. *Science in Nineteenth-Century America, a Documentary History.* New York, 1964.

4715 RODGERS, Andrew Denny. *John Torrey: A Story of North American Botany.* Princeton, 1942.

4716 ROTHENBERG, Marc. "The Educational and Intellectual Background of American Astronomers, 1825–1875." Doctoral dissertation, Bryn Mawr College, 1974.

4717 SMITH, David Eugene, and Jekuthiel GINSBURG. *A History of Mathematics in America before 1900.* Chicago, 1934.

4718 SMITH, Edgar F. *Chemistry in America: Chapters from the History of Science in the United States.* New York, 1914.

4719 STANTON, William. *The Leopard's Spots: Scientific Attitudes toward Race in America, 1815–59.* Chicago, 1960.†

4720 STONE, Bruce Winchester. "The Role of the Learned Societies in the Growth of Scientific Boston, 1780–1848." Doctoral dissertation, Boston University, 1974.

4721 STRUIK, Dirk J. *Yankee Science in the Making.* Rev. ed. New York, 1962.†

4722 SYDNOR, Charles S. *A Gentleman of the Old Natchez Region: Benjamin L. C. Wailes.* Durham, 1938.

4723 THOMPSON, Holland. *The Age of Invention; A Chronicle of Mechanical Conquest.* New Haven, 1921.

4724 WELKER, Robert Henry. *Birds and Men: American Birds in Science, Art, Literature, and Conservation, 1800–1900.* Cambridge, Mass., 1955.†

4725 WHITE, Morton Gabriel. *Science and Sentiment in America: Philosophical Thought from Jonathan Edwards to John Dewey.* New York, 1973.†

4726 WILKINSON, Norman B. *E. I. du Pont, Botanist: The Beginning of a Tradition.* Charlottesville, 1972.

4727 YOUNG, Robert T. *Biology in America.* Boston, 1922.

4728 ZOCHERT, Donald. "Science and the Common Man in Ante-Bellum America." *Isis,* LXV (1974), 448–473.

6. Medicine and Public Health

See also **955, 1787, 1808, 1810, 1998, 2552, 2574, 2579, 2690, 2703, 2868, 3068, 3679**

4729 BAIRD, Nancy D. "Asiatic Cholera's First Visit to Kentucky: A Study in Panic and Fear." *Filson Club Hist Q,* XLVIII (1974), 228–240.

4730 BAIRD, Nancy D. "Asiatic Cholera: Kentucky's First Public Health Instructor." *Filson Club Hist Q,* XLVIII (1974), 327–341.

4731 BREEDEN, James O. "Thomsonianism in Virginia." *Va Mag Hist Biog,* LXXXII (1974), 150–180.

4732 CASSEDY, James H. "An Early American Hangover: The Medical Profession and Intemperance, 1800–1860." *Bull Hist Med,* L (1976), 405–413.

4733 CHAMBERS, John S. *The Conquest of Cholera, America's Greatest Scourge.* New York, 1938.

4734 DAIN, Norman. *Concepts of Insanity in the United States, 1789–1865.* New Brunswick, 1964.

4735 DAIN, Norman. *Disordered Minds: The First Century of Eastern State Hospital in Williamsburg, Virginia, 1766–1866.* Williamsburg, Va., 1971.

4736 DAVIS, Nathan S. *Contributions to the History of Medical Education and Medical Institutions in the United States of America, 1776–1876.* Washington, D.C., 1877.

4737 DEUTSCH, Albert. *The Mentally Ill in America: A History of Their Care and Treatment from Colonial Times.* New York, 1949.

4738 DRAKE, Daniel. *Physician to the West: Selected Writings of Daniel Drake on Science and Society.* Ed. Henry D. SHAPIRO and Zane L. MILLER. Lexington, 1970.

4739 DUFFY, John, ed. *The Rudolph Matas History of Medicine in Louisiana.* 2 vols. Baton Rouge, 1958–1962.

4740 DUFFY, John. "Medical Practice in the Ante-Bellum South." *J S Hist,* XXV (1959), 53–72.

4741 DUFFY, John. "Medicine and Medical Practice in Early Pittsburgh." *W Pa Hist Mag,* XLV (1962), 333–343.

4742 DUFFY, John. "Hogs, Dogs and Dirt: Public Health in Early Pittsburgh." *Pa Mag Hist Biog,* LXXXVII (1963), 294–305.

4743 DUFFY, John. *History of Public Health in New York City, 1625–1866.* New York, 1968.

4744 DUFFY, John. *The Healers: The Rise of the Medical Establishment.* New York, 1976.

4745 DUNLOP, Richard. *Doctors of the American Frontier.* Garden City, N.Y., 1965.†

4746 FLEXNER, James T. *Doctors on Horseback: Pioneers of American Medicine.* New York, 1937.†

4747 GRIBBIN, William. "Divine Providence or Miasma? The Yellow Fever Epidemic of 1822." *N Y Hist,* LIII (1972), 283–298.

4748 GURR, Charles Stephen. "Social Leadership and the Medical Profession in Antebellum Georgia." Doctoral dissertation, University of Georgia, 1973.

4749 HAMMOND, E. Ashby. "Notes on the Medical History of Key West, 1822–1832." *Fla Hist Q,* LXVI (1967), 93–110.

4750 HORINE, Emmet F. *Daniel Drake, 1785–1852, Pioneer Physician of the Midwest.* Philadelphia, 1961.

4751 HURD, Henry M., et al. *The Institutional Care of the Insane in the United States and Canada.* 4 vols. Baltimore, 1916–1917.

4752 JONES, Thomas B. "Calvin Jones, M. D.: A Case Study in the Practice of Early American Medicine." *N C Hist Rev,* LIX (1972), 56–71.

4753 KAUFMAN, Martin. *Homeopathy in America: The Rise and Fall of a Medical Heresy.* Baltimore, 1971.

4754 KAUFMAN, Martin. *American Medical Education: The Formative Years, 1765–1910.* Westport, Conn., 1976.

4755 LARNER, John William, Jr. " 'Nails and Sundrie Medicines': Town Planning and Public Health in the Harmony Society, 1805–1840." *W Pa Hist Mag,* XLV (1962), 115–138, 209–227.

4756 LEWIS, Carl P., Jr. "The Baltimore College of Dental Surgery and the Birth of Professional Dentistry." *Md Hist Mag,* LIX (1964), 268–285.

4757 LUFKIN, Arthur W. *A History of Dentistry.* Philadelphia, 1938.

4758 MEANS, Richard K. *A History of Health Education in the United States.* Philadelphia, 1962.

4759 MILES, Wyndham D. "Washington's First Medical Journal: Duff Green's *Register and Library of Medical and Chirurgical Science,* 1833–1836." *Rec Col Hist Soc,* LXIX-LXX (1969–1970), 114–125.

4760 NASH, Roger John. "Within these Walls: The Ideology of the Movement to Institutionalize the Insane in America, 1830–1865." Doctoral dissertation, Northwestern University, 1973.

4761 NORWOOD, William Frederick. *Medical Education in the United States before the Civil War.* Philadelphia, 1944.

4762 PACKARD, Francis R. *History of Medicine in the United States.* 2 vols. New York, 1931.

4763 PICKARD, Madge E., and Roscoe Carlyle BULEY. *The Midwest Pioneer, His Ills, Cures, and Doctors.* Crawfordsville, Ind., 1945.

4764 POSTELL, William D. *The Health of Slaves on Southern Plantations.* Baton Rouge, 1951.

4765 RICHMAN, Allen Martin. "The Development of Medical Services in the United States Navy in the Age of Sail: 1815–1830." Doctoral dissertation, University of Minnesota, 1973.

4766 ROSENBERG, Charles E. *The Cholera Years: the United States in 1832, 1849, and 1866.* Chicago, 1962.

4767 ROTHSTEIN, William G. *American Physicians in the Nineteenth Century: From Sects to Science.* Baltimore, 1972.

4768 SAVITT, Todd L. *Medicine and Slavery: The Health Care of Blacks in Antebellum Virginia.* Urbana, 1978.

4769 SHAFER, Henry B. *The American Medical Profession, 1783–1850.* New York, 1936.

4770 SHRYOCK, Richard H. *The Development of Modern Medicine: An Interpretation of the Social and Scientific Factors Involved.* New York, 1947.

4771 SHRYOCK, Richard H. *Medicine and Society in America, 1660–1860.* New York, 1960.†

4772 SHRYOCK, Richard H. *Medicine in America: Historical Essays.* Baltimore, 1966.

4773 SHRYOCK, Richard H. "The Origins and Significance of the Public Health Movement in the United States." *Ann Med Hist,* I (1929), 645–665.

4774 SHRYOCK, Richard H. "A Century of Medical Progress in Philadelphia, 1750–1850." *Pa Hist,* VIII (1941), 6–28.

4775 SIGERIST, Henry E. *American Medicine.* New York, 1934.

4776 SMILLIE, Wilson G. *Public Health: Its Promise for the Future; A Chronicle of the Development of Public Health in the United States, 1607–1914.* New York, 1955.

4777 SMITH, Ashbel. *Yellow Fever in Galveston, Republic of Texas, 1839.* Ed. Chauncey D. LEAKE. Austin, 1951.

4778 STARR, Paul. "Medicine, Economy and Society in Nineteenth-Century America." *J Soc Hist,* X (1977), 588–607.

4779 TOP, Franklin H., ed. *The History of American Epidemiology.* St. Louis, 1952.

4780 VALLE, Rosemary K. "James Ohio Pattie and the 1827–1828 Alta California Measles Epidemic." *Calif Hist Soc Q,* LII (1973), 28–36.

4781 WILLIAMS, Ralph C. *The United States Public Health Services, 1798–1950.* Washington, D.C., 1951.

4782 YOUNG, James Harvey. "American Medical Quackery in the Age of the Common Man." *Miss Val Hist Rev,* XLVII (1961), 579–593.

4783 YOUNG, James Harvey. *The Toadstool Millionaires: A Social History of Patent Medicines before Federal Regulation.* Princeton, 1961.†

4784 YOUNG, James Harvey. *American Self-Dosage Medicines: An Historical Perspective.* Lawrence, Kansas, 1974.

INDEX

INDEX

INDEX

INDEX

INDEX

INDEX

INDEX

INDEX

INDEX

INDEX

INDEX

Houston, David F., 1465
Howard, John T., 4642
Howard, Milo B., Jr., 2308
Howard, Perry H., 2350
Howard, Robert P., 2500
Howard, Thomas W., 2485
Howard, Victor B., 3532
Howe, Daniel W., 1530, 2197, 2636
Howe, George F., 30
Howe, John R., 134
Howe, Mark De Wolfe, 434
Howell, Isabel, 3315
Hoyt, Elizabeth, 2173
Hoyt, William H., 839
Hruneni, George A., Jr., 866
Hryniewicki, Richard J., 3706
Hubach, Robert R., 173
Hubbell, Jay B., 4643
Huberich, Charles H., 3465
Hubner, Thurman W., 2055
Huch, Ronald K., 2922
Huculak, Mykhaylo, 1200
Hudson, Charles, 3707
Hudson, Frederic, 4568
Hudson, Winthrop S., 2923, 2924
Huehner, David R., 3082
Huff, Archie V., Jr., 532, 2198
Huggins, Nathan I., 3230
Hughes, Glenn, 4644
Hughes, J. R. T., 3864
Hugins, Walter E., 835, 1999, 2790
Hulbert, Archer B., 2563-65, 4419, 4420
Hull, Gary W., 2637
Hume, John F., 3533
Hungerford, Edward, 4421, 4422
Hunt, Alfred N., 2716
Hunt, Freeman, 4035
Hunt, Gaillard, 499, 796-97, 937
Hunter, Doreen M., 4645
Hunter, Louis C., 3865, 4204-05, 4423
Hunter, Lloyd A., 3284
Hunter, Robert F., 4424
Hunter, Robert M. T., 500
Hunter, William C., 4068
Hunting, Warren B., 1626
Huntington, Charles C., 3989
Huntington, Samuel P., 1768
Hurd, Henry M., 4751
Hurd, John C., 3231
Hurst, James W., 1659, 1660, 4036, 4096
Hurst, Lawrence, 1575
Husband, Michael B., 2566

Huse, Charles P., 4097
Hutchins, John G. B., 4314
Hutchinson, C. A., 2423
Hutchinson, William K., 3928
Hutton, Margaret, 2424
Hyde de Neuville, Guillaume, 1273
Hyden, Ralston, 1836

Ingalls, Walter R., 4206
Ingraham, Joseph H., 279
Innis, Harold A., 4315
Irelan, John R., 1001
Ireland, Robert M., 858-59, 2251-54
Irving, Washington, 280
Irwin, Leonard B., 3232
Irwin, Ray W., 978, 1069
Isham, Samuel, 4497
Israel, Fred, 1837

Jack, Theodore H., 1427, 2309
Jackson, Carlton L., 1368-69, 2310
Jackson, George S., 913
Jackson, Sidney L., 3083, 4269
Jacobs, Donald M., 3423-25
Jacobs, Melvin C., 2567
Jacobsen, Diane L., 3866
Jaffe, Bernard, 4703
Jaher, Frederic C., 2717, 3800, 4037
Jakle, John A., 369A
James, Bessie R., 914
James, D. Clayton, 3800
James, Edward T., 33
James, Edwin, 281
James, Janet W., 33, 3176
James, Marquis, 673, 697, 698
Jameson, J. Franklin, 501
Jamison, Albert L., 2995
Janssens, Agustín, 282
January, Alan F., 2199
Jarvis, Charles A., 3534
Jeffrey, Thomas E., 2174
Jenkins, J. S., 2000
Jenkins, John H., 2425
Jenkins, William S., 3647
Jenks, L. H., 4038
Jennings, Walter W., 3084
Jennings, Warren A., 2925-27
Jensen, Richard E., 2568
Jentz, John B., 4270
Jeremy, David J., 4207
Jervey, Theodore D., 666
Jessett, Thomas E., 3708

INDEX

INDEX

INDEX

INDEX

INDEX

INDEX

INDEX

INDEX

INDEX

INDEX

INDEX

290

INDEX